Praise for

DESTINED FOR WAR

A NATIONAL BESTSELLER
A *NEW YORK TIMES* NOTABLE BOOK OF THE YEAR
A *NEW YORK TIMES* EDITORS' CHOICE
A *LONDON TIMES* BOOK OF THE YEAR: POLITICS
A *FINANCIAL TIMES* BEST BOOK OF THE YEAR: POLITICS
AN AMAZON BEST HISTORY BOOK OF THE YEAR
SHORT-LISTED FOR THE 2018 LIONEL GELBER PRIZE

"Thucydides's Trap identifies a cardinal challenge to world order: the impact of a rising power on a ruling power. I read the book with great interest. I can only hope that the US-China relationship becomes the fifth case to resolve itself peacefully, rather than the thirteenth to result in war."

   —HENRY KISSINGER, former US secretary of state

"Graham Allison is one of the keenest observers of international affairs around. He consistently brings his deep understanding of history's currents to today's most difficult challenges and makes our toughest foreign policy dilemmas accessible to experts and everyday citizens alike. That's why I regularly sought his counsel both as a senator and as vice president. In *Destined for War,* Allison lays out one of the defining challenges of our time—managing the critical relationship between China and the United States."

   —JOE BIDEN, former vice president of the United States

"One of the most insightful and thought-provoking books I have ever read on the most important relationship in the world: the US and China. If Graham Allison is right—and I think he is—China and the US must heed the lessons in this superb study in order to build a strategic relationship that avoids a war which neither side would win."

   —GENERAL (RET.) DAVID PETRAEUS, chairman of the KKR Global Institute, former director of the CIA, and former commander of US Central Command

"The Chinese superpower has arrived. Could America's failure to grasp this reality pull the United States and China into war? [*Destined for War*] argue[s] persuasively that adjusting to this global power shift will require great skill on both sides if conflagration is to be avoided . . . [*Destined for War* is full of] wide-ranging, erudite case studies that span human history . . . [A] fine book."

— *New York Times Book Review*

"This summer's must-read book in both Washington and Beijing."

—NIALL FERGUSON, *Boston Globe*

"Please read this book, because it'll rattle you . . . [Allison is] a first-class academic with the instincts of a first-rate politician. He brings to the Thucydides Trap an impressive sweep of history and geopolitical and military knowledge. Unlike some academics, he writes interestingly . . . Allison isn't a pessimist. He argues that with skillful statecraft and political sensitivity these two superpowers can avoid war."

— *Bloomberg News*

"A brief but far-reaching book in which potted history is incisively deployed . . . Perhaps we can avoid war, Mr. Allison says, by negotiating a long peace with China."

— *Wall Street Journal*

"Mr. Allison does not say that war between China and the United States is inevitable, but he thinks it 'more likely than not.' This alarming conclusion is shared by many in Washington, where Mr. Allison's book is causing a stir . . . China and America could blunder into war in several ways, argues Mr. Allison . . . With Donald Trump in the White House, Mr. Allison worries that even a trade war might turn into a shooting war."

— *Economist*

"A provocative thesis on one of today's most pressing foreign policy issues and a page-turner of the first order, *Destined for War* is a must-read. Professor Allison writes with the propulsive narrative drive appropriate for such an immediate and danger-fraught topic. I can only hope that all senior policy experts read this timely book to prevent our country from falling into the trap Professor Allison so ably warns us against."

—CHRISTOPHER REICH, best-selling author of
Invasion of Privacy, The Patriots Club, and *Numbered Account*

"Do China and America want war? No. Might they be compelled into conflict by severe structural stress? Yes. Thankfully, Allison charts an essential course to avoid a catastrophic collision. *Destined for War* will be studied and debated for decades."

—KEVIN RUDD, former prime minister of Australia

"In *Destined for War,* Graham Allison has again done a great service. With an incisive review of the wars of yesterday and a deep understanding of today's international politics, Allison has provided American and Chinese leaders not just with a stark warning about the consequences of falling into the Thucydides's Trap, but also the insight to avoid it. For policymakers, scholars, and citizens on both sides of the Pacific Ocean, *Destined for War* is essential reading."

—ASH CARTER, former US secretary of defense

"Graham Allison is the Paul Revere of the nuclear age. He has been ringing the alarm for years trying to stir us from our slumber. In his brilliant book, Allison provides us with a heart-stopping look into a future that may end as abruptly as the past began."

—WILLIAM COHEN, former US secretary of defense

"In dissecting—and suggesting ways to bend—the dangerous arc of the US-China relationship, Graham Allison has written the most important foreign policy book of our time. This book should immediately be read by our new president. Placing *Destined for War* atop every government organization's reading list offers our generation of leaders the best hope for avoiding stumbling into Thucydides's notorious trap."

—ADMIRAL (RET.) SANDY WINNEFELD,
former vice chairman of the Joint Chiefs of Staff

"Drawing on a sweeping command of history and a keen ability to distill the essence of an argument, Graham Allison has provided the necessary guide for how to manage Sino-American relations into an uncertain future. Essential, even indispensable reading for every diplomat—and financier or businessman—who contemplates China and its relations with the world."

—KURT CAMPBELL, CEO, the Asia Group, and former
US assistant secretary of state for East Asian and Pacific affairs

"*Destined for War* is a must-read for anyone concerned about US-China relations, or peace. And by all who care about the ways US foreign policy is formed—and ought to be formed. A gifted combination of scholarship with truly accessible writing."

—AMITAI ETZIONI, professor of international affairs,
George Washington University, and author of
Avoiding War with China

"Reading *Destined for War* and drawing from its lessons could help to save the lives of millions of people."

—KLAUS SCHWAB, founder and executive chairman,
World Economic Forum

"Steeped in history and propelled by one of the most transformative developments in modern times—the rise of China—Graham Allison has written a gripping book that decisionmakers and citizens alike must read, digest, and act upon. Allison combines a historian's depth of knowledge with a policymaker's real world, practical understanding. He mines the recent and distant past to offer essential insights into the future—in so doing, changing the way we think about how America should act in the present."

—SAMANTHA POWER, former US ambassador to the United Nations and Pulitzer Prize–winning author of *A Problem from Hell*

"If any book can stop a world war, it is this one. Graham Allison makes a clear and compelling case that serious conflict between the United States and China is looming, but not inevitable. This gripping book is a must-read for policymakers in both nations as well as the general public."

—SAM NUNN, cochairman, Nuclear Threat Initiative, and former US senator (1972–1996)

"Might *Destined for War* be the policy book of the year? When Xi Jinping declares that the story in Graham Allison's book is serious enough to compel our attention, then we need to study the arguments in it. Deftly presented, clearly structured, and with a fine concluding exploration of the endless historical debate between great forces and contingency, *Destined for War* seems itself destined for much attention, argument, and constant classroom use."

—PAUL KENNEDY, author of
The Rise and Fall of the Great Powers

"As *Destined for War* demonstrates, recognizing the Thucydidean stress between the US and China is far from appeasement. Rather, Graham Allison shows why it is the fundamental starting point for a successful American strategy to deal with the rise of Chinese power that both upholds our vital national interests and avoids war."

—ROBERT D. BLACKWILL, Henry Kissinger Senior Fellow for
US Foreign Policy, Council on Foreign Relations, and former
US ambassador to India

"Graham Allison, with his usual conceptual clarity, uses the Thucydides's Trap to light up the big question of our day: how can the dominant power (the United States) avoid war with the rising power (China)? Allison provides historical perspective, while presenting the US perspective that he knows from the inside and the Chinese perspective that he has studied with uncommon depth."

—EZRA VOGEL, author of *Deng Xiaoping and the Transformation of
China*

"Read this book. You cannot get a better introduction to the dilemmas the US faces in its China policy or to the methods of applied history in understanding current affairs."

—ODD ARNE WESTAD, author of
Restless Empire: China and the World Since 1750

"It isn't often that a book comes along that should be mandatory reading for every member of Congress, cabinet member and, for that matter, any senior governmental official with a connection to foreign policy and national security. But Graham Allison's *Destined for War* is such a book."

—CHARLES E. COOK JR., editor, *Cook Political Report*

"*Destined for War* is a must-read for those who care about the long-term security and economic interests of the United States."

—US SENATOR DAN SULLIVAN (R-AK)

"Allison's book is essential reading both for the content and its impact. It is already being circulated in the White House and the Politburo, and will no doubt be added to political science reading lists in universities around the globe . . . Allison calls Obama's Asia pivot 'using an extra-strength aspirin to treat cancer.' With this book, we might finally be shifting to chemotherapy."

—Lowy Institute

"A pertinent study of the relationship between the United States and China . . . A timely, reasoned treatise by a keen observer and historian."

—*Kirkus Reviews* (starred review)

"Graham Allison has written what I think will be the definitive book on the relationship between China and the United States."

—DAVID RUBENSTEIN, cofounder and co–executive chairman, Carlyle Group

"The reason *Destined for War* is such an important book is that it asks: if China, with its current form of government and economic arrangement, rises to be twice as big as the United States, spending twice as much on everything, including its military, *then what happens?* Most people do not want to accept that this scenario is possible, let alone even contemplate what happens . . . If war happens, it would be an all-out catastrophe. So we need to do everything we possibly can to avoid it."

—LI LU, founder and chairman, Himalaya Capital Management

"Graham Allison has articulated an idea known as the Thucydides Trap. It states that, through history, the rise of an emerging power very often creates fear and anxiety among established powers, which can (in the worst-case scenario) lead to war. Schwarzman Scholars was designed to help defuse those tensions and create a more peaceful world."

—STEPHEN SCHWARZMAN, CEO, Blackstone Group

"Read every page . . . twice."
—ANTHONY SCARAMUCCI,
former White House communications director

"*Destined for War* by Graham Allison informs the moment like *Guns of August* did for Kennedy in [the] Cuban Missile Crisis. Important lessons."
—LLOYD BLANKFEIN, CEO, Goldman Sachs

"The US needs a strategy to deal with a China that is increasingly comfortable engaging aggressively in the world. A good primer on this is Graham Allison's recent book, *Destined for War*. Allison, a professor at Harvard's Kennedy School of Government, tells the story of China's truly meteoric rise over the past three decades, and makes the point that while we are playing checkers, the Chinese are not simply playing chess—they are playing a different game altogether: Go."
—ADMIRAL (RET.) JAMES G. STAVRIDIS, dean,
Fletcher School of Law and Diplomacy, Tufts University, and former
NATO Supreme Allied Commander Europe

DESTINED FOR WAR

BOOKS BY GRAHAM ALLISON

Essence of Decision:
Explaining the Cuban Missile Crisis
(with Philip Zelikow)

Nuclear Terrorism:
The Ultimate Preventable Catastrophe

Lee Kuan Yew:
The Grand Master's Insights on China,
the United States, and the World
(with Robert D. Blackwill and Ali Wyne)

Destined for War:
Can America and China Escape Thucydides's Trap?

DESTINED
FOR WAR

Can America and China
Escape Thucydides's Trap?

GRAHAM ALLISON

MARINER BOOKS

HOUGHTON MIFFLIN HARCOURT

Boston — New York

First Mariner Books edition 2018

For information about permission to reproduce selections from this book,
write to trade.permissions@hmhco.com or to Permissions, Houghton Mifflin Harcourt
Publishing Company, 3 Park Avenue, 19th Floor, New York, New York 10016.

hmhco.com

Library of Congress Cataloging-in-Publication Data is available.
ISBN 978-0-544-93527-3 (hardcover)
ISBN 978-1-328-91538-2 (pbk.)

Book design by Chloe Foster

Printed in the United States of America
7 2021
4500827931

Page 6 Source of data: World Bank (GDP: http://data.worldbank.org/indicator/NY.GDP.MKTP.CD?
locations=CN-US; Imports: http://data.worldbank.org/indicator/TM.VAL.MRCH.CD.WT?locations
=CN-US;Exports: http://data.worldbank.org/indicator/TX.VAL.MRCH.CD.WT?locations=CN-US;
Reserves: http://data.worldbank.org/indicator/FI.RES.XGLD.CD?locations=CN-US). *Page 9* Source
of data: International Monetary Fund, Economist Intelligence Unit. *Page 11* Source of data: International
Monetary Fund, World Economic Outlook Database, October 2016. *Page 42* Source of data: Courtesy of
the author. *Page 65* Source of data: The Maddison-Project, http://www.ggdc.net/maddison/maddison
-project/home.htm, 2013 version. *Page 76* Source of data: Kennedy, *The Rise and Fall of the Great Powers,*
p. 203. *Page 105* "American Aggression," *Toronto Star* (November 12, 1903), reproduced in *Literary Digest*
27, no. 26 (December 26, 1903), 909, P 267.3 v.27, Widener Library, Harvard University. *Page 141* Source
of data: Courtesy of the author. *Pages 168–69* Map by Mapping Specialists, Ltd., Fitchburg, WI. *Page 244*
Source of data: Courtesy of the author.

CONTENTS

PREFACE

Two centuries ago, Napoleon warned, "Let China sleep; when she wakes, she will shake the world." Today China has awakened, and the world is beginning to shake.

Yet many Americans are still in denial about what China's transformation from agrarian backwater to "the biggest player in the history of the world" means for the United States. What is this book's Big Idea? In a phrase, Thucydides's Trap. When a rising power threatens to displace a ruling power, alarm bells should sound: danger ahead. China and the United States are currently on a collision course for war — unless both parties take difficult and painful actions to avert it.

As a rapidly ascending China challenges America's accustomed predominance, these two nations risk falling into a deadly trap first identified by the ancient Greek historian Thucydides. Writing about a war that devastated the two leading city-states of classical Greece two and a half millennia ago, he explained: "It was the *rise* of Athens and the *fear* that this instilled in Sparta that made war *inevitable*."

That primal insight describes a perilous historical pattern. Reviewing the record of the past five hundred years, the Thucydides's Trap Project I direct at Harvard has found sixteen cases in which a major nation's rise has disrupted the position of a dominant state. In the most infamous example, an industrial Germany rattled Britain's established position at the top of the pecking order a century ago. The catastrophic outcome of their competition necessitated a new category of violent conflict: world war. Our research finds that twelve of these rivalries ended in war and four did not—not a comforting ratio for the twenty-first century's most important geopolitical contest.

This is not a book about China. It is about the *impact* of a rising China on the US and the global order. For seven decades since World War II, a rules-based framework led by Washington has defined world order, producing an era without war among great powers. Most people now think of this as normal. Historians call it a rare "Long Peace." To-day, an increasingly powerful China is unraveling this order, throwing into question the peace generations have taken for granted.

In 2015, the *Atlantic* published "The Thucydides Trap: Are the US and China headed for War?" In that essay I argued that this histori-cal metaphor provides the best lens available for illuminating relations between China and the US today. Since then, the concept has ignited considerable debate. Rather than face the evidence and reflect on the uncomfortable but necessary adjustments both sides might make, pol-icy wonks and presidents alike have constructed a straw man around Thucydides's claim about "inevitability." They have then put a torch to it—arguing that war between Washington and Beijing is not predeter-mined. At their 2015 summit, Presidents Barack Obama and Xi Jinping discussed the Trap at length. Obama emphasized that despite the struc-tural stress created by China's rise, "the two countries are capable of managing their disagreements." At the same time, they acknowledged that, in Xi's words, "should major countries time and again make the mistakes of strategic miscalculation, they might create such traps for themselves."

I concur: war between the US and China is not inevitable. Indeed, Thucydides would agree that neither was war between Athens and Sparta. Read in context, it is clear that he meant his claim about inev-itability as hyperbole: exaggeration for the purpose of emphasis. The point of Thucydides's Trap is neither fatalism nor pessimism. Instead, it points us beyond the headlines and regime rhetoric to recognize the tectonic structural stress that Beijing and Washington must master to construct a peaceful relationship.

If Hollywood were making a movie pitting China against the United States on the path to war, central casting could not find two better leading actors than Xi Jinping and Donald Trump. Each personifies his country's deep aspirations of national greatness. Much as Xi's appointment as leader of China in 2012 accentuated the role of the rising power, America's election of Donald Trump in a campaign that vilified China promises a more vigorous response from the ruling power. As personalities, Trump and Xi could not be more different. As protagonists in a struggle to be number one, however, they share portentous similarities. Both

- Are driven by a common ambition: to make their nation great again.
- Identify the nation ruled by the other as the principal obstacle to their dream.
- Take pride in their own unique leadership capabilities.
- See themselves playing a central role in revitalizing their nation.
- Have announced daunting domestic agendas that call for radical changes.
- Have fired up populist nationalist support to "drain the swamp" of corruption at home and confront attempts by each other to thwart their nation's historic mission.

Will the impending clash between these two great nations lead to war? Will Presidents Trump and Xi, or their successors, follow in the tragic footsteps of the leaders of Athens and Sparta or Britain and Germany? Or will they find a way to avoid war as effectively as Britain and the US did a century ago or the US and the Soviet Union did through four decades of Cold War? Obviously, no one knows. We can be certain, however, that the dynamic Thucydides identified will intensify in the years ahead.

Denying Thucydides's Trap does not make it less real. Recognizing it does not mean just accepting whatever happens. We owe it to future generations to face one of history's most brutal tendencies head on and then do everything we can to defy the odds.

INTRODUCTION

I have written my work, not as an essay to win the applause of the moment, but as a possession for all time.

—Thucydides, *History of the Peloponnesian War*

Here we are on top of the world. We have arrived at this peak to stay there forever. There is, of course, this thing called history. But history is something unpleasant that happens to other people.

—Arnold Toynbee, recalling the 1897 diamond jubilee celebration of Queen Victoria

Like other practicing historians, I am often asked what the "lessons of history" are. I answer that the only lesson I have learnt from studying the past is that there are no permanent winners and losers.

—Ramachandra Guha

A h, if we only knew." That was the best the German chancellor could offer. Even when a colleague pressed Theobald von Bethmann Hollweg, he could not explain how his choices, and those of other European statesmen, had led to the most devastating war the world had seen to that point. By the time the slaughter of the Great War finally ended in 1918, the key players had lost all they fought for: the Austro-Hungarian Empire dissolved, the German kaiser ousted, the Russian tsar overthrown, France bled for a generation, and England shorn of its treasure and youth. And for what? If we only knew.

Bethmann Hollweg's phrase haunted the president of the United States nearly half a century later. In 1962, John F. Kennedy was forty-five years old and in his second year in office, but still struggling to get his mind around his responsibilities as commander in chief. He knew that his finger was on the button of a nuclear arsenal that could kill hundreds of millions of human beings in a matter of minutes. But for what? A slogan at the time declared, "Better dead than red." Kennedy rejected that dichotomy as not just facile, but false. "Our goal," as he put it, had to be "not peace at the expense of freedom, but both peace and freedom." The question was how he and his administration could achieve both.

As he vacationed at the family compound on Cape Cod in the summer of 1962, Kennedy found himself reading *The Guns of August,* Barbara Tuchman's compelling account of the outbreak of war in 1914. Tuchman traced the thoughts and actions of Germany's Kaiser Wilhelm and his chancellor Bethmann Hollweg, Britain's King George and his foreign secretary Edward Grey, Tsar Nicholas, Austro-Hungarian emperor Franz Joseph, and others as they sleepwalked into the abyss. Tuchman argued that none of these men understood the danger they faced. None wanted the war they got. Given the opportunity for a do-over, none would repeat the choices he made. Reflecting on his own responsibilities, Kennedy pledged that if he ever found himself facing choices that could make the difference between catastrophic war and peace, he would be able to give history a better answer than Bethmann Hollweg's.

Kennedy had no inkling of what lay ahead. In October 1962, just two months after he read Tuchman's book, he faced off against Soviet leader Nikita Khrushchev in the most dangerous confrontation in human history. The Cuban Missile Crisis began when the United States discovered the Soviets attempting to sneak nuclear-tipped missiles into Cuba, a mere ninety miles from Florida. The situation quickly escalated from diplomatic threats to an American blockade of the island, military mobilizations in both the US and USSR, and several high-stakes clashes, including the shooting down of an American U-2 spy plane over Cuba. At the height of the crisis, which lasted for a tense thirteen days, Kennedy confided to his brother Robert that he believed the chances it would end in nuclear war were "between one-in-three and even." Nothing historians have discovered since has lengthened those odds.

Although he appreciated the dangers of his predicament, Kennedy repeatedly made choices he knew actually *increased* the risk of war, including nuclear war. He chose to confront Khrushchev publicly (rather than try to resolve the issue privately through diplomatic channels); to draw an unambiguous red line requiring the removal of Soviet missiles (rather than leave himself more wiggle room); to threaten air strikes to destroy the missiles (knowing this could trigger Soviet retaliation against Berlin); and finally, on the penultimate day of the crisis, to give Khrushchev a time-limited ultimatum (that, if rejected, would have required the US to fire the first shot).

In each of these choices, Kennedy understood that he was raising the risk that further events and choices by others beyond his control could lead to nuclear bombs destroying American cities, including Washington, DC (where his family stayed throughout the ordeal). For example, when Kennedy elevated the alert level of the American nuclear arsenal to Defcon II, he made US weapons less vulnerable to a preemptive Soviet attack but simultaneously relaxed a score of safety catches. At Defcon II, German and Turkish pilots took their seats in NATO fighter bombers loaded with armed nuclear weapons less than two hours away from their targets in the Soviet Union. Since electronic locks on nuclear weapons had not yet been invented, there was no physical or technical barrier preventing a pilot from deciding to fly to Moscow, drop a nuclear bomb, and start World War III.

With no way to wish away these "risks of the uncontrollable," Kennedy and his secretary of defense, Robert McNamara, reached deeply into organizational procedures to minimize accidents or mistakes. Despite those efforts, historians have identified more than a dozen close calls outside Kennedy's span of control that could have sparked a war. A US antisubmarine campaign, for example, dropped explosives around

Soviet submarines to force them to surface, leading a Soviet captain to believe he was under attack and almost fire his nuclear-armed torpedoes. In another incident, the pilot of a U-2 spy craft mistakenly flew over the Soviet Union, causing Khrushchev to fear that Washington was refining coordinates for a preemptive nuclear attack. If one of these actions had sparked a nuclear World War III, could JFK explain how his choices contributed to it? Could he give a better answer to an inquisitor's question than Bethmann Hollweg did?

The complexity of causation in human affairs has vexed philosophers, jurists, and social scientists. In analyzing how wars break out, historians focus primarily on proximate, or immediate, causes. In the case of World War I, these include the assassination of the Hapsburg archduke Franz Ferdinand and the decision by Tsar Nicholas II to mobilize Russian forces against the Central Powers. If the Cuban Missile Crisis had resulted in war, the proximate causes could have been the Soviet submarine captain's decision to fire his torpedoes rather than allow his submarine to sink, or a Turkish pilot's errant choice to fly his nuclear payload to Moscow. Proximate causes for war are undeniably important. But the founder of history believed that the most obvious causes for bloodshed mask even more significant ones. More important than the sparks that lead to war, Thucydides teaches us, are the structural factors that lay its foundations: conditions in which otherwise manageable events can escalate with unforeseeable severity and produce unimaginable consequences.

THUCYDIDES'S TRAP

In the most frequently cited one-liner in the study of international relations, the ancient Greek historian Thucydides explained, "It was the rise of Athens and the fear that this instilled in Sparta that made war inevitable."

Thucydides wrote about the Peloponnesian War, a conflict that engulfed his homeland, the city-state of Athens, in the fifth century BCE, and which in time came to consume almost the entirety of ancient Greece. A former soldier, Thucydides watched as Athens challenged the dominant Greek power of the day, the martial city-state of Sparta. He observed the outbreak of armed hostilities between the two powers and detailed the fighting's horrific toll. He did not live to see its bitter end, when a weakened Sparta finally vanquished Athens, but it is just as well for him.

While others identified an array of contributing causes of the Peloponnesian War, Thucydides went to the heart of the matter. When he turned the spotlight on "the rise of Athens and the fear that this instilled in Sparta," he identified a primary driver at the root of some of history's most catastrophic and puzzling wars. Intentions aside, when a rising power threatens to displace a ruling power, the resulting structural stress makes a violent clash the rule, not the exception. It happened between Athens and Sparta in the fifth century BCE, between Germany and Britain a century ago, and almost led to war between the Soviet Union and the United States in the 1950s and 1960s.

Like so many others, Athens believed its advance to be benign. Over the half century that preceded the conflict, it had emerged as a steeple of civilization. Philosophy, drama, architecture, democracy, history, and naval prowess—Athens had it all, beyond anything previously seen under the sun. Its rapid development began to threaten Sparta, which had grown accustomed to its position as the dominant power on the Peloponnese. As Athenian confidence and pride grew, so too did its demands for respect and expectations that arrangements be revised to reflect new realities of power. These were, Thucydides tells us, natural reactions to its changing station. How could Athenians not believe that their interests deserved more weight? How could Athenians not expect that they should have greater influence in resolving differences?

But it was also natural, Thucydides explained, that Spartans should see the Athenian claims as unreasonable, and even ungrateful. Who, Spartans rightly asked, provided the security environment that allowed Athens to flourish? As Athens swelled with a growing sense of its own importance, and felt entitled to greater say and sway, Sparta reacted with insecurity, fear, and a determination to defend the status quo.

Similar dynamics can be found in a host of other settings, indeed even in families. When a young man's adolescent surge poses the prospect that he will overshadow his older sibling (or even his father), what do we expect? Should the allocation of bedrooms, or closet space, or seating be adjusted to reflect relative size as well as age? In alpha-dominated species like gorillas, as a potential successor grows larger and stronger, both the pack leader and the wannabe prepare for a showdown. In businesses, when disruptive technologies allow upstart companies like Apple, Google, or Uber to break quickly into new industries, the result is often a bitter competition that forces established companies like Hewlett-Packard, Microsoft, or taxi operators to adapt their business models—or perish.

Thucydides's Trap refers to the natural, inevitable discombobulation that occurs when a rising power threatens to displace a ruling power. This can happen in any sphere. But its implications are most dangerous in international affairs. For just as the original instance of Thucydides's Trap resulted in a war that brought ancient Greece to its knees, this phenomenon has haunted diplomacy in the millennia since. Today it has set the world's two biggest powers on a path to a cataclysm nobody wants, but which they may prove unable to avoid.

ARE THE US AND CHINA DESTINED FOR WAR?

The world has never seen anything like the rapid, tectonic shift in the global balance of power created by the rise of China. If the US were a corporation, it would have accounted for 50 percent of the global economic market in the years immediately after World War II. By 1980, that had declined to 22 percent. Three decades of double-digit Chinese growth has reduced that US share to 16 percent today. If current trends continue, the US share of global economic output will decline further over the next three decades to just 11 percent. Over this same period, China's share of the global economy will have soared from 2 percent in 1980 to 18 percent in 2016, well on its way to 30 percent in 2040.

China's economic development is transforming it into a formidable political and military competitor. During the Cold War, as the US mounted clumsy responses to Soviet provocations, a sign in the Pentagon said: "If we ever faced a real enemy, we would be in deep trouble." China is a serious potential enemy.

The possibility that the United States and China could find themselves at war appears as unlikely as it would be unwise. The centennials recalling World War I, however, have reminded us of man's capacity for folly. When we say that war is "inconceivable," is this a statement about what is possible in the world — or only about what our limited minds can conceive?

As far ahead as the eye can see, the defining question about global order is whether China and the US can escape Thucydides's Trap. Most contests that fit this pattern have ended badly. Over the past five hundred years, in sixteen cases a major rising power has threatened to displace a ruling power. In twelve of those, the result was war. The four cases that avoided this outcome did so only because of huge, painful adjustments in attitudes and actions on the part of challenger and challenged alike.

The United States and China can likewise avoid war, but only if they can internalize two difficult truths. First, on the current trajectory, *war between the US and China in the decades ahead is not just possible, but much more likely than currently recognized.* Indeed, on the historical record, war is more likely than not. By underestimating the danger, moreover, we add to the risk. If leaders in Beijing and Washington keep doing what they have done for the past decade, the US and China will almost certainly wind up at war. Second, *war is not inevitable.* History shows that major ruling powers can manage relations with rivals, even those that threaten to overtake them, without triggering a war. The record of those successes, as well as the failures, offers many lessons for statesmen today. As George Santayana noted, only those who fail to study history are condemned to repeat it.

The chapters that follow describe the origins of Thucydides's Trap, explore its dynamics, and explain its implications for the present contest between the US and China. Part One provides a succinct summary of the rise of China. Everyone knows about China's growth but few have realized its magnitude or its consequences. To paraphrase former Czech president Václav Havel, it has happened so quickly that we have not yet had time to be astonished.

Part Two locates recent developments in US-China relations on the broader canvas of history. This not only helps us understand current events, but also provides clues about where events are trending. Our review stretches back 2,500 years, to the time when the rapid growth of Athens shocked a dominant martial Sparta and led to the Peloponnesian War. Key examples from the past 500 years also provide insights into the ways in which the tension between rising and ruling powers can tilt the chessboard toward war. The closest analogue to the current standoff—Germany's challenge to Britain's ruling global empire before World War I—should give us all pause.

Part Three asks whether we should see current trends in America's relations with China as a gathering storm of similar proportions. Daily media reports of China's "aggressive" behavior and unwillingness to accept the "international rules-based order" established by the US after World War II describe incidents and accidents reminiscent of 1914. At the same time, a dose of self-awareness is due. If China were "just like us" when the US burst into the twentieth century brimming with confidence that the hundred years ahead would be an American era, the rivalry would be even more severe, and war even harder to avoid. If it actually followed in America's footsteps, we should expect to see Chinese troops enforcing Beijing's will from Mongolia to Australia, just as Theodore Roosevelt molded "our hemisphere" to his liking.

China is following a different trajectory than did the United States during its own surge to primacy. But in many aspects of China's rise, we can hear echoes. What does President Xi Jinping's China want? In one line: to make China great again. The deepest aspiration of over a billion Chinese citizens is to make their nation not only rich, but also powerful. Indeed, their goal is a China so rich and so powerful that other nations will have no choice but to recognize its interests and give it the respect that it deserves. The sheer scale and ambition of this "China Dream" should disabuse us of any notion that the contest between China and the United States will naturally subside as China becomes a "responsible stakeholder." This is especially so given what my former colleague Sam Huntington famously called a "clash of civilizations," a historical disjunction in which fundamentally different Chinese and American values and traditions make rapprochement between the two powers even more elusive.

While resolution of the present rivalry may seem difficult to foresee, actual armed conflict appears distant. But is it? In truth, the paths to war are more varied and plausible (and even mundane) than we want to believe. From current confrontations in the South China Sea, the East China Sea, and cyberspace, to a trade conflict that spirals out of control, it is frighteningly easy to develop scenarios in which American and Chinese soldiers are killing each other. Though none of these scenarios seem likely, when we recall the unintended consequences of the assassination of the Hapsburg archduke or of Khrushchev's nuclear adventure in Cuba, we are reminded of just how narrow the gap is between "unlikely" and "impossible."

Part Four explains why war is *not* inevitable. Most of the policy community and general public are naively complacent about the possibility of war. Fatalists, meanwhile, see an irresistible force rapidly approaching an immovable object. Neither side has it right. If leaders in both societies will study the successes and failures of the past, they will find a rich source of clues from which to fashion a strategy that can meet each nation's essential interests without war.

The return to prominence of a 5,000-year-old civilization with 1.4 billion people is not a problem to be fixed. It is a *condition* — a chronic condition that will have to be managed over a generation. Success will require not just a new slogan, more frequent presidential summits, or additional meetings of departmental working groups. Managing this relationship without war will demand sustained attention, week by week, at the highest levels in both governments. It will require a depth of mutual understanding not seen since the Henry Kissinger–Zhou Enlai conversations that reestablished US-China relations in the 1970s. Most significant, it will mean more radical changes in attitudes and actions by leaders and the public alike than anyone has yet undertaken. To escape Thucydides's Trap, we must be willing to think the unthinkable —and imagine the unimaginable. Avoiding Thucydides's Trap in this case will require nothing less than bending the arc of history.

Part One

THE RISE OF CHINA

1

"THE BIGGEST PLAYER IN THE
HISTORY OF THE WORLD"

<hr>

You have no idea what sort of people the Athenians are. They are
always thinking of new schemes and are quick to carry them out.
They make a plan: if it succeeds, the success is nothing in comparison to what they are going to do next.

—Thucydides, Corinthian ambassador
addresses the Spartan Assembly, 432 BCE

Let China sleep; when she wakes, she will shake the world.

—Napoleon, 1817

Shortly after he became director of the Central Intelligence Agency
in September 2011, I went to see America's most successful modern general in his office in Langley, Virginia. David Petraeus and I had
first met in the 1980s when he was a doctoral student at Princeton and
I was dean of Harvard Kennedy School. We had stayed in touch ever
since, as he rose through the ranks of the US Army and I continued my
academic work while also serving several tours in the Pentagon. After
some preliminary discussion about his new job, I asked David whether
the old hands at the Agency had begun opening for him some of the
secret "jewel boxes"—the files containing the deepest, most heavily
classified secrets of the US government. He smiled knowingly and said,
"You bet," but then waited for me to say more.

After a pause, I asked what he had learned about "deep sleepers": individuals with whom the Agency had established a relationship, but whose assignment essentially consisted of going to live and prosper in a foreign country so as to develop a full understanding of its culture, people, and government. With a commitment to be helpful to their careers in unseen ways, the Agency only asked of these individuals that, when called upon — unobtrusively, perhaps just once or twice in a decade — they would provide their candid insights into what was happening in the country, and what was likely to happen in the future.

David was by this point leaning forward across the table as I opened a report from someone whose incisive, far-sighted understanding could inform Washington's response to the greatest geopolitical challenge of our lifetime. As I said to the new director, this individual had succeeded beyond all expectations. He had seen up close China's convulsions from the Great Leap Forward and Cultural Revolution in the 1960s to Deng Xiaoping's capitalist pivot in the 1980s. Indeed, he had established serious working relationships with many of the people who governed China, including China's future president, Xi Jinping.

I began reading the first set of questions from fifty pages of Q&A with this asset:

- Are China's current leaders serious about displacing the United States as the number-one power in Asia in the foreseeable future?
- What is China's strategy for becoming Number One?
- What are the major hurdles to China's executing its strategy?
- How likely is China to succeed?
- If it does succeed, what will be the consequences for its neighbors in Asia? For the US?
- Is conflict between China and the US inevitable?

This individual had provided invaluable answers to these questions and many more. He had pulled the curtain back on the thinking of the Chinese leadership. He had soberly assessed the risk that these two countries might someday violently collide. And he had given actionable intelligence that could help prevent the unthinkable from happening.

Lee Kuan Yew was, of course, no CIA spy. His mind, heart, and soul belonged to Singapore. But the longtime statesman, who died in 2015, was a font of wisdom hiding in plain sight. The report I gave to David was a sneak preview of *Lee Kuan Yew: The Grand Master's Insights on China, the United States, and the World,* a book that I coauthored in 2013 with Robert Blackwill and Ali Wyne. As the founder and long-serving leader of that tiny city-state, Lee took a small, poor, inconsequential fishing village and raised it to become a modern megalopolis. Ethnically Chinese, he was educated at Cambridge University and embodied a fusion of Confucian and upper-class English values. And until his death in 2015, he was also unquestionably the world's premier China watcher.

Lee's insights into what was happening in China, as well as the wider world, made him a sought-after strategic counselor to presidents and prime ministers on every continent — including every American head of state from Richard Nixon to Barack Obama. His keen understanding of China reflected not only his "singular strategic acumen,"[1] as Henry Kissinger called it, but also his intense need to know as much as he could about this sleeping giant. Though its economic and political might was not so obvious amid Mao's agrarian Marxism, China was nevertheless a colossus in whose shadow Lee's island nation struggled for enough sunlight to survive. Lee was one of the first to see China's true nature — and its full potential.

Uniquely, as Lee studied China and its leaders, they also studied him and his country. In the late 1970s, when Deng began to think about leading China on a fast march to the market, Chinese leaders looked to Singapore as a laboratory in not only economic but also political development. Lee spent thousands of hours in direct conversations with Chinese presidents, prime ministers, cabinet officers, and rising leaders of his "neighbor to the North."[2] Every Chinese leader from Deng Xiaoping to Xi Jinping has called him "mentor," a term of ultimate respect in Chinese culture.

My biggest takeaway from Lee for the new CIA director addresses the most troubling question about China's trajectory: What does its dramatic transformation mean for the global balance of power? Lee answered pointedly: "The size of China's displacement of the world balance is such that the world must find a new balance. It is not possible to pretend that this is just another big player. *This is the biggest player in the history of the world*."[3]

COULD THE US BECOME NUMBER TWO?

In my national security course at Harvard, my lecture on China begins with a quiz. The first question asks students to compare China and the United States in 1980 with their current rankings. Repeatedly, students are shocked at what they see. One glance at the chart with numbers from 2015 should explain why.

In a single generation, a nation that did not appear on any of the international league tables has vaulted into the top spot. In 1980, China's gross domestic product (GDP) was less than $300 billion; by 2015, it was $11 trillion—making it the world's second-largest economy by market exchange rates. In 1980, China's trade with the outside world amounted to less than $40 billion; by 2015, it had increased one hundredfold, to $4 trillion.[4] For every two-year period since 2008, the *increment of growth* in China's GDP has been larger than the entire econ-

China, as a percentage of the United States		
	1980	2015
GDP	7%	61%
Imports	8%	73%
Exports	8%	151%
Reserves	16%	3,140%

Figures as measured in US dollars. Source: World Bank.

omy of India.[5] Even at its lower growth rate in 2015, China's economy created a Greece every sixteen weeks and an Israel every twenty-five weeks.

During its own remarkable progress between 1860 and 1913, when the United States shocked European capitals by surpassing Great Britain to become the world's largest economy, America's annual growth averaged 4 percent.[6] Since 1980, China's economy has grown at 10 percent a year. According to the Rule of 72—divide 72 by the annual growth rate to determine when an economy or investment will double —the Chinese economy has doubled every seven years.

To appreciate how remarkable this is, we need a longer timeline. In the eighteenth century, Britain gave birth to the Industrial Revolution, creating what we now know as the modern world. In 1776, Adam Smith published *The Wealth of Nations* to explain how after millennia of poverty, market capitalism was creating wealth and a new middle class. Seventeen years later, an emissary from King George III (the same "mad King George" who lost the Revolutionary War to the US) arrived in China to propose establishing relations between the two nations. At that moment, British workers were massively more productive than their Chinese counterparts.[7] The Chinese were many, as they had been over the centuries. But they were poor. At the end of each day of labor, a Chinese worker had produced barely enough to feed himself and his family—leaving relatively little surplus for the state to pay soldiers or invest in armaments like a navy (which over four millennia Chinese emperors never did, bar one brief half-century exception) to project power far beyond its borders. Today workers in China are one quarter as productive as their American counterparts. If over the next decade or two they become just half as productive as Americans, China's economy will be twice the size of the US economy. If they equal American productivity, China will have an economy four times that of the US.

This elementary arithmetic poses a fundamental problem for Washington's effort to "rebalance" China's growing weight. In 2011, with considerable fanfare, then secretary of state Hillary Clinton announced an important "pivot" in American foreign policy, redirecting Washington's attention and resources from the Middle East to Asia.[8] In President Obama's words, "After a decade in which we fought two wars that cost us dearly, in blood and treasure, the US is turning our attention to the vast potential of the Asia-Pacific region."[9] He promised to increase America's diplomatic, economic, and military presence in the Asia-Pacific, and signaled the US determination to counter the impact of China's rise in the region. President Obama has featured this "rebalance" as one of the major foreign policy achievements of his administration.

As assistant secretary of state under Obama and Secretary Clinton, Kurt Campbell led this initiative. His 2016 book, *The Pivot: The Future of American Statecraft in Asia,* makes the best possible case for the "great rebalance" as more than aspiration. Despite his best efforts, however, he is unable to find many metrics to support his thesis. Measured in attention span of the president, time spent at National Security Council principals' and deputies' meetings, face time with leaders of the region, sorties flown, hours of ships on station, and dollars allocated, the pivot is hard to find. Ongoing wars in Iraq and Afghanistan combined with new wars in Syria and against ISIS across the Middle East to monopolize the administration's foreign policy agenda and dominate the president's days over his eight years in office. As one Obama White House official recalled: "It never felt like we pivoted away from the Middle East. About 80 percent of our main meetings at the National Security Council have focused on the Middle East."[10]

Even if American attention had not been focused elsewhere, Washington would have struggled to defy the laws of economic gravity. Compare the relative weight of the US and Chinese economies as if they were two competitors on opposite ends of a seesaw. The conclusion is as obvious as it is painful. Americans have been debating whether they should put less weight on their left foot (the Middle East) in order to put more weight on their right (Asia). Meanwhile, China has just kept growing—at three times the US rate. As a result, America's side of the seesaw has tilted to the point that soon both feet will be dangling entirely off the ground.

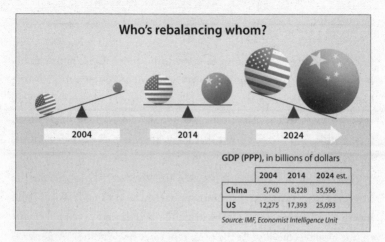

Who's rebalancing whom?

2004   2014   2024

GDP (PPP), in billions of dollars

	2004	2014	2024 est.
China	5,760	18,228	35,596
US	12,275	17,393	25,093

Source: IMF, Economist Intelligence Unit

This is the subtext of the first question on my class quiz. The second question pricks more delusions. It asks students: When might the US *actually* find itself number two? In what year might China overtake the United States to become the number-one auto market, the biggest market for luxury goods, or even the largest economy in the world, full stop?

Most students are stunned to learn that on most indicators, China has *already* surpassed the United States. As the largest producer of ships, steel, aluminum, furniture, clothing, textiles, cell phones, and computers, China has become the manufacturing powerhouse of the world.[11] Students are even more surprised to discover that China has also become the world's largest consumer of most products. America was the birthplace of the automobile, but China is now both the largest automaker and the largest auto market. Chinese consumers bought twenty million cars in 2015—three million more than were sold in the US.[12] China is also the world's largest market for cell phones and e-commerce, and has the largest number of Internet users.[13] China imported more oil, consumed more energy, and installed more solar power than any other nation.[14] Perhaps most devastatingly for America's self-conception, in 2016—as it has since the 2008 worldwide financial crisis —China continued to serve as the primary engine of global economic growth.[15]

BUT THAT'S IMPOSSIBLE!

For Americans who grew up in a world in which USA meant number one—and that would be every citizen since roughly 1870—the idea that China could unseat the US as the world's largest economy is unthinkable. Many Americans imagine that economic primacy is an unalienable right, to the point that it has become part of their national identity.

America's attachment to its position atop the world helps explain the firestorm that erupted at the International Monetary Fund/World Bank meeting in Washington in 2014 when the IMF issued its annual report on the global economy. As the press reported the headline: "America Is Now No. 2." In *MarketWatch*'s shout-out: "There's no easy way to say this, so I'll just say it: We're no longer No. 1."[16] More somberly, as the *Financial Times* summarized the IMF's message: "Now it is official. In 2014 the IMF estimates the size of the U.S. economy was $17.4 trillion and the size of China's economy was $17.6 trillion." The *FT* went on to note that "as recently as 2005, China's economy was less than half the size of the U.S. By 2019, the IMF expects it to be 20% bigger."[17]

The IMF had measured China's GDP using the yardstick of purchasing power parity, or PPP, which is the standard now used by the major international institutions whose professional responsibilities require them to compare national economies. As the CIA puts it, PPP "provides the best available starting point for comparisons of economic strength and wellbeing between countries." The IMF explains that "market rates are more volatile and using them can produce quite large swings in aggregate measures of growth even when growth rates in individual countries are stable. PPP is generally regarded as a better measure of overall wellbeing."[18] Measured by purchasing power parity, China has not only surpassed the US, but also now accounts for roughly 18 percent of world GDP, compared to just 2 percent in 1980.[19]

Among those for whom American primacy is an article of faith, the IMF announcement stimulated a vigorous search for metrics by which the US is still number one. These include GDP per capita, new data that

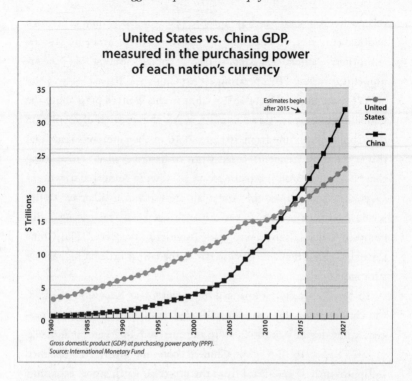

United States vs. China GDP, measured in the purchasing power of each nation's currency

Estimates begin after 2015 →

United States
China

$ Trillions

Gross domestic product (GDP) at purchasing power parity (PPP).
Source: International Monetary Fund

take better account of quality of life and well-being, and new ratio-nales for the previous standard that measured GDP at market exchange rates.[20] Since a number of my respected colleagues disagree, I asked the world's leading professor–central banker, former MIT professor Stan-ley Fischer, how we should measure the US economy against China's. Fischer wrote the textbook on Macroeconomics, taught Ben Bernanke (former head of the Federal Reserve System) and Mario Draghi (head of the European Central Bank), served as the chairman of the Central Bank of Israel, and now serves as the vice chairman of the US Fed. He knows whereof he speaks. And in his judgment, PPP truly is the best benchmark — and not just for assessing relative economic strength. "In comparing the size of national economies," he told me, "especially for the purposes of assessing comparative military potential, as the first ap-proximation, the best yardstick is PPP. This measures how many air-craft, missiles, ships, sailors, pilots, drones, bases, and other military-related items a state can buy and the prices it has to pay in its own national currency."[21] The International Institute for Strategic Studies' authoritative annual *The Military Balance* concurs, noting that "the arguments for using PPP are strongest for China and Russia."[22]

As I write this, the favorite story line in the Western press about the Chinese economy is "slowdown." A word-cloud search of reports on the Chinese economy from 2013 to 2016 in the elite press finds that this is the most frequently used word to describe what is happening there.[23] The question few pause to ask is: slowing compared to whom? Over this same period, the American press's favorite adjective to describe American economic performance has been "recovering." But compare China's "slowdown" with America's "recovery." Has China slowed to about the same growth rate as the US? A little bit higher? Or a lot more?

To be sure, since the financial crisis and Great Recession of 2008, the Chinese economy has indeed slowed, from an average of 10 percent in the decade prior to 2008 to the current 6 to 7 percent annually in 2015 and 2016. But while Chinese economic growth has declined by approximately one-third from the pre-crisis level, global economic growth has been cut nearly in half. The "recovering" US economy has averaged just 2.1 percent growth annually in the years since the Great Recession. The EU economies, meanwhile, have grown by 1.3 percent annually since then and continue to stagnate. The same is true of Japan, which has averaged just 1.2 percent growth during this period.[24] For all the noise about the Chinese economic slowdown, remember one incandescent fact: since the Great Recession, 40 percent of all the growth around the world has occurred in just one country: China.[25]

COULD ROME BE BUILT IN TWO WEEKS?

In 1980, American visitors to China were rare. The country had only recently "opened" to the West, and travel was still difficult. Those who went found a country that looked as if it had been plucked from the distant past: vast, rural, unchanging, inscrutable, asleep. They saw bamboo houses and crumbling Soviet-style apartment blocks, and city streets crowded only with throngs of bicycles, their riders wearing nearly identical drab Mao suits. Tourists who ventured across the water from Hong Kong saw the empty fields of Guangzhou and Shenzhen dotted with tiny villages. Wherever they went, Americans encountered grinding poverty: 88 percent of China's one billion citizens struggling to survive — as they had for millennia before the Industrial Revolution — on less than $2 a day.[26]

The once-empty streets of Beijing are now clogged with six million automobiles. Looking back on his secret diplomatic mission to China in the early 1970s, Henry Kissinger — the secretary of state who played a key role in reopening China to the West — said, "Remembering China in 1971, if anyone had shown me a picture of what Beijing looks like and said in 25 years Beijing will look like this, I would have said that's absolutely impossible."[27] The village of Shenzhen is today a mega-city of more than ten million people, with real estate prices that rival Silicon Valley's. Former Australian prime minister Kevin Rudd, an astute China watcher, has described the country's explosion as "the English Industrial Revolution and the global information revolution combusting simultaneously and compressed into not 300 years, but 30."[28]

When Americans complain about how long it takes to build a building or repair a road, authorities often reply that "Rome was not built in a day." Someone clearly forgot to tell the Chinese. By 2005, the country was building the square-foot equivalent of today's Rome *every two weeks*.[29] Between 2011 and 2013, China both produced and used more cement than the US did in the entire twentieth century.[30] In 2011, a Chinese firm built a 30-story skyscraper in just 15 days. Three years later, another construction firm built a 57-story skyscraper in 19 days.[31] Indeed, China built the equivalent of Europe's entire housing stock in just 15 years.[32]

When he first saw the "massive, beautifully appointed" Tianjin Meijiang Convention and Exhibition Center, which hosted the 2010 World Economic Forum's summer conference, *New York Times* columnist Thomas Friedman confessed to having gasped. It was built in just

8 months. Friedman noted the feat with amazement, but also dismay. It took almost as long for a Washington Metro crew to repair "two tiny escalators of 21 steps each at a red line station" near his home in Maryland.[33]

Friedman devotes an entire chapter of his book *Hot, Flat, and Crowded* to a fantasy about the far-reaching reforms the United States could enact if only it were "China for a day."[34] Today China is doing in hours what it takes years to accomplish in the US. I have been reminded of this daily when I see the bridge over the Charles River between my office at Harvard Kennedy School and Harvard Business School. It has been under reconstruction, snarling traffic, for 4 *years*. In November 2015, Beijing replaced the substantially larger, 1,300-ton Sanyuan Bridge in just *43 hours*.[35] Overall, China built 2.6 million miles of roads—including 70,000 miles of highways—between 1996 and 2016, connecting 95 percent of the country's villages and overtaking the US as the country with the most extensive highway system by almost 50 percent.[36]

Over the past decade, China has constructed the world's longest high-speed rail network: 12,000 miles of rail lines that carry passengers between cities at speeds of up to 180 miles per hour. In the US, that much new track would stretch from New York to California and back, twice. At 180 mph, one could go from Grand Central Terminal in New York City to Union Station in DC in just over an hour; from Boston to Washington in two. Indeed, China now has more high-speed rail tracks than the rest of the world combined.[37] During this same decade, California has been struggling mightily to build a single 520-mile high-speed connection between Los Angeles and San Francisco. Voters approved the project in 2008, but the state recently admitted it will not be finished until 2029, at a cost of $68 billion—9 years later and $35 billion more than was originally promised.[38] By then, China plans to have completed another 16,000 miles of high-speed rail connections.[39]

Beyond the skyscrapers, bridges, and fast trains lies the far more profound impact of China's human development. A generation ago, 90 out of every 100 Chinese lived on less than $2 a day. Today fewer than 3 in 100 do.[40] Average per capita income has risen from $193 in 1980 to over $8,100 today.[41] In assessing progress toward the UN's Millennium Development Goals for improving the lives of the world's poorest people, World Bank president Robert Zoellick noted in 2010, "Between 1981 and 2004, China succeeded in lifting more than half a billion people out of extreme poverty. This is certainly the greatest leap to overcome poverty in history."[42]

China's education, health care, and related indicators reflect similar improvements in its people's well-being. In 1949, Chinese citizens could expect to die at the age of thirty-six, and 8 in 10 could not read or write. By 2014, life expectancy had more than doubled, to seventy-six, and 95 percent are literate.[43] If China continues on its current growth path, millions of individuals will experience a hundredfold increase in living standards over their lifetimes. At the average per capita growth rate in the US over the past decade, Americans will have to wait 740 years to see an equivalent improvement. As the *Economist* has repeatedly explained to its readers, for the first time in modern history, Asia is now richer than Europe in terms of accumulated private wealth. Asia is expected to surpass North America around 2020, with China as the main driver of wealth accumulation (which includes total financial assets across households).[44]

In the blink of history's eye, China's economic growth has not only raised hundreds of millions from poverty, but also produced an extraordinary number of millionaires and billionaires. By one count, China surpassed the United States as the country with the most billionaires in 2015 and is now adding a new billionaire every week.[45] And while Chinese are among the most aggressive savers in the world — families typically save over 30 percent of their disposable income — one can hardly imagine what Karl Marx would say if he knew how many Chinese "Communists" are wearing Prada today. Chinese shoppers bought half of the world's luxury goods sold in 2015.[46] Louis Vuitton, Chanel, and Gucci now see Chinese as their primary customers. Sotheby's and Christie's highest-priced auctions are no longer held in New York and London, but in Beijing and Shanghai.

THE STEM REVOLUTION

A generation ago, China stood at the bottom of most international rankings of nations in education, science, technology, and innovation. But after two decades of determined investment in the country's human capital, it has become a global competitor. Today it rivals, and by some measures outperforms, the United States.[47]

The internationally recognized gold standard for comparing education performance among high school students is the Program for International Student Assessment. On the 2015 PISA test, China ranked sixth in mathematics while the United States ranked thirty-ninth. China's score was well above the OECD average, while the US score was significantly below. Even the highest-rated American state, Massachusetts, would stand just twentieth if it were measured as its own country in the rankings—a drop from its ninth-place rating when the test was last conducted, in 2012.[48] According to the most recent Stanford University comparison of students entering college in the fields of engineering and computer science, Chinese high school graduates arrive with a three-year advantage over their American counterparts in critical-thinking skills.[49]

In 2015, Tsinghua University passed MIT in the *U.S. News & World Report* rankings to become the number-one university in the world for engineering. Among the top ten schools of engineering, China and the US each had four.[50] In STEM subjects (science, technology, engineering, and mathematics), which provide the core competencies driving advances in science, technology, and the fastest-growing sectors of modern economies, China annually graduates four times as many students as the US (1.3 million vs. 300,000). And that does not include an additional 300,000 Chinese students currently enrolled in US institutions.[51] This gap has persisted for a decade despite the Obama administration's celebrated Educate to Innovate initiative to promote STEM education, launched in 2009. In every year of the Obama administration, Chinese universities awarded more PhDs in STEM fields than American universities.[52]

The impact of China's investments in education is already evident across the Chinese economy. Long known primarily as a low-cost producer of inexpensive consumer goods, China has seen its share of total global value-added in high-tech manufacturing increase from 7 percent in 2003 to 27 percent in 2014. The US National Science Foundation report that documented this growth also finds that over that same decade, the American share of this market declined from 36 to 29 percent. For example, in the fast moving field of robotics, in 2015 China not only registered twice as many applications for new patents, but also added two and a half times as many industrial robots to its workforce.[53] China is now the world leader in producing computers, semiconductors, and communications equipment, as well as pharmaceuticals.[54] In 2015, Chinese filed almost twice as many total patent applications as the second-place Americans and became the first country to generate more than one million applications in a single year.[55] On its current path, China will surpass the US to become the world leader in research-and-development spending by 2019.[56] As a 2014 American Academy of Arts and Sciences study warns: "If our nation does not act quickly to shore up its scientific enterprise, it will squander the advantage it has long held as an engine of innovation that generates new discoveries and stimulates job growth."[57]

In response to these trends, many Americans have sought refuge in the belief that for all its size and bluster, China's success is still essentially a story of imitation and mass production. This view has some grounding in reality: theft of intellectual property—both in the old-fashioned way, with spies, and increasingly by exploiting cyber methods as well —has been another key part of China's economic development program. As a Chinese colleague once explained to me, what Americans call R&D (research and development), Chinese think of as RD&T, where the T stands for theft. Of course, China only targets nations that have intellectual property worth stealing—the most important being the United States. "The amount of theft that's going on is simply staggering," FBI director James Comey said in 2014. "There's only two types of big corporations in America. Those who have been hacked by the Chinese, or those who don't yet know they've been hacked by the Chinese." A 2016 investigation by CBS's *60 Minutes* reported that China's corporate espionage has cost American companies hundreds of billions of dollars, leading a top Justice Department official to call Chinese cybertheft "a serious threat to our national security."[58]

Though it remains a hotbed of cyber piracy and corporate spying, with each passing year it is getting harder to dismiss China's growing power as an innovator in its own right. Consider supercomputers, which the White House Office of Science and Technology singled out as "essential to economic competitiveness, scientific discovery, and national security."[59] To ensure that the US could sustain its "leadership position" in supercomputing, President Obama established the National Strategic Computing Initiative in 2015 as a pillar of his Strategy for American Innovation. But since June 2013, the world's fastest supercomputer has been located not in Silicon Valley but in China. Indeed, in the rankings of the world's 500 fastest supercomputers—a list from which China was absent in 2001—today it has 167, two more than the United States. Moreover, China's top supercomputer is five times faster than the closest American competitor. And while China's supercomputers previously relied heavily on American processors, its top computer in 2016 was built entirely with domestic processors.[60]

Two further 2016 breakthroughs in China provide troubling pointers to the future: the launch of the world's first quantum communications satellite, designed to provide an unprecedented scope of hackproof communications, and completion of the largest radio telescope on earth, a device that has an unmatched capacity to search deep space for intelligent life. Each of these achievements demonstrates China's ability to undertake costly, long-term, pathbreaking projects and see them through to successful completion—a capability that has atrophied in the US, as demonstrated by the failure of multiple recent multibillion-dollar investments in mega-projects, from plutonium reprocessing at Savannah River in South Carolina (facing cancellation, despite $5 billion in taxpayer expenditures, after a recent estimate stated that the project would cost $1 billion annually and last decades), to what MIT called the "flagship" carbon capture and storage project at Kemper County, Mississippi ($4 billion in cost overruns, recently delayed by over two years, and facing an uncertain future).[61]

BIGGER BARRELS OF BIGGER GUNS

While GDP is not the only measure of a country's rise, it provides the substructure of national power. And while GDP does not translate instantly or automatically into economic or military strength, if history is our guide, nations with larger GDPs over time have proportionally greater influence in shaping international affairs.

Chinese never forget Mao's dictum: Power grows out of the barrel of a gun. They know that the Communist Party governs China, rather than successors of Chiang Kai-shek's Guomindang, for one and only one reason. Mao and his fighting comrades won the civil war. When in 1989 students and their supporters rose up in Tiananmen Square to protest, who crushed them to keep the Communist authorities in power? Chinese soldiers with guns and tanks. As China's economy has gotten bigger, its guns and tanks—and their twenty-first-century equivalents—have gotten better, and allowed for a new level of competition with other great powers, especially the United States. Just as technology start-ups like Facebook and Uber have used the concept of disruptive innovation to upend previously dominant firms, the Chinese military is developing new technologies that can counter ships, planes, and satellites that the US has developed over decades—and for a fraction of the cost. Today, states playing catch-up need not replicate investments that their competitors made in hardware and other "legacy" platforms. New technologies allow for asymmetric responses, like missiles that can be launched from the Chinese mainland to destroy aircraft carriers, or antisatellite weapons that for a million dollars can destroy a multibillion-dollar US satellite.[62]

Although it has devoted on average just 2 percent of its GDP to defense since the late 1980s (the US has spent closer to 4 percent),[63] three decades of double-digit economic growth have allowed Chinese military capabilities to expand eightfold.[64] Today its defense budget of $146 billion in market exchange rates (or $314 billion in PPP) ranks second only to that of the US, and is twice Russia's.[65] China's growing military might will be discussed in greater detail in chapter 6. For now, suffice it to say that China has already secured a number of advantages on the battlefield. The most authoritative assessment of the changing balance of military power in the region is a 2015 RAND Corporation study called "The U.S.-China Military Scorecard." The report finds that, by 2017, China will have an "advantage" or "approximate parity" in six of the nine areas of conventional capability: for instance, in launching attacks on air bases or surface targets, achieving air superiority, and preventing an opponent from using space-based weapons. The report concludes that over the next five to fifteen years, "Asia will witness a progressively receding frontier of U.S. dominance."[66] Like its economic progress, China's military advances are rapidly undercutting America's status as a global hegemon and are forcing US leaders to confront ugly truths about the limits of American power.

THE NEW BALANCE OF POWER

While serving as secretary of state, Hillary Clinton once suggested that in the twenty-first century the concept of balance of power was obsolete.[67] Lee Kuan Yew disagreed. He saw the idea as a fundamental building block in understanding relations among nations. But, he explained, "in the old concept, balance of power meant largely military power. In today's terms, it is a combination of economic and military, and I think the economic outweighs the military."[68]

This new balance of power has been called by another name: geoeconomics, which is the use of economic instruments (from trade and investment policy to sanctions, cyberattacks, and foreign aid) to achieve geopolitical goals. Robert Blackwill and Jennifer Harris explore the concept in their 2016 book, *War by Other Means: Geoeconomics and Statecraft*. They argue that China "is the world's leading practitioner of geoeconomics, but it has also been perhaps the major factor in returning regional or global power projection back to an importantly economic (as opposed to political-military) exercise."[69]

China primarily conducts foreign policy through economics because, to put it bluntly, it can. It is currently the largest trading partner for over 130 countries—including all the major Asian economies. Its trade with members of the Association of Southeast Asian Nations accounted for 15 percent of ASEAN's total trade in 2015, while the US accounted for only 9 percent. This imbalance will accelerate in the absence of the Trans-Pacific Partnership as China moves quickly to establish its own equivalent in an emerging co-prosperity area.[70]

This geoeconomic strategy harks back to Sun Tzu's maxim: "Ultimate excellence lies not in winning every battle, but in defeating the enemy without ever fighting." As Henry Kissinger's *On China* explains, victory for Sun Tzu was "not simply the triumph of armed forces," but "the achievement of the ultimate political objectives" that a military clash would be intended to secure: "Far better than challenging the enemy on the field of battle is . . . maneuvering him into an unfavorable position from which escape is impossible."[71] In economic relations today, China is doing just that.

Of course, mastery in international affairs requires more than just economic leverage. A government must have not only the economic heft but also the skill to wield economic instruments effectively. Here China has demonstrated a unique mastery in using hard instruments of "soft power." When parties are slow to recognize reality or determined to resist, China is ready to use the carrots and sticks of its economic power—buying, selling, sanctioning, investing, bribing, and stealing as needed until they fall into line. Nations that have become dependent on China's supply of key imports, and on Chinese markets for their exports, are particularly vulnerable: when disagreements arise, China simply delays the first and blocks the second. Notable cases include China's abrupt cessation of all exports of rare metals to Japan in 2010 (to persuade Japan to return several Chinese fishermen it had detained); its zeroing out of salmon purchases from what had been Norway's number-one market in 2011 (to punish Norway for the Nobel Peace Prize committee's selection of a noted Chinese dissident, Liu Xiaobo); and its prolonged inspection of bananas from the Philippines until they had rotted on the docks in 2012 (to change the Filipino government's calculations about a dispute over Scarborough Shoal in the South China Sea).

China enjoys such superiority in its balance of economic power that many other states have no realistic option but to comply with its wishes, even when the international system is on their side. In 2016, for instance, China flatly rejected an unfavorable ruling by the Permanent Court of Arbitration over a dispute with the Philippines in the South China Sea, setting the table for another contest of wills. In this standoff and others involving the South China Sea, China has demonstrated an ability to combine charm, largesse, bribes, and blackmail to find "compromises" that give it most of what it wants.

Better than bilateral bargaining, of course, are international institutions that give the designer the advantage. The United States led the way down this road in the aftermath of World War II when creating the Bretton Woods institutions: the IMF (to coordinate international finance), the World Bank (to provide below-market-rate loans to developing countries), and the GATT and its successor, the World Trade Organization (to promote trade). In both the IMF and the World Bank, one—and only one—country has a veto over any changes in governance of the institutions: the United States.

Predictably, as China's economy has grown, its leaders have become unhappy with these inherited arrangements, and have thus begun to forge new ones. After years of the United States' refusing to accommodate China's request for a larger share of the votes at the World Bank, in 2013 Beijing stunned Washington by establishing its own competitive institution, the Asian Infrastructure Investment Bank (AIIB). Despite an intense campaign by Washington to pressure nations not to join China's bank, fifty-seven signed up before it launched in 2015—including some of America's key allies, with the UK in the lead. They said no to the United States and yes to China in the hope of receiving loans at below-market rates and contracts for large construction projects funded by the bank. Their incentives were plain to see: even before the AIIB was established, the China Development Bank had surpassed the World Bank as the biggest financer of international development projects.[72] Including its commitment of $30 billion to the AIIB as starting capital, China's combined international development finance assets in 2016 were $130 billion larger than those of the six major Western development banks combined.[73]

This was not the first time China decided to start its own club rather than play by the West's rules. In the aftermath of the financial crisis and Great Recession of 2008, China organized the BRICS—Brazil, Russia, India, China, and South Africa—as a group of rapidly expanding economies capable of making decisions and taking actions without supervision from the United States or the G7. After Vladimir Putin sent Russian troops into Ukraine in 2014, the United States and European Union disinvited him to what was supposed to have been a G8 meeting and declared him "isolated." A month later, Xi Jinping and other leaders of the BRICS welcomed him with open arms at their summit.

Other Chinese initiatives have had similar effects. In September 2013, Xi Jinping announced China's intention to invest $1.4 trillion in building a "New Silk Road" of infrastructure to link sixty-five countries in Asia, Europe, and North Africa with a combined population of 4.4 billion people. Through the "Silk Road Economic Belt" and "21st-Century Maritime Silk Road"—collectively known as One Belt, One Road (OBOR)—China is constructing a network of highways, fast railroads, airports, ports, pipelines, power transmission lines, and fiber-optic cables across Eurasia. These modern physical links along what were once ancient Chinese trade routes will foster new diplomatic, trade, and financial ties. At this point, OBOR includes 900 projects at a cost exceeding $1.4 trillion. Even after adjusting for inflation, this amounts to 12 Marshall Plans, according to the investor and former IMF economist Stephen Jen.[74]

Largesse, economic imperialism—call it what you will. The fact is that China's economic network is spreading across the globe, altering the international balance of power in a way that causes even longtime US allies in Asia to tilt from the US toward China. In Lee Kuan Yew's succinct summary, "China is sucking the Southeast Asian countries into its economic system because of its vast market and growing purchasing power. Japan and South Korea will inevitably be sucked in as well. It just absorbs countries without having to use force . . . China's growing economic sway will be very difficult to fight."[75] Or in the Chinese version of the Golden Rule: He who has the gold, rules.

The implications of these developments for the relative position of China and the United States were captured memorably in a comment by one of America's wisest Asia hands. Having served for three decades in the US government, including assignments as ambassador to both the Philippines and South Korea, in 1998 Stephen Bosworth was appointed dean of the Fletcher School of Law and Diplomacy at Tufts University. In the decade that followed, he shifted his focus away from Asia to commit himself fully to that educational institution. Then, in 2009, he was asked by President Obama to become his special envoy for North Korea. When he returned from an initial two-week trip across the region after meeting with prime ministers and presidents, Bosworth reported that he could scarcely believe what he had seen. It was, he recalled, a "Rip Van Winkle experience." In "olden days"—by which he meant before 1998—when a crisis or issue arose, the first question Asian leaders always asked was: What does Washington think? Today, when something happens, they ask first: What does Beijing think?

Part Two

LESSONS FROM HISTORY

2

ATHENS VS. SPARTA

The final point was reached when Athenian strength attained a peak plain for all to see and the Athenians began to encroach upon Sparta's allies. It was at this point that Sparta felt its position was no longer tolerable and decided by starting this present war to employ all energies in attacking and, if possible, destroying the power of Athens.   —Thucydides, *History of the Peloponnesian War*

It was the rise of Athens and the fear that this instilled in Sparta that made war inevitable.

—Thucydides, *History of the Peloponnesian War*

As a freshman in college, I enrolled in a course on ancient Greek. Most of that first year consisted of learning a new alphabet, vocabulary, sentence structure, and grammar. But our professor promised us that if we studied hard, by the end of the second semester we would be reading Xenophon's *Anabasis*. And beyond that, he dangled a "prize" for those who excelled in the second year: reading Thucydides.

I can still hear his enunciation: Thucydides! He spoke the name of the Athenian historian with a combination of exuberance and reverence. For Professor Labban, classical Greece represented the first great steeple of civilization. Only by mastering the original language could we learn about it from the person he deemed the father of history. While he appreciated Herodotus, our professor insisted that Thucydides was the first to focus exclusively on capturing history "as it really happened."[1] His account combines a journalist's eye for detail, a researcher's search for truth among competing accounts, and a historian's ability to identify the root causes behind complex events. Thucydides was also, as Professor Labban taught us, the pioneer of what we now call realpolitik, or realism in international relations. Since I was a budding student of world politics, I became all the more determined to claim Professor Labban's prize—which I ultimately did.

Thucydides left few records of his own life. We know that he was born around the middle of the fifth century BCE and that he was a citizen of Athens, one of the two most powerful city-states of ancient Greece. We also know that he was a general who, exiled from his homeland, traveled around the Mediterranean region in the midst of a great war —a conflict that racked the ancient world, and which pitted his native Athens against the dominant power of the day, the city-state of Sparta, ultimately laying both low. Thucydides's *History of the Peloponnesian War* is the definitive account of this conflict, and one of the great works of Western civilization. To this day it remains a seminal text, studied and debated not only by historians and classicists, but also by military and civilian strategists at universities and war colleges around the world.

As Thucydides explains in the introduction to his work, the purpose of his chronicle is to help future statesmen, soldiers, and citizens understand war so that they can avoid mistakes made by their predecessors: "If my history be judged useful by those who desire an exact knowledge of the past as an aid to understanding the future—which in the course of human affairs must resemble if it does not reflect it—I shall be content."[2] As the original "applied historian," he shared the view later captured by Winston Churchill's quip: "The longer you can look back, the farther you can look forward."

From Thucydides, my second-year classmates and I learned about the long peace that preceded the great war between Athens and Sparta. We read about Athens's precious experiment in democracy and its unprecedented surge of creative achievement in every field. These ancient Greeks essentially invented philosophy, drama, architecture, sculpture, history, naval warfare, and more; what they did not create themselves, they took to heights never seen before in human history. Socrates, Plato, Sophocles, Euripides, Aristophanes, Ictinus (the architect of the Parthenon), Demosthenes, and Pericles remain giants in the advance of civilization.

Thucydides wrote his history so that we can understand how such remarkable states that had managed to exist peacefully for decades ultimately found themselves in a devastating war. While other observers emphasized proximate causes, Thucydides goes to the heart of the matter. "As to the reasons why Sparta and Athens broke the truce," he writes, "I propose first to give an account of the causes of complaint which they had against each other and of the specific instances where their interests clashed." But, he warns, "the real reason for the war is most likely to be obscured by such arguments."

Beneath these contributing factors lies a more fundamental cause, and he focuses his spotlight on it. What made war "inevitable," Thucydides tells us, "was the rise of Athens and the fear that this instilled in Sparta."[3]

This is the phenomenon that I have labeled Thucydides's Trap: the severe structural stress caused when a rising power threatens to upend a ruling one. In such conditions, not just extraordinary, unexpected events, but even ordinary flashpoints of foreign affairs, can trigger large-scale conflict.

How this dynamic drove Athens and Sparta to war emerges clearly in Thucydides's account. Having combined arms in a great war to expel the Persians, he writes, Athens and Sparta set out to manage their strategic competition peacefully. They successfully resolved a series of crises that threatened to ignite war, including negotiating a grand Thirty Years' Peace. They recognized that striking differences between the two states' cultures, political systems, and interests made vigorous competition unavoidable. But they also knew that war could bring disaster and were determined to find a way to secure their interests without it.

How, then, did these two great Greek city-states succumb to a conflict that had such catastrophic consequences for both? Every one of the six hundred pages in the *History of the Peloponnesian War* offers compelling details about the twists and turns along the path of this fatal war.[4] Stories about diplomatic encounters between the two principals and lesser Greek states like Melos, Megara, Corcyra, and many others offer instructive clues for statecraft. But Thucydides's main story line is the gravitational force that pulled Athens and Sparta toward their collision: the relentless rise of Athens and Sparta's growing sense that this was undermining its position of predominance in Greece. His main subject, in other words, is Thucydides's Trap, and the way it ensnared the ancient world's two most fabled powers despite their repeated attempts to avoid it.

RISE MEETS RULE

Before the Persian invasion of Greece in 490 BCE, Sparta had been the region's dominant power for more than a century. A city-state in the southern part of the Greek peninsula known as the Peloponnese, Sparta had to contend with several midsized powers on its land borders as well as a restive slave population known as the Helots, which outnumbered Spartan citizens seven to one.[5]

Sparta remains today a symbol of the ultimate military culture. From its families to its government, the organizing principle of the entire society aimed to maximize the vitality and strength of its fighting force. Spartan authorities allowed only physically perfect infants to live. They took sons from their families at the age of seven and enrolled them in military academies, where they were toughened, trained, and groomed for war. Men could marry at twenty but had to continue living in barracks, eating communal meals, and training daily. Only at age thirty, after twenty-three years of service to the Spartan state, did they earn full citizenship and the right to participate in the Assembly, which unlike its Athenian counterpart was dominated by conservative, aristocratic elders. Not until sixty were they finally exempt from military service. Spartan citizens prized military values above all else: courage, valor, and discipline. As Plutarch tells us, when Spartan mothers sent

their sons off to war, they told them to come back "bearing your shield
—or on it."[6]

Athens, by contrast, was a port city on a dry and bare promontory of
Attica that took pride in its culture. Isolated from the rest of mainland
Greece by high and sparsely populated mountains, Athens had always
been a trading nation, supplied by the merchants who crisscrossed the
Aegean Sea selling olive oil and timber, textiles and precious stones.
Unlike Sparta's garrison state, Athens was an open society, its acade-
mies enrolling students from across Greece. And after centuries of rule
by strongmen, Athens had also begun a bold, new political experiment
in what it called democracy. Its Assembly and the Council of Five
Hundred were open to all free men and made all key decisions.

Prior to the fifth century BCE, the Greek world was largely discon-
nected, divided into self-governing city-states. But the Persian invasion
in 490 BCE forced the Greeks to come together as never before to meet
a common threat. Later, at Thermopylae, a legendary suicide force of
three hundred elite Spartan warriors held off an entire Persian army,
sacrificing their lives to buy time for the combined Greek forces. At
Salamis, an allied fleet under Athenian command brilliantly destroyed
a Persian fleet despite being outnumbered three to one. In 479 BCE, the
combined Greek forces decisively defeated the invading Persian army
for the second time—and this time for good.

Conscious that it had played a pivotal role in the Greek victory, Athens aspired to take its place as one of the leading powers of Greece. And
indeed, in the wake of the Persian retreat, the city-state experienced a
remarkable economic, military, and cultural renaissance. Its economy
drew traders and sailors from across the Hellenic world to serve in its
merchant marine. As the volume of trade grew, Athens added a fleet of
trading ships to supplement its professional navy, which was already
more than twice the size of that of its nearest rival.[7] Distant Corcyra
was the only other Greek state with a substantial fleet, followed by
Sparta's key ally, Corinth. Neither power posed a real danger, however,
for the Athenians' stunning victories in the Persian wars had proved

that the skill of its sailors was even more important than the size of its fleet.

Over the course of the fifth century, Athens progressively turned the defensive alliance network it had formed to fight the Persians into a de facto maritime empire. Athens demanded that allies bear their share of the burden, brutally suppressing states such as Naxos that tried to escape its clutches. By 440 BCE, all Athenian colonies except the remote Lesbos and Chios had given up their own navies and were paying Athens for protection instead. Athens then massively expanded its maritime trade links throughout the region (creating a trading regime that left many smaller Greek states more prosperous and interconnected than ever before). Flush with gold, the Athenian government funded a cultural surge that built structures unlike any ever seen before (the Parthenon, for example) and staged frequent productions of the plays of Sophocles. Even as other parts of Greece looked on with growing resentment, Athenians saw the expansion of their empire as utterly benign. "That empire we acquired not by violence," they later claimed to the Spartans, but instead "because the allies attached themselves to us and spontaneously asked us to assume the command."[8]

The Spartans scoffed at this pretense. They knew the Athenians to be as ruthless and deceitful as they were. But their mistrust also reflected the stark contrast between the two powers' concepts of politics and culture. Sparta had a mixed political system that blended monarchy and oligarchy. It rarely intervened in the affairs of faraway nations, focusing instead on preventing a Helot rebellion at home and on securing its regional predominance. Spartans were proud of their distinctive culture. But, unlike the Athenians, they did not seek to persuade other states to follow their model. Despite its imposing infantry, Sparta was a conservative, status quo power.[9] As the Corinthian ambassador later put it to the Spartan Assembly, "The Athenians are addicted to innovation, and their designs are characterized by swiftness alike in conception and execution. You preserve what you have, invent nothing, and when forced to act you never go far enough."[10]

The Corinthian's caricature only slightly exaggerates. Athens projected audacity in every aspect of its national life. Athenians believed that they were advancing the frontiers of human achievement. They had no reservations about interfering in the affairs of other states, toppling oligarchic governments across the Greek islands and promoting democracies. They repeatedly sought to persuade neutral states (for example, Corcyra) to join in alliance. Most disconcertingly to Sparta, Athens's ambitions appeared to have no limit. As an Athenian diplomat stated bluntly to the Spartan Assembly shortly before the onset of war, "It was not we who set the example, for it has always been the law that the weaker should be subject to the stronger."[11]

Shortly after the Persian retreat, in an attempt to remind the Greek world of its overall dominance, the Spartan leadership had demanded that the Athenians not rebuild their city walls. This would have meant deliberately leaving themselves vulnerable to a land invasion—and thus to punishment by Sparta if they dared to disobey its commands. But Athens had no intention of returning to the status quo. Athenians believed that their painful sacrifices in the fight against the Persians had earned them a degree of autonomy. In this refusal, however, Spartan leaders saw evidence of disrespect. Others saw even more ominous signs of imperial ambitions that would threaten the established order.

For the moment, Athens's growing military power posed no material threat to Sparta. Together with its allied forces, the Spartans outnumbered the Athenian army by more than two to one. Most Spartans were confident in their confederation's position as the undisputed military hegemon of Greece. Nonetheless, as Athens's power continued to increase, some proposed a preemptive attack on Athens to remind the entire Greek world who was number one. These Spartan leaders reasoned that allowing Athens to rise unimpeded would eventually jeopardize Spartan hegemony. Although the Assembly overruled their initial appeals for war, as Athens's power grew, so did the influence of Spartan hawks.

For a time, Spartans continued to believe that diplomacy could restrain Athens's climb. After nearly sliding into all-out conflict in the middle of the century—a series of clashes collectively known as the

First Peloponnesian War—the two powers formalized their relations by a major treaty in 446 BCE. This famed Thirty Years' Peace laid the groundwork for a sophisticated regional security order. It prohibited members of one alliance from defecting to join the other, and established rules and a process for binding arbitration and non-interference, establishing precedents that are still used today to resolve disputes among nations. In the period that followed, Athens and Sparta agreed to settle their disputes through bilateral negotiation, and when that was not successful, with binding arbitration by a neutral party, such as the Oracle at Delphi. And while the agreement recognized Athens as an equal party, Spartans could also take comfort that its loyal allies Corinth, Thebes, and Megara, key members of the Peloponnesian League under Spartan control, were all located on Athens's doorstep.

For both states, the fruits of peace were as sweet as those of war were bitter. The treaty allowed Sparta and Athens to concentrate on their own spheres. Sparta retrenched and strengthened long-standing alliances with its neighbors. Athens continued to use its powerful navy to dominate—and extract gold from—its own subjects throughout the Aegean. It amassed a strategic reserve amounting to the previously unheard-of sum of 6,000 talents of gold, and was adding 1,000 talents per year in revenue. Even Sparta, with its famously stoic and conservative society, experienced its own, albeit smaller, cultural renaissance.[12]

This framework provided a period of unprecedented harmony within the greater Hellenic world, extending from the Côte d'Azur to the Black Sea. But the Thirty Years' Peace did not resolve the underlying causes of tension. It merely put them on hold. And under these conditions, as Thucydides tells us, it took very little to set the pyre alight.

THE SPARK

The spark came in 435 BCE. Initially, a local conflict did not appear to have much impact on Athenian interests. Corinth, an important Spartan ally, had provoked a showdown with Corcyra, a neutral power, over Epidamnus, a remote settlement in modern-day Albania.[13] Corcyra initially seemed to have the upper hand: its fleet of 120 warships routed Corinth in their first confrontation. But the humiliated Corinthians immediately began to prepare for a second campaign. They rapidly expanded their navy, recruiting sailors from all over Greece, and soon amassed an allied force of 150 ships. While it was still no match for Athens, Corinth now commanded the second-largest fleet in Greece. Terrified, neutral Corcyra appealed to Athens for help.

Corinth's actions in far-off Epidamnus now stirred fears about Sparta's malicious intentions and posed a strategic dilemma for Athens. The Athenians had two equally bad options. Aiding Corcyra directly would antagonize Corinth and potentially violate the Thirty Years' Peace. But doing nothing risked allowing Corinth to commandeer the Corcyraean fleet, tipping naval power dangerously in Sparta's direction.

The mood in the Athenian Assembly was grave. Athenians listened carefully as Corinthian and Corcyraean diplomats presented their respective cases. The debate stretched on for two days until Pericles, described by Thucydides as Athens's "first citizen," proposed a compromise solution: Athens would send a small, symbolic fleet to Corcyra with a directive not to engage unless attacked. Unfortunately, this attempt at a defensive deterrent proved too little to deter, but large enough to provoke. The Corinthians were enraged that the Athenians had taken up arms against them.

Sparta faced a similar strategic bind. If it supported Corinth's attack against Corcyra, Athens could reasonably conclude that Sparta aimed to match its naval capabilities and might be preparing for a preemptive war. On the other hand, if Sparta remained neutral, it would risk allowing Athens to become the decisive actor in the conflict and undermine Sparta's credibility with its other Peloponnesian League allies. This crossed a red line for Sparta, since maintaining stability in its immediate neighborhood was essential to the Spartan strategy for keeping the Helot threat in check.

Sparta and Athens were also at odds over another Spartan ally, Megara. In 432, Pericles had issued the Megarian Decree, an early instance of economic warfare that imposed sanctions on Megara as punishment for dishonoring Athenian temples and harboring runaway Athenian slaves. Though technically legal under its treaty with Sparta, the Megarian Decree was nonetheless provocative, and read by the Spartans as yet another sign of disrespect to the system over which Sparta presided. When Sparta demanded that Athens repeal the Megarian Decree, Pericles saw this as a challenge to his own credibility. Backing down would embolden Sparta to thwart Athens's rise elsewhere in the Greek world. It would also infuriate many Athenian citizens, who saw the decree as a national prerogative.

The Spartan king Archidamus II and Pericles were personal friends. Archidamus could see the situation from the Athenian point of view, and he recognized that his people were moved more by emotion than reason. Appealing to the Spartan virtue of moderation, Archidamus urged the Spartan Assembly not to demonize the Athenians or underestimate the Spartan government's response: "We always base our preparation against an enemy on the assumption that his plans are good."[14]

But Sparta's hawks disagreed. They argued that Athens had become so arrogant that it posed an unacceptable danger to Spartan security. They reminded the Assembly of Athens's frequent interventions in other Greek states, from Naxos and Potidaea to the present crises in Megara and Corcyra, and appealed to the audience's fear that Sparta's alliances were crumbling. And they demanded a harsh response, asserting that Athens "deserved double punishment for having ceased to be good and for having become bad."[15]

Sparta's pro-war faction had the simpler case, and its argument was reinforced by the Corinthian ambassador. Addressing the Spartan Assembly, he blamed Sparta's complacence for Athens's unchecked surge: "For all this you are responsible. You it was who first allowed them to fortify their city . . . You alone wait till the power of an enemy is becoming twice its original size, instead of crushing it in its infancy."[16] When the Corinthians suggested that they would withdraw from the alliance if Sparta did not act, every Spartan present must have been shocked and horrified. The message was clear: the rise of Athens could destroy a key alliance that for centuries had helped keep the Spartan homeland secure.

After vigorous debate, the Spartan Assembly voted for war. As Thucydides explains, "The Spartans voted that war should be declared because they were afraid of the further growth of Athenian power, seeing, as they did, that already the greater part of Greece was under the control of Athens."[17] The validity of Sparta's fears was by now irrelevant. The bulk of its leaders were convinced that Athens's aggrandizement threatened their power and security, and there was little that anyone — even their own king — could do to persuade them otherwise.

Why did the Athenians not anticipate how the Spartans would react? Thucydides himself cannot explain why Pericles failed to find a way to prevent conflicts over Megara and Corcyra from leading Athens into war with Sparta. But the history of international relations in the years since offer clues. When states repeatedly fail to act in what appears to be their true national interest, it is often because their policies reflect necessary compromises among parties within their government rather than a single coherent vision. Although Pericles had been reelected many times, he had few formal powers. The Athenian legal system was deliberately designed to limit the power of any single individual in order to avoid the risk of tyranny.[18] Pericles was therefore as much a politician as a statesman. His influence was limited to his power to persuade.

While the Megarian Decree clearly had caused relations with Sparta to reach a boiling point, Pericles saw the sanctions not as a provocation but as a necessary compromise.[19] Backing down was a non-starter. With the Athenian populace unwilling to bow to Spartan demands, Pericles concluded that repealing the decree might be even more dangerous than standing by it. If, after he met its demand, Sparta declared war anyway, Athens would then be disgraced as well as disadvantaged. So Pericles bent to popular pressure and reluctantly drew up plans for war.

Neither side had a clear military advantage, but both were fatally overconfident about their own capabilities. Having not suffered a military defeat in recent memory, the Spartans failed to understand the extent of Athenian naval power. One speaker later argued to the Spartan Assembly that its soldiers could quickly starve out the Athenians by burning their fields and storehouses—ignoring the fact that the Athenian fleet could resupply the city by sea. Meanwhile, the Athenian government, which had spent decades stockpiling gold, firmly believed that it held the winning hand. Pericles calculated that Athens could hold out for three years against an enemy siege if necessary—more than enough time, he thought, to defeat Sparta, perhaps by inciting a Helot rebellion. Of all the observers, only Spartan king Archidamus proved prescient, predicting that neither side held a decisive advantage, and that a war between them would last for a generation.

The war proved as devastating as Archidamus predicted. Three decades of bloodshed between Athens and Sparta brought the golden age of Greek culture to an end. The order that had developed after the Persian wars, based on agreed constraints and reinforced by a balance of power, collapsed—flinging the Greek city-states into levels of violence even their playwrights had not previously been able to imagine. When they captured Melos, for example, Athenian soldiers slaughtered all the adult males and sent the women and children into slavery—a violation of the rules of combat that Greeks had observed for centuries. This episode is immortalized in Thucydides's Melian Dialogue, where the Athenian ambassador captured the essence of realpolitik. "We shall not trouble you with specious pretenses—either how we have a right to our empire because we overthrew the Mede, or are now attacking you because of the wrong you have done us," he explained. Instead, "You know as well as we do that right is a question that only has meaning in relations between equals in power. In the real world, the strong do what they will and the weak suffer what they must."[20]

Most notably, the war sounded the death knell of the Athenian empire. Sparta emerged from the war victorious but sapped of its strength, its alliance network damaged and its wealth greatly depleted. Not for another two thousand years would the Greeks unite again of their own volition. The Peloponnesian War—and the original instance of Thucydides's Trap—was thus a watershed, not only in Greek history but also in the annals of Western civilization.

WAS WAR INEVITABLE?

Why did the competition between Greece's two great powers ultimately produce a war that destroyed what each cherished most? According to Thucydides, the fundamental explanation lies in the depth of the structural stress between a rising and a ruling power. As this rivalry led Athens and Sparta into successive standoffs, the most passionate voices in each political system grew louder, their sense of pride stronger, their claims about threats posed by the adversary more pointed, and their challenge to leaders who sought to keep the peace more severe. Thucydides identifies three primary drivers fueling this dynamic that lead to war: interests, fear, and honor.

National interests are plain enough. The survival of the state and its sovereignty in making decisions in its domain free from coercion from others are standard fare in discussions of national security. As Athens's relentless expansion "began to encroach upon Sparta's allies," Thucydides explains, Sparta "felt its position was no longer tolerable" and thus had no alternative but war. "Fear" is Thucydides's one-word reminder that facts about structural realities are not the whole story. Objective conditions have to be perceived by human beings—and the lenses through which we see them are influenced by emotions. In particular, ruling powers' fears often fuel misperceptions and exaggerate dangers, as rising powers' self-confidence stimulates unrealistic expectations about what is possible and encourages risk-taking.

But beyond interests and perceptions lies a third ingredient Thucydides calls "honor."[21] To many modern ears the word sounds pretentious. But Thucydides's concept encompasses what we now think of as a state's sense of itself, its convictions about the recognition and respect it is due, and its pride. As Athens's power grew over the fifth century, so too did its sense of entitlement. When approached by lesser Greek states like Megara and Corinth, the fact that they were allies of Sparta did not excuse them from showing proper deference. In the great historian's telling, as these three factors became increasingly intertwined they produced repeated face-offs Athens and Sparta could not avoid.

Despite their best efforts to prevent conflict, the leaders of the two states could not stop a relentless realignment from tipping into bloodshed. While each was playing chess against the other, at the same time, each was also contending with domestic political constituents who increasingly believed that failing to stand up to the other would be both dishonorable and disastrous. Ultimately, the leaders of Athens and Sparta were overwhelmed by their own domestic politics. Pericles and Archidamus understood the insight that America's greatest presidential scholar Richard Neustadt summarized in characterizing the American presidency: "Weakness," he observed, "remains the word from which to start."[22]

Was Thucydides right in claiming that the rise of Athens made war "inevitable"? Not literally, of course. His point was that as Athens grew more powerful and Sparta grew more anxious, the two countries chose paths that made it increasingly difficult to avoid war. As the stakes rose, Athenian assertiveness swelled into hubris; Spartan insecurity festered into paranoia. By forbidding interference in the other power's sphere of influence, the peace treaty unintentionally accelerated Athenian and Spartan competition over the remaining neutral states. Proximate crises in Corcyra and Megara brought to a head pressures that had been building for decades.

Thus Thucydides's Trap claimed its first victims. In spite of great statesmen and wise voices in both Athens and Sparta warning that war would mean disaster, the shifting balance of power led both sides to conclude that violence was the least bad option available. And the war came.

3

FIVE HUNDRED YEARS

It is a habit of mankind to entrust to careless hope what they long for, and to use sovereign reason to thrust aside what they do not desire . . . War is a violent teacher.

—Thucydides, on the defense of
the Athenian homeland, 424 BCE

What's past is prologue.   —William Shakespeare

History never repeats itself, but it does sometimes rhyme.

—Mark Twain

Only the dead have seen the end of war.   —George Santayana

The war between Athens and Sparta stands as the classic example of Thucydides's Trap. But the centuries since have seen many cases in which successors have been caught in the dynamics between rising and ruling powers that drive events toward war. Reviewing the past five hundred years, the Harvard Thucydides's Trap Project has identified sixteen cases in which an ascending power challenged an established power.* Twelve of these rivalries resulted in war.[1]

This chapter presents thumbnail sketches of the paths that led to five

---

* The full Thucydides's Trap Case File, part of the Belfer Center's Applied History Project at Harvard, is included as Appendix 1.

	Period	Ruling power	Rising power	Domain	Result
1	Late 15th century	Portugal	Spain	Global empire and trade	No war
2	First half of 16th century	France	Hapsburgs	Land power in Western Europe	War
3	16th and 17th centuries	Hapsburgs	Ottoman Empire	Land power in central and Eastern Europe, sea power in the Mediterranean	War
4	First half of 17th century	Hapsburgs	Sweden	Land and sea power in northern Europe	War
5	Mid- to late 17th century	Dutch Republic	England	Global empire, sea power, and trade	War
6	Late 17th to mid-18th centuries	France	Great Britain	Global empire and European land power	War
7	Late 18th and early 19th centuries	United Kingdom	France	Land and sea power in Europe	War
8	Mid-19th century	France and United Kingdom	Russia	Global empire, influence in Central Asia and eastern Mediterranean	War
9	Mid-19th century	France	Germany	Land power in Europe	War
10	Late 19th and early 20th centuries	China and Russia	Japan	Land and sea power in East Asia	War
11	Early 20th century	United Kingdom	United States	Global economic dominance and naval supremacy in the Western Hemisphere	No war
12	Early 20th century	United Kingdom supported by France, Russia	Germany	Land power in Europe and global sea power	War
13	Mid-20th century	Soviet Union, France, and UK	Germany	Land and sea power in Europe	War
14	Mid-20th century	United States	Japan	Sea power and influence in the Asia-Pacific region	War
15	1940s–1980s	United States	Soviet Union	Global power	No war
16	1990s–present	United Kingdom and France	Germany	Political influence in Europe	No war

of these wars. In reverse chronological order, we begin by exploring the rationale for Japan's attack on Pearl Harbor in December 1941, before examining a nineteenth-century prequel in which Japan's ascent set it on a course for war, first with China and then with Russia. We then trace Otto von Bismarck's manipulation of France to provoke its leader into starting a war that provided the critical enabler in unifying Germany; analyze the response of the dominant maritime Dutch Republic in the seventeenth century to England's naval buildup; and conclude with the Hapsburg challenge to France in the sixteenth century.

Readers who wonder whether a trade conflict could escalate into nuclear war should pay careful attention to the curious path that led Japan and the United States to Pearl Harbor. If the thought of a nation provoking its adversary into war to advance its own domestic agenda seems implausible, remember Bismarck. For insights into the ways in which naval rivalries can propel national governments to bloody war, the interplay between England and the Dutch Republic is instructive.

There are obviously substantial differences among these cases. Some feature monarchies; others, democracies. In some, diplomacy required weeks to exchange messages, while others had real-time communication. But in all the cases we find heads of state confronting strategic dilemmas about rivals under conditions of uncertainty and chronic stress. In retrospect, some readers may be tempted to dismiss their judgments as irrational or ill considered. With more reflection, however, we should be able to understand and even empathize with the pressures, hopes, and fears they felt—and the choices they made.

None of the conflicts were inevitable. But the weight of factors favoring war sometimes makes it difficult to see how the outcome could have been otherwise. Not that much imagination is required to consider how we would have voted in the Athenian Assembly after listening to Pericles make the case for war, or what counsel we might have given the Hapsburg Holy Roman emperor Charles V.

The basic contours of the dynamic Thucydides identified are evident in each of the cases. We see vividly what the Thucydides's Trap Project has named the "rising power syndrome" and the "ruling power syndrome." The first highlights a rising state's enhanced sense of itself, its interests, and its entitlement to recognition and respect. The second is essentially the mirror image of the first, the established power exhibiting an enlarged sense of fear and insecurity as it faces intimations of "decline." As in sibling rivalries, so too in diplomacy one finds a predictable progression reflected both at the dinner table and at the international conference table. A growing sense of self-importance ("my voice counts") leads to an expectation of recognition and respect ("listen to what I have to say") and a demand for increased impact ("I insist"). Understandably, the established power views the upstart's assertiveness as disrespectful, ungrateful, and even provocative or dangerous. In the Greek language, exaggerated self-importance becomes hubris, and unreasonable fear, paranoia.

JAPAN VS. UNITED STATES

Mid-twentieth century

On December 7, 1941, Japanese aircraft attacked the US Pacific naval headquarters at Pearl Harbor, Hawaii, sinking most of the American fleet stationed there. At the time, it seemed inconceivable that a small island nation with an economy and navy dwarfed in size by the United States would attack the most powerful country in the world. But from Japan's perspective, the alternatives appeared even worse.

Washington had attempted to use economic instruments, such as financial and trade sanctions, to coerce Japan to stop regional aggression, including against China. The Japanese government saw these constraints as a stranglehold that threatened its survival. Despite Japan's protestations, the United States failed to understand the consequences of its sanctions or anticipate Japan's response. Five days before the "surprise" attack on Pearl Harbor, Japan's ambassador to the United States delivered a clear warning. His government had concluded that Japan was "being placed under severe pressure by the United States to yield to the American position; and that it is preferable to fight rather than to yield to pressure."[2] Washington ignored the warning, remaining complacent, confident that Japan would not dare to choose war against an unquestionably superior force.

The road to Pearl Harbor had actually begun a half century earlier when America made its first pivot to Asia. Among the spoils from the Spanish-American War of 1898, the United States acquired its first major colony, the Philippines, as well as Guam. The next year, Secretary of State John Hay announced what he called the Open Door order, declaring that the United States would not permit any foreign power to colonize or monopolize trade with China. Instead, China would be "open" to all commercial interests (especially those of the US) on an equal basis.

To an industrializing, rapidly growing Japan, declarations by distant great powers that grandfathered their own colonies but prohibited the "land of the rising sun" from realizing its destiny seemed grossly unfair. Britain ruled India, as well as much of the rest of the world. The Netherlands had captured Indonesia. Russia had absorbed Siberia and seized Sakhalin Island, bringing it directly to Japan's border. European powers had also forced Japan to withdraw from the territories it had won in defeating the Chinese in 1894–95. And at this point the Americans proposed to declare game over? Not if Japan had anything to say about it.

After careful preparation, Japan went to war with Russia in 1904, defeating it handily and taking control of the Liaodong Peninsula, Port Arthur, the South Manchuria Railway, and half of Sakhalin. By then, it had already pushed China out of the island of Taiwan and occupied Korea. In 1931, Tokyo invaded the Chinese mainland, driving five hundred miles into the interior, leaving Japan in control of more than half the country. (Symbolized by the Rape of Nanking, the vicious 1937 campaign features prominently in high school textbooks read by every student in China today.)

Proclaiming "Asia for the Asians," in 1933 Tokyo announced a "Japanese Monroe Doctrine." It declared that hereafter "Japan is responsible for the maintenance of peace and order in the Far East," in what the country later christened the Greater East Asia Co-Prosperity Sphere. Japan's strategy reflected an uncompromising win-or-lose conviction: "If the sun is not ascending, it is descending."[3]

The self-proclaimed guardian of the Open Door found Japan's ambitions and actions unacceptable. As historian Paul Kennedy puts it, the United States had no choice but to respond to Japan's aggression, "seeing it as a threat to the Open Door order upon which, in theory, the American way of life was so dependent."[4] The American response began with economic rather than military means. First it imposed an embargo on exports of high-grade scrap iron and aviation fuel to Japan. Thereafter, Washington ratcheted up its sanctions to include essential raw materials such as iron, brass, and copper—and, finally, oil.

Franklin D. Roosevelt's August 1941 embargo proved to be the proverbial straw. As a leading analyst explains, "While oil was not the sole cause of the deterioration of relations, once employed as a diplomatic weapon, it made hostilities inevitable."[5] In desperation, Japanese leaders approved a plan to deliver a preemptive "knockout blow" at Pearl Harbor. The designer of the attacks, Admiral Isoroku Yamamoto, told his government, "In the first six months to a year of war against the US and England I will run wild, and I will show you an uninterrupted succession of victories." But he also warned them: "Should the war be prolonged for two or three years, I have no confidence in our ultimate victory."[6]

US policymakers reacted in shock over what they denounced as Japan's unprovoked attack. For being so starkly surprised, however, they had no one to blame but themselves.[7] Had they taken an afternoon to read Thucydides and think about the consequences of Athens's Megarian Decree, or reflect on Britain's efforts to contain the rise of Germany in the decade before 1914 (an episode that will be explored in full in the next chapter), they could have better anticipated Japan's initiative. Privately, some did. As sanctions tightened in 1941, American ambassador to Tokyo Joseph Grew insightfully noted in his diary, "The vicious circle of reprisals and counter reprisals is on . . . The obvious conclusion is eventual war."[8]

The contest between a rising and ruling power often intensifies competition over scarce resources. When an expanding economy compels the first to reach farther afield to secure essential commodities, including some under the control or protection of the second, the competition can become a resource scramble. The attempt to deny a state imports it judges crucial for survival can provoke war.

JAPAN VS. RUSSIA AND CHINA
Late nineteenth and early twentieth centuries

Japan's ascent to challenge China and Russia in the late-nineteenth century and early twentieth century was essentially a prequel to Pearl Harbor. It began in 1853, when US commodore Matthew Perry and his fleet of "Black Ships" overcame two centuries of Japanese isolation and resistance to repeated European overtures. Perry gave the emperor a stark choice: open Japanese ports for refueling and provisioning of American ships, or become the target of modern instruments of war he could hardly comprehend. Japan chose the first option and soon found itself mesmerized by modernization.

Less than two decades later, after the Meiji Restoration of 1868, Japan set off on a race of development to catch up with the Western powers.* Aided by Japanese technocrats who scoured the world for the best industrial products and practices that could be borrowed, adapted, or stolen, Japan's GNP nearly tripled between 1885 and 1899.[9] This economic surge deepened Tokyo's determination to stand on equal footing with the West. As Western powers continued carving out colonies and spheres of influence among Japan's neighbors, the country felt what historian Akira Iriye calls a "sense of urgency that they must act more energetically, both in the passive sense of avoiding victimization by the more aggressive West and also in the sense of extending their own power to join the ranks of the great powers."[10]

---

* In the Meiji Restoration, the emperor returned to a position of supreme national authority.

This urgency fueled a dramatic buildup of Japan's army and navy. Military expenditures jumped from 19 percent of the Japanese budget in 1880 to 31 percent in 1890.[11] As Japan grew more muscular, its attitudes toward its neighbors—many of whom were Western clients —hardened. In 1894, both China and Japan responded to a rebellion in Korea by sending troops.[12] They quickly came into conflict, and Japan defeated China, forcing it to hand over Korea, Taiwan, and southeastern Manchuria—home of Port Arthur, the strategic naval and trading port. Russia, however, had its own plans for southeastern Manchuria. Moscow and its European allies put so much pressure on Tokyo that only six days after it signed the Treaty of Shimonoseki with China, Japan was forced to relinquish its claims to Manchuria. In the process, Russia made it clear to Japan that it would not allow the emerging power to encroach on any territory it considered "vital."[13]

Predictably, this loss of face, and its geopolitical implications, left Japan seething. "With Manchuria and ultimately Korea in her hands," wrote a prominent Japanese academic in 1904, Russia "would be able, on the one hand, to build up under her exclusive policy a naval and commercial influence strong enough to enable her to dominate the East, and, on the other, to cripple forever Japan's ambition as a nation, slowly driving her to starvation and decay, and even politically annex her."[14] This nightmare seemed to be descending when Russia forced the Chinese to lease to it the Manchurian base at Port Arthur—and began work extending the Trans-Siberian Railway to provide a direct link between Moscow and the Yellow Sea.

After this "humiliation of 1895," Japan spent a decade "deliberately preparing for an eventual war with Russia."[15] In pursuing its own strategic and commercial interests, Russia built its railway on the very territory Japan had won in its decisive military victory over China—and then been stripped of by Western intervention. Weighing heavily on the Japanese psyche, this episode led to the conviction among Japan's leaders that they could no longer defer to Western demands. After completing its preparations for war in 1904, Japan demanded that Russia cede to it control of key parts of Manchuria. When Russia refused,

Japan launched a preemptive attack and achieved a stunningly decisive victory in the war that followed.

Japan's sense of urgency, anxiety, victimhood, and vindictiveness deepens our understanding of rising power syndrome. Tokyo's indignity at its treatment after it was too weak to object stoked its fierce determination to establish what it saw as its rightful place in the pecking order. This psychological pattern has played out again and again among ascending nations over the centuries.

GERMANY VS. FRANCE

Mid-nineteenth century

Prussia's victory over Denmark in 1864 and over Austria in 1866 left Europe's preeminent power in what the historian Michael Howard calls "that most dangerous of all moods; that of a great power which sees itself declining to the second rank."[16] As a French official explained at the time, "Grandeur is relative . . . A country's power can be diminished by the mere fact of new forces accumulating around it."[17]

The speed of Prussia's ascent shocked Paris and emboldened Berlin. As Prussia incorporated other German states, its population grew from one-third the size of France's in 1820 to four-fifths by 1870. Its iron and steel production surged from half of France's in 1860 to overtake it ten years later.[18] Prussia's military was also rapidly modernizing. By 1870 it had become a third larger than France's. As a military expert of the era noted: "France gaped in astonishment. Almost overnight a rather small and manageable neighbor had become an industrial and military colossus."[19] Indeed, the French empress captured the mood in Paris when she expressed her fear that she would one night "go to sleep French and wake up Prussian."[20]

Bismarck's driving ambition was to create a united Germany. But the leaders of the German-speaking principalities clung to their prerogatives as rulers of independent states. They would never have accepted subordination to Prussia had they not been "shaken out of their selfishness" by a shock that caused them to fear for their survival.[21] Bismarck calculated correctly that a war with France would provide just what was required. He and his generals also knew that they were well prepared to deal with French forces.[22]

To rally the reluctant southern princelings in a common cause, Bismarck recognized that it was important that France be seen as the aggressor. Given French emperor Napoleon III's alarm at Prussia's rise, Bismarck did not find it difficult to stimulate French fears. In a bold stroke, he proposed to place a German prince from the House of Hohenzollern on the Spanish throne. That would effectively box France in between German powers on both sides. As Bismarck expected, Paris panicked at the specter of encirclement. As noted in the leading biography of Bismarck, the French foreign secretary believed "that the Hohenzollern candidacy for the Spanish throne constituted a serious attempt to change the European Balance of Power to the detriment of the French Empire. The honor and interests of France had been severely injured."[23] Under pressure domestically for having stood by as the Prussian threat had grown, and believing that his army would crush Berlin in battle, Napoleon demanded that the Prussian king forever renounce putting one of his relatives on the Spanish throne.[24] Prussia refused. As tension mounted, the fear of war was stoked further by the Ems Telegram (a half-true press dispatch that Bismarck manipulated to magnify French fears), prompting Napoleon to declare war on Prussia. As Bismarck had foreseen, Prussian troops, with the assistance of select units from the principalities, swiftly defeated France in a victory that gave birth to a united German empire.

Bismarck provides a textbook example of exploitation of the ruling power syndrome: taking advantage of exaggerated fears, insecurities, and dread of changes in the status quo to provoke a reckless response. Modern behavioral scientists have explained this at the basic psychological level, noting that people's fears of loss (or intimations of "decline") trump our hopes of gain—driving us to take often unreasonable risks to protect what is ours. Especially in cases of "imperial overstretch" in which a great power's "global interests and obligations [are] . . . far larger than the country's power to defend them all simultaneously,"[25] states may foolishly double down in their attempt to maintain the status quo.

ENGLAND VS. DUTCH REPUBLIC

Mid- to late seventeenth century

During the "golden age" of the Dutch Republic in the first half of the seventeenth century, the Netherlands emerged as Europe's leading maritime power, dominating trade, shipping, and finance. Bolstered by a growing navy, however, a resurgent England soon challenged the Dutch Republic's established order and its networks of free trade. Both saw the competition as existential. As the English academic George Edmundson has noted, each nation was "instinctively conscious that its destiny was upon the water, and that mastery of the seas was a necessity of national existence."[26] Both believed there were only two choices in this zero-sum game: "either the voluntary submission of one of the rivals to the other, or a trial of strength by ordeal of battle."[27]

The Dutch Republic's position in the world of the seventeenth century stood on two pillars: free trade and freedom of navigation. A "borderless" world enabled the tiny Netherlands to translate high productivity and efficiency into outsized political and economic heft — a feat London thought came at its own expense. There was, as political scientist Jack Levy puts it, "widespread belief in England that the Dutch economic success was built on the exploitation of England."[28]

During the first half of the century, England was too weak to challenge the Dutch-imposed order. But its resentment grew, and between 1649 and 1651 London doubled the size of its fleet from thirty-nine to eighty major ships, bringing it to rough parity with its rival.[29] Emboldened by its growing strength, London claimed sovereignty over the seas around its island, and in 1651 passed the first Navigation Act, giving it the exclusive authority to regulate commerce within its colonies and mandating that English trade be carried by English vessels. London justified these aggressive policies on the grounds that "the economic expansion of England must involve freedom from her virtually 'colonial' status in relation to the Dutch."[30] Dutch leader Johan de Witt, on the other hand, contended that the free trade system his country had built was both a "natural right and the law of nations."[31] The Netherlands also saw England's mercantilist policies as a direct threat to its survival, with a defiant De Witt declaring: "We would shed our last drop of blood" before we "acknowledge [England's] imaginary sovereignty over the seas."[32]

Before coming to blows, both sides tried to step back from the brink. The English proposed a mutual defense pact and political confederation in 1651, which the Dutch rejected as a transparent attempt by the larger nation to dominate them politically. The Netherlands countered by proposing economic agreements that London feared would serve only to perpetuate the Dutch Republic's already formidable advantages. Ultimately, beginning in 1652 the two sides fought three wars in less than a quarter century. As Edmundson concludes, these "were the inevitable outcome of a long-continued clashing of interests, which were of fundamental importance and indeed vital to the welfare of both nations."[33]

These wars remind us that adjusting existing arrangements, institutions, and relationships to reflect a shifting balance of power encounters what the Thucydides's Trap Project calls "transitional friction." In this dynamic, rising powers typically believe institutions are not changing fast enough, and see delay as evidence that the established state is determined to contain it. Ruling powers believe the rising state is overreaching in demanding more rapid adjustments than are either merited or safe.

HAPSBURGS VS. FRANCE
First half of sixteenth century

In the early sixteenth century, the growing power of the House of Hapsburg threatened French preeminence in Europe. Tensions came to a head when King Charles I of Spain (subsequently known as King Charles V) challenged King Francis I for the position of Holy Roman emperor. Francis and his entourage had long expected that he would succeed his grandfather Maximilian I in that position.

As the ruler of Western Europe's predominant land power and a monarch who had conquered considerable portions of Italy, including Milan, Francis had, as Pope Leo X declared, "surpassed in wealth and power all other Christian kings."[34] So when the pope chose King Charles instead, Francis was livid. In the words of the leading historian of the period, the jilted French king immediately "forecast war—not against the Infidel, but between himself and Charles."[35]

After being crowned Holy Roman emperor, Charles rapidly extended his rule over the Netherlands, much of modern-day Italy, and an empire in the New World, thus bringing Europe closer to a universal monarchy than it had been since the ninth century. In establishing unchallenged dominion over his far-flung territories,[36] which he described as "the empire on which the sun never sets," Charles relied primarily on military superiority.

Although Charles did not openly say so, many Europeans—Francis in particular—suspected he secretly sought world domination.[37] "Whether Charles V aspired to a universal empire or not," one historian observes, "the fact remained that . . . his dominions were already too universal and injured too many interests not to provoke widespread resentment."[38] Francis led the list of resenters. Not only did Charles cast a shadow on the French king's glory. By continuous expansion, he also raised the prospect that the Hapsburgs and their allies would encircle France.[39]

Calculating that the best way to improve his own position was to exploit his adversary's weakness, Francis encouraged his allies to invade Hapsburg-controlled territory in modern-day Spain, France, and Luxembourg.[40] Charles reacted by enlisting English forces to help blunt France's aggression, sending his own troops to invade French-held territory in Italy and ultimately leading a series of inconclusive wars with France. Intermittent war between France and Spain dragged on, ultimately outliving both of the rulers who had precipitated it.

This contest between France and the Hapsburgs casts light on the multiple ways misperceptions mislead states just as surely as they do individuals. We typically see ourselves as more benign than we are, and are quicker to attribute malign motives to potential adversaries. Because states can never be certain about each other's intent, they focus instead on capabilities. Defensive actions taken by one power often seem threatening to its opponent, as Robert Jervis's "security dilemma" reminds us.[41] A rising power may discount a ruling state's fear and insecurity because it "knows" itself to be well-meaning. Meanwhile, its opponent misunderstands even positive initiatives as overly demanding, or even threatening. Sparta's flat rejection of Athens's attempt to provide assistance to Spartan victims of the great earthquake in 464 BCE reflects this inclination.

The Franco-Hapsburg example also reminds us of the risks as well as the rewards of alliances. Seeking to hedge against a shifting balance of power, both states can respond by strengthening existing alliances or forming new ones. Each is more willing to enter into arrangements it had previously rejected. Each tends to underestimate differences between its own interests and those of new allies, and exaggerate benefits of engaging new partners. As states become more deeply concerned with preserving their credibility, they may take on new allies that end up hurting more than helping.

In Francis's manipulation of his allies as pawns to provoke Charles, and in the Hapsburg king's entry into league with the English monarch, we can hear echoes of Sparta's willingness to set aside its own hostility to Corinth and the objections of those who argued—correctly, as it turned out—that an alliance between the two powers would create more problems than it solved.

4

BRITAIN VS. GERMANY

By all means, keep anyone else from having a fleet if possible. Otherwise, pick the strongest as your friend.

— Thucydides, *History of the Peloponnesian War*

They build navies so as to play a part in the world's affairs. It is sport to them. It is life and death to us.

— Winston Churchill, speech to the House of Commons, March 1914

Since Germany is particularly backward in sea power, it is a life-and-death question for her, as a World Power and great cultural state, to make up the lost ground.

— Admiral Alfred Tirpitz, advice to Kaiser Wilhelm II, 1899

On October 24, 1911, a thirty-six-year-old political phenomenon became First Lord of the Admiralty, responsible for the Royal Navy, the guardian of Britain and its empire. Born in Blenheim Palace to one of England's first families, educated at Harrow and Sandhurst, tested on the battlefield in three imperial wars, elected to Parliament at age twenty-five, and the author of eleven widely read books and scores of articles, Winston Churchill personified the audacity of a small island nation that governed a quarter of humanity.

On his fourth day in office, Churchill sent a memorandum to his cabinet colleagues reminding them of their cardinal responsibility.

Echoing the Roman injunction "If you want peace, prepare for war," he wrote: "Preparation for war is the only guarantee for the preservation of the wealth, natural resources, and territory of the state." Adequate readiness required a proper understanding of three things: the "probable danger that may arise"; history's lessons for the "best general method" to meet the threat; and how to apply the era's "war material" in the most efficient manner.[1]

In 1911, the "probable danger" was imminent and impossible to miss: Germany's accelerating military buildup, particularly its fleet, which had more than doubled in size over the previous decade.[2] The "best general method" to meet this danger was equally clear: maintaining Britain's naval primacy. According to the Two-Power Standard, announced in 1889, Britain declared that it would maintain a fleet of battleships equal to the numbers deployed by its next two competitors combined. Churchill's openness to technological advances and drive to adopt them also ensured the "most efficient application" of the "war material of the era." He not only built more warships, but applied superior technology to make them more lethal: better armed, with new fifteen-inch guns; faster, powered by oil instead of coal; and supplemented by a new instrument of war, the airplane.[3]

In the thousand days between his memorandum and the outbreak of World War I, Churchill led a Herculean effort to maintain British naval supremacy, simultaneously making bold diplomatic strokes to broker détente with Germany and seizing every advantage should war come. His urgency sprang from his conviction that the German surge at sea signaled not a national security challenge but an existential threat to Britain's survival. Churchill knew that on British warships "floated the might, majesty, dominion, and power of the British Empire." If its navy were destroyed, he wrote later, the empire "would dissolve like a dream." All of Europe would pass "into the iron grip and rule of the Teuton and of all that the Teutonic system meant." To avoid that catastrophe, he insisted, the Royal Navy was "all we had."[4]

Britain thus faced an excruciating dilemma, one that strategists even today struggle to escape in planning exercises.[5] On the one hand, naval superiority was non-negotiable. Without it, British outposts in India, South Africa, and Canada—not to mention Britain itself—were vulnerable. Moreover, Britain's long-term security demanded that no hegemon seize control of Western Europe. As Churchill later put it, "For four hundred years the foreign policy of England has been to oppose the strongest, most aggressive, most dominating Power on the Continent."[6] A hegemon triumphant over its opponents on land could devote its resources to building a navy bigger than Britain's—and the coastline opposite the British Isles provided an ideal launchpad for invasion. Therefore no British government could tolerate a challenge to its naval dominion or an attempt to overturn the Continent's balance of power. On the other hand, Churchill and other British leaders recognized that the very effort to prevent Germany from building a dominant navy or overpowering its European rivals could bring about a war more horrible than any before in history.

The British were right to think of their strategic dilemma in apocalyptic terms. When World War I ended in 1918, their world indeed lay in ruins. A half millennium in which Europe had been the political center of the world came to a crashing halt.

The war was a catastrophe born more of miscalculation than ignorance. Europe's leaders had sufficient warning that war could devastate their social order and economies. But an all-too-rational struggle over predominance produced conditions of tectonic stress—primarily between Britain and Germany, but also between Germany and Russia—in which statesmen deemed the risk of war preferable to the perceived alternative of national destruction or capitulation.

The Great War's development followed the same bleak pattern—and many of the same dynamics—as other Thucydidean conflicts over the centuries. Britain was beset by anxieties typical of many ruling powers; Germany was driven by the ambition and indignation characteristic of many up-and-comers. The heat of their rivalry, along with recklessness and myopia across Europe, stoked an assassination in Sarajevo into a global conflagration.[7] Britain had no vital national interests at stake in the Balkans. Nevertheless, it was pulled into the fire, partly because of entangling alignments, but mainly because it feared that a powerful Germany left unchecked across the Continent would threaten its existence.

Churchill later wrote that while British leaders did not believe war was inevitable and sought to prevent it, the possibility of bloodshed "was continually in their thoughts." For a decade before 1914, he recalled, "those whose duty it was to watch over the safety of the country lived simultaneously in two different worlds of thought." They inhabited "the actual visible world with its peaceful activities and cosmopolitan aims," but also "a hypothetical world, a world 'beneath the threshold' . . . a world at one moment utterly fantastic, at the next seeming about to leap into reality—a world of monstrous shadows moving in convulsive combinations through vistas of fathomless catastrophe."[8]

Churchill's nightmare became reality in August 1914. Just days before war exploded across Europe, Churchill wrote to his wife: "Everything tends towards catastrophe and collapse . . . A wave of madness has swept the mind of Christendom . . . But *we all drift on in a kind of dull cataleptic trance*."[9] His letter concludes by noting "how willingly and proudly I would risk—or give—if need be—my period of existence to keep this country great and famous and prosperous and free. But the problems are very difficult. One has to try to measure the indefinite and weigh the imponderable."[10]

THE CROWE MEMORANDUM

The cold logic that set Berlin and London on a collision course was captured vividly seven years before the war in what historians call the Crowe Memorandum. In late 1905, King Edward VII had asked his government why the British were "displaying a persistently unfriendly attitude toward Germany"—a country whose sovereign, Kaiser Wilhelm II, also happened to be Edward's nephew. Why, the king wanted to know, was Britain so suspicious of a nation it had once considered as a possible ally, and now so "eager to run after France," a nation once thought its greatest foe?[11]

The man charged with answering the king's question was the Foreign Office's leading Germany expert, Eyre Crowe. Crowe was half German, married to a German woman, had been raised in Germany, and loved German culture. But he resented Prussia's militaristic influence over its fellow German states—a patchwork of kingdoms that, until recently, had shared a common language but little else. By 1871, however, Prussia's leading statesman, Otto von Bismarck, had brought together these disparate states to form a single nation under the leadership of the Prussian king (and now German emperor) Wilhelm I, grandfather of Wilhelm II. After a year of research into the king's question, Crowe delivered a diplomatic gem on New Year's Day 1907.[12]

"The healthy activity of a powerful Germany," Crowe allowed, was good for the world. Instead of fearing Germany's overseas expansion in principle, he wrote, Britain should applaud German competition for "intellectual and moral leadership" and "join in the race." But what if Germany's ultimate goal was "to break up and supplant the British Empire"? Crowe knew that German leaders had indignantly denied "any schemes of so subversive a nature," and it was possible that Germany did not "consciously cherish" them. At the same time, Britain could ill afford to trust German assurances. Germany might seek "a general political hegemony and maritime ascendancy, threatening the independence of her neighbors and ultimately the existence of England."

In the end, Crowe concluded that Germany's *intentions* were irrelevant; its *capabilities* were what mattered. A vague policy of growth could at any time shift into a grand design for political and naval dominance. Even if Germany accrued power gradually without a premeditated plan for domination, its resulting position would be just as formidable and menacing. Moreover, whether or not Germany had such a plan, it "would clearly be wise to build as powerful a navy as she can afford." Germany's growing wealth and power fueled its naval expansion, and German naval supremacy was "incompatible with the existence of the British Empire." Thus, whether Germany consciously sought to supplant it or not, Britain had no prudent alternative but to

stand up to perceived German encroachments and outbuild Germany's
naval expansion.[13]

THE END OF THE BRITISH CENTURY?

Fin de siècle Britons could be forgiven for fearing things could only go
downhill. Over the previous two centuries, an island twenty miles off
the European mainland had acquired an empire spanning every continent. By 1900, it encompassed modern-day India, Pakistan, Burma,
Malaysia, Singapore, Australia, New Zealand, and Canada, along with
much of the African continent.[14] It exerted a strong influence, sometimes equivalent to de facto control, over Latin America, the Persian
Gulf, and Egypt. By "ruling the waves" with a peerless navy, Britain
really did rule an "empire on which the sun never set."

The birthplace of the Industrial Revolution, Britain had become the
"workshop of the world," and by 1880 it accounted for almost a quarter of the world's manufacturing output and trade.[15] Its investments
powered global growth, and its fleets protected global trade. As my colleague Niall Ferguson has explained, Britain was "both policeman and
banker to the world . . . the first true superpower."[16] Britain thus saw
itself, and expected others to see it, as number one.

But if Britain had indisputably owned the nineteenth century, some
Britons doubted its claim on the twentieth. Undercurrents of anxiety
surfaced at the Festival of the British Empire, the 1897 diamond jubilee
for Queen Victoria. The embodiment of British rectitude and primacy,
Victoria had occupied the throne since the 1830s, and her descendants
populated the royal families of Europe, including Germany. To mark
the occasion, the era's most famous author, Rudyard Kipling, originally composed a poem glorifying Britain's imperial mission to civilize
the world. In a sign of the times, however, it was replaced with his
more contemplative "Recessional," which raised a disquieting prospect: "Far-called our navies melt away; / On dune and headland sinks
the fire: / Lo, all our pomp of yesterday / Is one with Nineveh and

Tyre! / Judge of the Nations, spare us yet, / Lest we forget—lest we forget!"[17]

Just a month after the jubilee, a twenty-two-year-old Winston Churchill confronted this specter of decline in his first official political speech. Atop a small platform facing a crowd of his countrymen, Churchill insisted that Britons would "continue to pursue that course marked out for us by an all-wise hand and carry out our mission of bearing peace, civilization and good government to the uttermost ends of the earth." Dismissing those who claimed that "in this Jubilee year our Empire has reached the height of its glory and power, and that now we shall begin to decline, as Babylon, Carthage, Rome declined," Churchill called on his audience to "give the lie to their dismal croaking." Instead, British citizens should stand up and show "by our actions that the vigor and vitality of our race is unimpaired and that our determination is to uphold the Empire that we have inherited from our fathers as Englishmen."[18]

Nonetheless, the "croakers" had something to croak about. There *were* alarming signs that Britain was declining relative to other powers.[19] In 1899, war with the Boers (descendants of Dutch settlers in what is today South Africa) broke out. Britain had not fought a well-trained adversary with modern weapons for a half century. The numerically inferior but determined Boers inflicted a series of humiliating defeats on their more powerful enemies. As he had done earlier in India and Sudan, Churchill rushed to join the fight, only to be captured by the Boers. The world's newspapers followed the tale of his subsequent escape and flight to freedom.[20] Britain eventually won the war, but at immense cost, shaking its imperial reputation. The German general staff studied the Boer War carefully, concluding, as Paul Kennedy puts it, that "Britain would find it impossible to defend India against a Russian assault," and "without a total reorganization of its military system, the empire itself would be dissolved within two decades."[21]

Meanwhile, a host of rivals were chipping away at the substantial head start in science and industry that had cemented Britain's number-one position following its hard-fought victory over Napoleonic France in 1815. After the American Civil War and Bismarck's success in unifying Germany in 1871, Britain watched others adopt its technologies, grow their economies faster, and emerge as peer competitors.[22] London worried about four rivals in particular: Russia, France, the United States, and Germany.

With the biggest army in Europe, its third-greatest fleet, a rapidly growing industrial base, and the largest landmass of any nation, Russia cast quite a shadow. New railways enabled Moscow to project power farther and faster than ever before, while its continuous expansion moved its borders steadily closer to British spheres of influence in central, western, and southern Asia.[23] What is more, Russia's alliance with France raised the prospect that Britain might have to fight both rivals at once, not only in Europe but also in India.

Despite its weak industrial base, France was an imperial competitor—indeed, the world's second-largest empire. Colonial disputes led to frequent friction with London and occasional war scares. In 1898, France was forced to back down from a confrontation over Fashoda (in the modern state of South Sudan) when it realized it had no chance of winning a naval conflict. But maintaining the Two-Power Standard to match the combined power of the expanding French and Russian navies put increasing pressure on British budgets.[24]

The United States, meanwhile, had emerged as a continental power that threatened British influence in the Western Hemisphere (explored in more detail in chapters 5 and 9). With a population almost twice that of Britain, seemingly endless natural resources, and a hunger for growth, America would have surprised the world had it *not* outstripped Britain's industrial might.[25] The US economy overtook Britain's (although not its empire overall) by about 1870 and never looked back. By 1913, Britain accounted for only 13 percent of global manufacturing output, down from 23 percent in 1880; the US, by contrast, had risen to 32 percent.[26] Backed by a modernizing navy, Washington had begun asserting itself ever more aggressively in the Western Hemisphere. After London and Washington went to the brink of war over Venezuela's borders in 1895 (see chapter 5), the British prime minister advised his finance minister that war with the United States "in the not distant future has become something more than a possibility: and by the light of it we must examine the estimates of the Admiralty." He warned that war with the US was "much more of a reality than the future Russo-French coalition."[27]

Another industrial phenomenon with growing naval ambitions lay much closer to home. Since its victory over France and unification under Bismarck, Germany had become the strongest land power in Europe, with an economic dynamism to match. German exports were now fiercely competitive with British products, making Berlin a formidable commercial rival. Before 1900, however, the British Empire saw it more as an economic than a strategic threat. Indeed, a number of senior British politicians favored a German alliance, and some tried to broker one.[28]

By 1914, London's calculations had changed completely. Britain found itself fighting alongside its former rivals Russia and France (and later the US) to prevent Germany from gaining strategic mastery in Europe. The story of how that happened—how, among a range of competitors, Germany became Britain's main adversary[29]—is a testament to the fear felt by a ruling power when a rising one appears to endanger its security. In Britain's case, that fear was concentrated by a growing German fleet that could only be intended for use against the Royal Navy.

GERMANY'S "PLACE IN THE SUN"

The story of Germany's rise, and its decision to build a navy so alarming to the British, is in many ways a simple one. It is the story of a country that experienced rapid, almost dizzying development in a very short time, but saw its path to global greatness blocked by what it considered an unjust and covetous incumbent.

Ever since Bismarck melded a patchwork of dozens of states into one German Empire following the triumphant wars against Austria (1866) and France (1870–71), Germany had emerged as an economic, military, and cultural phenomenon dominating the European continent. The Germans were no longer the objects of other people's history but the subject of their own story of national greatness.

As America's greatest Cold War strategist George Kennan later explained, Bismarck's deft diplomacy ensured that when it came to managing Europe's clashing interests and alignments, Germany always found itself in the majority. Bismarck did what was required to keep the vengeful French isolated, and he stayed on good terms with Russia.[30] The tsar still had the largest army in Europe, but Germany had the strongest and best-trained fighting force overall.[31]

Moreover, the seesaw on which Germany and Britain occupied opposite ends was shifting relentlessly. By 1914, Germany's population of sixty-five million was 50 percent larger than Britain's.[32] Germany grew to become Europe's leading economy, surpassing Britain by 1910.[33] By 1913, it accounted for 14.8 percent of global manufacturing output, overtaking Britain's 13.6 percent.[34] Prior to unification, it had produced only half the steel Britain did; by 1914, it produced twice as much. Writing in 1980—before the rise of China—Paul Kennedy wondered "whether the relative productive forces—and, by extension, the relative national power—of any two neighboring states before or since had altered in such a remarkable way in the course of one man's lifetime as occurred here between Britain and Germany."[35]

Britons experienced Germany's industrial growth most immediately in the form of German exports displacing British products at home and abroad. Between 1890 and 1913, Britain's exports to Germany doubled—but were still worth only half the value of its imports from Germany, which had tripled.[36] A best-selling book in 1896, *Made in Germany,* warned Britons that "a gigantic commercial State is arising to menace our prosperity, and contend with us for the trade of the world."[37]

Germany was overtaking Britain not only in the heavy industry and factory products of the First Industrial Revolution, but also in the electrical and petrochemical advances of the Second Industrial Revolution.

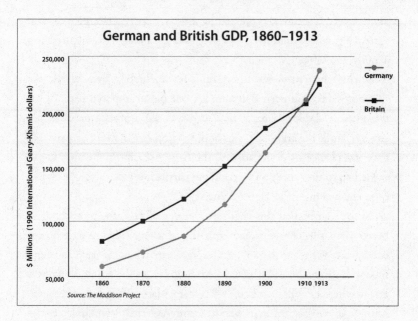

German and British GDP, 1860–1913

Source: The Maddison Project

By the turn of the century, Germany's organic-chemical industry controlled 90 percent of the global market.[38] In 1913, Britain, France, and Italy together produced and consumed only about 80 percent of the electricity that Germany did.[39] By 1914, Germany had twice as many telephones as Britain, and almost twice as much railway track.[40] German science and technology had surpassed Britain's to become the best in the world, fostered by a supportive government and nourished by esteemed universities.[41] Between 1901, when Nobel Prizes were first awarded, and 1914, Germany won eighteen prizes overall, more than twice as many as the United Kingdom and four times as many as the United States. In physics and chemistry alone, Germany won ten Nobels—almost twice as many as the UK and the US combined.[42]

Despite their rapid economic growth and impressive national achievements, many Germans felt shortchanged. The future, they believed, belonged not to the European "Great Powers" but to what had come to be known as "World Powers": superpowers whose size, population, and resources would allow them to dominate the twentieth century. America and Russia were continent-sized powers. Britain had a vast overseas empire, protected by a huge fleet. To compete on that scale, Germany would need its own colonies, along with the means to acquire and safeguard them.[43]

During this era many other countries, including Japan, Italy, the United States, and even Belgium, set out on an imperial path. What was notable about Germany, however, was the combination of its desire to change the colonial status quo, the immense national power that gave it a chance of doing so, and the strong sense that because it had come late to the table during the rapid partitioning of the globe, it had been cheated out of its rightful due.[44]

No one embodied this combustible mix of resentment and hubris better than the new German emperor, Kaiser Wilhelm II, who ascended to the throne in 1888. Privately, Bismarck compared his young monarch to a balloon: "If you do not hold fast to the string, you never know where he will be off to."[45] Two years later, Wilhelm untethered himself, dismissing the man who had united Germany and made Berlin the capital of a European Great Power.[46] His new government let lapse a secret treaty Bismarck had negotiated with Russia to prevent it from joining any French attack on Germany, and Paris soon seized the opportunity to end its isolation through an alliance with Moscow.[47]

Driven to see Germany become a World Power, and with his gaze expanding beyond Europe, the kaiser required a *Weltpolitik,* or global foreign policy. In the summer of Queen Victoria's jubilee, the kaiser chose Bernhard von Bülow as his foreign minister, declaring that "Bülow will be my Bismarck."[48] Bülow was not coy about his ambition, announcing that "the days when Germans granted one neighbor the earth, the other the sea, and reserved for themselves the sky, where pure doctrine reigns —those days are over. We don't want to put anyone in the shadow," he affirmed, "but we too *demand our place in the sun.*"[49]

Weltpolitik was as much about domestic politics as about the world beyond Germany's borders. While colonial gains over the next twenty years were unimpressive,[50] the vision of world expansion captured the German imagination. In 1897, Hans Delbrück, one of Germany's best-known historians and editor of a widely read magazine, spoke for many of his compatriots in arguing that "phenomenal masses of land will be partitioned in all corners of the world in the course of the next few decades. And the nationality that remains empty-handed will be excluded for a generation to come from the ranks of those great peoples that define the contours of the human spirit."[51] Bülow was even more direct: "The question is not, whether we want to colonize or not," he explained, "but that we *must* colonize, whether we like it or not."[52]

The "entire future" of Germany "among the great nations" depended on its becoming a World Power, Delbrück said. But one nation stood in the way. "We can pursue [a colonial] policy with England or without England," he asserted. "With England means in peace; against England means—through war." In either case, there could be "no step backward."[53] Germany would no longer be forced to swallow the dictates of the powers that were, but would stake its own claim to the world that was to come. Bülow told the Reichstag in 1899 that Germany could no longer "permit any foreign power, any foreign Jupiter, to tell us: 'What is to be done? The earth is already partitioned.' In the coming century," he announced, "Germany will be either the *hammer* or the *anvil*." In a speech at the launch of a battleship that same year, the kaiser was equally unsubtle: "Old empires pass away and new ones are in the process of being formed."[54] The Germans seeking World Power status were ultimately, as Michael Howard has written, "not concerned with expanding within what they saw as a British dominated world-system. It was precisely that system which they found intolerable, and which they were determined to challenge on a basis of equality."[55]

The thought that Germany might elbow Britain from the top spot, or at the very least become its equal, gave the kaiser immense psychological satisfaction. Wilhelm had decidedly mixed feelings about Britain—the birthplace of his mother, Queen Victoria's eldest daughter—and what he referred to as his "damned family" there. On the one hand, he was fluent in English and devoted to his grandmother Queen Victoria. He was thrilled when she made him an honorary admiral in the Royal Navy, proudly wearing its uniform whenever he could. As late as 1910, he told former president Theodore Roosevelt, visiting

Berlin on a European tour, that war between Germany and Britain was "unthinkable": "I was brought up in England . . . I feel myself partly an Englishman," he said with passion. And then, "with intense emphasis," he told Roosevelt: "I ADORE ENGLAND!"[56]

At the same time, Wilhelm could not conceal his resentment or his rivalrous ambitions. Margaret MacMillan's insightful 2013 work, *The War That Ended Peace,* unmasks the kaiser's profound insecurity, describing him as "an actor who secretly suspected that he was not up to the demanding role he had to play." Damaged at birth, his left arm remained shriveled the rest of his life. He resented the insistence of his British mother that her homeland was congenitally superior to Germany. Thus, his efforts to win the respect of his British royal relations often backfired. Although Wilhelm was always most welcome at the Royal Yacht Club's annual regatta in Cowes, his uncle (the future King Edward) was exasperated by his domineering manner, calling him "the most brilliant failure in history." To compete, Wilhelm established an even more elaborate regatta week of his own at Kiel, where he entertained European royalty, including his cousin Tsar Nicholas.[57] But as Theodore Roosevelt noted, "The head of the greatest military empire of the day was as jealously sensitive to English opinion as if he were some parvenu multi-millionaire trying to break into the London social world."[58]

Spurred on by what he saw as Britain's chronic condescension, the kaiser grew ever more determined to secure Germany's rightful place in the sun. He concluded, however, that the reigning global empire would not grant him or his countrymen the respect and influence they deserved—not, that is, until Germany could demonstrate that it was Britain's equal, not only in hosting the best sailing regatta but in building a navy to match.[59]

"OUR FUTURE LIES ON THE WATER"

In 1890, an American naval strategist, Captain Alfred T. Mahan, published *The Influence of Sea Power upon History.* Using Britain as his prime example, Mahan identified naval strength as the main determinant of great-power success—the key to military triumph, colonies, and wealth. The book arrived like a bolt of lightning in capitals from Washington and Tokyo to Berlin and St. Petersburg. It had no keener reader than Kaiser Wilhelm himself, who in 1894 said that he was "trying to learn it by heart." He ordered copies for every ship in his fleet.[60] Mahan's thinking shaped the kaiser's conviction that Germany's future lay "on the water." In the historian Jonathan Steinberg's words, "For the Kaiser, the sea and the navy were symbols of the British Empire's greatness, a greatness which he both admired and envied."[61] A navy that rivaled Britain's would not only enable Germany to achieve its destiny as a World Power, but also end its intolerable position of vulnerability to coercion by a superior British fleet.

The kaiser had felt the weight of Britain's heavy hand after he sent a provocative telegram to the Boer leadership in southern Africa in 1896, indicating that he might offer support against the British. London was outraged. As a senior British Foreign Office official told the German ambassador, any intervention could mean war, and "a blockade of Hamburg and Bremen." Twisting the knife, he noted that "the annihilation of German commerce on the high seas would be child's play for the English fleet."[62] This was a brute fact, hard to ignore. Germany had less than half Britain's battleships. How could Germany hope to play a global role when the British fleet could force it to back down on command? The Venezuela border crisis of 1895–96 between Washington and London reinforced the lesson. In the kaiser's words: "only when we can hold out our mailed fist against his face, will the British lion draw back, as he did recently before America's threats."[63]

Wilhelm chose Alfred Tirpitz in 1897 to build that mailed fist as head of his naval department. For Germany to join America, Russia, and Britain as one of the four World Powers, Tirpitz told the kaiser, it would need a powerful navy to match. "To make up the lost ground" was, he warned, "a life-and-death question."[64] Margaret MacMillan characterizes Tirpitz as "a Social Darwinist with a deterministic view of history as a series of struggles for survival. Germany needed to expand;

Britain, as the dominant power, was bound to want to stop that."[65] Instructively, Tirpitz compared this struggle to business competition: "The older and stronger firm inevitably seeks to strangle the new and rising one before it is too late. That," he said after the war, "was the key to the Anglo-German conflict."[66]

While in public Tirpitz emphasized that Germany needed to expand its navy to protect the country's commerce,[67] in private he and the kaiser agreed that the primary purpose of the new German navy should be as a weapon against British dominance. In the first memorandum for his master, in June 1897, the same month as Britain's triumphant jubilee, Tirpitz stated that "the most dangerous enemy at the present time is England. It is also the enemy against which we most urgently require a certain measure of naval force as a political power factor."[68]

Tirpitz's ultimate goal was a German navy "equally as strong as England's."[69] But recognizing that building such a fleet would take time, he argued that even a smaller fleet could be a significant "political power factor." An overstretched Britain, with its fleet committed around the world and minding the threat of a rapid German attack against its coastal towns, would treat Germany with more respect.[70] Moreover, according to what Tirpitz called his "risk theory," if his fleet became strong enough to cause serious damage to the Royal Navy, leaving it vulnerable to attack by other great powers, this would deter the British from attacks on Germany. The core of this strategy was spelled out in the explanatory documents to the Second Naval Law: "Germany must have a battle fleet so strong that, even for the adversary with the greatest sea-power, a war against it would involve such dangers as to imperil his position in the World."[71] Realizing that the period between the initiation of Germany's naval buildup and the point where its fleet could defend itself against the British would be a "danger zone,"[72] Bülow counseled that "we must operate carefully, like the caterpillar before it has grown into a butterfly."[73]

Germany would do its best not to get drawn into a fight with the British before its fleet was strong enough. And there was no point in any kind of security arrangement before the new fleet had forced Britain to acknowledge Germany's new status. In the meantime, Bülow hoped Britain would make his task easier by getting entangled in a war with Russia, allowing Germany quietly to increase its economic and naval strength. Eventually, once German naval might was a fait accompli, Britain would be forced to come to terms with the new reality.[74]

Tirpitz had promised the kaiser that a large fleet of battleships would promote German patriotism and unity. He was skillful in mobilizing public opinion in support of the proposed naval program and in lobbying the Reichstag. The First Naval Law, passed in 1898, called for a total of nineteen battleships. The kaiser was delighted, and readily agreed when the following year Tirpitz recommended accelerating the expansion program, offering his master the tempting prospect that Britain would lose any "inclination to attack us and will as a result concede to Your Majesty sufficient naval presence . . . for the conduct of a grand policy overseas." The Second Naval Law was signed in 1900, doubling the size of the future fleet to thirty-eight battleships.[75]

When King Edward VII visited Germany for the Kiel Regatta in June 1904, his nephew hosted a dinner for him at the Imperial Yacht Club. In contrast to Tirpitz's efforts to disguise Germany's ambitions, Kaiser Wilhelm took pleasure in showing off as much of his navy as possible to his uncle. His shipbuilding program was clearly on track to produce a fleet that would rival Britain's. As the kaiser pronounced in the toast to his uncle, "As a little boy, I was allowed to visit Portsmouth and Plymouth . . . I admired the proud English ships in those two splendid harbors. Then there awoke in me the wish to build ships like these someday, and when I was grown up to possess as fine a navy as the English."[76] Within a month of Wilhelm's rash display at Kiel, Britain had made its first official plans for war with Germany.[77]

"MOST BULLIES, WHEN TACKLED, ARE COWARDS"

As early as 1900, the British Admiralty had acknowledged that Germany would within a few years overtake Russia as the world's third-largest naval power after Britain and France. The Admiralty realized that this meant London would need to review the Two-Power Standard and maintain a counterbalancing British fleet in the North Sea.[78]

In 1902, citing Germany's 1900 Naval Law, the First Lord of the Admiralty told the cabinet: "I am convinced that the great new German navy is being carefully built up from the point of view of a war with us."[79] In that same year, his director of naval intelligence had concluded that Britain would "have to fight for command of the North Sea, as we did in the Dutch wars of the seventeenth century." Although some in both Britain and Germany had for a time accepted Tirpitz's justification that Germany's fleet was needed to protect its commerce, this pretense was unsustainable. As Paul Kennedy notes, when the reality sank in and London realized that the German fleet's real target was Britain itself, "the effect upon Anglo-German relations was disastrous — and irremediable."[80]

Deteriorating Anglo-German relations coincided with rapidly shifting power dynamics in and beyond Europe, and with Britain's reassessment of its global posture.[81] In the face of a range of rising powers, Britain gradually acknowledged it could no longer maintain naval supremacy everywhere. American, Japanese, Russian, and many other fleets were growing, but only Germany's buildup took place just a few hundred nautical miles from Britain.[82] The Admiralty tacitly conceded supremacy in the Western Hemisphere to the United States, and in 1902 Britain ended its "splendid isolation" to sign a defensive alliance with Japan, allowing it to reduce the Royal Navy's burden in the Far East.[83]

While primarily aimed against Russia, the Japanese alliance also ended any need for an understanding with Germany over China and opened the door to greater cooperation with France. Britain and France both saw Japan and Russia edging toward war, and neither wished to find itself fighting each other by being dragged into the conflict by their respective allies.[84] They also saw the opportunity to settle other long-standing disputes, in 1904 signing the Entente Cordiale, which resolved outstanding colonial questions. This was not an alliance, but

Berlin nevertheless saw it as a threat to its diplomatic position. Unwisely, it tried to pull Britain and France apart through provocations in Morocco. Unsurprisingly, this pushed London and Paris closer together.

Meanwhile, in the Far East, Japan had decisively defeated Russia by 1905 in their contest over Manchuria and Korea. The sinking of the Russian fleet meant that Germany moved up to third place among navies of the world, after Britain and France.[85] Russia's decline at first seemed like good news for Britain, since it meant that Moscow posed less of a threat to London's interests. But it also meant that Russia would not be an effective ally for France against Germany for some time. There was now the real prospect that Germany would be able to upset the balance of power in Europe.[86]

Would London let Berlin rewrite the European order, or would it defend the status quo? Its security interests dictated the latter. Eyre Crowe had described Britain's role in maintaining the balance of power — preventing any single state from dominating the Continent — as a virtual "law of nature." A senior figure in British military planning warned, "There is no doubt that within measurable distance there looms a titanic struggle between Germany and Europe for mastery."[87] Britain began taking steps to make the outcome of such a struggle more favorable. The Entente Cordiale did not commit Britain to France's defense, but in 1905–6 London and Paris began secret military talks. In 1907, Britain signed a convention with Russia, putting their colonial disputes on ice, and thereby creating a trilateral alignment between Britain and the Franco-Russian alliance that became known as the Triple Entente.

Thus, in the wake of the Russo-Japanese War, Britain focused on the prospect that a rising Germany would become the European hegemon. If Germany dominated the Continent, it would be able to mobilize sufficient resources to undermine British naval supremacy — leaving Britain vulnerable to invasion.[88] As King Edward put it in 1909, if Britain remained aloof in a future struggle, "Germany would have the power of demolishing her enemies, one by one, with us sitting back with folded arms, and she would then probably proceed to attack us."[89]

Berlin drew different lessons from the Russo-Japanese War. In Japan's preemptive strike against the Russian fleet at Port Arthur—an attack that foreshadowed Pearl Harbor less than four decades later—the Germans saw a model for a British sneak attack on their own North Sea fleet at Kiel. They had repeatedly analyzed Britain's surprise attack at Copenhagen in 1807, in which it captured the Danish fleet before Napoleon could co-opt it. As historian Jonathan Steinberg notes, the kaiser "believed unreservedly" in the possibility of such an attack. Indeed, in late 1904 his ambassador to Britain had to reassure him in person that this was not imminent. In early 1907, when rumors spread in Kiel that the British were about to attack, nervous parents took their children out of school. German fears were not entirely misplaced. To paraphrase Henry Kissinger, even paranoids have enemies. Britain's new First Sea Lord—Admiral John "Jacky" Fisher, appointed as the country's highest uniformed naval officer in October 1904—*did* actually recommend on a number of occasions that the Royal Navy should "Copenhagen" the German fleet. The first time he put it to King Edward in late 1904, his monarch's response was "My God, Fisher, you must be mad!" But when the admiral explained the idea again four years later, the king listened more carefully. Fisher believed that deterring an adversary with bellicose statements was the best way to avoid war, but Germany's leaders found in British rhetoric more than sufficient cause to redouble their naval investments.[90]

Ironically, Germany's naval chief was also guilty of fundamentally misjudging the effects his actions would have on the opposing power. Tirpitz had assumed Britain would not become aware of the growing force across the North Sea, and that London would not be able to realign itself diplomatically to neutralize other adversaries and to avoid coming to terms with Germany. Both assumptions proved wrong.[91] Tirpitz had also assumed that Britain would neither be able to concentrate its fleet against Germany nor be willing to spend the money required to match the German shipbuilding program. In this, he would be proved wrong once again.[92]

Britain did all that Germany thought it would not do and more. Fisher led a reorganization of the Royal Navy to focus its strength on the German threat. In 1906, he wrote to King Edward: "Our only probable enemy is Germany. Germany keeps her *whole* Fleet always concentrated within a few hours of England. We must therefore keep a Fleet twice as powerful concentrated within a few hours of Germany."[93] Diplomatic realignments with France, Japan, and (in a less formal way) the United States meant that Fisher could safely execute his naval rebalance, devoting 75 percent of British battleships to counter Germany's fleet.[94]

In his 1907 memorandum, Crowe had advised that merely demanding that Germany stop its naval expansion would only encourage Berlin to build faster. The Germans would understand only one language: action. Britain should demonstrate its determination to outbuild the Germans, forcing them to see the futility of the program on which they had embarked. This approach surely resonated with King Edward, who had once remarked of his nephew, "Willy is a bully, and most bullies, when tackled, are cowards."[95]

Not only did Britain increase the size of its fleet, but Fisher also oversaw the development of a new class of battleship, the *Dreadnought*. First launched in 1906, the *Dreadnought*-class battleship was faster, larger, and more heavily armored than all its predecessors, and its twelve-inch guns gave it double the firepower and striking distance.[96] All other navies would now have to build their own dreadnoughts if they wished to compete. Tirpitz learned about Britain's new weapon program in early 1905. By the fall of that year, he had submitted to the Reichstag a new supplement that increased naval spending by 35 percent over the law of 1900, and provided for the building of two dreadnoughts annually. In addition, he began preparations for widening the Kiel Canal, at great cost, to allow German dreadnoughts to move quickly from the Baltic to their projected battle space in the North Sea.[97]

Fisher noted with an eagle eye the milestones on the path to conflict.[98] In 1911, he predicted that war with Germany would come when the widening of the Kiel Canal was finished. Indeed, he foresaw a German surprise attack, probably on a three-day holiday weekend. His predicted date for the "Battle of Armageddon"? October 21, 1914. (In fact, the Great War began two months earlier—in August 1914, on a holiday weekend, a month after the canal had been completed.)[99]

The naval race assumed a momentum of its own, fueled by growing popular fervor and anxiety in both countries. The Germans introduced supplements to the naval laws, increasing the size or production rate of their fleet. These supplements tended to follow British developments such as the dreadnought or perceived humiliations on the international stage: in 1906, after the Tangiers Crisis; in 1908, as Germany feared "encirclement"; and in 1912, following the Agadir Crisis.[100]

In 1908–9, Britain accused Germany of secretly building ships at a higher rate than its public declarations. Germany rejected mutual inspections, prompting fears that the only basis for assessing the German threat was its ship construction capability. Now it was Britain's turn to be gripped by panics of surprise attacks, and by demands from its own population—who were avid consumers of "invasion literature"—for a faster buildup.[101] Even though the Committee of Imperial Defence had assessed in 1903 and again in 1908 that the Royal Navy could still protect the homeland, the public cried for more dreadnoughts. After

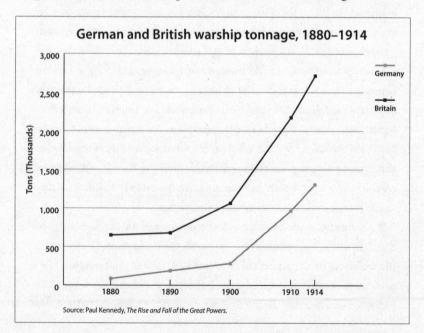

Source: Paul Kennedy, *The Rise and Fall of the Great Powers.*

initial doubts, Chancellor of the Exchequer David Lloyd George eventually proposed tax hikes to pay for the new construction, asserting, "We don't intend to put in jeopardy the naval supremacy which is so essential not only to our national existence, but, in our judgment, to the vital interests of Western civilization."[102]

Crowe's memorandum warned that Germany had acted like a "professional blackmailer" in the colonial domain, and concessions only made blackmailers ask for more. Relations might improve when Britain took a "resolute stand," as they had done with France after the Fashoda crisis in East Africa.[103] Yet, as with Tirpitz's "risk fleet" (the naval force he felt would deter London and eventually persuade it to acknowledge Germany's global status), Britain's firmness and diplomatic realignments failed to produce the desired results.

As the decade went on, Germany became increasingly strident in its claims of victimhood and impending disaster.[104] By the time of the 1908 Bosnian crisis—when Austria-Hungary's annexation of Bosnia and Herzegovina precipitated an international backlash, forcing Berlin to come to the aid of its ally in Vienna—the German press argued that "peace-loving" Germany had been encircled by a military alliance of Britain, Russia, and France, and that it could only depend on Austria-Hungary, which therefore needed strong German support.[105] Austria-Hungary's many nationalities were increasingly at odds with one another, and Balkan complications threatened to spill over into Austrian territories. Serbia, Vienna's biggest headache, was supported by Russia. Germany, like Britain, feared that the collapse of its partner would leave it vulnerable to its rival's aggression. When King Edward had toured Europe in 1907, presumably to seek further conspirators against Germany, the kaiser told an audience of three hundred that his uncle was "Satan. You cannot imagine what a Satan he is!"[106]

It is instructive to compare Edward's and Wilhelm's understanding of the consequences of British determination to resist German encroachments. Both believed their countries' rivalry an aberration from what they thought natural ethnic alignments. Both chalked it up to the other's envy. In 1908, Edward felt that continued British strength and vigilance would make Germany "accept the inevitable and be friendly with us." But he was incorrect: by 1912 the kaiser had a much more fatalistic outlook, angrily arguing that out of "fear of our growing big" the British would support Berlin's adversaries in the "imminent struggle for existence" against "the Germanic peoples of Europe."[107] Alliances tightened, producing what Henry Kissinger has termed a "diplomatic doomsday machine" that later allowed an assassination in the Balkans to cascade into a world war.

War almost broke out in summer 1911, when Germany sent a naval vessel, the *Panther,* to Agadir, hoping to secure a naval base on the Atlantic — thereby challenging French dominance in Morocco. France asked Britain for support. The British cabinet feared that Berlin aimed to embarrass Paris and weaken its ties to London. In a speech at Mansion House, Lloyd George made clear that war would be preferable to an ignominious capitulation that would undermine Britain's great-power status. Germany eventually backed down and the hostility passed peacefully, but many Germans felt they had won insufficient concessions, and their frustration and anger toward Britain grew.[108] Much of Germany's population and leadership believed colonies essential for its survival, and it now seemed that Germany's vital expansion might be thwarted, with fatal consequences.[109]

Churchill had been home secretary at the time of the Agadir Crisis and believed that Britain should defend France if attacked by Germany. He agreed with Lloyd George's directness and was glad to see that "the bully [was] climbing down." It seemed that British strength and determination to stand up to aggression had dissuaded the Germans from "any fresh act of provocation" in the crisis, and that "all would," as Churchill told his wife, "come out smooth and triumphant." But the risk of war had been real. Churchill knew that for Britain the true stakes in such a conflict were not the independence of Morocco or Belgium, but preventing "France from being trampled down and looted by the Prussian Junkers — a disaster ruinous to the world, and swiftly fatal to our country."[110]

Staggered by his government's lack of readiness during the 1911 crisis when appointed several months thereafter as First Lord of the Admiralty, Churchill turned his attention to Britain's vulnerabilities. His "mind was full of the dangers of war" and his heart utterly committed to making Britain, in the late Martin Gilbert's words, "invulnerable at sea . . . Every deficiency would have to be made good, every gap filled, every contingency anticipated." But for Churchill, preparation did not mean fatalism. While he did everything in his power to make Britain ready for battle, he categorically rejected "the theory of inevitable wars" and hoped that by postponing the "evil day," conflict might be prevented—since with time, positive developments in foreign societies could take effect, such as more peaceful "democratic forces" superseding the Junker class in Germany's government.[111]

Churchill thus made a strenuous effort to slow or stop the naval race. In 1908, Kaiser Wilhelm had rebuffed a British suggestion to limit the arms race; additional Anglo-German discussions from 1909 to 1911 had gone nowhere. But Churchill was not dissuaded. In January 1912, he told Sir Ernest Cassel, an intermediary to the kaiser, that if Germany cut the pace of its naval program, this would bring about "an immediate détente." Cassel proposed to the kaiser that he accept British naval superiority and reduce his own program, in return for Britain's assisting Germany in its quest for colonies. London and Berlin would refrain from aggressive actions against each other. The kaiser, as Cassel reported upon his return, was "enchanted, almost childishly so." But when Britain's secretary of state for war, Richard Haldane, went on a follow-up mission to Germany, the Germans were willing to offer only a reduction in the pace of their naval program in return for Britain's neutrality in the case of a European war. Britain could not assent to Germany's overturning the balance of power. Although Britain was willing to pledge not to join any attack against Germany, the kaiser angrily rejected the British position.[112]

On March 12, 1912, the kaiser approved a supplementary Naval Law that called for an additional three battleships and for the German fleet to be kept in greater readiness. A week later, Churchill announced to Parliament that Britain would replace the Two-Power Standard. Hereafter, it would maintain a 16-to-10 advantage in dreadnoughts against its main competitor. Moreover, Churchill announced that for every new German battleship emerging from the supplementary German Naval Law, Britain would build *two* new ones. He also proposed a moratorium, which he called a "naval holiday," in which Britain would match any German suspension of its building program. For instance, Churchill hypothesized publicly, if in 1913 Germany would forgo building three ships, Britain would forgo building the five it would otherwise have constructed in response. The Germans rejected Churchill's proposal (which he repeated the following year), seeing it as an attempt to lock in place British dominance and undermine domestic support for the German navy. Nonetheless, a year later, in February 1913, lacking political support for increased naval expenditure, Tirpitz announced that he would essentially accept the 16-to-10 battleship ratio.[113]

The naval race appeared to be over. Although Germany had managed to dramatically close the gap of its warship tonnage to Britain's —from 7.4 to 1 in 1880, to 3.6 to 1 in 1890, and then to only 2.1 to 1 in 1914[114]—Britain still had 20 dreadnoughts to Germany's 13 when the war began.[115] Despite its immense financial and diplomatic cost, Germany's naval buildup had failed in overtaking Britain. Indeed, as Churchill later argued, the German naval program "closed the ranks of the Entente. With every rivet that von Tirpitz drove into his ships of war, he united British opinion . . . The hammers that clanged at Kiel and Wilhelmhaven were forging the coalition of nations by which Germany was to be resisted and finally overthrown."[116]

Did the Anglo-German naval race cause World War I? No. Arms races do not inevitably produce conflict. As Michael Howard has shown, the "longest and perhaps the bitterest arms race in modern history" was between the French and British navies for ninety years after 1815— although that race ended not in war but with the Entente Cordiale.[117]

Yet the arms race between Berlin and London did in many ways lay the foundation for war. While Germany's growing economic challenge to England had not made strategic rivalry between the two nations inevitable (or even prevented Britain's elite from considering Berlin as a

possible ally), the growth of the German navy and its geographic proximity to Britain posed a unique existential threat. The mistrust and
fear that Germany's naval program provoked in the British contributed
to London's identification of Berlin as its primary enemy. And once
this concept took hold, it shaped Britain's views of Germany's other
actions. While Britain faced many rivals, only Germany was capable
of disrupting the European balance and building naval capabilities that
could imperil Britain's survival.[118] Although Tirpitz had for the moment accepted his adversary's superiority in the North Sea by 1913, the
British knew that his concession stemmed primarily from domestic and
financial constraints, and that if and when conditions changed, so too
would his plans.[119] What some called Britain's "victory" in the naval
race did not ease its fears about the danger posed by Germany. Thus,
when in 1914 Germany invaded France and the Low Countries, war
seemed preferable to the prospect of Germany achieving dominance on
the Continent and then threatening Britain's survival.

A second, parallel Thucydidean dynamic is key to understanding
why Britain and Germany went to war in 1914. At the same time that
Germany's rise was provoking British fears, Berlin could see a pressing
threat to its own interests in the form of Russia, a rising challenger to
Germany's status as the greatest land power in Europe.[120] The loss of
the war against Japan in 1905 and a period of simmering revolutionary
unrest had dealt Russia a crushing blow. But it now appeared to be taking shape as a revitalized, modern military power right on Germany's
borders. In 1913, Russia announced what it called the "grand program"
for expanding its army with an array of initiatives. It was expected that
by 1917 the Russian army would outnumber Germany's by three to
one. Germany's plan for a two-front war called for quickly defeating
France before turning east to deal with the slow-moving Russian jug-
gernaut. By 1914, heavy French investment had allowed the development of a Russian railway system that would shorten its mobilization period to two weeks, as opposed to the six weeks assumed in the
German plan.[121]

Russia's rapid development, along with a general fatalism about an eventual European war, encouraged an aggressive attitude among Germany's political and military leadership. Some espoused preventive war while there was still a chance to beat Russia—especially since a successful war might allow Germany to break out of its "encirclement." In 1914 they were presented with an opportunity either to quash Russian influence in the Balkans or to defeat Russia militarily before it was too late.[122]

On June 28, the nephew to Austro-Hungarian emperor Franz Joseph and next in line to the throne was assassinated by a Serbian nationalist in Bosnia. In the confrontation between Austria-Hungary and Serbia that followed, Russia backed Serbia. In July, Berlin gave its infamous "blank check" to Vienna—assuring Austria-Hungary that it would receive, as the kaiser put it, "Germany's full support" in its retaliation against Serbia, even if this caused "serious European complications."[123]

Germany was willing to risk war with Russia, and therefore with France, in 1914 primarily because of the related fears that its sole ally would collapse if Austria-Hungary did not crush its enemies in the Balkans and the prospect of being helpless in a future conflict with Moscow. Berlin's backing emboldened Vienna to issue a stern ultimatum to Belgrade on July 23, demanding, among other things, that Serbia permit Austro-Hungarian agents to enter its territory in their pursuit of the assassin's network. The Germans were aware that Vienna had designed the ultimatum to be rejected. The Austro-Hungarian ambassador to Belgrade was instructed that, however the Serbians replied, "it must come to a war." After a week of desultory diplomacy, events began to take on their own momentum, overwhelming those who now feared the consequences of earlier decisions. When he arrived back from vacation and read the Serbian reply that accepted all of Vienna's demands, the kaiser told his war minister that this had removed "all reason for war." The war minister retorted that his sovereign "no longer had control of the affair in his own hands."[124] That same day, Vienna declared war on Belgrade.

In what is now known as the July Crisis, the simultaneous Thucydidean dynamics between London and Berlin, and between Berlin and

Moscow, became interlocked. Germany's determination to prop up its ally and forestall the menace of a rising Russia led to its declaration of war against the tsar—and his ally, France. The German general staff's war plan for a quick defeat of France called for invasions of Luxembourg and Belgium. But by invading Belgium on the way to crushing France, Germany crossed a red line for Britain.

The prospect of Germany's defeat of France led London to fear the arrival of the European hegemon that it had spent centuries trying to prevent. The violation of Belgian neutrality—which Britain was sworn to protect under the 1839 Treaty of London—helped to energize British public opinion and unite the governing Liberal Party, which had been divided over whether to enter the conflict. But Britain went to war primarily because of its assessment that its vital national interests would be violated if Germany was successful in becoming the hegemon of Europe. The security factors driving Britain and Germany into war were clear. As Foreign Secretary Edward Grey stated to Parliament on August 3, Britain could not tolerate "the whole of the west of Europe opposite us . . . falling under the domination of a single power."[125]

As Paul Kennedy neatly puts it, the leaders of Britain and Germany considered that their clash in 1914 was "but a continuation of what had been going on for at least fifteen or twenty years," and had begun "because the former power wished to preserve the existing status quo, whereas the latter, for a mixture of offensive and defensive motives, was taking steps to alter it."[126]

"DIVERTING THE DEADLY CURRENT"

Among the paradoxes of 1914 is the disjunction between years of warning about and preparing for war, on the one hand, and on the other, shock at the rapidity with which the Continent plunged into chaos.[127] Archduke Franz Ferdinand was killed on June 28. On July 9, the most senior official at the British Foreign Office doubted "whether Austria will take any action of a serious character," and expected "the

storm [to] blow over." Until being told on July 25 of the Austrian ultimatum to Serbia, Churchill's and the cabinet's attention was mainly on
the threat of civil strife in Ireland.[128] Less than two weeks later, Europe
was at war.

Germany invaded Luxembourg on August 2, and Belgium on August 4. That day, London demanded that Germany withdraw from
Belgium by eleven p.m., British time. Churchill found himself in the
Admiralty, waiting for Britain's ultimatum to expire. When Big Ben
struck eleven and no German pledge to honor Belgian neutrality had
been received, Churchill took the next step. The "war telegram" flew
to Royal Navy ships around the world: "Commence hostilities against
Germany."[129]

Structural stress made the war that devastated Europe more likely
—but not inevitable. Many statesmen later found it comforting to believe that nothing could have prevented the conflict. Churchill was not
one of them. Yet even Churchill, an accomplished historian as well as
a policymaker, struggled to understand what he and his colleagues had
done—and left undone. A decade after he issued the war telegram, he
published *The World Crisis,* a multivolume work of penetrating analysis
and elegant prose setting forth "the manner in which I endeavored to
discharge my share in these hazardous responsibilities."[130]

Could the war have been avoided? Churchill admitted that contemplating the conflict's origins left "a prevailing sense of the defective
control of individuals upon world affairs." But he refused to succumb
to determinism. He identified missed opportunities to assuage reasonable security concerns on both sides, to prevent "or at the very least
[delay] the fatal exodus from the diplomatic field," and perhaps to "divert the deadly current" flowing toward war. He stretched his imagination, asking: "Could we in England perhaps by some effort, by some
sacrifice of our material interests, by some compulsive gesture, at once
of friendship and command, have reconciled France and Germany in
time and formed that grand association on which alone the peace and
glory of Europe would be safe?" He answered: "I cannot tell."[131]

Nearly a century after Churchill reflected on this dilemma, there are still no easy answers for how Britain could have resisted the currents dragging Europe into war while preserving British vital interests.[132] The parallels between this case and our contemporary challenge with China are inevitably inexact, but still unsettling. Like Germany, China feels it has been cheated out of its rightful place by nations that were strong when it was weak. Like Germany, China has the will and the means to change the status quo.

Meanwhile, like Britain, the United States jealously guards its primacy on the world stage, and is determined to resist Chinese attempts to revise the global political order. Both nations naturally see their own actions as just and reasonable, and their opponent's as suspect and dangerous. As we shall see in the next chapter, Americans might be more understanding of China today if they were aware of the behavior of another rising power that was even more rapacious and belligerent at that stage in its own development—Theodore Roosevelt's United States.

Despite American aggressiveness, London succeeded in avoiding war with a rising US, healing old wounds and laying the ground for a future close relationship. It would be foolhardy, however, to trust that the unusual constellation of factors producing that fortunate outcome will repeat itself. Misplaced optimism and business as usual in both Washington and Beijing are likely to result in a dynamic more closely resembling Britain and Germany's encounter than Britain and America's "great rapprochement."

The magnitude of the catastrophe that befell Europe, and the possibility of its repetition in the great contest of the twenty-first century, should encourage us to follow Churchill's example. We should stretch our imagination in asking whether changes in what leaders in both nations now consider essential could "divert the deadly current" of our own time. We should pray that we can avoid one day echoing Chancellor Bethmann Hollweg's pathetic answer on the cause of Europe's war: "Ah, if we only knew."[133]

Part Three

———

A GATHERING STORM

5

IMAGINE CHINA WERE
JUST LIKE US

It is impossible for Athenians either to enjoy peace and quiet themselves, or to allow anyone else to.

> —Thucydides, Corinthian ambassador
> addresses the Spartan Assembly, 432 BCE

According to the law of nature one rules whatever one can. We did not make this law. We found it when we came to power, and we shall leave it to those who come after us.

> —Thucydides, Athenians to Melians, 416 BCE

> O would some power the gift to give us
> To see ourselves as others see us!
>
> —Robert Burns

Americans enjoy lecturing Chinese to be "more like us." Perhaps they should be more careful what they wish for. Historically, how have emerging hegemons behaved? To be more specific, how did Washington act just over a century ago when Theodore Roosevelt led the US into what he was supremely confident would be an American century?

On April 19, 1897, a thirty-eight-year-old political phenomenon joined the administration of President William McKinley as the second-ranking civilian leading the Department of the Navy. Born to one of the first families of New York, educated at Harvard, hardened as a cowboy in the Dakota Badlands, tempered as a police commissioner in New York City, and established as a public intellectual who had already published fifteen widely discussed books, Roosevelt was, in the words of his heavyweight sparring partner, "a strong, tough man; hard to hurt and harder to stop."[1]

Seven days after taking office as assistant secretary of the navy, TR gave McKinley a lengthy private memorandum describing the current conditions of the navy (unacceptable), the necessity for its rapid buildup (to secure peace in the Western Hemisphere), and the dangers posed by Spanish control of Cuba, which lay precariously close to the US coast.[2] Before the month was out, and without informing his boss or President McKinley, the new assistant secretary had also sent instructions to the leadership of the Naval War College—then the government's cockpit of war planning. They were to develop operational plans in case of war with Spain (over Cuba) or Japan (over Hawaii, whose Tokyo-friendly monarch the US had helped overthrow in 1893).[3]

Although the United States was just emerging on the world stage, Roosevelt knew in his bones that the hundred years ahead should be an American era, and he was committed to do everything in his power to make it so. Believing determination to be the handmaid of destiny, TR seized, and on occasion even manufactured, every opportunity to define that century on his own terms. In the decade that followed his arrival in Washington, the US declared war on Spain, expelling it from the Western Hemisphere and acquiring Puerto Rico, Guam, and the Philippines; threatened Germany and Britain with war unless they agreed to settle disputes on American terms; supported an insurrection in Colombia to create a new country, Panama, in order to build a canal; and declared itself the policeman of the Western Hemisphere, asserting the right to intervene whenever and wherever it judged necessary —a right it exercised nine times in the seven years of TR's presidency alone.[4]

Never before or since has a president so fundamentally shaped the country's sense of its role in the world. TR led the nation to a new understanding of what it meant to be an American. National greatness, he insisted, rested on two imperatives: the mission to advance civilization at home and abroad, and the muscle to achieve it—in particular a superior military composed of men who embodied strength, courage, and the will to fight.

TR lionized the rugged settlers who endured sacrifice and survived by dint of their resilience, self-confidence, savvy—and readiness to use violence. In his telling, "the chief feature of frontier life was the endless war between the settlers and the red men."[5] For a bookish, asthmatic, upper-class, prep school and then Harvard student, Roosevelt's post-graduate years in the Dakota Badlands were formative. There, he found himself face-to-face with danger in a Darwinian struggle for survival. He fought hand to hand against Indians and desperadoes, was shot, bled, and almost died on multiple occasions—but survived by causing others to bleed and die. In his view, this made him a man more than any other experience in his life. It also convinced him that those unable or unwilling to fight for themselves would perforce be ruled by others who were. "All the great masterful races have been fighting races," he declared in his first public speech as assistant secretary. "The minute that a race loses the hard-fighting virtues," he warned, "then, no matter what else it may retain, no matter how skilled in commerce and finance, in science or art, it has lost its proud right to stand as the equal of the best. Cowardice in a race, as in an individual, is an unpardonable sin."[6] Roosevelt's four-volume *Winning of the West* proclaimed his gospel of Americanism. The first volume, published when he was just thirty-one, details the nation's relentless advance across the continent, driven by "Manifest Destiny": the conviction that "America's incorporation of all adjacent lands was the virtually inevitable fulfillment of a moral mission delegated to the nation by Providence itself."[7] Likening its importance to a combination of the Civil War and the emancipation of slaves, TR called America's westward expansion the "crowning and greatest achievement" of the English-speaking peoples' march of civilization "over the world's waste spaces."[8]

Moreover, for TR, America's mission did not end at its Pacific coast.

Along with like-minded military and congressional figures, he raised the banner of expansionism not just to expel Spain from Cuba and the Western Hemisphere, but also to make the United States a power in the Atlantic and Pacific. As Roosevelt put it after the Hawaiian coup: "I believe in more ships; I believe in ultimately driving every European power off of this continent, and I don't want to see our flag hauled down where it has been hauled up."[9]

Claiming the Americas for Americans would require military might, especially naval superiority. As a student at Harvard, Roosevelt had begun a serious scholarly study of the War of 1812. When later published as *The Naval War of 1812,* it became the conflict's authoritative account. The head of the Naval War College made it mandatory reading, giving copies to the captain of every ship in the US Navy. TR's analysis highlighted one central finding. "The simple truth," the future president wrote, was that "the side which possessed the superiority in force, in the proportion of three to two, could not well help winning."[10]

No one who had read *The Naval War of 1812* was surprised when the new assistant secretary of the navy made a forceful case for a bigger, stronger navy to serve as the backbone of American global power. In his speech to the Naval War College seven weeks after taking office, TR counseled "preparation for war is the surest guaranty for peace," warning ominously that the US "cannot stand still if it is to retain its self-respect." Diplomacy was "an excellent thing." But, he insisted, "ultimately those who wish to see this country at peace with foreign nations will be wise if they place reliance upon a first-class fleet of first-class battleships rather than on any arbitration treaty which the wit of man can devise."[11]

America followed TR's advice. In 1890, the navy did not possess any battleships. By 1905, it had built twenty-five and became a leading naval power.[12] Even Britain would come to realize that it did not want to fight with America in its own backyard, especially with a rising Germany much closer to home.

The United States proved more interested in using its newfound economic and military prowess to reinforce its growing influence than to expand its borders. Although TR looked wistfully at western Canada (still a dominion of the British Empire), most expansionists did not believe acquiring more territory in the Americas was feasible. Instead, the US would settle for dominance of a hemisphere made up of respectful, compliant neighbors free from interference by outside foreign powers. In practical terms, this meant communicating clearly that US interests in its hemispheric sphere of influence were non-negotiable and backing this up by, as Roosevelt said, "power, and the willingness and readiness to use it."[13]

Roosevelt had no patience for those who opposed his agenda. In his view, "Every expansion of civilization makes for peace . . . Every expansion of a great civilized power means a victory for law, order, and righteousness."[14] Even when acknowledging that the United States acted in self-interest, TR insisted that expanding US influence would improve the lives of those not yet capable of governing themselves. His justification for the American occupation of the Philippines typifies what the historian Albert Weinberg wryly referred to as a "virile conception of international altruism." TR called on his countrymen to recognize "our duty toward the people living in barbarism to see that they are freed from their chains," and that "we can free them only by destroying barbarism itself." In words that would have made Rudyard Kipling and Cecil Rhodes smile, TR argued, "The missionary, the merchant, and the soldier may each have a part to play in this destruction, and in the consequent uplifting of the people."[15]

Today, many Americans find these words uncomfortable, imperialist, or racist—though one can hear echoes in twenty-first-century claims about American leadership in upholding an international rules-based liberal order. Like most Americans of his time, Roosevelt believed that the advance of civilization was "fraught with lasting benefits" for all societies, since "the best that can happen to any people that has not already a high civilization of its own is to assimilate and profit by American or European ideas."[16] What he called "our share of the world's work" obliged the US to follow in the footsteps of England, France, and Germany in spreading "the ideas of civilization and Christianity."[17] As he promised in his first State of the Union address, the US would "do for [Filipinos] what has never before been done for any people of the tropics—make them fit for self-government after the fashion of the really free nations."[18]

In TR's mind, Providence had called upon the United States to play a unique role as guardian and evangelist of Western civilization. In his mission to "expand" that civilization, he also enlarged the American empire in ways that shook its global competitors to the core. As my colleague Joseph Nye has written, "Roosevelt was the first president to deliberately project American power on the global stage."[19] From the Caribbean to the Philippines, from Venezuela to Panama to Alaska, he heralded America's newfound capabilities and far-reaching purpose in the name of establishing the same control over the hemisphere that previous generations of Americans had achieved over the frontier.

Four of these episodes in particular describe the trajectory of America's ascendance and capture the intensity of its drive to become a world power: *the* world power. As Roosevelt put it: "The twentieth century looms before us big with the fate of many nations. If we stand idly by, if we seek merely swollen, slothful ease and ignoble peace, if we shrink from the hard contests where men must win at hazard of their lives and at the risk of all they hold dear, then the bolder and stronger peoples will pass us by, and will win for themselves the domination of the world."[20]

THE SPANISH-AMERICAN WAR

Well before he joined the McKinley administration, Roosevelt had been eager for war with Spain. For a man who believed that "every true patriot . . . should look forward to the day when not a single European power will hold a foot of American soil,"[21] Spain's control of territory a mere ninety miles from the United States was an affront. TR was not the first American policymaker to be aggravated by Cuba's status. In 1823, Secretary of State John Quincy Adams likened Cuba to an apple that would break its "unnatural connection" with Spain and fall into

American hands.[22] Yet despite frequent unrest and a series of independence movements, Spain controlled Cuba for another seven decades.[23]

Roosevelt intended to break this "unnatural" link. He insisted that the US needed to "drive the Spaniards out of Cuba" — although as he noted in a letter in 1895, his first wish would be "an immediate war with Great Britain for the conquest of Canada."[24] Roosevelt's anti-Spanish position gave the newly elected President McKinley reservations about appointing him assistant navy secretary, since in his inaugural address McKinley had pointedly pledged to avoid "wars of conquest" and "the temptation of territorial aggression," noting that "peace is preferable to war in almost every contingency."[25]

McKinley's concerns about Roosevelt were not unfounded. Within weeks of joining the administration, Roosevelt told Mahan, "Until we definitely turn Spain out of those islands (and if I had my way that would be done tomorrow), we will always be menaced by trouble there."[26] The leading popular newspapers of the day, owned by William Randolph Hearst and Joseph Pulitzer, were also calling for war. "You furnish the pictures, and I'll furnish the war," Hearst had famously told one of his illustrators.[27]

Four months after taking office at the Department of the Navy, Roosevelt presented McKinley with a full invasion plan that promised victory in six weeks.[28] TR would soon have the opportunity to go from planning to participating in a US invasion of Cuba. On February 15, 1898, an explosion sank the USS *Maine* battleship in Havana Harbor, killing 266 Americans. Despite pressure from Roosevelt, the media, and an outraged public, McKinley refused to retaliate immediately, instead ordering an inquiry to determine what happened. Roosevelt was apoplectic. Weeks before the incident he had told a colleague, "I have been hoping and working ardently to bring about our interference in Cuba."[29] Now he raged that the "blood of the murdered men of the Maine calls not for indemnity but for the full measure of atonement, which can only come by driving the Spaniard from the New World."[30] The president, TR remarked to his brother-in-law, had "no more backbone than a chocolate éclair."[31]

After his official inquiry concluded that a mine had caused the explosion, McKinley had no choice but to declare war.[32] TR immediately resigned from his position as assistant secretary, secured a commission as a lieutenant colonel in the US Army, and organized the First US Volunteer Cavalry Regiment—the Rough Riders. TR and his Riders became legend during the Battle of San Juan, helping capture San Juan Hill in a chaotic firefight on July 1, 1898. In the thick of battle, TR demonstrated the manly courage about which he had written. A fellow soldier marveled at the way he "moved about in the midst of the shrapnel explosions . . . Theodore preferred to stand up or walk about sniffing the fragrant air of combat." Roosevelt later recalled the battle as the greatest day of his life.[33]

The United States defeated Spain before the end of August and signed a peace treaty in December. For Spain, the terms were severe: Cuba gained its independence, and Spain ceded Puerto Rico, Guam, and the Philippines to the US.[34] In the aftermath of the war, historian and Roosevelt confidant Brooks Adams declared that the events of 1898 would become "the turning point in our history." Looking ahead, he predicted that "we may dominate the world, as no nation has dominated it in recent time . . . I look forward to the next ten years as probably the culminating period of America."[35]

ENFORCING THE MONROE DOCTRINE

Following the Spanish-American War, and after a brief stint as governor of New York, Roosevelt accepted the invitation to rejoin McKinley's administration by running as his vice president in the 1900 presidential election. The McKinley-Roosevelt ticket won handily. When an assassin killed McKinley in September 1901, TR was thrust into the Oval Office after just six months on the job. During his first year as president, Roosevelt was presented an opportunity to assert the full force of American power after years of frustration over the diffidence of his predecessors. This chance came in 1902 when Germany, supported by Britain and Italy, imposed a naval blockade on Venezuela after it refused to repay long-standing debts. Germany then upped the ante by sinking Venezuelan ships and threatening to attack the port of Puerto Cabello.

Sensing what the definitive Roosevelt biographer Edmund Morris described as "the circlings of a distant predator" and suspecting that Germany sought a permanent naval outpost in Venezuela, President Roosevelt seized the occasion to send Europe an unmistakable message.[36] He warned Berlin that the United States would "be obliged to interfere by force if necessary" if Germany did not withdraw its ships within ten days.[37] He then demanded that the Europeans settle their differences with Venezuela through arbitration, which he would arrange. He instructed the German ambassador Theodor von Holleben to "tell the Emperor that it is not safe to try to bluff me, because poker is the American national game and I am prepared to call his bluff." And to ensure that the kaiser could not miss the point, he continued: "If he does not instantly withdraw his warships from Venezuelan waters, I shall not hesitate to use the forces at my command to crush them."[38] Indeed, Roosevelt warned the kaiser that "there was no spot in the world where Germany in the event of a conflict with the United States would be at a greater disadvantage than in the Caribbean Sea."[39]

Roosevelt's demand that Germany defer to the US invoked a doctrine set forth by James Monroe in 1823: the Western Hemisphere was no longer open for European colonization or foreign interference.[40] While sweeping in scope, the Monroe Doctrine was originally aspirational rather than operational and remained so for the remainder of the nineteenth century. Since the US lacked the means to enforce it, it posed no barrier to the British when they took the Falkland Islands from Argentina in 1833, nor did it prevent them from maintaining a sizable naval presence along Nicaragua's coastlines or from temporarily seizing the Nicaraguan port in Corinto in 1895. The Germans also spoke dismissively of the doctrine, and sent warships from time to time to settle commercial disputes in small countries like Haiti.[41]

Well before he was president, TR had been determined to give the doctrine teeth. After British forces occupied Corinto, TR worried that Venezuela would be next. "If we allow England to invade Venezuela nominally for reparation, as at Corinto," he wrote to Senator Henry Cabot Lodge, a fellow member of the expansionist lobby, "our supremacy in the Americas is over."[42] President Grover Cleveland's reluctance to take a hard line against the British in Venezuela dismayed Roosevelt, who later observed that "the clamor of the peace faction has convinced me that this country needs a war."[43] The Cleveland administration eventually warned the British not to violate the Monroe Doctrine with encroachments from its colony in British Guiana into territory also claimed by Venezuela, asserting that "today the United States is practically sovereign on this continent, and its fiat is law upon the subjects to which it defines its interposition." Sensing that Cleveland meant what he said, the British reluctantly agreed to determine the proper border with arbitration rather than test the limits of American patience with a *de facto* claim to the disputed territory.[44]

Roosevelt glowed, insisting that the United States had grown "sufficiently powerful to make what it said of weight in foreign affairs," and belittled those who questioned whether it was sensible (or legal) for the US to threaten Britain over its actions in a remote part of South America. The Monroe Doctrine, Roosevelt wrote, "is not a question of law at all. It is a question of policy . . . To argue that it cannot be recognized as a principle of international law is a mere waste of breath."[45]

Roosevelt demonstrated the same resolve in his faceoff with Berlin and London. His ultimatum persuaded both countries to withdraw from Venezuelan waters and to settle their dispute at The Hague on terms satisfactory to the US. The results vindicated Roosevelt in his determination that "the Monroe Doctrine should be treated as the cardinal feature of American foreign policy." But, he warned, "it would be worse than idle to assert it unless we intended to back it up, and it can be backed up only by a thoroughly good navy."[46] The US naval advantage in the Caribbean spoke more decisively than words ever could.

As he later told a Chicago audience, "If the American nation will speak softly and yet build, and keep at a pitch of the highest training, a thoroughly efficient navy, the Monroe Doctrine will go far."[47] The world would soon find out just how far Roosevelt intended to take it.

THE PANAMA CANAL

Since the sixteenth century, great powers in Europe had dreamt of a canal connecting the Atlantic and Pacific Oceans. But attempts to construct such a canal had proved futile. France embarked on a serious project in the 1880s led by the celebrated Ferdinand de Lesseps, who had built the Suez Canal in the 1860s. But the undertaking bogged down in a series of failures. American and British projects in Panama and neighboring Nicaragua had also failed to advance. As American power grew, Roosevelt vowed to succeed where others had stumbled, and to ensure that this passage was his country's to control.

For Roosevelt, a canal through Central America was also required for national security. Without it, American warships based on the Atlantic coast had to travel fourteen thousand miles on a journey of over two months around Chile's Cape Horn to reach the West Coast and protect American interests in the Pacific (and vice versa). Thus, for example, the Puget Sound–based battleship *Oregon* transited all of North and South America in order to reach Cuba during the Spanish-American War.[48] Since this canal was a "necessity" in TR's view, he would allow nothing to stand in its way—not distant great powers like France, and certainly not second-rate nations like Colombia, which had controlled Panama as a province since 1821.

When the Colombian government rejected his proposal to build a canal through its territory in Panama, TR refused to take no for an answer. As he later remarked, "I took the Isthmus, started the canal, and then left Congress—not to debate the canal, but to debate me."[49] Critics accused him of manufacturing a revolution to seize part of Colombia in a shameful episode of gunboat diplomacy. Roosevelt was unapologetic, declaring that "by far the most important action I took in foreign affairs during the time I was president related to the Panama Canal."[50]

Historian David McCullough described this saga as "the great material set piece" of Roosevelt's presidency. In his definitive account of the canal's construction, he wrote that for Roosevelt, "first, last, and always, the canal was the vital—the indispensable—path to global destiny for the United States of America."[51] As TR told Congress: "If ever a government could be said to have received a mandate from civilization to effect an object the accomplishment of which was demanded in the interest of mankind, the United States holds that position with regard to the interoceanic canal."[52]

When in August 1903 the Colombian Senate unanimously rejected the treaty for the US to build the canal because of concerns over financial terms and sovereignty, Roosevelt seethed at what he saw as a display of "dismal ignorance." As he said to his secretary of state, John Hay, "I do not think the Bogota lot of jack rabbits should be allowed permanently to bar one of the future highways of civilization."[53] In response, Roosevelt "determined that I would do what ought to be done without regard to them."[54]

At first, Roosevelt relied on an imaginative reading of an 1846 US-Colombia treaty to argue that, in effect, America already had permission to build the canal. "I feel we are certainly justified in morals," Roosevelt confided to a US Senate ally, "and therefore justified in law, under the treaty of 1846, in interfering summarily and saying that the canal is to be built and that they must not stop it."[55] But when the French engineer and businessman Philippe Bunau-Varilla brought news that a revolution was brewing in Panama, TR switched horses.

At a White House meeting on October 9, 1903, Bunau-Varilla (who had significant financial interests riding on the canal's completion) asked the president directly whether the United States would support a Panamanian insurrection against Colombian rule. Roosevelt demurred —but also refused to say that the US would protect its supposed allies, the Colombians, from an independence movement. Instead, he said, "I have no use for a government that would do what that government has done," and noted later that Bunau-Varilla "would have been a very dull man" had he missed his signal.[56]

After confirming that Bunau-Varilla's report about a potential revolution was accurate, TR sent navy ships to shadow the Panamanian coast and ordered the army to plan for a potential US landing.[57] Secretary of State Hay informed Bunau-Varilla about these preparations. By November 2, the USS *Nashville* was visible from the shore of Colón, and nine more gunboats would soon take up positions on Panama's Atlantic and Pacific coasts.[58]

On November 3, the rebels issued their declaration of independence. A contingent of marines landed and shut the main railway to prevent the Colombian military from reaching Panama City, while the US ships blocked the Colombians from landing naval reinforcements. TR also warned the Colombian government that if it tried to oppose Panamanian independence, it should expect to see American forces on its territory. Less than seventy-two hours after the Panamanian rebels declared independence, the US was the first to recognize the new nation and establish diplomatic relations.[59]

Bunau-Varilla quickly negotiated a treaty that gave the US rights "in perpetuity" to the future canal in return for $10 million up front and $250,000 annually. The deal was, Roosevelt's secretary of state admitted privately, "very satisfactory, vastly advantageous to the United States, and we must confess, with what face we can muster, not so advantageous to Panama."[60] The arrangement only proved more imbalanced in the years that followed. For example, while Panama continued to receive only $250,000 annually from the canal, the US Treasury collected about $1 million in profits from the canal in 1921, close to $14 million in 1925, and over $18 million each year from 1928 to 1930.[61] Moreover, this does not include the impact of reduced shipping costs, which made products cheaper for American consumers and US goods more competitive in foreign markets. By 1970, tolls exceeded $100 million annually, and by the end of the twentieth century, when the United States finally transferred ownership back to Panama under the

terms of a treaty signed by President Jimmy Carter, the canal was col-
lecting $540 million in tolls.[62] Overall, comparing the amount the US
paid annually to Panama under the final treaty and the amount it (or
France) would have paid under six earlier (and less coercive) contracts,
TR's hard bargain likely deprived Panama of yearly revenue anywhere
from 1.2 to 3.7 times its annual GDP.[63]

To the end of his life, TR insisted that the revolution in Panama had
been a natural expression of its people's desire for independence and
a canal.[64] Though cheering the outcome, even Roosevelt's supporters
called that view what it was: poppycock. As his secretary of war, Elihu
Root, told TR: "You have shown that you were accused of seduction
and you have conclusively proved that you were guilty of rape."[65]

ALASKA BOUNDARY DISPUTE

Around the same time he was encouraging the Panamanian independence movement, TR was also stirring up a disagreement with America's northern neighbor—and its imperial patron, Britain—over the
border between western Canada and the future US state of Alaska.

We can see the results of the Alaskan border dispute vividly on the
map. From the body of Alaska, a "fat tail" extends some five hundred
miles south, separating Canada from the Pacific Ocean. The United
States had inherited the ill-defined boundary between British Columbia and the Alaska panhandle when it purchased Alaska from Russia in
1867. And for many years Washington had been content to let the border remain murky.[66] Sporadic attempts were made to clarify the boundary after British Columbia joined the Canadian Federation in 1871. But
they went nowhere until gold was discovered in the Canadian Yukon
in 1897. Suddenly the question of the boundary's definition took on
new urgency for one simple reason: the gold was in Canada, but the US
controlled the critical routes from the ocean into the Klondike, which
was largely inaccessible by land. Canada claimed that its border should
be measured not thirty miles from the coast (as was the US practice),
but rather thirty miles from the extremities of the small islands *off the*

coast. This interpretation of the border would guarantee Canada direct access to the sea and would have given Canada ownership of Juneau, Skagway, Lynn Canal, and Glacier Bay.[67]

Roosevelt was incredulous over the Canadian claim, which he declared "exactly as indefensible as if they should now claim the island of Nantucket."[68] After sending troops to protect US claims, TR threatened "drastic" action if required. Privately, he warned the British ambassador that it was "going to be ugly" if Canada or Britain tried to stand in his way.[69] In deference to pleading from Secretary of War Root, Roosevelt agreed to submit the boundary dispute to an international tribunal—but only after Root assured him that the tribunal would simply ratify the American position. True to his word, Root designed the tribunal so that each side chose three members, thus ensuring that a 3–3 tie would be the worst outcome. Leaving nothing to chance, Roosevelt appointed three close allies who shared his thinking —Lodge, Root, and former senator George Turner—even though the rules called for "impartial jurists." There was no doubt about how Canada's two members would vote, either.[70] This made the third and final commissioner representing the Canadian side, Lord Chief Justice Alverstone of Britain—the crucial swing vote.

Root assured TR that the British (via Alverstone) would back the US claim because it was so clearly in their interest. Given the deference it had shown in settling the 1895 and 1902 Venezuela disputes, the British government would not confront the US on a secondary issue like this. Leaving nothing to chance, however, TR took advantage of Supreme Court Justice Oliver Wendell Holmes Jr.'s visit to London to have him warn the British colonial secretary that if the commission deadlocked, "I shall take a position which will prevent any possibility of arbitration hereafter." He also instructed Hay to remind London that if the tribunal could not come to an agreement "now," the US would be forced "to act in a way which will necessarily wound British pride."[71] TR was more explicit with his own tribunal members: "I want no snap judgements," he counseled, "but in the event of specious and captious objections on the part of the English, I am going to send a brigade of

American regulars up to Skagway and take possession of the disputed
territory and hold it by the power and the force of the United States."[72]

London bowed under the pressure. In October 1903, the tribunal
rendered its 4–2 decision, giving the United States a sweeping victory
on all claims. Alverstone had cast the critical vote. The two Canadian
commissioners refused to sign the final ruling, protesting that they
were "powerless to prevent" the machinations of the US and Britain.
In Canada, the verdict "set off one of the most concentrated explosions
of resentment" in the country's history, according to Canadian historian Norman Penlington. The press claimed that Canada had been "sac-
rificed," "tricked," and "robbed," deriding Alverstone for selling out
Canada to satisfy the insatiable American president.[73] The *Washington
Morning Post,* on the other hand, reported that Roosevelt and his administration "regard the award as far and away the greatest diplomatic
success which the United States have gained for a generation."[74] In exchange for a few minor concessions to Canada, the US maintained an
unbroken coastal strip: twenty-five thousand square miles of coast and
islands along the Alaskan panhandle and a swath of the pristine Tsongas
wilderness that would become America's largest national forest. When
all was said and done, the land TR won from territory claimed by Canada added roughly another Rhode Island to American territory.[75]

IMAGINING A "XI COROLLARY"

Fresh from victories over Spain, Germany, and Britain, and dominant
from Alaska to Venezuela, Roosevelt declared in his 1904 State of the
Union speech that the US had assumed responsibility for the peace and
stability of its geopolitical neighborhood. In the future, TR stated,
"chronic wrongdoing, or an impotence which results in a general loos-
ening of the ties of civilized society, may in America, as elsewhere,
ultimately require intervention by some civilized nation, and in the
Western Hemisphere the adherence of the United States to the Monroe
Doctrine may force the United States, however reluctantly, in flagrant

Political cartoon from the *Montreal Star* (1903) depicting the American eagle as a vulture in search of new prey following US actions in Panama and Alaska.

AMERICAN AGGRESSION.

AMERICAN EAGLE—"Let me see; what else is there in sight now?"
Star (Montreal).

cases of such wrongdoing or impotence, to the exercise of an international police power."[76] This resolution became known as the Roosevelt Corollary to the Monroe Doctrine.

In the remaining years of his presidency, TR showed just what kind of "wrongdoing or impotence" he had in mind. He sent the US military to intervene in the Dominican Republic, Honduras, and Cuba during periods of unrest that threatened American commercial interests. Although he tried and failed to overthrow a government of Mexico that he found objectionable, his successor, William Howard Taft, encouraged Mexican revolutionaries based in the US to arm and organize against Mexican president Porfirio Díaz, supported them when they deposed Díaz, and subsequently backed a coup that overthrew *them* when they also began to pose problems for the United States. American marines or warships intervened in Latin America twenty-one times in the thirty years between the announcement of the Roosevelt Corollary and Franklin Roosevelt's Good Neighbor policy of the mid-1930s, which repudiated the style of interventionism that the new president's cousin and predecessor had embraced so fervently.

After leaving office, TR told a friend: "If I must choose between a policy of blood and iron and one of milk and water, I am for the policy of blood and iron. It is better not only for the nation but in the long run for the world."[77] Yet the impact of TR's "civilizing mission" and "police power" rankled many in the hemisphere.[78] In 1913, the Argentine political leader Manuel Ugarte spoke plainly to the newly elected Woodrow Wilson, noting that many Latin American countries "have become open season for the vilest of instincts that in the United States itself are not condoned since they violate notions of public responsibility and opinion . . . As a result of such behavior the United States has gradually become the most unpopular nation among us." Díaz had famously captured this sentiment with his lament, "Poor Mexico! So far from God and so close to the United States."[79]

As we watch Beijing's renewed assertiveness in its neighborhood, and the South and East China Seas along its border in particular, should we hear echoes of TR's actions in the Caribbean? If China were to become half as demanding now as the US was then, will American leaders today find a way to adapt as adroitly as the British did? Reviewing the record to this point, the differences between Xi and TR are more striking than the similarities. However, there are few signs that Americans are preparing to accept Britain's fate. Watching the trend lines, Thucydides would likely say: buckle up—we ain't seen nothing yet.

6

WHAT XI'S CHINA WANTS

The admiration of the present and succeeding ages will be ours, since we have not left our power without witness . . . We have forced every sea and land to be the highway of our daring, and everywhere, whether for evil or for good, have left imperishable monuments behind us.

—Thucydides, Pericles's Funeral Oration, 431 BCE

Heaven is above, earth is below, and that in between heaven and earth is called China. Those on the peripheries are the foreign. The foreign belong to the outer, while China belongs to the inner.

—Shi Jie, "On the Middle Kingdom," 1040 CE

The greatest Chinese dream is the great rejuvenation of the Chinese nation. —Xi Jinping, 2012

What does President Xi Jinping want? In one line: to "Make China Great Again."

This primal ambition was clear to the world's premier China watcher from the day Xi became president. Lee Kuan Yew knew Xi well, and understood that China's unbounded aspiration was driven by an indomitable determination to reclaim past greatness. Ask most China scholars whether Xi and his colleagues seriously believe that China can displace the United States as the predominant power in Asia in the foreseeable future. They will duck the question with phrases like "It's complicated . . . on the one hand . . . but on the other . . ." When I put this question to Lee during a meeting shortly before his death in 2015, his piercing eyes widened with incredulity, as if to ask, "Are you kidding?" He answered directly: "Of course. Why not? How could they not aspire to be number one in Asia and in time the world?"[1]

Lee foresaw the twenty-first century as a "contest for supremacy in Asia."[2] And as Xi rose to the presidency in 2012, Lee announced to the world that this competition was accelerating. Among all foreign observers, Lee was the first to say of this largely unknown technocrat, "Watch this man."

Indeed, for the only time in a half century of assessing foreign leaders, Lee compared the new Chinese president to himself. Both men were shaped by trials that left deep grooves in their souls. For Lee, the "whole world collapsed" when Japan invaded Singapore in 1942. "It was," he recalled, "the single biggest political education of my life." Most important, "for three and a half years I saw the meaning of power."[3] Similarly, Xi was schooled in the struggle to survive the madness of Mao's Cultural Revolution. Reflecting on that experience, he noted that "People who have little experience with power, those who have been far away from it, tend to regard it as mysterious." In contrast, Xi learned to "look past the superficial things: the flowers and the glory and the applause." Instead, as he said, "I see the detention houses, the fickleness of human relationships. I understand politics on a deeper level."[4]

Xi emerged from the upheaval with what Lee called "iron in his soul."[5] In what is surely the most unusual comparison anyone has ever made between Xi and another international leader, Lee likened him to Nelson Mandela, "a person with enormous emotional stability who does not allow his personal misfortunes or sufferings to affect his judgment."[6]

Xi's vision for China is similarly iron-willed. His "China Dream" combines prosperity and power—equal parts Theodore Roosevelt's muscular vision of an American century and Franklin Roosevelt's dynamic New Deal. It captures the intense yearning of a billion Chinese: to be rich, to be powerful, and to be respected. Xi exudes supreme confidence that in his lifetime China can realize all three by sustaining its economic miracle, fostering a patriotic citizenry, and bowing to no other power in world affairs. And while these extraordinary ambitions engender skepticism among most observers, neither Lee nor I would bet against Xi. As Lee said, "This reawakened sense of destiny is an overpowering force."[7]

"Making China Great Again" means:

- Returning China to the predominance in Asia it enjoyed before the West intruded.
- Reestablishing control over the territories of "greater China," including not just Xinjiang and Tibet on the mainland, but also Hong Kong and Taiwan.
- Recovering its historic sphere of influence along its borders and in the adjacent seas so that others give it the deference great nations have always demanded.
- Commanding the respect of other great powers in the councils of the world.

At the core of these national goals is a civilizational creed that sees China as the center of the universe. In the Chinese language, the word for China, *zhong guo* (中国), means "Middle Kingdom." "Middle" refers not to the space between other, rival kingdoms, but to all that lies between heaven and earth. As Lee summarized the world view shared by hundreds of Chinese officials who sought his advice (including every leader since Deng Xiaoping), they "recall a world in which China was dominant and other states related to them as suppliants to a superior, as vassals came to Beijing bearing tribute."[8] In this narrative, the rise of the West in recent centuries is a historical anomaly, reflecting China's technological and military weakness when it faced dominant imperial powers. Xi Jinping has promised his fellow citizens: no more.

THE WORLD ACCORDING TO CHINA

As befits the oldest continuous civilization on earth, the Chinese have a uniquely long sense of history. In no other country do modern leaders explain policy decisions by "invoking strategic principles from millennium-old events."[9] In 1969, when to everyone's surprise President-elect Richard Nixon chose a Harvard professor, Henry Kissinger, to be his national security adviser, Kissinger's new boss told him that he intended to explore an opening to China. Kissinger had made his career studying and writing about European history, not Asia. Knowing that he needed a crash course, he began with a weekend tutorial from his Harvard colleague John King Fairbank, the founding dean of modern China studies in the United States. In Fairbank's summary, classical Chinese foreign policy consisted of three key tenets: demand for regional "dominance," insistence that neighboring countries recognize and respect China's inherent "superiority," and willingness to use this dominance and superiority to orchestrate "harmonious co-existence" with its neighbors.[10]

From Fairbank, Kissinger learned "the disesteem of physical coercion deeply embedded in Confucian teaching." For China, "the military functioned as a last resort." Fairbank also explained that China's concept of international order mirrors its internal governance. In Fairbank's classic summary, "Chinese tended to think of their foreign relations as giving expression externally to the same principles of social and political order that were manifested internally." As a result, "China's foreign relations were accordingly hierarchic and non-egalitarian."[11] Just as it suppressed dissent and demanded that all its citizens bow to the power of the central government, so too did it expect regional powers to prostrate themselves before Beijing.

Finally, Fairbank taught that Chinese civilization was profoundly ethnocentric and culturally supremacist, seeing itself as the apex of all meaningful human activity. "The Chinese Emperor was conceived of and recognized as the pinnacle of a universal political hierarchy, with all other states' rulers theoretically serving as vassals."[12] In this system, as in the Confucian social system within China, order or harmony derived from hierarchy. The fundamental duty of states as well as individuals was Confucius's commandment: "Know thy place." Thus foreign rulers had to acknowledge their (lower) place by performing the ritual kowtow, touching their forehead to the ground. This time-honored gesture spoke to a very real history—thousands of years in which China had stood alone as Asia's political, economic, and cultural hegemon, its periphery arrayed with "a host of lesser states that imbibed Chinese culture and paid tribute to China's greatness." To Chinese leaders, Kissinger learned, this "constituted the natural order of the universe."[13]

Reflecting its civilization's centripetal orientation, Chinese foreign policy traditionally sought to maintain international hierarchy, not to expand its borders through military conquest. As Kissinger wrote after leaving office, China's sense that it should "tower over its geographical sphere . . . did not necessarily imply an adversarial relationship with neighboring peoples." And while, "like the United States, China thought of itself as playing a special role," it "never espoused the American notion of universalism to spread its values around the world." Instead, it "confined itself to controlling the barbarians immediately at its doorstep, strove for tributary states like Korea to recognize China's special status, and in return, conferred benefits such as trading rights." In sum, China "expanded by cultural osmosis, not missionary zeal."[14]

Millennia of Chinese dominance ended abruptly in the first half of the nineteenth century when the Qing Dynasty came face-to-face with the power of an industrializing, imperial Western Europe. The following decades were marked by military defeat, foreign-influenced civil war, economic colonization, and occupation by outside powers—first by the European imperialists and later by Japan.

For much of this period, foreign powers exerted greater influence in China than the Chinese government itself. When the Qing tried to prohibit British merchants from selling opium to Chinese in the 1830s, London dealt them a quick, decisive defeat in the First Opium War, begun in 1839. When the Qing sued for peace, the British pressed their advantage with the Treaty of Nanjing, which ceded control of Hong Kong to Britain, opened five ports to trade with foreigners, and granted British citizens immunity from local law.[15] The subsequent Treaty of Bogue forced the Qing Empire to recognize Britain as a nation equal to China. And thirteen years later, in 1856, the French joined the British in the Second Opium War, eventually burning the imperial Summer Palace in Beijing to the ground in 1860. The defeated Chinese were forced to legalize both foreign merchants' attempts to hook them on opium and foreign missionaries' efforts to convert them to Christianity.[16]

Foreign warships were also granted the right to navigate the length of China's rivers at will, penetrating deep into the Chinese heartland. On one occasion, a gunboat ventured 975 miles inland up the Yangtze.[17] As Stapleton Roy, a seasoned diplomat who was born in Nanjing and served as US ambassador to China from 1991 to 1995, recalls: "From 1854 to 1941, U.S. gunboats cruised China's inland rivers to protect American interests. As recently as 1948, during the Chinese civil war, as a thirteen-year-old I was evacuated from Nanjing to Shanghai on an American destroyer that had cruised some two hundred miles up the Yangtze River to China's then capital city."[18]

The Qing's efforts to defend China's sovereignty through military development proved futile. For centuries, China had treated Japan as a tributary state. But in 1894, a modernizing Japan attacked, seizing Manchuria, Taiwan, and the vassal state of Korea. Five years later, the rebels of a Chinese uprising known as the Boxer Rebellion attacked foreign enclaves under a banner that read, "Revive the Qing and destroy the foreign." In response, an eight-nation alliance of imperial powers invaded China's major cities and engaged in a "carnival of loot."[19] One American diplomat, Herbert G. Squiers, managed to fill several railroad cars with stolen art and porcelain, some of which is still rumored to be held by the Metropolitan Museum in New York today.[20]

The exhausted Qing administrators held out as long as they could, but in 1912 the disgraced dynasty collapsed, plunging the country into chaos. Warlords divided China and fought a civil war that lasted for almost forty more years. Japan exploited this weakness in 1937, invading and occupying much of the country in a brutal campaign that killed as many as twenty million Chinese. Every high school student in China today learns to feel the shame of this "century of humiliation." The lesson is unmistakable: Never forget — and never again!

Not until Mao Zedong's Chinese Communists won the civil war in 1949 did China's victimhood ultimately end. Although the once-grand empire was in ruins, it was at last back in Chinese hands. Thus Mao could declare with pride, "The Chinese people have stood up!"

Throughout the famine of the Great Leap Forward, the mayhem of his Cultural Revolution, and his relentless purges, Mao's achievement has remained the core of the Communist leadership's claim to legitimacy: his Party saved China from domination by foreign imperialists. And today, after three decades of frantic economic expansion, China believes that it is finally returning to its proper place in the world. But recovering that primacy will be possible only when China becomes not just wealthy but also strong — as Xi did in the crucible of the Cultural Revolution.

WHO IS XI JINPING?

Xi was born a princeling of the revolution, the son of a trusted colleague of Mao, Vice Premier Xi Zhongxun, who had fought alongside him in the Chinese civil war. Destined to grow up in Beijing's "cradle of leaders," he awoke shortly after his ninth birthday in 1962 to discover that a paranoid Mao had arrested his father. In the days that followed, his father was humiliated and eventually imprisoned for the duration of the Cultural Revolution. During what Xi describes as a "dystopian" period, Red Guards repeatedly forced him to denounce his own father. When his school closed, Xi spent his days defending himself in street fights and stealing books from shuttered libraries to try to educate himself.[21] Sent to the countryside by Mao to be "reeducated," Xi found himself living in a cave in a rural village in Yan'an, shoveling dung and snapping to the demands of his peasant foreman. Depressed by deprivation and abuse, his older half-sister, Xi Heping, hanged herself from a shower rail.

Instead of suicide, Xi chose to embrace the reality of the jungle. There—in his apt word—he was "reborn." As one of his longtime friends told an American diplomat, he "chose to survive by becoming redder than red"—and doing whatever it took to claw his way back to the top.[22] Xi was nothing if not persistent. The leader of 1.4 billion people and a Communist Party with 89 million members was actually rejected the first *nine* times he sought to join the Party, succeeding finally on his tenth attempt.

With assistance from former friends of his father, he managed to return to Beijing and become a student at the prestigious Tsinghua University. After graduation, he took an entry-level staff job in the Central Military Commission. To earn his stripes, he then returned to the countryside for what Xi's biographer Kerry Brown characterized as the "harsh and unglamorous political training" of a provincial official.[23] But there he steadily worked his way up the hierarchy, and, in 1997, won—just barely—a seat on the Party's Central Committee. (When the ballots for the 150 slots were counted, he came in 151st. Only because Party leader Jiang Zemin decided to make an exception and expand the membership to 151 was he included.)[24] When he was sent to be the Party chief in the province of Zhejiang in 2002, Xi oversaw spectacular economic growth: exports increased 33 percent annually for his four years in office.[25] He also proved adept at identifying and supporting promising local entrepreneurs, including Jack Ma, whose Alibaba is now a global titan that rivals Amazon.

While Xi demonstrated his skills as an administrator, he kept a low profile, avoiding the ostentatious displays of wealth common among many of his colleagues. When names of potential future Party leaders began circulating in 2005, his was not one. But then, in early 2007, a high-level corruption scandal swept Shanghai. Chinese president Hu Jintao and his colleagues on the Politburo Standing Committee felt a desperate need to act quickly and decisively. Knowing of Xi's reputation for rectitude and discipline, they chose him to put out the fire. He did so with a combination of decisiveness and finesse that won the admiration of all his peers. By the summer of 2007, his name topped internal Party lists of the most capable individuals likely to find a place in the next generation of leaders.

Xi was rewarded when the top four hundred Party leaders who composed the Central Committee and its alternates met in October 2007 to select the nine-man Standing Committee that would lead the nation for the next five years.* He emerged not only as a member of the Standing Committee, but also as heir apparent to President Hu. As unassuming as he was ambitious, Xi had assiduously kept his head down as he climbed the Party ladder, narrowly beating the favorite Li Keqiang to become next in line for the top spot. When the press first announced that he was the likely successor to Hu, he was so unknown outside inner Party ranks that a widely circulated joke asked, "Who is Xi Jinping?" The answer: "The husband of Peng Liyuan"—the famous folksinger to whom he is married.[26]

After Mao's death in 1976, the Party made every effort to prevent potential autocrats from rising to power. Its selection criteria emphasized not only competence but temperament as well—seeking men who were sound, safe, and preferably uncharismatic. The leader became just one member of a team of nine senior Party technocrats who made policy decisions by consensus. Traditionally, Standing Committee members are doppelgängers. In official photos, dressed in identical suits, shirts, and ties, it is often difficult for foreign counterparts to distinguish them from each other. Hu Jintao fit this mold so well that he frequently read his talking points from note cards, sometimes even in one-on-one meetings. Xi was assumed to be cut from the same cloth —an agreeable spokesman for the collective leadership.

Little did they know. By the end of his second year as president, Xi had so firmly concentrated power in his own hands that he was often referred to as the "Chairman of Everything." Unlike his go-along

---

* Xi Jinping later reduced the Standing Committee from nine to seven members.

to get-along predecessors, he has sidelined other figures so completely that he has no deputy or obvious successor. Though his vice premier, Li Keqiang, continued on paper to lead the economic reform program, decision making on all key issues in fact shifted to a newly created Leading Group for Financial and Economic Affairs, headed by Xi's trusted colleague Liu He, reporting directly to the president. Wielding a highly visible anticorruption campaign to masterful effect, he purged dozens of powerful rivals previously thought to be untouchable, including the former head of China's internal security service, Zhou Yongkang — the first Standing Committee member ever prosecuted for corruption. In his consolidation of power, Xi has taken more than a dozen titles for himself, including chairman of a new national security council and commander in chief of the military, a title that even Mao was never given. And he has had himself anointed China's "Core Leader" — a term symbolic of his centrality to the state that Hu had allowed to lapse. Most significant, as of this writing Xi appears to be setting the stage to defy traditional term limits and remain in power beyond 2022.[27] *

REALIZING CHINA'S DREAM

According to Xi's political mentor, Singapore's Lee Kuan Yew, a nation's leader must "paint his vision of their future to his people, translate that vision into policies which he must convince the people are worth supporting, and finally galvanize them to help him in their implementation."[28] Having painted a bold vision of the China Dream, Xi is aggressively mobilizing supporters to execute a hugely ambitious agenda of action advancing on four related fronts:

- Revitalizing the Party, cleansing it of corruption, restoring its sense of mission, and reestablishing its authority in the eyes of the Chinese people.

---

* This assessment proved correct in March 2018 when the National People's Congress amended the constitution to eliminate presidential term limits.

- Reviving Chinese nationalism and patriotism to instill pride in being Chinese.
- Engineering a third economic revolution.★ Xi knows this will entail politically painful structural reforms to sustain China's historically unsustainable rates of growth.
- Reorganizing and rebuilding China's military so that it can, as Xi says, "fight and win."

Any one of these initiatives would be more than enough for most heads of state to attempt in a decade. But Xi and his team have chosen to address all four at once, seeing them as critically interdependent. Many Western interlocutors, including advisers friendly to China, have warned him about overload. Indeed, a number of serious scholars placed their bets that Xi would not make it to the end of his first term in the autumn of 2017. Yet Xi exudes what China scholar Andrew Nathan has described as "Napoleonic self-confidence."[29] As former Australian prime minister Kevin Rudd (who has known Xi since the 1980s when they were both lower-level government officials) puts it, Xi has a "deep sense of national mission, a clear political vision for the country," and is "very much a man in a hurry."[30]

Chinese officials are keenly aware of the hurdles they face. For example, Xi's key economic adviser Liu He — whom I have known for two decades, since he was a student at Harvard Kennedy School — keeps a list of more than two dozen problems, among them: demographics (will China become old before it can become rich?); the challenges of fostering innovation; maintaining social stability while downsizing inefficient state-owned enterprises; and meeting energy demands without making the environment unlivable. He has analyzed each with deeper insight and more nuance than any Western observer

---

★ The first economic revolution, under Deng Xiaoping, began China's march to the market in 1978 with special economic zones and the first stage of privatization. The second acceleration of reform and opening to the outside world was overseen by Jiang Zemin, who fostered decades of hyperfast growth.

I have read. Aware of the risks, Xi and the Party continue to double down on all fronts.

In my own lengthy conversations with Liu, he traced the source of this confidence back to the Wall Street–initiated global financial crisis of 2008.[31] Without boasting, he reviews the record of Chinese performance in response to this challenge. Alone among the world's largest economies, China managed to weather the crisis and subsequent Great Recession without falling into negative growth.[32] Because they had rejected the Washington Consensus to liberalize China's financial markets, when the 2008 crisis struck, China's leaders had more tools with which to respond—and they used them. Like the Obama administration, Chinese officials in 2009 provided an unprecedented $586 billion fiscal stimulus. As a result, the Chinese can now travel on fast trains between their major cities. In contrast, they ask, what did the US get for its $983 billion infusion?[33]

To convince the rest of the Chinese leadership and his fellow citizens that his China Dream is not just rhetoric, Xi has flouted a cardinal rule of political survival: never state an unambiguous objective and a date in the same sentence. Within a month of becoming China's leader in 2012 Xi announced two bold objectives and specified deadlines for meeting each. To realize its dream, China will achieve "Two Centennial Goals." First, it will build a "moderately prosperous society" (double 2010 GDP per capita, to around $10,000) by 2021, when it celebrates the 100th anniversary of the Chinese Communist Party. Second, it will become a "modernized, fully developed, rich and powerful" nation by the 100th anniversary of the People's Republic in 2049.*

Precipitously, the first deadline arrives in the ninth year of his sched-

---

* It is worth noting that Chinese officials and public documents choose their economic yardsticks purposefully. When assessing the size of the Chinese economy in public, officials almost always use market exchange rates (MER) to measure GDP, rather than PPP, to make the economy appear smaller and less threatening. Behind closed doors, when comparing China and the US, they use PPP (see discussion in chapter 1). In this case, Xi's Two Centennial Goals are measured in MER. Measured in PPP, the first has already been achieved.

uled ten-year term as president. If China reaches that goal, its economy will be 40 percent larger than that of the United States (measured in PPP), according to the IMF.[34] If China meets the second target by 2049, its economy will be triple America's. Moreover, in Xi's plan, economic supremacy is just the substructure of the dream. American businessman Robert Lawrence Kuhn is one of the few Westerners with regular access to Xi's inner circle. When talking among themselves, Kuhn notes, Xi's team emphasizes that being number one means being first not only in economic terms, but also in defense, science, technology, and culture.[35] Making China great again is thus not just a matter of making it rich. Xi means to make it powerful, make it proud, and make the Party, as the primary driver for the entire venture, once again the worthy vanguard of the people.

XI'S NIGHTMARE

When Xi Jinping has nightmares, the apparition he sees is Mikhail Gorbachev. Shortly after taking power, Xi asked his close colleagues a rhetorical question: "Why did the Soviet Union collapse?" As he never tires of reminding them, "It is a profound lesson for us." After careful analysis, Xi concluded that Gorbachev made three fatal errors. He relaxed political control of society before he had reformed his country's economy. He and his predecessors allowed the Communist Party to become corrupt, and ultimately hollow. And he "nationalized" the Soviet military, requiring commanders to swear allegiance to the nation, not the Party and its leader. As a result, this "left the Party disarmed." When opponents rose up to overthrow the system, in Xi's words, there was nobody left who "was man enough to stand up and resist."[36]

Xi could see that in the years since the 1989 Tiananmen Square incident, the Chinese Communist Party (CCP) had been walking a path dangerously close to Gorbachev's. Particularly after the mantra of the era declared "To be rich is glorious," almost everyone who was powerful enough to do so became wealthy. This included many Communist Party leaders, government officials, and military officers. As this wealth became visible in ostentatious displays of luxury, citizens rightly began to question the Party's moral core and fidelity to its mission. As Xi warned Party officials, "The wavering of idealistic faith is the most dangerous form of wavering. A political party's decline often starts with the loss or lack of idealistic faith."[37] It also undermines public confidence and trust.

Xi knows that the supreme leader's credibility ultimately depends on a chain of command in which his order will cause a soldier to shoot his fellow citizens. Discussing Gorbachev's fate, he and Lee Kuan Yew came to the same conclusion. In Lee's words: "The day Gorbachev said to the masses in Moscow: do not be afraid of the KGB, I took a deep breath. He is sitting on top of a terror machine that holds the damn pile together, and he says: do not be afraid." Lee was not surprised by the results because "He had jumped into the deep end of the pool without learning how to swim." For good measure, Lee added: "Between being loved and feared, I have always believed Machiavelli was right. If nobody is afraid of me, I am meaningless."[38]

The first imperative in realizing Xi's China Dream is to relegitimize a strong Party to serve as the vanguard and guardian of the Chinese state. Shortly after taking office, Xi told his Politburo colleagues that "winning or losing public support is an issue that concerns the CCP's survival or extinction." And he bluntly warned them: "Corruption could kill the Party." Quoting Confucius, he vowed to "govern with virtue and keep order through punishments."[39] This was not an idle threat. Xi launched an anticorruption campaign of unprecedented scale led by his closest associate, Wang Qishan. Under Wang, 18 task forces headed by trusted lieutenants report directly to Xi. Since 2012, more than 900,000 Party members have been disciplined and 42,000 expelled and prosecuted in criminal courts. Among those have been 170 high-level "tigers," including dozens of high-ranking military officers, 18 sitting or former members of the 150-person Central Committee, and even former members of the Standing Committee.[40] In pursuing this campaign, Xi and his inner circle have also been developing a strategy to formalize it in ways that advance the rule of law.

In contrast to Gorbachev's glasnost—openness to ideas—Xi has demanded ideological conformity, tightening control over political discourse. He has insisted that the media vigorously promote the Party's interests. Indeed, he has even prototyped a system to track every citizen's financial, social, and digital behavior as part of a massive "social credit" database reminiscent of George Orwell's *1984*.[41] At the same time, Xi has moved to cement the Party's centrality in China's governance. Deng Xiaoping sought to separate Party from government, and strengthen China's state bureaucracy vis-à-vis the Party. Xi has flatly rejected that idea, proclaiming, in effect, "It's the Party, stupid." Shortly after Xi took power, an op-ed in *People's Daily* crystallized his position: "The key to running things well in China and realizing the China Dream lies in the Party."[42]

MAKING CHINA PROUD AGAIN

Xi knows that a clean Party is not enough. Even as Deng's market reforms broadened rapid economic growth after 1989, the Party still struggled to articulate its *raison d'être*. Why should the Chinese people allow it to govern them? The Party's answer is the second priority of Xi's China Dream: a renewed sense of national identity embraced with pride by a billion Chinese. In their fierce communism, Mao and his fellow revolutionaries had subordinated being Chinese to a global (and decidedly Western) ideology. But for many Chinese, the Marxist notion of a "new socialist man" always seemed alien. Nationalism has proved to be a far more effective, durably native concept.[43]

Xi is reinventing the Party as the twenty-first-century successor of the imperial mandarins—the guardians of a proud civilization with a historical mandate to rule. "Several thousand years ago, the Chinese nation trod a path that was different from other nations," says Xi. "It is not a coincidence that we started up 'socialism with Chinese characteristics.' It was decided by our country's historical inheritance."[44] China scholar Mark Elliott has highlighted "a bright line drawn directly from empire to republic. The People's Republic has become the successor state of the Qing . . . and increasingly has come to rely upon this equation for its legitimacy."[45]

Xi has led a revival of classical Chinese thought, ordering officials nationwide to attend lectures on the "brilliant insights" of Confucius and other Chinese philosophers to encourage "national self-confidence," while declaring that "the Chinese Communist Party is the successor to this fine traditional Chinese culture."[46] Much as the splendor of the Roman Empire became an inspiration during the Italian Renaissance, the glory of the Chinese nation's "golden age" (*shengshi* 盛世), remembered as the era before the Qing Dynasty's fall, is now a source of pride in modern China. It is no coincidence that the intensely retrospective term "rejuvenation" (*fuxing* 复兴) — so central to Xi's China Dream — can also be translated as "renaissance."

Meanwhile, the phrase *wuwang guochi* (勿忘国耻), or "never forget our national humiliation," has become a mantra that nurtures a patriotism grounded in victimhood and infused with a demand for payback. As Geoff Dyer has explained, "The Communist Party has faced a slow-burning threat to its legitimacy ever since it dumped Marx for the market." Thus the Party has evoked past humiliations at the hands of Japan and the West "to create a sense of unity that had been fracturing, and to define a Chinese identity fundamentally at odds with American modernity."[47]

During the 1990s when many Western thought leaders were celebrating the "end of history" with the apparent triumph of market-based democracies, a number of observers believed that China, too, was on a path to democratic government. Today, few in China would say that political freedoms are more important than reclaiming China's international standing and national pride. As Lee put it pointedly, "If you believe that there is going to be a revolution of some sort in China for democracy, you are wrong. Where are the students of Tiananmen now?" he asked provocatively. And he answered bluntly: "They are irrelevant. The Chinese people want a revived China."[48] So long as Xi can deliver on his promise to restore China's past greatness, the Party's future (and his own) would seem secure.

SUSTAINING THE UNSUSTAINABLE

Xi knows the Chinese people's support for sweeping Party rule still depends largely on its ability to deliver levels of economic growth no other nation has achieved. But continuing China's extraordinary economic performance will require perpetuating a unique high-wire act. Xi's unambiguous promise of 6.5 percent growth per year through 2021 demands what some have described as "sustaining the unsustainable."

There is general agreement about what China must do to continue growing at that pace for many years to come. The key elements are stated in China's most recent five-year economic plan, including: accelerating the transition to domestic consumption-driven demand; restructuring or closing inefficient state-owned enterprises; strengthening the base of science and technology to advance innovation; promoting Chinese entrepreneurship; and avoiding unsustainable levels of debt.

At its current position on the development spectrum, China needs many more years of high growth rates to catch up to the living standards of the world's most advanced economies. China's per capita income is still less than one-third that of South Korea or Spain, and one-fifth that of Singapore or the US. As it steadily moves from the manufacture of basic goods to higher-value products and services, incomes should increase. But Xi is wary of the middle-income trap that has ensnared many developing countries as rising wages erase their competitive edge in manufacturing. This is the impetus for what he calls "supply-side reforms," which aim to rebalance China's export-led economy with domestic consumption and services. In fact, China's service sector grew by 8 percent in 2015, and for the first time accounted for over 50 percent of GDP.[49]

To reduce inefficiency in state-owned enterprises, Beijing has promised to "ruthlessly bring down the knife on zombie enterprises"—companies that operate despite being technically insolvent—cutting four million jobs in the process.[50] Meanwhile, the "Made in China 2025" plan calls for raising the quality and technological sophistication of Chinese products.

Xi is also determined that China become a world leader in science, technology, and innovation by the mid-twenty-first century. He has boosted R&D spending, incubated tech start-ups, and called for a "robot revolution." (In 2016, China employed more robots than any other country.)[51] He believes that China's concentration of power in government gives it inherent advantages over Western competitors because it "can pool resources in a major mission."[52] Unlike the US in recent years, it can also sustain commitments over a decade or longer if required, as it has demonstrated in becoming the leader in fast trains, solar power, supercomputers, and other arenas.

Xi is equally committed to restoring a livable environment by tackling rampant pollution, estimated by some to kill four thousand Chinese every day.[53] Smog in Beijing has become so bad in some seasons that the government has been forced to close coal plants and factories before events like the Olympics or the G-20 meeting. Some rivers are so saturated with industrial waste that one in Wenzhou literally caught fire in 2014. According to World Bank estimates, China's increasingly unlivable environment costs it several percent of GDP annually.[54] To reverse these trends, China has embarked on what the Natural Resources Defense Council called its "greenest Five-Year Plan ever": sixteen of the thirty-three targets concern the environment, and all are mandatory.[55]

The IMF describes corporate debt, currently at 145 percent of GDP, as "a key fault line in the Chinese economy."[56] But some of this debt can be shifted to government, which has a much lower debt ratio at 17 percent of GDP.[57] China is also moving cautiously toward a more free-floating currency with fewer restrictions on capital controls. At the same time, it seeks to avoid what some Chinese see as dangers in the Western-style unregulated casino that gives the global financial system too much sway over national economic policy.

Many Western analysts also highlight the consequences of the ruthless one-child policy imposed by Deng Xiaoping in 1980. While it contributed to the objective of lifting a half billion people up from abject poverty in a single generation, it has left China with a serious demographic problem (Xi repealed the one-child policy in 2015). Nonetheless, the number of new entrants into the workforce will continue increasing until 2041. With an additional 300 million Chinese moving from poor rural areas to new cities and workers' productive lives lengthening, Beijing still has decades to mitigate this risk.[58]

Given the scope and ambition of Xi's plan, most Western economists and many investors are bearish. But most of these economists and investors have lost money betting against China for the past thirty years. As the former chair of President Reagan's Council of Economic Advisers, Martin Feldstein, puts it: "Not all of these policies have to succeed . . . If enough of them succeed well enough, 6.5% growth over the next few years might not be out of reach."[59]

Domestic reforms are matched by similarly dramatic changes to China's role in the global economy. In 2013, Xi announced a multidecade, multitrillion-dollar infrastructure project called One Belt, One Road (OBOR). Its goal is a transportation and technology network spanning Eurasia and nearly all countries bordering the Indian Ocean. The plan will effectively export some of China's excess industrial capacity and provide a cushion for the construction, steel, and cement industries, which have struggled in recent years as the country completed many of its highest-priority infrastructure projects. The planned projects abroad are massive. From an 1,800-mile, $46 billion corridor of roads, railways, and pipelines running through Pakistan, to hydroelectric dams and tin mines in Myanmar, to a new naval installation in Djibouti in the Horn of Africa, China is moving at a pace never seen in these countries.

But OBOR is about much more than simply rechanneling excess industrial capacity. Just as the original Silk Road not only spurred trade but also stimulated geopolitical competition (including the nineteenth-century "Great Game" that pitted Britain against Russia for control of Central Asia), OBOR will allow China to project power across several continents. OBOR's promise to integrate the countries of Eurasia reflects a vision in which the balance of geostrategic power shifts to Asia. In this, one can hear echoes of claims made a century ago

by Halford Mackinder, a founding father of geopolitics. In 1919, he
named Eurasia the "World Island" and declared famously, "Who rules
the World Island commands the World."[60] By 2030, if current targets
are met, Mackinder's conception of Eurasia could for the first time become a reality. OBOR high-speed railways will cut the time required
to move freight from Rotterdam to Beijing from a month to two days.
Mackinder's vision may even come to overshadow Mahan's thesis about
the centrality of sea power that has so dominated the minds of strategists for more than a century (as we saw in chapters 4 and 5).

A MESSAGE FOR AMERICA: BUTT OUT

Once both China's dominant economic market and its physical infrastructure have integrated its neighbors into China's greater co-prosperity area, the United States' post–World War II position in Asia will become untenable. Asked to distill China's message to the US, a Chinese
colleague answered: Back off. His colleague proposed a more candid
two-word summary: Butt out.

As realistic students of history, Chinese leaders recognize that the
role the US has played since World War II as the guardian of regional
stability and security has been essential to the rise of Asia, including
China itself. But they believe that as the tide that brought the US to
Asia recedes, America must leave with it. Much as Britain's role in the
Western Hemisphere faded at the beginning of the twentieth century,
so must America's role in Asia as the region's historic superpower re-
sumes its place. As Xi told a gathering of Eurasian leaders in 2014, "In
the final analysis, it is for the people of Asia to run the affairs of Asia,
solve the problems of Asia and uphold the security of Asia."[61]

The attempt to persuade the United States to accept the new reality has recently become most intense in the South China Sea. An area
approximately the size of the Caribbean and bordered by China, Taiwan, and six nations of Southeast Asia, the sea includes several hundred
islands, reefs, and other features, many of which are under water at
high tide. During the mid-twentieth century, while China was focused

internally, other nations claimed islands in the South China Sea and engaged in construction projects there. In 1956, for example, Taiwan occupied Itu Aba, the largest feature in the Spratly Islands, and garrisoned hundreds of troops there.[62] In September 1973, South Vietnam formally annexed ten of the Spratly Islands and deployed hundreds of troops to them to defend its claim.[63]

Fearful that its interests were being trampled by its neighbors, in 1974 China seized control of the islands closest to its border — the Paracels — from Vietnam.[64] In 2012, China took control of Scarborough Shoal from the Philippines. Since then, it has enlarged its claims, asserting exclusive ownership of the entire South China Sea and redefining the area by redrawing the map with a "nine-dash line" that encompasses 90 percent of the territory. If accepted by others, its neighboring countries have observed that this would create a "South China Lake."

China has also undertaken major construction projects on features throughout the sea, building outposts on seven different features in the Spratly Islands. By June 2015, China had reclaimed more than 2,900 acres of land, compared to Vietnam's 80, Malaysia's 70, the Philippines' 14, and Taiwan's 8.[65] As part of its efforts, China has built ports, airstrips, radar facilities, lighthouses, and support buildings,[66] all of which expand the reach of its ships and military aircraft and allow Beijing to blanket the region with radar and surveillance assets.

The Pentagon has no doubt about what is driving this undertaking. As a recent Defense Department report notes, China's "latest land reclamation and construction will also allow it to berth deeper draft ships at outposts; expand its law enforcement and naval presence farther south into the South China Sea; and potentially operate aircraft — possibly as a divert airstrip for carrier-based aircraft — that could enable China to conduct sustained operations with aircraft carriers in the area."[67]

China's longer-term objective is also clear. For decades it has chafed at the operation of US spy ships in waters adjacent to its borders. China asserts that under the UN Convention on the Law of the Sea the United States must request permission for these ships to operate in China's Exclusive Economic Zone, which extends two hundred nautical miles from China's shores—a claim the US flatly rejects. Nonetheless, the construction of radar facilities on features in the South China Sea, as well as airstrips and ports, will make it easier for China to track (and harass) US ships conducting surveillance. The ability to project power in the area will also give China greater influence over the $5.3 trillion in trade that passes through the South China Sea every year.[68] As it slowly muscles the United States out of these waters, China is also absorbing the nations of Southeast Asia into its economic orbit and pulling in Japan and Australia as well. It has so far succeeded without a fight. But if fight it must, Xi intends to win.

"FIGHT AND WIN"

Despite all the other challenges on his agenda, Xi is also simultaneously reorganizing and rebuilding China's armed forces. Russia's foremost expert on the Chinese military, Andrei Kokoshin, calls it "unprecedented in scale and depth."[69] The question many have asked is: Why now? Such a major reorganization is disenfranchising hundreds of influential generals who have built personal fiefdoms, carrying significant political risk for Xi. And the sight of thousands of uniformed soldiers protesting unemployment and pension cuts, which occurred in October 2016, is not one any Chinese leader wants to see.[70]

But Xi has judged it necessary to ensure the military's unquestioned loyalty to the Party, and specifically to its leader. Expecting that his other far-reaching initiatives will encounter resistance, he needs to know he can count on those who hold the guns from which political power grows. As China scholar William Kirby has pointed out, "The military has played a decisive role at every major turning point in modern Chinese political history."[71] Xi's goal is a military command structure that exerts effective control over the armed forces of the Party. He wants commanders who will "unswervingly adhere to the Party's absolute leadership" and specifically to its commander in chief.[72] In the tumult of the anticorruption campaign and subsequent reorganization of the top military brass, he has carefully picked loyal officers who he trusts will stand with him, come what may.

Xi also believes that a military that is "able to fight and win wars" is essential to realizing every other component of the China Dream. "To achieve the great revival of the Chinese nation," he has argued, "we must ensure there is unison between a prosperous country and strong military."[73] While all great powers build strong militaries, the "Strong Army Dream" is especially important to China as it seeks to overcome its humiliation at the hands of foreign powers.

In 1991, Chinese leaders were stunned by the devastating effectiveness of the US military during Operation Desert Storm in Iraq. These views were reinforced in 1999 during NATO's Kosovo campaign (when US stealth bombers accidentally bombed the Chinese embassy in Belgrade). And the Chinese military continues studying America's latest advances in warfare, including the use of drones for both intelligence and air strikes. In 1991, the US defeated Saddam Hussein's military forces in a month with fewer than 150 US combat deaths. In this brief, lopsided war, Americans enjoyed what military planners call "full-spectrum technological dominance" by combining new technologies like space-based navigation and surveillance systems, long-range precision-guided bombs, and radar-evading stealth aircraft. America's ability to exploit these new tools was bolstered by organizational changes that allowed the three military services—army, navy, and air force—to operate with greater synergy. The United States also surgically targeted the Iraqi military's command-and-control systems, essentially leaving Iraqi commanders blind and deaf.[74] Watching that spectacle, Chinese leaders determined to acquire the technical capabilities to counter and ultimately surpass what they sometimes refer to as "American magic." Those ambitions are captured in China scholar Michael Pillsbury's oft-cited assessments for the Department of Defense.[75]

Other lessons for the Chinese military emerged from the 1996 Taiwan Strait Crisis. Fearing that Taiwan was straying toward independence, Beijing sought to discipline Taipei by a show of force in which

Chinese "missile tests" bracketed the island, threatening the commercial shipping on which Taiwan's economy depends. When President Clinton responded by sending two aircraft carriers to the area in the largest deployment of US military power in Asia since the Vietnam War, the Chinese government had no option but to retreat. The episode made few waves in the United States. But in China it dredged up painful memories of the century of humiliation and shook the confidence of military leaders, who pledged to do whatever was necessary to avoid such an indignity again.

Xi's military reforms today largely mirror those of the Goldwater-Nichols Act of 1986, which the US successfully implemented to improve joint operations prior to the Gulf War and other military conflicts of the 1990s. China is integrating its intelligence, surveillance, and reconnaissance capabilities across the full spectrum of land, air, and sea weaponry. And it has already replaced its traditional seven internally-focused military regions with five new theater commands charged with joint operations against external enemies.[76]

Spotlighting corruption as an existential threat to the military, Xi has taken bold steps to crack down on rampant graft, which had included the outright buying of rank. Under that banner, Xi has made the historic—and previously autonomous—power centers in the People's Liberation Army once again fully accountable to the Party. He eliminated the military's four General Departments, which under Hu Jintao grew dangerously independent and notoriously corrupt. The overhaul reorganized the General Departments into fifteen separate bodies that all report directly to the Central Military Commission—the chairman of which is again Xi Jinping.

Such bureaucratic reshuffling is not usually a portentous event. But in Xi's case it underscores Beijing's deadly serious commitment to building a modern military that can take on and defeat all adversaries—in particular the United States. While Chinese military planners are not forecasting war, the war for which they are preparing pits China against the US at sea. The powers that dominated China during the century of humiliation all relied on naval supremacy to do so. As one Chinese analyst warns: "Ignoring the oceans is a historical error we committed, and now even in the future we . . . pay a price for this error."[77] Xi is determined to not make the same mistake, strengthening the naval, air, and missile forces of the PLA crucial to controlling the seas, while cutting 300,000 army troops and reducing the ground forces' traditional dominance within the military.[78] Chinese military strategists, meanwhile, are preparing for maritime conflict with a "forward defense" strategy based on controlling the seas near China within the "first island chain," which runs from Japan, through Taiwan, to the Philippines and the South China Sea.[79] US Naval War College professors James Holmes and Toshi Yoshihara note that, like the German kaiser and Theodore Roosevelt before them, "the Mahanian conceit that national greatness derives from sea power beguiles many Chinese strategists." We should therefore expect China to "attach extraordinary value to fighting and winning in the waters that fall within the near-seas," they conclude.[80]

Former national security adviser Brent Scowcroft was the first to explain the consequence of the humiliation of 1996 when American carriers forced China to back down. Its military shopping list was thereafter predictable: weapon systems to ensure that if such a confrontation with the US happens again, Beijing will prevail. Today, China's arsenal of more than one thousand antiship missiles based on the mainland and its coastal fleet make it impossible for any US warship to operate safely within a thousand miles of China's coast. Sixty-two submarines patrol adjacent waters armed with torpedoes and missiles that can attack surface ships. An array of antisatellite weapons gives China the capacity to jam or even destroy US intelligence, surveillance, and communication satellites over this area. Together, these capabilities have degraded the position of Pacific military dominance to which the US had become accustomed since the Battle of Midway in 1942. No longer does the United States have uncontested control of the sea and air along the thousand-mile-wide corridor of ocean bordering China. Exploiting asymmetric advantages, China has capitalized on its geographic proximity to the battlefield, which provides, as one naval planner notes, a landmass equivalent of a million aircraft carriers. With an arsenal of million-dollar missiles, it can attack and sink multibillion-dollar carriers.

Fielding "anti-access/area-denial" (*A2/AD*) military capabilities that threaten US carriers and other capital ships, China has been steadily pushing the US Navy out of its adjacent seas. American ships continue to show their flags, conducting occasional freedom-of-navigation patrols into the Taiwan Strait and South China Sea. The US has also signaled that, in case of war, its carriers would remain behind the first island chain—putting them beyond the reach of Chinese land-based missiles. From that distance carrier-based aircraft would be unable to reach targets on the Chinese mainland. Thus the US Navy has been struggling to find a way these aircraft carriers and their planes can remain relevant. The Pentagon's main effort to do so is outlined in a doctrine called Air-Sea Battle.[81] This calls for the air force to send long-range bombers with stand-off missiles to destroy Chinese land-based antiship missile batteries—allowing US carriers to safely move up close enough to China's borders to join the fight. As discussed further in chapter 8, Air-Sea Battle has many drawbacks, not the least of which is its dramatic escalation of any standoff.

As discussed in chapter 1, the authoritative 2015 RAND study "The U.S.-China Military Scorecard" found that by 2017 China will have an "advantage" or "approximate parity" in six of the nine areas of conventional capability that are critical in a showdown over Taiwan, and four of nine in a South China Sea conflict. It concludes that over the next five to fifteen years, "Asia will witness a progressively receding frontier of US dominance."[82] This will pose for the US the prospect of a conventional conflict it could actually lose.

Of course, just because China wants to be *able* to "fight and win" does not mean that it *wants* to fight. Clearly, it does not. But as it pursues its objectives, its rivalry with the US is exacerbated by deep cultural differences. This clash of cultures has never been more consequential for the world than it is today.

7

CLASH OF CIVILIZATIONS

We have a form of government that does not emulate the practices of our neighbors . . . In our approach to warfare, we also differ from our opponents . . . In matters of goodness, we also contrast with most people . . . Our efforts have no equivalent among people who do not share these values.

— Thucydides, Pericles's funeral oration, 431 BCE

Contemplate the great contrast between the two national characters, a contrast of which you have little perception, having never yet considered what sort of antagonists you will encounter in the Athenians, and how widely, how absolutely different they are from yourselves.

— Thucydides, Corinthian ambassador addresses the Spartan Assembly, 432 BCE

It is my hypothesis that the fundamental source of conflict in this new world will not be primarily ideological or economic. The great divisions among humankind will be cultural . . . The clash of civilizations will dominate global politics.

— Samuel Huntington, "The Clash of Civilizations?," 1993

When Lord George Macartney arrived in Beijing from London in 1793, he might as well have come from Mars. As the envoy of King George III, he was on a mission to establish diplomatic relations between Great Britain and Qing China. But the Chinese officials with whom he met had no idea who he was, where he came from, or what he was talking about. They had no conception of his proposal for "diplomatic relations." China had never established such a connection with any other country—never, indeed, allowed any country to open an embassy on its soil. Nor had it ever posted an ambassador abroad. The Chinese government did not even have a foreign ministry.[1] Moreover, indignity of indignities, the "red haired barbarians" who had ventured into their midst could not even speak their language. Macartney's "interpreter" was a Chinese priest from Naples who spoke no English. Thus, to converse, he translated the words of his mandarin hosts into Latin, so that Macartney, who had studied the language decades earlier at Trinity College, could nominally understand.[2]

London had instructed Macartney to establish a permanent diplomatic mission in Beijing but also to open new ports and markets for British goods, and negotiate a more flexible system for conducting trade in the coastal province of Canton. Macartney was also to rent a compound where British merchants could operate year-round, and to gather intelligence on "the present strength, policy, and government" of China.[3] To impress his hosts and generate interest in British exports, Macartney brought as gifts for the emperor an array of exemplary British products, including artillery pieces, a chariot, telescopes, porcelain, textiles, and a diamond-studded wristwatch.[4]

After a journey of nine months from Britain, Macartney and his entourage arrived at the Chengde Mountain Resort in Rehe, where they were to await an audience with the Qianlong emperor.[5] But from his initial encounter with his counterparts to his last, Macartney proved unable to connect. According to millennia-long Chinese custom, when beholding the divine emperor, mere mortals were required to perform nine kowtows, prostrating themselves flat on the ground. Macartney proposed instead that he would follow British protocol, bowing on one knee as he would before his own sovereign. He proposed further that a Chinese official of his rank should do likewise before a portrait of King George III that he had brought as a gift. His Chinese handlers scoffed. "Such an equivalence was out of the question," writes the French scholar-politician Alain Peyrefitte, summarizing the episode. "There was only one Emperor, and that was the Son of Heaven. Other monarchies were mere 'kinglets.'"[6] As Macartney saw it, he had come from the most powerful nation on earth to a poor, backward country that he was doing a favor by treating as Britain's equal. Through his hosts' eyes, however, this British representative had come as a vassal to pay tribute to the Son of Heaven.

His hosts made Macartney wait in Chengde for six days. Then on September 14, 1793, at three a.m., they awakened the British entourage, marched them three miles in the darkness to the emperor's court, and then had them wait another four hours until the emperor appeared.[7] (Not coincidentally, Henry Kissinger's first meeting with Mao repeated this same script.) When he finally had his audience, Macartney followed English practice with one knee bowed. The official Chinese dispatch of the event, however, reported a different story, claiming: "When the ambassador entered His Majesty's presence, he was so overcome with awe and nervousness that his legs gave way under him, so that he groveled abjectly on the ground, thus to all intents and purposes performing an involuntary kowtow."[8]

Macartney delivered the letter from King George outlining his proposals, anticipating that over the next week or so he would negotiate details with his Chinese counterparts. For his hosts, however, the meeting signified the end of Britain's successful expression of tribute, and they suggested that Macartney head home before the weather turned cold.[9] Days later — and only after panicked importuning on his part — Macartney received a written response from the emperor. It noted King George's "humble desire to partake of the benefits of Chinese civilization" and recognized that his envoy "had crossed the seas and paid his respects at my court." But the emperor flatly rejected all of Macartney's proposals. Specifically, the request to establish a foreign embassy in Beijing "could not possibly be entertained." Acknowledging that "the tea, silk, and porcelain which the Celestial Empire produces are absolutely necessary to European nations and to yourselves," China would allow foreign merchants to continue current arrangements that permitted them to exchange goods at the port of Canton. But additional trading sites and a compound where the British could reside year-round were out of the question.

Summarizing his view of the encounter, the emperor's letter concluded: "If you assert that your reverence for Our Celestial dynasty fills you with a desire to acquire our civilization, our ceremonies and code of law differ so completely from your own that, even if your envoy were able to acquire the rudiments of our civilization, you could not possibly transplant our manners and customs to your alien soil."[10] With that, Macartney sailed back to London.

It would not be fair to call an encounter that had no chance to succeed an epic failure. Rather than build a bridge, Macartney's diplomatic mission exposed the gulf between China and the West. Though today Beijing and capitals around the world engage in trade and diplomatic relations, fundamental differences between these two ancient systems remain. Globalization has smoothed transactions but not erased primal fault lines.

CLASH OF CIVILIZATIONS

Exactly two hundred years after the Macartney mission, the American political scientist Samuel Huntington published a landmark essay in *Foreign Affairs* titled "The Clash of Civilizations?" It asserted that the fundamental source of conflict in the post–Cold War world would not be ideological, economic, or political, but instead cultural. "The clash of civilizations," Huntington predicted, "will dominate global politics."[11] Huntington's thesis provoked a firestorm of criticism. He was writing in an increasingly politically correct culture, one in which most academics were minimizing distinctions among civilizations or cultures from their analyses. Respondents challenged Huntington's concept of civilization and questioned his account of the boundaries between them.

Nevertheless, in the years since the article was published, the policy community has incorporated this still-difficult-to-define concept of civilization into studies of war, in particular the ongoing war between Western democracies and Islamic terrorist groups like al-Qaeda and ISIS. To a lesser but still considerable degree, it has also shaped the thinking of policymakers, military planners, and scholars who study US-China relations—and the danger of violent conflict between these two superpowered civilizations.

Huntington defined civilization as an entity that constitutes the most expansive level of cultural organization. "A civilization is the highest cultural grouping of people and the broadest level of cultural identity people have short of that which distinguishes humans from other species," he wrote. "It is defined both by common objective elements, such as language, history, religion, customs, institutions, and by the subjective self-identification of people." Civilizations may include several nation-states or only one, and may overlap with other civilizations or include subcivilizations. According to Huntington, China and a few other states form the "Confucian" civilization, while the United States fits into a group of states that collectively comprise the "Western" civilization. Acknowledging that the "lines between [civilizations] are seldom sharp," Huntington argued that they are nonetheless "real."[12]

Huntington by no means ruled out future violent conflicts between groups within a common civilization. His point, rather, was that in a post–Cold War world, civilizational fault lines would not dissolve in a global convergence toward liberal world order—as one of Huntington's former students, the political scholar Francis Fukuyama, had predicted in his 1989 article "The End of History?"[13]—but become more pronounced. "Differences do not necessarily mean conflict, and conflict does not necessarily mean violence," Huntington allowed. "Over the centuries, however, differences among civilizations have generated the most prolonged and the most violent conflicts."[14]

Huntington was keen to disabuse readers of the Western myth of universal values, which he said was not just naive but inimical to other civilizations, particularly the Confucian one with China at its center. "The very notion that there could be a 'universal civilization' is a Western idea, directly at odds with the particularism of most Asian societies and their emphasis on what distinguishes one people from another," he wrote.[15] That is, the West believes that a basic set of values and beliefs—including individualism, liberalism, equality, liberty, rule of law, democracy, free markets, and the separation of church and state —should be embraced by all of humanity. To the contrary, Asian cultures prize their unique sets of values and beliefs that distinguish them from other people.

In the book-length version of his argument *The Clash of Civilizations and the Remaking of World Order,* Huntington identifies five key ways in which Western and Confucian societies tend to differ. First, as he notes, Confucian cultures reflect an ethos that reinforces "the values of authority, hierarchy, the subordination of individual rights and interests, the importance of consensus, the avoidance of confrontation, 'saving face,' and, in general, the supremacy of the state over society and of society over the individual." He points out the contrasts between these attitudes and "American beliefs of liberty, equality, democracy, and individualism." Furthermore, he underlines Americans' "propensity to distrust the government, oppose authority, promote checks and balances, encourage competition, and sanctify human rights."[16]

Huntington also observes that the main Confucian culture, China, defines identity in racial terms: "Chinese are those of the same 'race, blood, and culture.'" Putting the point provocatively, he notes that "for Chinese and those of Chinese descent living in non-Chinese societies, the 'mirror test' becomes the test of who they are: 'go look in the mirror.'" This concept of Chinese culture is both incredibly narrow and enormously expansive, as it leads the Chinese government to believe that "people of Chinese descent, even if citizens of another country, are members of the Chinese community and hence in some measure subject to the authority of the Chinese government."[17]

In line with that notion, Huntington argues that China's view of external affairs is essentially an extension of its concept of internal order. Both reflect a Confucian emphasis on harmony through hierarchy —with China's leader at the top. As Confucius said, just as "there are not two suns in the sky, there cannot be two emperors on earth."[18]

But while China projects its internal order outward, it has a nearly visceral mistrust of any external interference in its domestic affairs. As Macartney's failed mission to eighteenth-century China suggests, long before the century of humiliation, Chinese were wary of foreigners who landed on their shores. They prohibited them from learning Chinese or living among the general population. Strands of this suspicion persist into the present. American historian Crane Brinton captures the depth of resentment in an anecdote in his book *Anatomy of a Revolution*: "We Americans will for a long time share the blame for that sign in a Shanghai park, 'Dogs and Chinese not allowed.'"[19] Similarly, as a colleague of mine was told by a deputy mayor of Shanghai, he would know that China was rich again when every upper-middle-class family in Shanghai had an American houseboy. In Huntington's view, this memory of the past fueled the broad consensus "among Chinese leaders and scholars that the United States was trying to 'divide China territorially, subvert it politically, contain it strategically and frustrate it economically.'"[20]

Finally, Huntington claimed that, as members of a society that has existed for thousands of years, Chinese think in fundamentally different time scales than Westerners. As he put it, they "tended to think of the evolution of their society in terms of centuries and millennia and to give priority to maximizing long-term gains." Huntington contrasts this with "the primacy in American beliefs of forgetting the past, ignoring the future, and focusing on maximizing immediate gains."[21]

Huntington's five features of Confucian civilization are necessarily sweeping, but they do identify the general sturdy strands of Chinese culture that have persisted through the centuries. What is more, they provide pointers to ways in which it is distinct, and in some ways incompatible, with the cultures of Western nations like the United States. Being overtaken by a rival who shares common values — such as Britain grudgingly watching an upstart America surpass its power but largely preserve its cultural, religious, and political beliefs — is one thing. It would be quite another to be surpassed by an adversary whose values are so strikingly different. Hillary Clinton spoke for most Americans when she said, "I don't want my grandchildren to live in a world dominated by the Chinese."[22] To understand how broad differences in cultural inclinations can translate into confrontation, we need to examine more closely how Americans and Chinese differ in their view of the nature and purpose of government.

THE US AND CHINA

Who are we? What is our rightful place in the world? What constitutes order—both within our society and in relations with other nations? Short answers to such profound questions risk caricature, but they highlight fundamental differences between America and China. Entirely independent of the structural stress of Thucydides's Trap, these contrasts—and in some cases opposites—nonetheless tend to make US-China relations that much harder to manage.

Despite their many differences, the United States and China are alike in at least one respect: both have extreme superiority complexes. Each sees itself as exceptional—literally without peers. While Muhammad Ali's "I am the greatest" rightly captures American swagger, China's conception of itself as the unique link between humans and the heavens might be even more immodest. The clash of these two number ones will require painful adjustment. Will it be more difficult for the Chinese to rationalize a cosmology in which there are two "suns," or for the US to accept that it must live with another, and possibly superior, superpower? Lee Kuan Yew had doubts about America's ability to adapt to a new reality: "For America to be displaced, not in the world, but only in the western Pacific, by an Asian people long despised and dismissed with contempt as decadent, feeble, corrupt, and inept is emotionally very difficult to accept. The sense of cultural supremacy of the Americans will make this adjustment most difficult."[23]

In some ways, Chinese exceptionalism is more sweeping than its American counterpart. "The empire saw itself as the center of the civilized universe," explains scholar Harry Gelber. "The Chinese scholar-bureaucrat did not think of a 'China' or a 'Chinese civilization' in

America and China, clash of cultures

	America	China
Self-perception	"Number one"	"Center of universe"
Core value	Freedom	Order
View of government	Necessary evil	Necessary good
Form of government	Democratic republic	Responsive authoritarianism
Exemplar	Missionary	Inimitable
Foreigners	Inclusive	Exclusive
Time horizon	Now	Eternity
Change	Invention	Restoration and evolution
Foreign policy	International order	Harmonious hierarchy

the modern sense at all. For him, there were the Han people and, beyond that, only barbarism. Whatever was not civilized was, by definition, barbaric."[24] The Chinese, notes Kevin Rudd, take great pride in their resilience and civilizational achievements, and this exceptionalism imbues their very way of thinking, having "generated a self-reverential body of philosophical thought."[25]

Americans, too, revere their civilizational achievements, especially political ones, with nearly religious fervor. The country's revolutionary history has imparted a passion for freedom unequaled around the globe. It is enshrined in the core of the American political creed, the Declaration of Independence, which proclaims that "all men are created equal" and that they are "endowed by their Creator with certain unalienable rights." The Declaration specifies that these rights include "life, liberty, and the pursuit of happiness," and that these are not matters of opinion but rather "self-evident" truths. Seeking to explain to his colleagues in the House of Lords what motivated the rebellious American colonists, William Pitt the Elder identified "this spirit of independence, animating the nation of America . . . It is not new among them; it is, and ever has been their established principle. They prefer poverty with liberty, to golden chains and sordid affluence; will die in defense of their rights, as men — as freemen."[26] As the great twentieth-century American social historian Richard Hofstadter said, "It has been our fate as a nation not to have ideologies, but to be one."[27]

In contrast, China abides by Confucius's first commandment: "Know thy place."[28] For Chinese, order is the central political value, and the alternative to order is chaos. Harmonious order is created by a hierarchy in which everyone in society not only has a place but knows it. In traditional China, the emperor stood at the pinnacle of the hierarchy and maintained order. As Henry Kissinger explains, "The Chinese Emperor was both a political ruler and a metaphysical concept . . . The Emperor was perceived as the linchpin of the 'Great Harmony' of all things great and small."[29] Liberty, as Americans understand the term, would upset the hierarchy and invite chaos.

These philosophical differences between China and the US are reflected in each country's concept of government. The American idea was summed up in the most widely read pamphlet during the American Revolution, Thomas Paine's *Common Sense*. In it, Paine explained, "Society in every state is a blessing, but Government, even in its best state, is but a necessary evil; in its worst state an intolerable one."[30] Though animated by a deep distrust of authority, America's Founding Fathers recognized nonetheless that society required a government. Otherwise, who would protect citizens from foreign threats, or violations of their rights by criminals at home? But they wrestled with a dilemma. A government powerful enough to perform its essential functions would tend toward tyranny. To manage this challenge, they designed, as Richard Neustadt taught us, a government of "separated institutions sharing power."[31] This deliberately produced constant struggle among the executive, legislative, and judicial branches that meant delay, gridlock, and even dysfunction. But it also provided checks and balances against abuse. As Justice Louis Brandeis explained eloquently, their purpose was "not to promote efficiency, but to preclude the exercise of arbitrary authority."[32]

The Chinese conception of government and its role in society could hardly be more different. History has taught the Chinese the primacy of order and the indispensability of government in achieving that order. As Lee Kuan Yew observed, "The country's history and cultural records show that when there is a strong center (Beijing or Nanjing), the country is peaceful and prosperous. When the center is weak, then the provinces and their counties are run by little warlords."[33] Accordingly, the sort of strong central government that Americans see as a necessary evil is, for their Chinese counterparts, the principal agent advancing order and the public good at home and abroad.

For Americans, democracy—government of, by, and for the people—is the only legitimate form of government. It is required to protect citizens' rights and allow them to flourish. As Thomas Jefferson put it, "The republican is the only form of government which is not eternally at open or secret war with the rights of mankind."[34] The political legitimacy of any government, Americans believe, can only be derived from the consent of the governed.

Most Chinese would disagree. They believe that political legitimacy comes from performance. In his provocative TED Talk, "A Tale of Two Political Systems," the Shanghai venture capitalist Eric Li challenges democracy's presumed superiority. He recounts, "I was asked once, 'The Party wasn't voted in by election. Where is the source of legitimacy?' I said, 'How about competency?'" He goes on to remind his audience, "We all know the facts. In 1949, when the Party took power, China was mired in civil war, dismembered by foreign aggression, average life expectancy at that time, 41 years old. Today it is the second largest economy in the world, an industrial powerhouse, and its people live in increasing prosperity."[35] In short, performance justifies one-party rule.

America's government was conceived as a democratic republic, whereas China's—under the Qing emperors and Communist Party leaders—might best be characterized as responsive authoritarianism. Competing conceptions of political legitimacy have become a sore point in US-China relations. In Kissinger's apt summary, "The conviction that American principles are universal has introduced a challenging element into the international system because it implies that governments not practicing them are less than fully legitimate."[36] He goes on to explain how this tenet, which we take for granted, predictably breeds resentment among nations who are made to feel they live in a benighted political system awaiting redemption by American values. Needless to say, this type of righteousness does not go over well in China.

When it comes to promoting their fundamental political values internationally, the US and China have distinctively different approaches. Americans believe that human rights and democracy are universal aspirations, needing only America's example (and sometimes an imperialistic nudge) to be realized everywhere. For this reason, Huntington called the United States "a missionary nation," one driven by the belief "that the non-Western peoples should commit themselves to the Western values of democracy, free markets, limited government, human rights, individualism, the rule of law, and should embody these values in their institutions."[37] Much like Teddy Roosevelt's belief around the turn of the twentieth century that the spread of American power represented the spread of civilization itself, most Americans in the early twenty-first century believe that democratic rights will benefit anyone, anywhere in the world. Throughout the twentieth century, leaders in Washington have translated that belief into a foreign policy that has sought to advance the cause of democracy, even, on occasion, attempting to impose it on those who have failed to embrace it themselves.

In contrast, Chinese believe that others can look up to them, admire their virtues, and even attempt to mimic their behavior. But they do not try to convert them to these values. As Kissinger notes, "China did not export its ideas but let others come to seek them. Neighboring peoples, the Chinese believed, benefitted from contact with China and civilization so long as they acknowledged the suzerainty of the Chinese government. Those who did not were barbarian."[38]

Chinese leaders are also deeply suspicious of American efforts to convert them. As the grandfather of China's economic liberalization, Deng Xiaoping, warned fellow members of China's Communist Party, "Their talk about human rights, freedom and democracy is designed only to safeguard the interests of the strong, rich countries, which take advantage of their strength to bully weak countries, and which pursue hegemony and practice power politics."[39]

Chinese attitudes toward foreign political systems have a counterpart in Chinese views of foreigners in general. American society is as inclusive as China's is exclusive. As a "nation of immigrants," most Americans are proud of the fact that anyone can become an American. As George Washington wrote in 1783, "The bosom of America is open to receive not only the Opulent, and respectable Stranger, but the oppressed and persecuted of all Nations and Religions; whom we shall welcome to a participation of all our rights and privileges, if by decency and propriety of conduct they appear to merit the enjoyment."[40] In contrast, to be Chinese one has to be born Chinese. US labor markets are open, diverse, and flexible. This gives the nation a marked advantage in the global competition for talent: half of the 87 American startup companies worth more than $1 billion in 2016 were founded by immigrants.[41]

American and Chinese time horizons—their sense of past, present, and future—are as different as night and day. Americans look forward to celebrating the country's 250th birthday in 2026, while Chinese note proudly that their history spans five *millennia*. Americans mark July 4, 1776, as the birth of their nation, but China has no recorded genesis. Thus, unlike every other nation that traces its development along a path of rise and fall, China sees itself as a fixture of the universe: it always was; it always will be. US leaders refer to the "American experiment," and their sometimes haphazard policies follow in kind. By contrast, Chinese leaders see themselves as trustees of a sacred inheritance, and act accordingly.

Because of their expansive sense of time, Chinese are careful to distinguish the acute from the chronic, the urgent from the important. Can anyone imagine an American political leader suggesting that a major foreign policy problem be put on the proverbial shelf for a generation—as Deng Xiaoping did with Japan on the issue of the Senkaku/Diaoyu Islands by accepting an eventual, rather than immediate, solution to the dispute? Ever more sensitive to the demands of the news cycle and popular opinion, US politicians seek alliterative and enumerated bullet-point policy plans that promise quick resolution. Chinese are strategically patient: as long as trends are moving in their favor, they are comfortable waiting out a problem.

Americans think of themselves as problem solvers. Reflecting their short-termism, they see problems as discrete issues to be addressed and solved now—so that they can move on to the next ones. In Lee Kuan Yew's words: "When they fail, they pick themselves up and start afresh. The American culture is that we start from scratch and beat you. What kind of mindset do you need for that? It is part of their history. They went into an empty continent and made the best of it."[42] In what has been called the United States of Amnesia, every day is new, every crisis "unprecedented." This contrasts sharply with the institutional memory of the Chinese, who recognize that there is nothing new under the sun.

Indeed, Chinese believe that many problems can only be managed, and that each solution inevitably yields more problems. Challenges are thus long term and iterative. Issues they face today resulted from a process that has evolved over the past year, decade, or even century. New policy actions taken today will simply impact that continuing evolution. For instance, since 1949 Taiwan has been ruled by what Beijing considers rogue Chinese nationalists. Although Chinese leaders insist that Taiwan remains an integral part of China, they have been willing to pursue a long-term strategy involving thickening economic and social entanglements to slowly integrate the island back into China.

The US-China gap most relevant for Thucydides's Trap emerges from competing conceptions of world order. Chinese believe in harmony through hierarchy, both at home and abroad. The ways Beijing treats its own citizens is an instructive proxy for how China is likely to relate to other nations when it becomes the world's dominant power. America's democratic ideals carry over only so far into its foreign policy. On the one hand, Americans aspire to an international rule of law that is essentially American domestic rule of law writ large. On the other, they recognize the realities of power in the global Hobbesian jungle, where it is better to be the lion than the lamb. Washington often tries to reconcile this tension by depicting a world in which the United States is the "benevolent hegemon," acting as lawmaker, policeman, judge, and jury.

Americans urge other powers to accept a "rule-based international order." But through Chinese eyes, this appears to be an order in which Americans make the rules, and others obey the orders. A former chairman of the Joint Chiefs of Staff, Martin Dempsey, became familiar with the predictable resentment this elicited from China. "One of the things that fascinated me about the Chinese is whenever I would have a conversation with them about international standards or international rules of behavior, they would inevitably point out that those rules were made when they were absent from the world stage," Dempsey remarked. "They are no longer absent from the world stage, and so those rules need to be renegotiated with them."[43]

If Huntington is correct—and I believe he is—that civilizational differences are growing more, not less, significant as sources of conflict, statesmen in China and the United States today should exercise greater modesty about what they can accomplish. Misunderstandings are easy; empathy and consensus elusive. In a globalized world, and a time of instant communication and rapid travel that makes the Macartney mission look positively Stone Age, the "clash of civilizations" could shape not only future diplomacy but also the course of war.

STRATEGIC CULTURE CLASH

As they shaped American policy toward China, American policymakers from Henry Kissinger and Brent Scowcroft to President Obama's national security adviser Tom Donilon have noted distinctive traits in how their Chinese counterparts think about the use of military force. In deciding whether, when, and how to attack adversaries, Chinese leaders have for the most part been rational and pragmatic. Thus the "logic of the situation" provides the best initial guide for answering questions about when China is likely to be deterred from taking military action against the United States, or how it will respond to a threat or an attack. Beyond that, however, policymakers and analysts have identified five presumptions and predilections that provide further clues to China's likely strategic behavior in confrontations.

First, in both war and peace Chinese strategy is unabashedly realpolitik, unencumbered by any serious requirement to rationalize behavior in terms of international law or religious norms. This allows the Chinese government to be ruthlessly flexible, since it feels few constraints from prior rationales and is largely immune to critics who point out its inconsistencies. So, for example, when Henry Kissinger arrived in China, he found interlocutors unblinkered by ideology and brutally candid about China's national interests. Whereas in 1973 Nixon and Kissinger felt it necessary to frame their compromise to end the Vietnam War as "peace with honor" and to assure a "decent interval" to dampen American domestic political reactions, Mao felt no need to pretend that in establishing relations with capitalist America to strengthen Communist China's position vis-à-vis the Soviet Union, he was somehow bolstering a larger socialist international movement.

While its practical approach to international politics arguably gives it an edge over the United States, so too does China's obsessively holistic strategic world view. Chinese planners see everything as connected to everything else. In the tradition of Sun Tzu, the evolving context in which a strategic situation occurs is critical, because it determines the *shi* of that situation. *Shi* has no direct Western translation, but is most closely described as the "potential energy" or "momentum" inherent in any situation at a given moment. It comprises geography and terrain, weather, balance of forces, surprise, morale, and many other elements. "Each factor influences the other," Kissinger explains, "giving rise to subtle shifts in momentum and relative advantage."[44] Thus a skilled strategist spends most of his time patiently "observing and cultivating changes in the strategic landscape" and moves only when they are in optimal alignment. Then, with "his potential that of a fully drawn crossbow" (in Sun Tzu's words), he strikes swiftly, with precise timing, surging "downhill" with a momentum that appears unstoppable, breaking his opponent like "a grindstone against eggs."[45] To an observer, the result appears inevitable. As sinologist François Jullien writes, if a master strategist's action "is taken at the ideal moment, it is not even detectable: the process that leads to victory is determined so far in advance."[46] Or, like "setting a stone in motion on a steep slope," says Sun Tzu, "the force applied is minute, but the results are enormous."[47]

War for Chinese strategists is primarily psychological and political; military campaigns are a secondary concern. In Chinese thinking, an opponent's perception of facts on the ground may be just as important as the facts themselves. Creating and sustaining the image of a civilization so superior that it is the "center of the universe," for example, deters enemies from challenging Chinese dominance. The sheer size of the Chinese economy relative to those of outsiders also plays a role in subduing them—for instance, through access or denial to trade. If psychological deterrence and economic incentives fail, the barbarians outside China's borders can be set against one another in a contest in which everyone would lose except China. Eroding the enemy's material capability and morale, and backing him into an alley from which there is no exit, is far better than defeating him on the battlefield.

Chinese seek victory not in a decisive battle but through incremental moves designed to gradually improve their position. To quote Kissinger again: "Rarely did Chinese statesmen risk the outcome of a conflict on a single all-or-nothing clash: elaborate multi-year maneuvers were closer to their style. Where the Western tradition prized the decisive clash of forces emphasizing feats of heroism, the Chinese ideal stressed subtlety, indirection, and the patient accumulation of relative advantage."[48] In an instructive analogy, David Lai illustrates this by comparing the game of chess with its Chinese equivalent, *weiqi*—often referred to as *go*. In chess, players seek to dominate the center and conquer the opponent. In *weiqi,* players seek to surround the opponent. If the chess master sees five or six moves ahead, the *weiqi* master sees twenty or thirty. Attending to every dimension in the broader relationship with the adversary, the Chinese strategist resists rushing prematurely toward victory, instead aiming to build incremental advantage. "In the Western tradition, there is a heavy emphasis on the use of force; the art of war is largely limited to the battlefields; and the way to fight is force on force," Lai explains. By contrast, "The philosophy behind *go* is to compete for relative gain rather than seeking complete annihilation of the opponent forces." In a wise reminder, Lai warns that "It is dangerous to play *go* with the chess mindset. One can become overly aggressive so that he will stretch his force thin and expose his vulnerable parts in the battlefields."[49]

Current American debate about what is called "gray zone" conflict (or, in Russia, "hybrid warfare") proceeds in apparent ignorance of centuries over which China has perfected many more than fifty shades of warfare in which the actual use of combat forces is the last resort. As Sun Tzu explains in *The Art of War,* "The highest victory is to defeat the enemy without ever fighting."[50] China's history of domestic political upheaval and struggle between competing kingdoms has led its strategists to favor means other than fighting.

Recognizing these strategic predispositions, of course, is but a first step. In order to avoid a war with China, or navigate a conflict once it has begun, US leaders would also need to consider how the different strategic world views in Washington and Beijing might bring them to blows, and how that difference might shape a clash as it unfolds. Both capitals agree that today the greatest point of tension lies in the South China Sea. To understand how strategic "misalignment" could lead to tragic outcomes there, we must fully recognize China's perspective on this region.

CHINA SEES CHINA SEAS

As a consequence of its ongoing restoration of power and influence in East Asia, from China's perspective the US position in the western Pacific is waning. Chinese actions in the region have endeavored to hasten this retreat, most visibly in the South China Sea.

For decades, Americans have been missing the big picture in East

Asia, not least because of the difficulty in "seeing ourselves as others see us," to paraphrase Robert Burns. Every president since Nixon has believed that the United States was welcoming China into the international economic and political order. But as Kissinger says plainly, every Chinese leader he has met believes that America's strategy is to "contain" China. If anything, China's highly pragmatic reading of American intentions was only reinforced by the Obama administration's highly publicized "pivot" away from Europe and the Middle East to Asia. As then secretary of state Hillary Clinton described this shift in 2011: "Our post–World War II commitment to building a comprehensive and lasting transatlantic network of institutions and relationships has paid off many times over — and continues to do so. The time has come for the United States to make similar investments as a Pacific power."[51]

The effect of this announcement on China was predictable given its leaders' realpolitik mindset, and was also impossible to miss during diplomatic encounters in the years that followed. In 2014, Kevin Rudd and Brent Scowcroft each came back from separate, extensive conversations in China with identical views of what they call the striking, and indeed alarming, "consensus" in the Chinese leadership. According to both statesmen, China's leaders believe that America's grand strategy for dealing with China involves five to's: to isolate China, to contain China, to diminish China, to internally divide China, and to sabotage China's leadership. As Rudd explained, these convictions "derive from a Chinese conclusion that the US has not, and never will, accept the fundamental political legitimacy of the Chinese administration because it is not a liberal democracy." Moreover, according to Rudd, this is based on "a deeply held, deeply 'realist' Chinese conclusion that the US will never willingly concede its status as the preeminent regional and global power, and will do everything within its power to retain that position."[52]

From a Chinese perspective, the US campaign against China in the South China Sea — including its encouragement of the Philippines in 2013 to take its cause to the Permanent Court of Arbitration in The Hague, its recruitment of a chorus condemning China when it dismissed the court's finding that favored the Philippines, and its conduct of highly publicized freedom-of-navigation operations in the area— provides more than enough evidence for its views. And so America continues its game of chess while China rearranges the stones on its *go* board, working methodically to end these incursions by effecting a gradual yet overwhelming change in this nearby theater.

As the contest in the South China Sea unfolds, it will be shaped by the basic strategic assumptions and blind spots of both adversaries. In our attempt to assess the course it will take, therefore, and in particular whether or when China might use lethal military force to advance its interests, what clues can we draw from Chinese civilization, culture, and strategic traditions?

First, it seems clear that China will bring a long-term perspective to the standoff with the United States in the South China Sea, understanding it as part of a historical evolution, and expecting that the future will be shaped by the realities of geography, economics, and attention span. So the Chinese will be patient in the "long game" with the US—a contest in which they steadily accrue advantages, confident that they will outlast the Americans in the region. While the US may at times be fixated by events in the South China Sea or East China Sea, Chinese will expect Americans to eventually pivot back to ongoing wars in the Middle East, or Russian threats to Europe, or its problems at home.

It is also safe to assume that the Chinese government will be ruthlessly realistic in assessing the military correlation of forces between China and the US, and thus in forecasting the outcome of any potential military encounter. Because it will take at least another decade or more for China's military capabilities to match those of the US, even in arenas closest to China, Beijing will be cautious and prudent about any lethal use of force against the US. Instead, by gradually changing facts on the ground and in the waters throughout the South China Sea and adapting to resistance it encounters, as in the game of *weiqi,* the Chinese will win by the accumulation of overwhelming advantages.

Furthermore, China will be "strategic" with Chinese characteristics, treating military force as a subordinate instrument in the orchestration of its foreign policy, which seeks not victory in battle but the achievement of national objectives. It will bolster diplomatic and economic connections with its neighbors, deepening their dependency on China, and use economic leverage to encourage (or coerce) cooperation on other issues. In doing so, it hopes to increase influence on its periphery while also undermining the relationships between its neighbors and the United States. It may even attempt to "use barbarians against barbarians" to prevent a balancing coalition from forming against China —for instance, by playing Japan against South Korea, or Russia against the US. In time, Beijing will achieve such a preponderance of power that others in the region will simply accept its dominance not just as inevitable, but also as irresistible.

Although it will treat warfare as a last resort, should China conclude that long-term trend lines are no longer moving in its favor and that it is losing bargaining power, it could initiate a limited military conflict to teach an adversary a lesson. As political scientist Taylor Fravel has shown in a study of its twenty-three territorial disputes since 1949, China employed force in only three of them. As these cases suggest, China becomes more likely to resort to force if it believes an adversary is shifting the balance of forces against it at a time of domestic unrest. In his analysis of Beijing's attacks on India in 1962, the Soviet Union in 1969, and Vietnam in 1979, Fravel also demonstrates that China tends to use its military against opponents of comparable or greater strength, while it is more willing to negotiate with weaker adversaries.[53]

In sum, as long as developments in the South China Sea are generally moving in China's favor, it appears unlikely to use military force. But if trends in the correlation of forces should shift against it, particularly at a moment of domestic political instability, China could initiate a limited military conflict, even against a larger, more powerful state like the US. How such a conflict might occur is the focus of the next chapter.

8

FROM HERE TO WAR

Consider the vast influence of accident in war before you are engaged in it. It is a common mistake in going to war to begin at the wrong end, to act first, and wait for disaster.

—Thucydides, Athenian ambassador
to Spartan Assembly, 432 BCE

Never, never, never believe any war will be smooth and easy, or that anyone who embarks on the strange voyage can measure the tides and hurricanes he will encounter. The statesman who yields to war fever must realize that once the signal is given, he is no longer the master of policy but the slave of unforeseeable and uncontrollable events. —Winston Churchill

War is the province of chance. In no other sphere of human activity must such a margin be left for this intruder. It increases the uncertainty of every circumstance and deranges the course of events.

—Carl von Clausewitz

Would a Chinese leader barely in control of his own country after a long civil war dare to attack a superpower that had crushed Japan and ended World War II five years earlier by dropping atomic bombs? As American troops pushed North Korean forces toward the Chinese border in 1950, General Douglas MacArthur could not imagine so. But Mao did. MacArthur was dumbstruck. Chinese forces rapidly beat American troops back to the line that had divided North and South Korea when the war began. That 38th parallel continues to mark the border between the two Koreas today. By the time the war ended, nearly three million had perished, including 36,000 American troops.

Similarly, in 1969, Soviet leaders could not imagine that China would react to a minor border dispute by launching a preemptive strike against a power with overwhelming nuclear superiority. But that is precisely what Mao did when he started the Sino-Soviet border war. The gambit showed the world China's doctrine of "active defense." Mao sent an unmistakable message: China would never be intimidated, not even by adversaries that could wipe it off the map.

In the years ahead, could a collision between American and Chinese warships in the South China Sea, a drive toward national independence in Taiwan, jockeying between China and Japan over islands on which no one wants to live, instability in North Korea, or even a spiraling economic dispute provide the spark to a war between China and the US that neither wants? For most readers, it may seem hard to imagine — since the consequences would be so obviously disproportionate to any gains either side could hope to achieve.[1] Even a non-nuclear war conducted mostly at sea and in the air could kill thousands of combatants on both sides. Moreover, the economic impact of such a war would be massive. As a 2016 RAND study found, after just one year of a severe non-nuclear war, American GDP could decline by up to 10 percent and Chinese GDP by as much as 35 percent — setbacks on par with the Great Depression.[2] And if a war did go nuclear, both nations could be utterly destroyed. Chinese and American leaders know they cannot let that happen.

Unwise or undesirable, however, does not mean impossible. Wars occur even when leaders are determined to avoid them. Events or actions of others narrow their options, forcing them to make choices that risk war rather than acquiesce to unacceptable alternatives. Pericles did not want war with Sparta. The kaiser did not seek war with Britain. Mao initially opposed Kim Il-sung's attack on South Korea in 1950 for fear of blowback. But events often require leaders to choose between bad and worse risks. And once the military machines are in motion, misunderstandings, miscalculations, and entanglements can escalate to conflict far beyond anyone's original intent.

To better understand these dangers, Washington and Beijing have developed scenarios, simulations, and war games. These often begin with an unexpected incident or accident. Individuals assigned to play the hand of China or the US take it from there. Participants in these exercises are repeatedly surprised to find how often and easily small sparks lead to large wars. This chapter reviews four historical cases in which China initiated limited war, summarizes four concepts that war planners study to understand sources of conflict, and sketches five plausible paths to war between today's two greatest powers.

Korea, 1950–53. On June 25, 1950, Kim Il-sung (the grandfather of current North Korean leader Kim Jong-un) launched a surprise invasion of South Korea. By the fourth day, North Korea had captured Seoul, the South's capital. Within a month, South Korean forces were on the verge of surrender.

Just in the nick of time, a United Nations–authorized force composed mainly of American troops came to the rescue. Led by General Douglas MacArthur, the supreme commander for allied powers in Japan, three US Army divisions entered the war, backed by the same B-26 and B-29 bombers that had demolished much of Japan. In the next three months, they drove the North Koreans back to the 38th parallel.

Expecting the war to be over by Christmas and with little thought about how China might react, MacArthur's forces crossed the 38th parallel and advanced rapidly toward the Yalu River, which marks the border between North Korea and China. Korea would finally be unified under an American-supported government in Seoul. Ignoring repeated warnings from Chinese propaganda and tactical signs from captured Chinese troops, American intelligence officers discounted the possibility that China might intervene on behalf of the North. The Chinese civil war had come to an end less than a year earlier. That savage conflict had torn the country apart and claimed up to 3.5 million lives.[3] Why would a regime still reeling from that war risk its survival by attacking the nuclear power that had forced imperial Japan to surrender unconditionally?[4]

At the beginning of November, however, MacArthur awoke to find the vanguard of a 300,000-strong Chinese army slamming US and allied forces. Caught off guard, American units suffered severe losses. One regiment of the US First Cavalry Division lost 600 men in close combat in a matter of hours. In the weeks that followed, what MacArthur and his fellow commanders had dismissed as a "peasant army" not only halted the allied advance but beat UN forces back to the 38th parallel.[5]

Losing a war he thought he had won, MacArthur called on President Harry Truman to authorize him to use nuclear weapons against China.[6] Instead of accepting the rogue five-star general's plan, Truman fired him. The war dragged on in stalemate for two more years before an armistice was finally signed by Truman's successor, President Dwight Eisenhower, in 1953. As the historian T. R. Fehrenbach notes, "For more than a hundred years, Chinese military forces had been objects of contempt, possessing neither skill, means, nor the will to fight."[7] No longer.

Sino–Soviet border, 1969. Nineteen years after the Chinese sprang their winter surprise on US and allied forces, China faced down the world's second superpower. At the height of Sino-Soviet tensions in the late 1960s, the two powers clashed in a series of minor incidents across their disputed border along the frozen Ussuri River in Siberia. Soviet troops were "on the move," Mao claimed, and the USSR had "again and again" increased its forces there in an attempt, the *People's Daily* reported, to create an "anti-China ring of encirclement."[8]

In a sequence of actions and reactions, both sides built up their forces along the border, pitting more than 650,000 Chinese troops against 290,000 Soviet soldiers and 1,200 aircraft. Mao had threatened a massive "People's War" that would be "a contest of human power and morale." According to the highest-ranking Soviet official ever to defect to the West, Arkady Shevchenko, the Politburo was terrified by a "nightmare vision of invasion by millions of Chinese" that made Soviet leaders "almost frantic."[9]

The Soviet forces were much better armed and trained, and they were backed by a dominant air force. Moreover, they had an arsenal of over 10,000 nuclear weapons, including 500-kiloton, SS-12 tactical nuclear missiles that Moscow had deployed to the border region. Although China had tested a nuclear device in 1964, it had developed only a handful of warheads and had no way to deliver them against Moscow. As late as November 1968, Mao himself admitted that China, "in a sense, is still a non-nuclear power. With this little nuclear weaponry, we cannot be counted as a nuclear country. If we are to fight a war, we must use conventional weapons."[10] Many Soviet military leaders believed a preemptive nuclear first strike was the only way to end the growing Chinese threat. In fact, the Soviet Union was so serious about attacking China that it quietly approached the Nixon administration to gauge how the US would react. As Kissinger, then the US national security adviser, later reflected, "The Soviet Union was much closer to a preemptive attack than we realized" at the time.[11] Only after Washington warned that it would not stand by idly did Moscow shelve this option.[12]

Still, facing an angry Soviet Union, Mao adopted an unexpected strategy: he poked the bear. China's military planned an attack that would "strive for suddenness of action" and teach Moscow a "bitter lesson."[13] On March 2, 1969, the PLA ambushed Soviet border troops on Zhenbao Island in the Ussuri River, followed shortly by a second attack, killing ninety-one Soviets at the cost of thirty Chinese.[14]

Why did China make such a reckless gambit? To Mao, it was a defensive action of last resort—a demonstration of China's broader strategic concept of "active defense," or what Mao described as "defense through decisive engagements."[15] The Chinese planned the ambush more to deliver a psychological blow than a military defeat. As Michael Gerson concludes, its objective was to "deter future Soviet aggression or coercion against China" and "forcibly demonstrate China's courage, resolve, and strength in the face of what was perceived to be a looming Soviet threat."[16]

Taiwan Strait Crisis, 1996. Beyond Mao, China has continued to use military force selectively in ways that risk a wider war in order to send strong messages to its opponents. In 1996, fearing that Taiwanese president Lee Teng-hui was undermining the long-standing "One China" formula and moving toward independence, Beijing again chose a military option. In an effort to defeat Lee in Taiwan's 1996 election, China sought to intimidate Taiwanese voters by launching a barrage of missiles that bracketed the island and threatened commercial shipping on which it depended.

In this case, the Clinton administration's forceful response surprised the Chinese. The United States sent the USS *Nimitz* and USS *Independence* aircraft carrier battle groups to Taiwan's aid. China backed down. Indeed, its attempt to sway Taiwanese voters backfired, as President Lee won and the US strengthened its bond with Taiwan.[17] But Beijing's misjudgment deepened American military planners' appreciation of ways in which China's propensity for aggressive brinkmanship, coupled with an accident or misunderstanding, could provoke war.[18]

China Seas, today. As noted in chapter 7, gazing out from their coastline, Chinese leaders see China Seas. From their perspective, the constant presence of US naval ships in their waters and daily intelligence flights along their borders are anomalies—unwelcome hangovers from the Second World War. As China has developed the capability to do so, it has attempted to force the United States to back off. Thus, for example, in December 2013, as the guided-missile cruiser USS *Cowpens* was observing the PLA Navy's first aircraft carrier, the *Liaoning*, on its maiden deployment, its captain received a stern message from the commander of the carrier ordering him to leave the area. The *Cowpens* captain's response noted that he was conducting appropriate, legal operations in international waters and would therefore ignore the order. Minutes later, a PLA Navy ship cut across the *Cowpens*'s path, leaving its captain only two options: ram the ship, or take evasive action that would avoid collision but appear to the Chinese as backing down. He chose the latter.[19]

The *Cowpens* incident was one of scores in recent years in which PLA Navy vessels and aircraft have engaged in deliberate provocations, risking "accidental" collisions and testing American officers' limits. The US Navy, for its part, has instructed its ships to avoid confrontation and deescalate when faced with these tactics. It has not always been successful, however. In April 2001, a US surveillance aircraft flying near Hainan Island collided with a Chinese fighter jet that was harassing it to demonstrate Beijing's opposition to these intelligence-gathering flights. The Chinese pilot was killed, while the US pilots were forced to make a crash landing in Chinese territory, sparking the first international crisis of the George W. Bush administration. The American crew, who were detained by the Chinese after their emergency landing, were freed after ten days. But the Chinese held the plane for longer, allowing them an opportunity to extract its top-secret surveillance technology. Since that incident the PLA has been altering the landscape and balance of forces in its adjacent waters. By building islands, deploying missile batteries, and constructing airfields across the South China Sea, it is creating new facts on the ground to pose greater threats to US forces in these critical sea-lanes.

Together, these four cases suggest that when considering when and how China may use military force, it is not sufficient to ask what we would do in its shoes. For Chinese leaders, military force is an instrument in an orchestra of engagement, one they may use preemptively to surprise a stronger opponent who would not have done likewise.

SPARKS, BACKGROUND CONDITIONS, ACCELERANTS, AND ESCALATION LADDERS

In war scenarios, analysts use basic concepts familiar from the US Forest Service. Arsonists cause only a small fraction of fires. Discarded cigarettes, smoldering campfires, industrial accidents, and bolts of lightning are much more common sources. Fortunately, in the forest as well as in relations among nations, most sparks do not ignite a blaze.

Background conditions often determine which sparks become fires. While Smoky the Bear's warning that "only you can prevent forest fires" warns campers and hikers about sparks, the Forest Service also posts additional warnings after long dry spells or periods of extreme heat, occasionally closing high-risk areas. Moreover, it regulates the storage of flammable chemicals, propane tanks, and gas depots, becoming increasingly stringent as conditions worsen.

In relations between China and the United States today, relevant background conditions stretch from geography, culture, and history, to lessons each government has drawn from recent instances of military engagement. Unlike Germany and Britain, the US and China are on opposite sides of the globe. Noting that fact, Chinese strategists sometimes remind Americans wryly that there is currently little chance of an accidental collision between US and Chinese ships in the Caribbean. If the US Navy would follow their example in the East and South China Seas and stay in its own hemisphere, they say, there would be no risk of colliding with Chinese ships. Furthermore, what Pentagon planners call the "tyranny of distance" raises questions about America's ability to sustain a campaign against China in those bodies of water.

The most pertinent background conditions, however, are the Thucydidean syndromes of rising and ruling powers that China and the United States display in full. Indeed, these features are more acute in light of China's century of humiliation, particularly the smoldering anger over atrocities it suffered at the hands of Japanese invaders and occupiers. Disputes between Japan and China over islands in the East China Sea thus present special risks. If the government of Prime Minister Shinzo Abe or his successor succeeds in revising Japan's pacifist constitution and strengthening its military capabilities, including amphibious landings to seize disputed islands, China will do more than take note.

"History," Kissinger observed in his first book, "is the memory of states."[20] This memory bears heavily on future national decisions. Both the American and Chinese militaries acknowledge that the US has lost, or at least failed to win, four of the five major wars it has entered since World War II.[21] (Korea was at best a draw, Vietnam a loss, and Iraq and Afghanistan unlikely to turn out well. Only President George H. W. Bush's war in 1991 to force Saddam Hussein's Iraq to retreat from

Kuwait counts as a clear win.) Reflecting on that record, former secretary of defense Robert Gates stated the obvious: "In my opinion, any future defense secretary who advises the president to again send a big American land army into Asia or into the Middle East or Africa should 'have his head examined,' as General MacArthur so delicately put it."[22] In recent decades, Americans—and the policymakers sending American troops to war—have also displayed an ever-lower tolerance for losing American lives in combat. The impact of this casualty aversion is severe: military planners now rule out entire categories of operations because of their risk to soldiers, while politicians speak less and less of victory and more and more of protecting troops. Chinese leaders know this and have factored it into their planning. In offline conversations, some have been known to quip that they have several million surplus single males ready to die for their country.

Like gasoline to a match, accelerants can turn an accidental collision or third-party provocation into war. One cluster of accelerants is captured by what Clausewitz called the "fog of war." Extending Thucydides's insight about war as "an affair of chances," in *On War* Clausewitz observes that "war is the realm of uncertainty. Three quarters of the factors on which action in war is based are wrapped in a fog of greater or lesser uncertainty."[23] This profound uncertainty can lead a commander or policymaker to act aggressively when a fuller set of facts would advise caution, and vice versa.

In 1964, two days after North Vietnamese ships attacked the intelligence-gathering destroyer USS *Maddox* in the Gulf of Tonkin, US intelligence reported a second attack on the ship. Provoked by this North Vietnamese audacity, Secretary of Defense Robert McNamara led the campaign that persuaded Congress to pass the Gulf of Tonkin Resolution, essentially declaring war on North Vietnam. Only decades later did McNamara learn that the report about the attack was incorrect. As McNamara wrote, "Ultimately, President Johnson authorized bombing in response to what he thought had been a second attack that hadn't occurred." A false alarm played a key role in putting the United States on the path to failure in Vietnam.[24]

The advent of disruptive weapons that promise "shock and awe" makes the fog and uncertainty even worse. With attacks on command-and-control systems, including the satellites that have become essential for targeting data and communications, enemies can paralyze a nation's military command. In the 1991 "Desert Storm" war with Saddam Hussein, US forces demonstrated version 1.0 of this option. They destroyed Saddam's intelligence and cut the communication links between him and Iraqi commanders in the field. Isolated, his forces hunkered down, making US aircraft attacks on them, as some pilots noted, like "shooting fish in a barrel."

Antisatellite weapons are one accelerant that military planners expect to play a big role in any US-China conflict. Long a subject of science fiction, such weapons are today a fact of life. In 2007, China successfully destroyed a weather satellite, and it regularly tests its antisatellite capabilities in less dramatic fashion. Satellites provide a crucial link in almost every US military endeavor, from warning of opponents' ballistic-missile launches and providing imagery and weather forecasts to planning operations. Global positioning satellites put the "precision" in almost all the military's precision-guided munitions and allow ships, planes, and ground units to know where they are on the battlefield. The US depends on this technology more than any of its competitors. Without it, the commander in chief cannot relay orders to platoons on the ground, vessels at sea, and everyone in between. Antisatellite weapons run the gamut from "kinetic" ones that physically destroy their targets, littering space with orbital debris, to quieter systems that use lasers to jam or "dazzle" satellites, rendering them inoperable.

Cyberspace provides even more opportunities for disruptive technological transformations that could provide a decisive advantage, on the one hand, but might also risk uncontrolled escalation, on the other. The details of offensive cyberweapons remain heavily classified and are constantly evolving. But the public has seen glimpses of them in some cases, such as America's cyberattack against Iran's nuclear program.[25] America's primary cyberspace organizations, the National Security Agency and the US Cyber Command, as well as their Chinese counterparts, can now use cyberweapons to silently shut down military networks and critical civilian infrastructure like power grids. Moreover, by employing proxies and assembling an international web of compromised computers, they can disguise the origins of a cyber-operation, slowing the victim's ability to identify the attacker.

Like antisatellite weapons, cyberweapons could create a decisive advantage in battle by disrupting the command-and-control and targeting information on which modern militaries depend—and do so without bloodshed. This presents a dangerous paradox: the very action that attackers believe will tamp down conflict can appear reckless and provocative to the victims. Even if the physical battlefield remained restricted to the South China Sea, cyber-capabilities allow each combatant to reach into the other's vulnerable infrastructure—for example, by closing down electrical grids, hospitals, or parts of the financial system. Similarly, cyberattacks that disrupted communication would intensify the fog of war, creating confusion that multiplies the chances of miscalculation.

While both the US and China now have nuclear arsenals that could survive the other's first strike and still allow for retaliation, neither can be sure its cyber-arsenals could withstand a serious cyberassault. For example, a large-scale Chinese cyberattack against the US military's networks could temporarily cripple Washington's ability to respond with its own cyberattacks, or even to operate some of its critical command-and-control and surveillance systems. This creates a dangerous use-it-or-lose-it dynamic in which each side has an incentive to attack key links in the other's computer networks before they themselves are disabled.

A faction in Beijing or Washington might call for a small-scale cyberattack to send a covert shot across the opponent's bow that would kill no one and cause no public alarm, but would signal the threat of larger-scale cyberattacks on military or civilian infrastructure. But if the opponent did not interpret the action that way, rapid tit-for-tat escalation in the cyber-domain could ensue. With both sides conscious of the use-or-lose mindset and each fearful of its own vulnerabilities, either might misinterpret an attack under way or retaliate disproportionately while its own cyberweapons were still intact.

An array of dangerous accelerants in cyberspace might inadvertently bring the United States and China into conflict. First, a denial and deception campaign could sufficiently convince investigators that China was not involved in an offensive attack, leading them to hold a third party accountable instead. Such a campaign might employ false personas on social media, co-opted media organizations, or false-flag indictors left behind in malware to distract US investigators from getting to ground truth. If such a campaign were effective, it would make the fog of war much denser.

Another accelerant might involve compromising the confidentiality of sensitive networks. Some are obvious, such as those that operate nuclear command-and-control. Others, however, may be perceived quite differently by each side. Take China's Great Firewall, a collection of hardware and software that enables Beijing to monitor and block vast segments of online content. Washington could disable a system essential to the Great Firewall, intending it as a modest, private warning. But for Chinese leaders who regard the ability to control the information citizens see as vital, the operation could be misconstrued as the tip of a spear aimed at regime change.

Compared with the bluntest instruments of war, especially nuclear bombs, cyberweapons offer the promise of subtlety and precision. But this promise is illusory. Increased connectivity among systems, devices, and "things" creates a domino effect. Unable to determine how the hacking of one system may affect others, attackers would find it difficult to narrowly tailor the effects of their operation and avoid unintended escalation. In 2016, 180,000 Internet-connected industrial control systems were operating around the world.[26] Along with the proliferation of the so-called Internet of Things, which encompasses some 10 billion devices worldwide, the number of enticing targets is growing rapidly. Collateral damage in the cyberdomain could be as deadly and disruptive as it is in traditional warfare. Hacking a military target, for example, could inadvertently disable a system used by a medical or financial complex. While American cyber commanders repeatedly affirm that in cyber offense, the US has the biggest rocks, they also acknowledge that the US lives in the glassiest house.

In the 1960s, futurist Herman Kahn (one of the Cold War strategists parodied by Peter Sellers's movie character Dr. Strangelove) proposed a 44-rung escalation ladder from "subcrisis maneuvering" up to full-scale nuclear war.[27] Kahn's first rung was the "ostensible crisis"—the spark. He explained that in a crisis, two powers would rarely proceed methodically and incrementally up the ladder. Background conditions and accelerants could cause them to skip rungs. As they move up the ladder, each state would assess its position relative to the adversary's at each rung and calculate how it would compare at rungs further up the ladder. This in turn might shape a willingness to accept stalemate or defeat rather than escalate to more destructive levels of war. Often, one state has an advantage over several steps, only to be at a disadvantage higher up the ladder. While each would prefer to settle at a point where it has the upper hand, it must find terms acceptable to an adversary who knows that he has the option of escalating to more destructive levels of conflict at which he then holds the advantage.

Nobel Prize–winning economist Thomas Schelling likened the fundamental strategic competition among nuclear superpowers to a game of chicken. In the classic form of the game played by thrill-seeking teenagers in the 1950s, two hot-rodders face off, each putting the left wheel of his car on the center line of the road. From opposite directions, they drive toward each other at full speed. The one who swerves first is the chicken, and the other gets the girl. If neither swerves, the cars collide and both die.

By "shouldering" ships and "buzzing" aircraft to occupying or constructing islands, states can force an adversary to play this deadly game: proceed on course and risk a fatal collision, or avoid it, but at the cost of submission. Rivals who consistently yield rather than risk a crash can be nudged step by step off the road, or out of sea-lanes, entirely. Each party knows this, and knows that the other knows. So, as Schelling taught us, strategic conflict short of hot war is essentially a contest in risk-taking. The state that can persuade its adversary that it is more committed to achieving its objective, or more reckless in pursuit of it, can force the adversary to be more responsible—and yield.

AN ACCIDENTAL COLLISION AT SEA

Potential sparks are frighteningly mundane. Currently, American and allied warships and aircraft are operating in greater proximity to their Chinese counterparts than ever before. US Navy guided-missile destroyers periodically conduct freedom-of-navigation operations near Chinese-controlled islands in disputed waters in the South China Sea. Suppose that during routine operations an American destroyer passes near Mischief Reef, one of China's constructed islands on which it has built runways for aircraft and installed air and missile defenses. (In imagining this scenario and the others that follow, readers may wish to refer to the map of China and its surroundings on pages 168–69). As the ship nears the contested site, Chinese coast guard vessels harass the destroyer, just as they did during the *Cowpens* incident. Unlike that encounter, however, the US destroyer declines to swerve (or is unable to do so in time), collides with a Chinese ship, and sinks it, killing all on board.

The Chinese government now has three options. The dovish course would be to avoid escalation by allowing the American destroyer to leave the area and to protest its actions through diplomatic channels. At the other end of the spectrum, it could adopt an eye-for-an-eye approach and sink the destroyer using aircraft or missiles stationed on Mischief Reef. But refusing to be the "chicken," while also not wanting to escalate, Beijing could opt for what it believes is a middle course. As the US destroyer attempts to leave the area, a PLA Navy cruiser blocks its way, insisting that the destroyer entered Chinese territorial waters and demanding that its crew surrender and face justice for the deaths of the coast guard personnel.

China might well believe that it is deescalating the situation by pursuing a policy that allows for a diplomatic solution akin to the deal that permitted the American crew to return home following the 2001

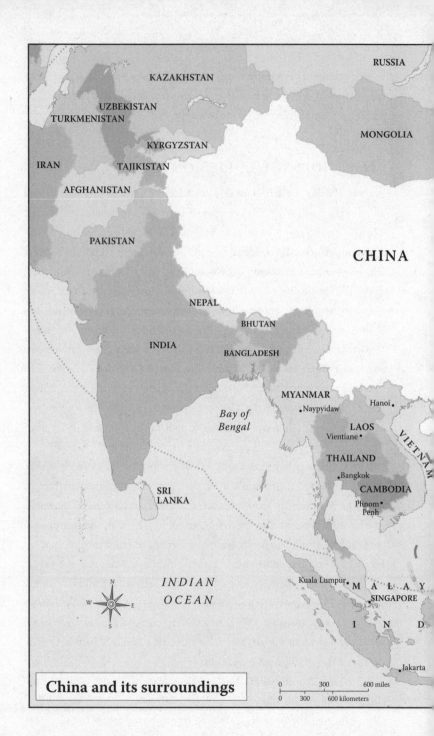

China and its surroundings

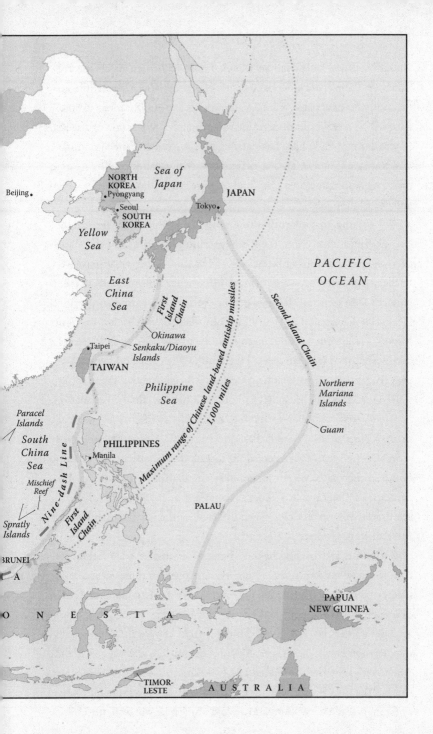

aircraft collision near Hainan Island. From an American perspective, however, China's reckless harassment of the destroyer caused the collision in the first place. China's attempt to arrest US sailors in international waters would undermine the principles of the law of the sea. Surrendering would have far-reaching repercussions: if the US military will not stand up to China to defend operations conducted by its own navy, what message does that send to America's allies, including Japan and the Philippines?

Not willing to undermine its credibility by surrendering, the destroyer could simply sink the Chinese cruiser blocking its path. Alternatively, to avoid further bloodshed and to show a degree of sensitivity to the nationalistic pressures Chinese leaders face at home, the US could choose to use a show of force to get the cruiser to back down peacefully. US Pacific Command in Hawaii, in consultation with leaders in Washington, could order nearby aircraft to fly to the area, send an aircraft carrier stationed in Japan toward the South China Sea, and forward-deploy B-2 bombers to Guam. American officials believe these actions will signal their seriousness without risking any further escalation.

Events look different to Beijing, especially as the fog of war rolls in. As China sees it, the US has already sunk a Chinese vessel. Now scores of American aircraft are aloft, threatening attacks on the Chinese cruiser, other naval vessels, or military installations on nearby islands. Mindful of their public's outcry, Chinese leaders are especially conscious that any further bloodshed inflicted by the United States would force them to retaliate aggressively.

But events are running beyond Beijing's control. As US fighter jets rush to the scene to assist the stranded destroyer, a Chinese antiaircraft battery panics and fires on the oncoming aircraft. The US aircraft take desperate evasive action, and the destroyer begins firing on Chinese antiaircraft sites on the island. Under attack, the local Chinese commander bombards the destroyer with antiship missiles on the island. The missiles hit their intended target, killing hundreds of sailors and sinking the ship. Those who escape are now stranded in small lifeboats.

Chinese leaders are desperate to avoid a full-scale war with the United

States, but also cannot admit their chain of command broke down. They claim their actions were a proportionate and defensive response because the American destroyer, responsible for the sinking of a Chinese coast guard vessel, was the aggressor. US officials are stunned that China has sunk a $3 billion destroyer and killed hundreds of American sailors. Though wary of going to war with China, those in the White House Situation Room cannot back down: video of the ship's wreckage and stranded US sailors on cable news and social media has made that impossible. Many in Congress are calling on the administration to authorize war plans based on the doctrine formerly named Air-Sea Battle, which calls for massive air strikes against missile and radar systems on the Chinese mainland. Realizing that attacks on China's mainland would trigger war, the president authorizes Pacific Command to instead destroy China's military bases on disputed islands in the South China Sea. The president reasons that this is a proportionate response, since these islands were directly responsible for the sinking of the destroyer. Furthermore, eliminating these military bases will allow US ships to rescue the sailors stranded nearby. Most important, such an action would target only China's artificial islands, leaving its mainland untouched.

President Xi Jinping and other Chinese officials do not make this distinction. For years they have told the public that China has undisputed sovereignty over these islands. For them, they are an integral part of China proper, and America has just attacked them. (Americans who scoff should recall that the Japanese attack on Pearl Harbor struck neither the mainland nor even a US state, yet still rallied a nation to war.) Many in China are demanding that Xi order the PLA to destroy US military bases in Guam, Japan, and elsewhere in the Pacific. Some want China to attack the United States itself. No one is calling for China to exercise restraint. As millions of its citizens' social media postings are reminding the government, after its century of humiliation at the hands of sovereign powers, the ruling Communist Party has promised: "never again."

Still, President Xi clings to the hope that war can be avoided, an impossibility if China begins attacking US military bases in Guam or

Japan, killing soldiers and civilians and triggering retaliatory attacks on the Chinese mainland. Seeking a proportionate response to the US attack on China's island bases, Xi instead approves an alternative plan proposed by the head of the PLA's new Strategic Support Force: using laser, electronic, and kinetic weapons to destroy or disable all US military satellites in orbit above the crisis area, and cyberattacks to cripple American command-and-control systems throughout the Asia-Pacific region. The goal is to deescalate: Xi hopes that the US will be shocked into backing down.

But from the American perspective, these "blinding" attacks are indistinguishable from the first stage of a coordinated attack on the US aircraft carrier and its strike group sailing from Japan—an event for which the PLA has spent decades developing its "carrier-killer" antiship ballistic missiles. The 90,000-ton carrier, a floating city of 5,500 sailors which the US describes as sovereign American territory, is simply too big to lose. The president is not willing to take the risk. On the advice of the Joint Chiefs of Staff, the president reluctantly approves the only plan ready on short notice that has a chance of saving the carrier: a war plan based on Air-Sea Battle. Using those assets still operational after the Chinese attack, the US military begins destroying China's "kill chains," which are the various satellite and surveillance systems that allow Beijing to accurately target American carriers with its antiship missiles. It also launches massive cruise missile and stealth bomber attacks on PLA missile sites and air bases on the Chinese mainland, which could at any moment be used to sink American vessels anywhere within the first island chain.

The attacks provoke exactly what they intended to avoid. Its mainland now under attack, and the targeting systems needed to operate China's antiship weapons about to be lost, China must use them or lose them. Xi authorizes attacks on all US warships within range, including the carrier group. American aircraft and naval escorts intercept Chinese bombers and fighter jets flying to the carrier, but a swarm of DF-21D ballistic missiles—the so-called carrier killers—launched at the carrier prove too much to handle. Enough reach their target to sink the carrier, killing most of the 5,500 sailors on board—far more than died during Pearl Harbor. The dynamics of playing chicken with cyber- and space weapons over the South China Sea have stoked a tiny spark into a roaring fire.

TAIWAN MOVES TOWARD INDEPENDENCE

If Taiwan were an independent nation, it would be among the most successful countries in the world. Its hardworking population of twenty-three million has developed a market economy twice the size of the Philippines, Thailand, or Vietnam. Although many in Taiwan want independence, China views it as a province. Beijing is prepared to do whatever it takes to keep Taipei from asserting its sovereignty. No other country has been prepared to fight China over the matter.

Suppose, however, that the Chinese government were to substantially increase repression at home, including in Hong Kong, where China had promised to maintain considerable autonomy and freedom when Britain returned control of the city in 1997. Enraged that the Chinese government is backtracking on its promises, residents of Hong Kong take to the streets to demand that Beijing uphold its commitment to "One Country, Two Systems." As the protests drag on for weeks with no resolution in sight, Xi orders the Chinese military to do what it did in Tiananmen Square in 1989: crush the protests.

The ensuing violence shocks the Taiwanese, particularly the younger generation. Pro-independence and anti-Beijing sentiment soars. In this atmosphere, the Taiwanese president is emboldened to ramp up rhetoric emphasizing her people's hard-won rights and democracy. Her political allies go further, insisting that what has occurred in Hong Kong proves that Taiwan can never guarantee its citizens' freedom without being a sovereign, independent country. To signal his disapproval of Chinese regression in Hong Kong, the American president pointedly announces his respect for the Taiwanese president's strong stance and declares that the 1979 Taiwan Relations Act fully commits the US to defend Taiwan against a Chinese invasion.

This is a major break from the long-standing US policy of "strategic ambiguity" on the issue, and the Taiwanese president interprets it as tacit endorsement of a move toward independence. In an interview with the *New York Times,* she announces that Taiwan will apply for full membership to the United Nations (a move that China has long opposed) and rejects the so-called 1992 Consensus, under which both parties had agreed to the One China concept while allowing for differing interpretations of what it actually meant. To punish Taiwan's insubordination and scare it into backing down, China conducts an enhanced version of its Taiwan Strait Crisis response by barraging Taiwanese waters with "tests" of ballistic and cruise missiles, severely interrupting the commercial shipping that constitutes the island's lifeline to the world. When Taipei still refuses to withdraw its membership application, China uses other weapons, including mine-laying drones, to further disrupt shipping into and out of Taiwan.

As a small island nation, Taiwan imports 70 percent of its food and most of its natural resources, including energy.[28] A sustained blockade would cause its economy to grind to a halt and produce large-scale food shortages. Despite opposition to Taiwan's application to join the United Nations, the US administration feels obliged to prevent its strangulation. Many pro-Taiwan members of the US Congress are demanding that the White House send aircraft carriers to Taiwan's aid, just as Bill Clinton did during the 1995–96 crisis.[29] But the administration knows that Chinese antiship ballistic missiles would now pose a serious threat to any US carriers moving into the area, and the American public has little stomach for another war.

Instead, US Pacific Command offers to escort commercial shipping through the affected seas, a gesture of support but not of willingness to fight. (Readers will recall how this symbolic maneuver backfired for Athens when it sent a minimum deterrent to support Corcyra.) The escort campaign puts US warships at risk of being sunk by the Chinese missile barrage, either deliberately or accidentally—an event that could instantly kill more than one thousand Americans and spark calls for retaliation. In this scenario, a Chinese antiship missile—ostensibly fired as part of ongoing test barrages—sinks the USS *John P. Murtha*, an amphibious transport dock ship acting as an escort to civilian shipping. All of the nearly eight hundred sailors and marines aboard are killed—more than the US lost in the first year of the Iraq War.

China insists that the sinking was accidental; the *Murtha* merely got in the way of a missile fired at a random patch of ocean. But in Washington, the secretary of defense and the chairman of the Joint Chiefs urge the president not to be deceived by this explanation, but instead to authorize Pacific Command to execute its Air-Sea Battle plan to strike PLA antiship missile launch sites on the mainland.

In this or related cases, America's recent history of military intervention and combat casualties would play an outsized role in shaping Washington's response. Mindful of the quagmires in which his predecessors found themselves in Iraq and Afghanistan, a president might well tip the scales against war. Sensitive to a resurgence of populist, isolationist sentiment, he might be averse to honoring the nation's commitments to Taiwan. Even so, the death of eight hundred sailors and marines in one dramatic incident would likely shock Americans into demanding retribution.

Confronted with the sinking of the *Murtha*, the president accedes to pressure from military and political advisers, and agrees to preemptively strike antiship and other ballistic-missile systems on the Chinese mainland. Because China's conventional and nuclear missiles are kept in the same locations, and their command-and-control systems are intertwined, Beijing mistakenly believes the United States is trying to eliminate its nuclear arsenal in a surprise first strike.

In a desperate attempt to "deescalate by escalating"—an Orwellian doctrine that is nevertheless a pillar of Russian military strategy—China fires one of its land-based, nuclear-tipped ballistic missiles into an empty tract of ocean south of Okinawa. The nuclear threshold has been crossed. And while no lives have been lost in the strike, it is but a short step from here to all-out nuclear war.

WAR PROVOKED BY A THIRD PARTY

The spark to a Sino-American clash need not initially involve American or Chinese military forces. Instead, it might result from a confrontation with or between third-party allies. We came close to such a scenario in 2010, when North Korea sank the South Korean warship *Cheonan*, killing forty-six South Korean sailors. China supported North Korea's denial of involvement. Seoul, meanwhile, insisted that Pyongyang be held accountable. Ultimately, the two Koreas and their allies stepped back from the brink. But with a new set of background conditions and accelerants today, it is not clear that it would be so easy to avoid war, especially if the third parties involved were less inured to the sort of slow, grinding tensions that the Korean Peninsula has endured for decades.

Besides South Korea, the other major American ally in China's immediate vicinity is Japan, a country with a post–World War II history of pacifism, but whose politics have become increasingly militaristic in recent years. Conservative Japanese politicians have spoken ever more stridently about revising the pacifist constitution imposed on their country by the United States. They have also been chafing against Chinese claims of sovereignty in the East and South China Seas. In a crisis involving its historical rival Beijing, any steps Tokyo takes would certainly be shaped by these memories, and by the Japanese government's shifting attitude toward military force.

A likely flashpoint is the Senkaku Islands (known in China as the Diaoyu Islands), located near valuable fishing grounds, trade routes, and potential oil reserves in the East China Sea. The United States temporarily controlled the islands after World War II, but in the early 1970s returned them to Japan, which had claimed them since the nineteenth century. But in the 1970s, China also claimed sovereignty over the islands. Chinese ships regularly pass through these waters, raising tensions between Beijing and Tokyo and risking a collision that could set off a chain reaction.

Consider a scenario that provided the story line for a recent war game designed by the RAND Corporation.[30] A group of Japanese ultranationalists sets sail for the Senkakus in small civilian watercraft. On social media, they explain they are headed for Kuba Jima, one of the smaller islands, which they intend to claim and occupy on behalf of Japan. They land and begin building unidentified structures. Taking a page out of the Chinese playbook, they live-stream their activities for the world to see. China reacts swiftly, its coast guard arriving within hours with officers who arrest the Japanese dissidents and take them back to the Chinese mainland for trial. Does Japan allow them to face justice in a Chinese court? It could. Instead, rather than lose face, Japan dispatches some of its own coast guard vessels in the area to intercept the ship carrying the arrested ultranationalists and prevent them from being taken to China.

A pileup ensues as both the PLA Navy and the Japan Maritime Self-Defense Force deploy warships and fighter planes to the area. Neither side backs down. To make matters worse, some of the Japanese vessels land amphibious troops to occupy Kuba Jima, doubling down on the nationalists' actions. A skirmish has become a military confrontation. In an urgent call, the Japanese prime minister reminds the US president that Tokyo expects the United States to uphold the seven-decade-old US-Japan mutual defense treaty, noting that senior officials have repeatedly confirmed that the US commitment applies to the Senkakus.[31]

As the standoff enters its third day, the president and his National Security Council must decide: Does the United States wholeheartedly respond to Japan's appeal, putting air power over the disputed island to protect the Japanese troops now on the ground there? Or is there a more restrained course that will satisfy the Japanese without antagonizing China and further escalating the tense naval standoff? The president opts for the latter, directing the Japan-based US carrier strike group to take up a patrol station outside the range of the PLA's land-based carrier-killer missiles, but keeping aircraft and submarines close enough to aid Japanese vessels and territory if things get ugly.

They do. The next morning, a Chinese destroyer collides with a Japanese fishing boat in the crowded waters off the Senkakus, and soon fighter jets from both sides are provocatively buzzing their opponent's warships. The standoff erupts into a brief, bloody naval battle as a Japanese captain, fearing for his ship's safety, downs one of the low-flying Chinese fighters, and the PLA Navy warships, in return, sink his vessel.

Both sides are at the edge of war at this point, and so is the United States, which is in a position to sink Chinese vessels with its hidden attack submarines or to send its carrier's air wing into action. At this juncture, however, before the next decision has been made, something unexpected happens. All communications between Japanese forces on and around the Senkakus and their headquarters go dark.

A cyberattack has severely disrupted one of the Japanese military's command-and-control systems. The United States and Japan immediately blame China. The attacker has even left the telltale signs of the PLA's offensive hacking unit. There is little hesitation in Washington or at US Pacific Command about what to do next. To prevent the Japanese naval force from being annihilated while it is incommunicado, US submarines sink three PLA Navy warships off the Senkakus with torpedoes. China, Japan, and the United States have now fired their opening shots in a three-nation war.

But what if it was not the PLA that launched the cyberattack after all? What if it was a carefully timed false-flag operation by Russia, seeking to draw the United States and China into a conflict in order to distract Washington from its wrestling match with Russia over Ukraine? By the time intelligence agencies around the world learn the truth, it will be too late. Moscow has played its hand brilliantly.

From the Senkakus, the war zone spreads as China attacks more Japanese vessels elsewhere in the East China Sea. Tokyo is desperate for the United States to commit its carrier strike group to the fight. If Washington makes that call, the same point of no return may well be crossed as in the previous scenario: the destruction of one of the crown jewels of the US Navy and the loss of life of all aboard could be the tragedy that the US administration is forced to avenge with widening attacks on Chinese forces in a full-scale Pacific war.

NORTH KOREAN COLLAPSE

Everyone recognizes that North Korea is a ticking time bomb. At any moment, the regime of Kim Jong-un could well collapse into chaos, threatening the vital national interests not only of the US and China, but also of South Korea and Japan. Each year the North Korean regime remains in power, its nuclear arsenal grows larger. Pyongyang is currently thought to have about twenty warheads and could have as many as one hundred by 2020.[32] At the same time, North Korea's missile program continues to advance, and it is rapidly acquiring the capability to deliver one or more of these nuclear warheads against targets in South Korea, Japan, American bases in Guam and Okinawa, and even Hawaii. For many American strategists, this is a red line North Korea can never be allowed to cross. For China, the prospect of South Korea conquering the North and bringing US troops to China's borders is as unacceptable today as it was in 1950. But if the government in Pyongyang collapsed, it is difficult to imagine a South Korean president surviving politically if she or he declined to send troops to pacify the peninsula. Indeed, current US war plans reportedly call for American and South Korean troops to march north to stabilize the country and ultimately reunite the nations.

While these issues have been discussed at some length in "Track II" conversations between former American and Chinese officials, the two governments have not seriously considered options to mitigate the risks posed by competing contingency plans that could pit American and Chinese troops against each other. Analysts have identified a dozen paths to war that begin with the collapse of the North Korean regime. For our purposes, three suffice.

First, if Kim Jong-un were to die without an obvious heir, military factions might vie for power, setting off a civil war and plunging the country into chaos. In the ensuing vacuum, the military commander in control of thousands of artillery pieces along the border with South Korea could blame Seoul for Kim's death and threaten to destroy the city, which is just thirty miles across the border. Fearing the commander will make good on his threat, US aircraft could seek to preemptively destroy the artillery pieces under his control. China, meanwhile, would be worried that a desperate North Korean commander's bombardment of Seoul would provide a pretext for US–South Korean forces to invade and reunify the peninsula under Seoul's control. Unbeknown to Washington, an anxious Beijing determined to restrain North Korea could send its special forces into the area — where they might be killed in the US attack on the artillery. Beijing would see the US attack on its forces as deliberate and retaliate. Unaware that they have killed Chinese troops, US commanders would respond, moving up the escalation ladder.

North Korea's increasingly sophisticated intermediate-range missiles serve as the driver for a second sequence. As North Korea descends into chaos following Kim's death, Americans do their best to destroy weapon systems capable of delivering a nuclear warhead against South Korea, Japan, or the US territory of Guam. The US Joint Special Operations Command has a long-standing mission to secure "loose nukes" and has trained to enter the North to take control of its nuclear weapons facilities before rogue commanders could pirate these weapons to international arms bazaars. But since the sites where these weapons are held are thought to be near China's borders, it is very likely that if and when US troops arrive, they will find Chinese special forces already there. As General Raymond Thomas, the former head of Joint Special Operations Command, has warned, trying to secure North Korea's nuclear weapons would result in a "vertical track meet" between Chinese and US–South Korean forces.[33] Each nation's special operations forces, unaware of the other's presence, could find themselves in a firefight that results in scores of deaths. Despite the fact that this outcome was accidental, each could see the engagement as an intentional ambush by the other to which it felt obliged to retaliate.

Third, fearing instability on its border, China could send large numbers of troops into North Korea to stabilize the area and establish a buffer state between it and America's military ally in South Korea. Under strong pressure from its population to liberate those who have lived under the most brutal regime on earth, the South Korean government could also send troops marching north. Because American troops and aircraft stationed in South Korea are integrated with South Korean troops in operational military plans, American and Chinese troops would then engage each other directly, as they did in 1950. The reader need not be reminded how that turned out.

FROM ECONOMIC CONFLICT TO MILITARY WAR

Could a trade conflict escalate into a hot war that ends with nuclear weapons exploding on the territory of the adversary? Unlikely but not impossible: remember Pearl Harbor.

Imagine an American administration that comes into office determined to reverse the tide that has allowed China's economy to become larger than its own. The new president's economic team presents him an analysis that identifies a clear culprit: Chinese cheating—on trade agreements, currency, intellectual property, industrial subsidies, and artificially cheap exports. To begin leveling the playing field, the president orders his Treasury secretary to label China a "currency manipulator," which requires Washington to initiate talks with China. As negotiations open, the president tweets that the bilateral trade deficit has grown by more than 250 percent since China first joined the WTO in 2001 and stands at more than $345 billion today.[34] At a press conference later that day, he releases a report from his Council of Economic Advisers that finds that over the past fifteen years, aided and abetted by concessions China won when joining the WTO, Beijing has run a $3.86 trillion trade surplus with the US. "It is time not only for change, but for payback," he says, demanding that China pledge to eliminate the surplus within two years. As the talks between Treasury officials break down, the secretary of state reminds his Chinese counterpart that the Trade Act of 1930 allows the president to impose sanctions of up to 50 percent on selected imports from countries that "discriminate" against the US.

China responds to this threat by agreeing to stop intervening in currency markets. But since the Chinese government has been buying renminbi, the withdrawal of its support causes the currency's value to decline sharply, further disadvantaging the sale of American goods in China. At the same time, Chinese customs officials begin delaying selective US food exports at their border, claiming that they failed health inspections—forcing the US to either ship them back home or allow them to rot on the docks. Some US factories in China begin experiencing "spontaneous" slowdowns, stoppages, and protests. Beijing also begins selling some of the more than $1 trillion in US treasuries it holds, causing turbulence in bond markets and a rise in interest rates.

Global markets react as investors begin selling US stocks. Major indexes fall dramatically, and bond market volatility soars. Despite the market turmoil, Washington persists in confronting China on trade, demanding "equal trade without a deficit."

To bolster its case, the White House publishes two reports that the press calls economic bombshells. The first, from the Director of National Intelligence, details China's strategy for dominating the semiconductor industry by a combination of purchases of American and international companies, licensing their technologies, investing in Silicon Valley start-ups, and establishing market relationships with key buyers. In each of these areas, China has found ways around the Committee on Foreign Investment in the United States, a secret multiagency panel that seeks to protect US national security from foreign economic intervention. The second is a Treasury Department report on China's massive cybereconomic theft. Based on US intelligence data, the report assesses the value of the intellectual property stolen at $1.23 trillion. The president demands compensation in full. He announces that until payment is received, he is imposing tariffs on Chinese companies that have been exploiting stolen intellectual property, including telecommunications company Huawei and appliance manufacturer Midea. China retaliates with its own tariffs on equivalent American products.

As they move up this escalation ladder, US financial markets suffer a series of cyber glitches similar to the 2010 "flash crash" when high-frequency traders caused the stock market to lose $1 trillion in a half hour (although it quickly recovered).[35] Unlike that singular incident, such flash crashes happen repeatedly over the course of a week, and though each time the markets bounce back, they do not recover their losses. In investigating the cause, the FBI discovers that malicious software has been inserted in critical financial systems. While the digital signatures point to China, agents cannot dismiss the possibility of a false flag. Investigators conclude that if the malware is activated, the damage will be not just a temporary denial of service, but also the loss of transaction records and financial accounts.

The secretary of the Treasury advises the president that even rumors about the malware could raise questions about the integrity of the entire American financial system and cause panic. For the president, this conjures up memories of 2008, when the US government bailed out the financial industry because it feared that the failure of one major bank could have a knock-on effect that collapsed the entire system.[36]

While the White House is deliberating, foreign hackers activate malware inside the networks of the three largest US banks. The news is devastating: account information for hundreds of thousands of customers is permanently erased. Going online to check their balance, they discover that their account has disappeared — leaving them, in effect, bankrupt. Their stories light up social media and TV broadcasts. Fearing they could be next, millions of Americans attempt to withdraw their life savings from banks and mutual funds. This paralyzes even the financial institutions that have not been attacked. The president and his advisers begin to think in apocalyptic terms, some recalling former Federal Reserve chairman Ben Bernanke's warning in 2008 that unless decisive action is taken immediately, "we may not have an economy on Monday."[37]

To prevent China's cyberwarriors from doing any more damage, the president decides to launch a cyberattack on the source. But despite US Cyber Command's best efforts, the attack is only partially effective, as more financial institutions are hacked. The president's military advisers recommend air strikes to destroy all known locations of China's cyberwar units.

Hoping to avoid a shooting war with Beijing, the president reaches deep into the Pentagon's black bag of secret capabilities. He orders the military to use a heretofore undisclosed drone to attack the Shanghai headquarters of PLA Unit 61398—China's most sophisticated cyber-warriors. Beyond stealthy, the drone uses "adaptive camouflage" that its designers liken to Harry Potter's invisibility cloak, allowing it to blend in to its surroundings.[38] By using this option, the US seeks to create "plausible deniability."

This hope proves misguided. The Chinese have penetrated the US military's computer networks so thoroughly that not only do they know about the invisible drones, they also know they are forward-deployed at Kadena Air Base in Japan. Confident that the US was the source of the attack, Beijing retaliates by launching missile strikes on Kadena, killing scores of US troops (and some of their families) as well as hundreds of civilians in the surrounding communities.

The Japanese public insists that its government—and the government of its US ally—respond to this unprovoked Chinese attack. A trade war has become a shooting war with events spiraling beyond the control of Washington and Beijing.

War between the United States and China is not inevitable, but it is possible. Indeed, as these scenarios illustrate, the underlying stress created by China's disruptive rise creates conditions in which accidental, otherwise inconsequential events could trigger a large-scale conflict. In making choices to push back against bullying, meet long-standing treaty commitments, or demand the respect their nation deserves, leaders on both sides may fall into a trap that they know exists but which they believe they can avoid. The relentless advance of new technologies, from antisatellite and cyberweapons to others whose names remain classified, multiplies effects that will not be fully understood before they are used in a real conflict. On current trajectories, a disastrous war between the United States and China in the decades ahead is not just possible, but much more likely than most of us are willing to allow.

Part Four

———

WHY WAR IS NOT INEVITABLE

9

TWELVE CLUES FOR PEACE

That war is an evil is a proposition so familiar to everyone that it would be tedious to develop it. No one is forced to engage in it by ignorance, or kept out of it by fear. If both should happen to have chosen the wrong moment for acting, advice to make peace would not be unserviceable. This, if we did but see it, is just what we stand most in need of at the present juncture.

—Thucydides, Hermocrates addresses the Sicilians, 424 BCE

Fortunately, escaping Thucydides's Trap is not just a matter of theory. The past five hundred years offer at least four cases in which rising and ruling powers successfully steered their ships of state through treacherous shoals without war.

The first of these cases occurred in the late fifteenth and early sixteenth centuries, when Spain rose to rival and eventually replace Portugal as the world's dominant sea power. The most recent is the rise of Germany to predominance in Europe since the end of the Cold War. The two most instructive cases of these good-news stories come from the twentieth century: the first when the United States deposed the United Kingdom as the leading global power; the second when an ascending Soviet Union threatened America's position as the unipolar power. Together, they offer a rich set of clues for leaders seeking to make the rise of China a fifth case of no war.

SPAIN VS. PORTUGAL

Late fifteenth century

For most of the fifteenth century, Portugal's fleet ruled ocean trade routes, overshadowing its Iberian rival and neighbor, the Spanish kingdom of Castile. Portugal's success reflected its historical development. In 1249, its people became the first Europeans to escape Muslim rule, creating a nation largely along Portugal's modern-day borders. Then, in 1348, the Black Death killed one-third of the country's population, leaving too few able-bodied workers to farm the rocky soil.[1] Enterprising Portuguese turned to the Atlantic and in time became Europe's most skilled and successful fishermen. The country's maritime prowess grew further after 1415, when the Portuguese captured their first overseas territory, near the Strait of Gibraltar. Determined to enrich his country and crown, the great prince Henry the Navigator supported the development of new seafaring technologies, including the fast and nimble caravel, improved rigging for boats, and detailed maps.[2] Pioneering the field of nautical science to great effect, Portugal essentially "launched the movement of European expansion."[3] In 1488, its explorers were the first Europeans to round the Cape of Good Hope in search of trade routes to India and its lucrative spice trade.

During most of the fifteenth century, Portugal had a free hand to establish its predominance because the kingdom of Castile was preoccupied by internal conflicts.[4] But that changed in 1469 with the marriage of the eighteen-year-old Isabella of Castile to the seventeen-year-old Ferdinand of Aragon, merging the two kingdoms into a unified Spain. Together they reclaimed territory from Moorish occupiers, recaptured Granada, and, in 1492—the same year they sponsored the first voyage of a Genoese sailor named Christopher Columbus—expelled the Moors completely from the Iberian Peninsula.

As its internal affairs normalized, Spain's economy began to grow. Revenues to the crown rose thirtyfold between 1474 and 1504.[5] Enriched, a rising Spain was emboldened to seek gold, spices, and new trade relationships across the sea—just as its neighbor Portugal had been doing for nearly a century. Spain's timing was fortuitous. With the death of Henry the Navigator in 1460, Portuguese patronage of innovation declined, as did its strict prohibition on exporting its ship-building and mapmaking expertise. By the 1480s, other nations had begun to exploit these skills and match Portugal's mastery of the Atlantic. When Christopher Columbus approached Henry's successor, King John II, for funds to sail west in search of a new route to India and royalties for lands discovered, King John said no. So Columbus turned to Ferdinand and Isabella, requesting three ships, the titles of Admiral of the Ocean and Viceroy of the lands he might discover, and one-tenth of colonial revenue.[6] The Spanish king and queen agreed.[7]

When Columbus returned triumphant, King John saw he had made a big mistake. Thanks to Columbus's discovery, Spain emerged as a serious rival for overseas empire and sea routes, threatening Portugal's virtual monopoly. Each nation worried about the potential for conflict, especially in new lands, as the leaders of both feared the enormous expenditure of blood and treasure an all-out war between these two military powerhouses would require.[8]

Fortunately for both, Ferdinand and Isabella decided to appeal to a higher authority: the representative of God on earth, Pope Alexander VI. (As it happened, the pope was of Spanish descent and had recently been elected with the support of Spain.) Acting as arbitrator, Alexander VI drew a line from north to south running from pole to pole dividing the Western Hemisphere. Lands west of the boundary would belong to Spain, territory east to Portugal. Judging this arrangement unfairly favorable to Spain, Portugal at first rejected the pope's proposal. Nevertheless, it became the basis for negotiations leading to the Treaty of Tordesillas, which was signed in 1494. (The agreed line cut through modern-day Brazil, and explains why Brazilians speak Portuguese while most of the rest of South America speaks Spanish.) Rulers in both capitals proclaimed it a triumph. Spain legitimized its stake in the venture of exploration; Portugal confirmed its claim to what it believed was the preferred route to India. As historian A. R. Disney notes, Tordesillas "became a basic charter of empire, defining respective spheres of 'conquest' well into the eighteenth century."[9]

The papal role in defining these spheres of influence created incentives to honor the treaty's terms. Each country's rulers were subject to papal authority, up to and including excommunication. Both nations justified their conquests as a mission to convert the heathen to Christianity. Indeed, when new colonial aspirants in England, France, and the Netherlands emerged over subsequent decades, Spain and Portugal embraced the Vatican-approved framework as guardians of the status quo even more tightly. Thus there were no significant hostilities between the two countries for almost a century.

Clue 1: Higher authorities can help resolve rivalry without war.
Ever since the Dutch legal scholar Hugo Grotius coined the idea of a single, global society of nation-states in the seventeenth century, theorists have dreamed of a world governed by international law. In the aftermath of World War II, statesmen wrestled with this aspiration in creating the United Nations. Its charter established a framework of international law and organizations overseen by a Security Council to which members are, in theory, subordinate. Tellingly, however, the five great powers of the time — the United States, the Soviet Union, China, Britain, and France — each insisted on retaining a unilateral veto power over decisions by the council.

The UN Charter calls on each member state to accept constraints on its behavior, including its use of military force against other members. The interpretation of these constraints, however, is left to the members. Article 51 of the charter gives each state the "right of self-defense." The US stretched this right to new limits in 2003 when it argued that its attack on Iraq was justified by "preemptive self-defense," claiming that Saddam Hussein had weapons of mass destruction and posed an "imminent threat." More recently, President Obama pushed even further in unilaterally ordering attacks on groups the US designated as "terrorists" in seven countries.[10]

In the narrative offered by proponents of international law, the past seven decades have seen a steady advance in the acceptance of the international "rules-based system." Realists disagree, especially when it comes to the use of military force. There, they note that strong states have repeatedly flouted that system when they judge it in their national interest to do so. In 2016, for example, the US led the campaign to condemn China's wholesale rejection of the Permanent Court of Arbitration's finding that struck down Beijing's claims to the South China Sea. Some observers saw this as hypocrisy, recalling that Washington had similarly rejected the International Court of Justice's judgment against it when the CIA mined harbors in Nicaragua in the 1980s in an effort to overthrow that nation's Sandinista government.[11] Clearly, at this point, subordination to international authorities has substantial limits. Nevertheless, to the extent that states can be persuaded to defer to the constraints and decisions of supranational authorities or legal frameworks, as the rulers of Spain and Portugal did in the fifteenth century, these factors can play significant roles in managing conflicts that would otherwise end in war.

GERMANY VS. BRITAIN AND FRANCE

1990s–present

Henry Kissinger has pointed to an ironic twist of fate: "Seventy years after having defeated German claims to dominating Europe, the victors are now pleading, largely for economic reasons, with Germany to lead Europe."[12] In 1989, after the Berlin Wall's collapse, British prime minister Margaret Thatcher urged President George H. W. Bush to block the rush to reunification, warning that "the Germans will get in peace what Hitler could not get in war."[13] In fact, although the actions of a more powerful, united Germany have sometimes caused resentment, Germany's ascent to predominance in Europe has occurred not just without war, but also in a context in which military conflict with its European neighbors has become virtually inconceivable. The reasons for these developments are suggestive.

World War II ended with Soviet troops occupying the eastern part of Germany, while US-led troops held the west. This division constituted for many European strategists the solution to the "German problem" that had been at the root of two twentieth-century world wars. When the Iron Curtain "descended across the Continent," as Churchill put it, the competition between the Soviet Union and the "Free World" became Europe's primary fault line. In response, the US organized the North Atlantic Treaty Organization. In the oft-repeated quip of NATO's first secretary general, its mission was "to keep the Soviets out, the Americans in, and the Germans down."[14]

Determined not to repeat the patterns of international politics that had made Europe a killing field for so much of the twentieth century, wise European leaders like Jean Monnet and Robert Schuman fostered thick economic interdependence among the nations of Europe, and especially between France and Germany. This trade network soon grew into the European Common Market in which goods traded freely without tariffs. This became the first building block in a larger and more ambitious European project aimed at subordinating elements of national sovereignty to supranational European institutions. In the treaty establishing the European Coal and Steel Community, one of the key precursors to the EU, Monnet described an institution that would "lay the first concrete foundations of the European Federation which is indispensable for the maintenance of peace."[15] Some of the visionary statesmen who orchestrated this effort even imagined a united Europe analogous to the United States. Yet everyone, including the Germans themselves, seemed to agree that Germany would remain a junior partner. Having internalized the Holocaust and other crimes against humanity committed by the Nazi regime, Germans distrusted themselves, and readily accepted a subordinate role in European institutions.

But in the final chapter of the Cold War, when the Berlin Wall crumbled, the prospect of Germany's reunification arose. West Germany's European partners in particular were dead set against it. Prime Minister Thatcher and President François Mitterrand went repeatedly to President George H. W. Bush urging him to prevent unification. As the

French ambassador to Germany argued publicly, unification "would give birth to a Europe dominated by Germany, which no one in the East or the West wants."[16] Nonetheless, President Bush and his national security team moved ahead. They insisted, however, that a unified Germany remain inside NATO—not leaving it disarmed or neutral, as the Soviet leader Mikhail Gorbachev sought. For Bush, a unified Germany leading European institutions would become a centerpiece in his vision of a "Europe whole and free."[17]

As Thatcher and Mitterrand foresaw, Germany's growing economic strength increasingly gave it the dominant political voice on the Continent. In 1989, German GDP was roughly equal to that of Britain and France; today, it is 40 percent larger.[18] When the EC (European Community) became the EU (European Union) and most of its members surrendered their national currencies to create a common euro, the European Central Bank was naturally located in Germany. Nonetheless, even as Germany's prominence increased, it held fast to a strategy of integration with its neighbors. As the noted German scholar Helga Haftendorn has argued, the EU allowed German power to be channeled toward a greater good, and created "a 'Europeanized Germany' rather than a 'German Europe.'"[19]

As of this writing, the European experiment remains uncertain. When the global financial crisis stressed the contradictions baked into the euro (namely, a common monetary policy without common fiscal authority) and forced Germans to bail out Greece and others, many predicted the end of the common European currency. Yet the euro remains alive. As Europe has been flooded by refugees from countries convulsed by post–Arab Spring chaos, Euro-skeptics have again brought out their placards proclaiming "the end is near." The June 2016 "Brexit" vote for the UK to leave the EU was for many the final sign of the post–Cold War order's imminent collapse. But as the architects of the European project understood, while crises that threaten the survival of the union are inevitable, collapse is not. Indeed, from their perspective, crises present opportunities to strengthen integration in ways that political resistance would otherwise make impossible.

Though an economic powerhouse and increasingly active political leader, Germany has remained a military eunuch. In 1945, it was forcibly disarmed and demilitarized as part of denazification. The US security guarantee, and in particular the US "nuclear umbrella" that remained after reunification, reassured Germany's neighbors by removing any reason for Germany to increase its military. Over time, Germany's leaders have rationalized this situation by embracing a postmodern conception of international order that sees security as essentially a natural state of affairs. Along with most of its European counterparts, Germany's military today is thus more symbolic and ceremonial than operational. In that sense, a militarily neutered Germany is not a "normal" state in international politics.

Clue 2: States can be embedded in larger economic, political, and security institutions that constrain historically "normal" behaviors. Germany is the poster child of an economic and political giant that remains a military dwarf. It is economically integrated with its neighbors and protected by an American security overlord with a nuclear umbrella. If a combination of economic stress, immigrants, and a revival of populist nationalism were to unravel the EU, would an increasingly powerful Germany still pose no threat to its neighbors? If the US were to weaken or even withdraw NATO's security blanket, would we see a renationalization of the military forces of Europe, including in Germany? And if that were to occur, could Thucydidean dynamics make war between Germany and some of its neighbors again thinkable? Or, alternatively, have the cultural changes in Germany become so deeply internalized that it is no longer imaginable that Germans recover their martial traditions?[20]

UNITED STATES VS. BRITAIN
Early twentieth century

Teddy Roosevelt's success in guiding the US to displace Britain as dominant in the Western Hemisphere reflected changes in the underlying correlates of power. In the last three decades of the nineteenth century, the United States had risen from the ashes of its civil war to become an economic colossus. In 1850, the populations of Britain and America were roughly equal. By 1900, there were twice as many Americans as Britons.[21] The American economy surpassed Britain's in 1870, and grew to twice its size by 1914.[22] In 1880, Britain had accounted for 23 percent of global manufacturing output. By 1914, its market share had fallen to 13 percent as America's rose to 32 percent.[23]

Anglo-American relations remained tense after their acrimonious separation. In the War of 1812, the British burned the White House while Americans assaulted British Canada. During the Civil War, Britain had seriously considered supporting the Confederacy, a fact that many Americans (including TR) had not forgotten.[24] As American power grew, so did its demand for respect and influence in its domain. In 1895, when a territorial dispute arose between Venezuela and British Guiana, Secretary of State Richard Olney demanded that Britain accept arbitration under the Monroe Doctrine, arguing that "the United States is practically sovereign on this continent."[25] London rejected Washington's demands, with British colonial secretary Joseph Chamberlain insisting that "Great Britain is an American Power with a territorial area greater than the United States themselves."[26] But when President Grover Cleveland responded with a thinly veiled threat of war, the British agreed to arbitration.[27]

Not long after Cleveland's message, British prime minister Lord Salisbury advised his finance minister that war with the US "in the not distant future has become something more than a possibility." He instructed the Admiralty to review its budgets accordingly, warning that the US was a more likely adversary than the Franco-Russian alliance.[28] While the US Navy was still small compared to the Royal Navy, it was growing, especially after the Spanish-American War and Teddy Roosevelt's ascendance to the presidency. The First Lord of the Admiralty, the Earl of Selborne, described the situation starkly: "If the Americans choose to pay for what they can easily afford, they can gradually build up a navy, fully as large and then larger than ours."[29]

Facing multiple rising challengers and bogged down in a trouble-some South African war, Britain could no longer confront all threats head-on. Although the US was the most powerful of its rising rivals, Germany and Russia posed a more proximate danger. Moreover, unlike Europe — where Britain could serve as a balancer among competing powers — the Western Hemisphere had no competitors to the US that London could enlist as British allies. Britain's Canadian dominion, for its part, had no capability to defend itself.[30]

These hard truths shaped British leaders' mindset of accommodation aimed at avoiding military conflict with the US at virtually any cost. The Admiralty was at this time the cockpit of British national secu-rity policy. In 1904, its highest-ranking naval officer, First Sea Lord Jacky Fisher, bluntly told his civilian superiors that Britain should "use all possible means to avoid such a war," because, he warned, "under no conceivable circumstances could we escape an overwhelming and humiliating defeat by the United States." Further, he spelled out the humiliating implication: "leaving Canada to her fate no matter what the cause of quarrel or merits of the case."[31] As Selborne had summa-rized: "I would never quarrel with the United States if I could pos-sibly avoid it."[32] Reflecting that judgment, Britain exempted the US from the canonical Two-Power Standard, which committed the UK to maintaining a number of battleships equal to those of the next two largest competitors combined.[33]

Moreover, aware that it could not contest American dominance in the Western Hemisphere without reducing naval forces protecting more important areas (including the homeland itself), the British Ad-miralty ignored repeated army requests for operational plans to defend Canada in the case of war with America. Instead it simply recom-mended that good Anglo-American relations be maintained.[34] Britain's recognition of this uncomfortable reality drove successive concessions over disputes in the Western Hemisphere. As a result, historian Anne Orde concluded, "by the end of 1903 . . . Britain had acquiesced in American supremacy in the Western Hemisphere from Venezuela to Alaska."[35] In part, British willingness to yield to American demands reflected the belief that both states shared not just an ethnic and linguistic heritage, but also a common political culture and model of governance. But the principal driver was cold realism.[36]

Facing more ominous threats closer to home, Britain's choices were constrained. Had Russia and then Germany not appeared such potent threats in this period, would Britain have played a tougher hand? That is unclear. But what is clear is that at this point the relative balance of power had shifted so far that British officials could not see war as a viable means to constrain America's rise. As Prime Minister Lord Salisbury wistfully reflected in 1902: "It is very sad, but I am afraid America is bound to forge ahead and nothing can restore the equality between us. If we had interfered in the Confederate Wars it was then possible for us to reduce the power of the United States to manageable proportions. But *two* such chances are not given to a nation in the course of its career."[37]

In comparing British responses to two rising powers, the Germans to the east and the Americans to the west, the greatest twentieth-century international historian, Ernest May, identified "Britain's choice of forbearance toward the United States" as the "key to what happened," along with "Germany's choice to put display of independence and of military and naval power ahead of all else." While President Roosevelt could be bellicose over minor disputes, he was, in May's words, "careful to avoid the Kaiser's mistake of threatening Britain's actual security." Britain could convince itself that the US Navy might serve British interests in the Western Hemisphere or East Asia. This judgment was encouraged by the vast Atlantic Ocean separating the two countries, which diminished America's direct security threat to Britain. Germany was much closer, and its navy was clearly intended to deter or fight Britain. Facing a challenging strategic horizon, Britain chose, as May pointed out, "to make a virtue of necessity and to yield to the Americans in every dispute with as much good grace as was permitted." By 1906, when a new Liberal government came to power, Foreign Secretary Edward Grey announced that maintaining good relations with the US had become Britain's "cardinal policy."[38]

British leaders' skill in finding ways to satisfy even unreasonable American demands without sacrificing vital British national interests is a textbook example of well-executed diplomacy. By laying the foundation for what historians have called the Great Rapprochement, Britain helped to heal long-standing hostility between the two nations to the point that when war came in 1914, it could count on the US as an essential source of materiel and finance for its war effort. After German submarines began attacking American ships, Washington joined the war alongside London. Had Britain been unable to obtain American loans and supplies, and later American military partnership, Germany might well have triumphed in World War I. In negotiating the peace at Versailles, the US and Britain stood shoulder to shoulder. And when after the war, the United States established the Washington Naval Treaty setting national limits on the number of capital warships each nation would be allowed, Britain was rewarded with a position of parity with the US, even though its postwar debts meant it could not compete with an American naval buildup.[39] When less than a generation later the world was again consumed by war, the two nations fought as intimate allies and worked together after World War II to shape the peace, cementing what Washington and London still call the "special relationship."

Clue 3: Wily statesmen make a virtue of necessity—and distinguish needs and wants. Brute facts are hard to ignore. As the US surpassed Britain in all important dimensions, Americans' determination to have their way became evident. From the disputes in Venezuela to the contest with Canada over the fat tail of Alaska, Britain could have chosen or chanced war. But it knew that the cost of war would be large and the likelihood of victory small. It also faced other, more serious strategic threats closer to home. So Britain wisely made the best of its lot, managing to accommodate American demands without sacrificing its own vital interests. And it did so in ways that impressed upon America's governing class the interests the

US and UK shared, while minimizing interests that divided them—thus paving the way for greater cooperation (and greater benefits for London) in the future. At a time when its global empire was so firmly linked to its sense of self, Britain could have easily—but mistakenly—judged its security stake in the Americas to be essential. But it was not. Far from diminishing its global stature or jeopardizing its security posture, Britain's shift of its fleet from the Western Hemisphere proved a timely rebalancing of its own forces before World War I and prolonged its influence in international affairs.

Clue 4: Timing is crucial. Windows of opportunity open, often unexpectedly, only to close without warning. Prime Minister Lord Salisbury's candid observation captures this poignantly. If British leaders had concluded in 1861 that a rising US continental hegemon would pose an intolerable threat to core British interests, then the smart option might have been to intervene on behalf of the Confederacy in the American Civil War and "reduce" US power to "manageable proportions." Had Britain done so, it is possible that at the beginning of the twentieth century there would have been two weaker, likely rival, and perhaps even warring nations on the territories of the United States. Under those conditions, with command of the sea and a secure position in Canada, Britain would likely have found two Americas far less demanding in territorial disputes in Venezuela, Alaska, and elsewhere. But in the history of nations, as in the life of individuals, opportunities missed are opportunities forgone.

Preventive intervention presents a classic conundrum for individuals that becomes exponentially more vexing in the case of democratic nations. When the cost of intervention is lowest and the effectiveness of action highest, the need to act is ambiguous and uncertain. By the time the necessity for action is obvious to all the players whose support or acquiescence is required, the cost of effective intervention has risen, sometimes to levels that make it prohibitive. For governments, especially democratic governments in which many parties have to agree before action can be taken, this conundrum tilts the scales markedly toward procrastination rather than prevention —whether in dealing with rising rivals or recurring humanitarian catastrophes.

Clue 5: Cultural commonalities can help prevent conflict. Because Britain and the US shared a language and political culture, influential Britons could console themselves with the thought that although Britain was by most measures no longer number one, its values would remain dominant. They could dismiss those who argued that Britain faced a choice between conflict with the US and the elimination of their way of life and historic mission. Quite the opposite: many Englishmen embraced the thought that the "English-speaking peoples" would continue to rule the world. As future prime minister Harold Macmillan put it during World War II, "These Americans represent the new Roman Empire and we Britons, like the Greeks of old, must teach them how to make it go."[40]

SOVIET UNION VS. UNITED STATES
1940s–1980s

The idea that the Soviet Union seriously challenged American global leadership in the post–World War II period is hard for most Americans today to conceive. Since the collapse of the USSR in 1991, Americans have seen Russia as a declining power: weak, confused, and more recently, under Vladimir Putin, blinded by anger. Communism as an ideology that people could voluntarily embrace has been consigned to the dustbin of history. Command-and-control economics and politics have repeatedly shown that they do not work. Students at Harvard are thus confounded when I make them read a chapter from the most popular economics textbook of the mid-twentieth century, Paul Samuelson's *Economics: An Introductory Analysis,* published in 1964. It foresaw Soviet GNP overtaking that of the US by the mid-1980s.[41]

The twentieth century was defined by a cascade of world wars: the

First, the Second, and the specter of a Third that could well have been the last. In that final contest, the adversaries believed the stakes were so high that each was prepared to risk the death of hundreds of millions of its own citizens to defeat the other. After a struggle of four decades, in 1989, the Berlin Wall came tumbling down; in 1990, the Warsaw Pact collapsed; and on Christmas Day 1991, the Evil Empire imploded. The Cold War thus ended with a whimper rather than the final bang leaders on both sides rightly feared. This stands as a rare US victory in the years since World War II. How did the Cold War go so right when so many of America's hot wars since 1945 have gone so wrong? What insights can statesmen glean from that ordeal for today?

The term "cold war" was coined by none other than George Orwell —of *1984* fame. After the deadliest war in history, the US and Soviet Union both emerged exhausted. That conflict had forced them to fight as allies, since victory over the Nazis necessitated cooperation. (As Churchill quipped, if Hitler had invaded hell, he "would make at least a favorable reference to the devil in the House of Commons."[42]) As it became clear that Soviet armies would remain in Eastern European countries they had liberated from the Nazis, American policymakers struggled to design a strategy for a postwar world in which its onetime ally was emerging as its greatest foe.

The starting point for this strategy was a Manichaean conviction about the Soviet Union. These statesmen saw it as an adversary as "incompatible with democracy as Nazism or fascism," to quote America's first secretary of defense, James Forrestal.[43] In his historic Long Telegram from Moscow just nine months after V-E Day, George Kennan (then America's chargé d'affaires in Moscow) warned that expansionist Soviet communism was a "political force committed fanatically to the belief that with the US there could be no permanent modus vivendi." At its core, Kennan said, Soviet Communists believed it was necessary that "our society be disrupted, our traditional way of life destroyed, the international authority of our state be broken, if Soviet power is to be secure."[44] Confronting such an adversary, America could survive only by destroying the USSR, or transforming it.

The rush of Soviet aggression in the immediate postwar period validated this analysis for American policymakers. A Soviet-sponsored coup in Czechoslovakia in 1948, the victory of Chinese Communists in 1949, and Soviet-supported North Korea's invasion of South Korea in 1950 all presented the specter of communism on the march. In 1949, the Soviets tested their first atomic bomb, denying the US monopoly control of the "absolute weapon."[45] And although the Soviet economy was devastated during World War II, Russian society recovered much faster than it did following World War I.[46] In the first decade after the Second World War, the Soviet economy more than doubled, increasing by half again in the next decade.[47] Much of this new wealth was devoted to military spending. As Robert Gates, a senior US intelligence official during the Cold War who would later serve as secretary of defense, notes: "The USSR proceeded to undertake the largest military buildup in history over a twenty-five-year period, with profound consequences for the international balance of power."[48] As a result, in 1956 when Khrushchev famously claimed, "History is on our side, we will bury you," no one laughed.

Before the nuclear age, such a threat would have required all-out war—a hot war as intense as the one the US, Britain, and their allies had just fought against Hitler's Germany. In that war, the goal could be nothing less than the enemy's unconditional surrender. But while the US arguably had an opportunity to attack and defeat the Soviet Union immediately after World War II—and seriously considered the option—it declined to do so.[49] After the Soviets tested their first atomic bomb, American strategists began wrestling with the thought that in the contest with the Soviet Union, war as they knew it might soon be obsolete.[50]

In the greatest leap of strategic imagination in the history of American diplomacy, over a four-year period from Kennan's Long Telegram and Secretary of State George Marshall's commencement speech at Harvard (in which he pointed to the Marshall Plan) to Paul Nitze's NSC-68 (a top-secret memo outlining the military foundations for this competition), American leaders we now refer to as the "wise men" developed a comprehensive strategy for a form of combat never previously seen.[51] Clausewitz taught us to understand war as the extension of international politics by other means.[52] After foreign policy, diplomacy, and negotiation have done all they can to secure a nation's interest, armies, navies, and air forces can continue that effort with other instruments of influence. But what if direct engagement of armies risked national suicide? Under such conditions, alternatives had to be explored. Thus, they invented "cold war" as the conduct of war by every means short of bombs and bullets used by the principal combatants directly against each other. The US and Soviet Union made systemic, sustained assaults against each other along every azimuth except one: direct military attacks. This included economic warfare, information warfare, covert actions, and even proxy wars in Korea (where Soviet pilots flew covert missions against US forces), Vietnam (where Soviet soldiers manned air defenses that shot down dozens of American aircraft), Angola, and Afghanistan (where CIA-backed mujahideen covertly fought Soviet troops).

In conducting this new form of war, both sides recognized that "cold" conflict could easily turn "hot." To guard against that risk, they accepted—for the time being—many unacceptable facts on the ground. These included Soviet domination of the captive nations of Eastern Europe and the Communist regimes in China, Cuba, and North Korea. In addition, the rivals wove an intricate web of mutual constraints around the competition—constraints that President John F. Kennedy called "the precarious rules of the status quo."[53] To reduce the risk of surprise nuclear attacks, for instance, they negotiated arms-control treaties that provided greater transparency and instilled greater confidence in each party that the other was not about to launch a first strike. To avoid accidental collisions of aircraft or ships, they negotiated precise rules of the road for air and sea. Over time, both competitors tacitly agreed to each other's three no's: no use of nuclear weapons, no direct overt killing of each other's armed forces, and no military intervention in each other's recognized sphere of influence.[54]

For twenty-first-century American students, perhaps the biggest

surprise about the Cold War is the fact that the US actually had a coherent, bipartisan grand strategy that it sustained for four decades.
Most people can remember "containment." In reality, the US had a
complex Cold War strategy that was built on three big ideas. The first
identified the Soviet Union as an existential threat to America's core
interests—literally a threat to the nation's existence. Under the flag
of Marxist-Leninist ideology, Soviet forces threatened to engulf key
countries in Europe and Asia, much as the forces of Islam had spread
like wildfire in the seventh century. The Soviet Union was not only
consolidating an outer empire of occupied countries in Eastern Europe,
but also threatening a combination of internal subversion and external
intimidation in US-allied nations including Greece, France, and Italy.
As NSC-68 stated: "The Soviet Union, unlike previous aspirants to
hegemony, is animated by a new fanatic faith, antithetical to our own,
and seeks to impose its absolute authority over the rest of the world."
Absent a vigorous response, American strategists believed that societies
demoralized by a devastating war and exhausted economically could
soon fall victim to Communist expansion.

The second pillar of US Cold War strategy answered the fundamental question about the purpose of American foreign policy. As NSC-68
boldly put it in one line, the purpose was "to preserve the US as a free
nation with our fundamental institutions and values intact." This mantra deserves a pause for reflection. In a world in which "American leadership" has been seen by many as a requirement for the US to serve as a
global police force responsible for defending those unable or unwilling
to defend themselves, the Cold Warriors' unambiguous commitment
to "America first" will strike many internationalists as anachronistic, or
even offensive. But these statesmen made no apology: the survival and
success of the United States as a free nation was not only what Americans should and did care about most. It was the essential prerequisite for
American power achieving any larger objective in the world.

A third big idea built upon the second. It called for an unprecedented departure from America's historic aversion to entangling alliances. While the US had the option of withdrawing to Fortress Amer-

ica, as it had done after World War I and in prior centuries, the Cold Warriors judged that this path was no longer viable in an increasingly interconnected world. America's survival and well-being required building nothing less than a new international order. But in contrast to the romanticism of post–World War I leaders like Woodrow Wilson, who imagined that they had concluded "the war to end all wars," Cold War strategists recognized that surviving the Soviet threat would be a long-term project — very long-term.

The foundation of this undertaking would be the economic and strategic centers of gravity: Europe and Japan. In a surge of initiative, these pragmatic visionaries created the Marshall Plan (to rebuild Europe); the International Monetary Fund, the World Bank, and the General Agreement on Tariffs and Trade (to provide basic global economic order); the North Atlantic Treaty Organization and the US-Japan alliance (to ensure that Europe and Japan were deeply integrated into the campaign against the Soviet Union); and the United Nations — all as building blocks of a global order they sought to construct, floor by floor, over decades. This order aimed to defeat the Soviet adversary and thereby advance the cause of peace, prosperity, and freedom for Americans first, their allies second, and other nations thereafter.

In confronting the Soviet Union, this strategy sought simultaneously to sustain three lines of effort: to *contain* Soviet expansion, to *deter* the Soviets from acting against vital American interests, and to *undermine* both the idea and the practice of communism. Containment prevented the USSR from acquiring additional capabilities. Even more importantly, it aimed to defeat the Marxist narrative of a historically inevitable advance. Soviet expansion could be stopped not by fighting Soviet troops but rather by deterrence — credibly threatening to retaliate against Soviet aggression in ways that would impose unacceptable costs.

Undermining the Soviet adversary began with the demonstration that US-led free market democracies trumped Soviet command-and-control economics and authoritarian politics in delivering what citizens wanted. But it also sought to magnify contradictions

within Soviet strategy by intervening in nations' domestic affairs to encourage nationalism in Soviet satellites like Poland or allies like China
—confident that national identities would prove more durable than
dreams to create a "new socialist man." Furthermore, the US strategy
advanced the values of freedom and human rights by persuading Soviet
leaders to make written commitments to common ideals in the UN
Declaration on Human Rights and the Helsinki Accords, confident
that these were the rightful heritage of mankind. And to supplement
these efforts, it sustained a campaign of overt and covert actions inside
the Soviet Union and its satellites to undermine Communist ideology
and governments.[55]

**Clue 6: There is nothing new under the sun—except nuclear
weapons.** Some observers claim the twenty-first century is so different from the past that lessons from previous experience are no longer
relevant. To be sure, it is difficult to find precedents for current levels
of economic integration, globalization, and ubiquitous worldwide
communication, or global threats from climate disruption to violent
Islamic extremism. But as my colleagues Carmen Reinhart and Kenneth Rogoff remind us in their analysis of 350 financial crises over
the past eight centuries, many previous generations have imagined
that *This Time Is Different*.[56] Reinhart and Rogoff side with Thucydides in reasoning that, as long as men are men, we can anticipate recurring patterns in human affairs. After all, one of the best-selling
books in Europe in the decade before World War I was Norman Angell's *The Great Illusion*. It persuaded millions of readers, including
many in high places like Viscount Esher (who was in charge of rebuilding the British Army after its poor showing in the Boer War
that ended in 1902), that economic interdependence had made war
an illusion: "futile" because "the war-like do not inherit the earth."[57]

Nonetheless, in one decisive respect, the late twentieth and early
twenty-first centuries are different from anything that preceded
them: *nuclear weapons have no precedent*. Einstein observed after the
US dropped atomic bombs on Hiroshima and Nagasaki that nuclear

weapons have "changed everything except our way of thinking." Yet over time the thinking of those who have shouldered responsibility for nuclear weapons has been changing. Statesmen know that today's arsenals include single nuclear bombs with more explosive power than all of the bombs that have been dropped in all the wars in history. They know that a full-scale nuclear Armageddon could actually extinguish life on earth. Thus nuclear weapons have what students of international relations call a "crystal ball effect."[58] Any leader contemplating a nuclear attack on a state with a nuclear arsenal capable of retaliation must confront the specter of killing tens or even hundreds of millions of his own people. Understandably and repeatedly, this has led them to think again.[59]

Clue 7: MAD really does make all-out war madness. After exploding its first bomb in 1949, the Soviet Union rapidly developed a nuclear arsenal so substantial and sophisticated that it created what nuclear strategists recognized as mutual assured destruction: MAD. This described a condition in which neither the US nor the USSR could be sure of destroying its opponent's arsenal with a nuclear first strike before the enemy could launch a fatal nuclear response. Under such conditions, one state's decision to kill another is simultaneously a choice to commit national suicide.

Technology, in effect, made the US and USSR (and now Russia) inseparable Siamese twins. While each still had a head and brain and will to act, their backbones have been fused to become one. In their united breast beats a single heart. On the day that heart stops beating, both unquestionably die. As awkward and uncomfortable as this metaphor is, it captures the defining fact about the US relationship with the Soviet Union in the Cold War. And it remains the defining truth many twenty-first-century Americans imagine somehow vanished when the Cold War ended. Both the US and Russia retain superpower nuclear arsenals. Thus, however evil, however demonic, however dangerous, however deserving to be strangled Russia is, the US must struggle to find some way to live with it — or face dying together. In Ronald Reagan's oft-quoted one-liner: "A nuclear war cannot be won and must therefore never be fought."[60]

Today, China has also developed a nuclear arsenal so robust that it creates a twenty-first-century version of MAD with the United States. The US recognizes this reality in its deployments of ballistic missile defenses, which exclude Russia and China from the threat matrix they are required to meet (since under current conditions, it is not feasible to mount a credible defense against them).[61] Thus in a second case, as Churchill noted about the Soviet Union, a "sublime irony" has made "safety the sturdy child of terror and survival the twin brother of annihilation."[62]

Clue 8: Hot war between nuclear superpowers is thus no longer a justifiable option. The constraints imposed by MAD on the contest between the Soviet Union and the United States are relevant for American strategists thinking about China today. From the 1950s through the 1980s, the rise of the Soviet Union to superpower status created what came to be recognized as a "bipolar world." Both nations believed that their survival required that they bury or convert the other. But if President Ronald Reagan was right, this had to be achieved without war.

The central implication for US strategy toward China from the US-Soviet competition is therefore as uncomfortable to accept as it is impossible to deny: once two states have invulnerable nuclear arsenals, hot war is no longer a justifiable option. Both nations must integrate this brute fact in their foreign policies. To repeat: we are inseparable Siamese twins. This means both must compromise in ways they would otherwise find intolerable and restrain themselves and their allies from taking actions that could escalate to all-out war.

The Cold War seared this truth into the psyche and operations of the American national security community as it confronted the Soviet Union. But today, many policymakers dismiss this as "ancient history." Nobody in the current generation of American leaders participated in that history. Few have experienced it vicariously. And while China has been slow in building a superpower nuclear arsenal and, unlike Putin's Russia in recent years, has never engaged in nuclear saber rattling, some Chinese military officers still quote Mao's audacious claim that even after losing 300 million citizens in a nuclear exchange, China would still survive.[63]

It will take repeated, candid conversations between US and Chinese political leaders—as well as discussions among military officers, enlivened by war games in which both parties threaten or even use nuclear weapons—to help leaders on both sides internalize the unnatural truth that war is no longer an acceptable option. Helping leaders across both societies realize the implications of this big idea poses a still larger challenge.

Clue 9: Leaders of nuclear superpowers must nonetheless be prepared to risk a war they cannot win. The "nuclear paradox" is inescapable. In a competition constrained by MAD, neither nation can win a nuclear war—but this is not the end of the matter. Paradoxically, each must demonstrate a willingness to risk losing such a war—or find itself nudged off the road. Think again about the game of chicken discussed in chapter 8. Consider each clause of the paradox. On the one hand, if war occurs, both nations lose. There is no value for which rational leaders could reasonably choose the deaths of hundreds of millions of their own citizens. In that sense, in the Cuban Missile Crisis President Kennedy and Chairman Khrushchev were partners in a struggle to prevent mutual disaster. But this is the condition for both nations, and the leaders of both nations know it. Thus, on the other hand, if either nation is unwilling to risk waging (losing) a nuclear war, its opponent can win any objective by creating conditions that force the more responsible power to choose between yielding and risking escalation to war. In order to preserve vital interests and values, therefore, leaders must be willing to choose paths that risk destruction.

An analogous, but fortunately less deadly, dynamic can be seen in the economic and cyber-competition between the US and China.

During the 2012 presidential campaign, Republican candidate Mitt Romney announced, "On day one of my presidency I will designate China a currency manipulator and take appropriate counteraction."[64] The political and economic establishment rejected his threat as reckless rhetoric that risked a catastrophic trade war. The establishment likewise rejected similar threats by President Donald Trump during the 2016 presidential campaign. But if there are no circumstances in which Washington is willing to risk a trade confrontation with China, why would Chinese leaders stop "playing the US like a fiddle and smiling all the way to the bank" (to use Romney's mixed metaphor)[65] or "raping our country" (as Trump put it)[66] by undervaluing their currency, subsidizing domestic producers, protecting their own market, and stealing intellectual property? Just as the US must be willing to risk economic warfare with China in order to incentivize constraints that preserve its economic interests, so too must Washington keep nuclear warfare in its toolkit in order to credibly deter real and potential adversaries such as China.

From the collection of cases, three further lessons emerge:

Clue 10: Thick economic interdependence raises the cost—and thus lowers the likelihood—of war. In the decades before World War I, the UK and German economies became so thickly interwoven that one party could not impose economic pain on the other without harming itself. Many hoped that this entangling web of trade and investments would prevent war. They were wrong. But when war did break out, the economic consequences for Berlin and London were extraordinary.

Similarly, current US-Chinese economic relations are so interdependent that they create an analogue of MAD that has been labeled MAED: mutual assured economic destruction.[67] The United States is the largest market for Chinese exports, and China is America's largest creditor. If war prevented the US from buying Chinese goods, and China from buying American dollars, the economic and social impact on each would almost certainly outweigh any benefits that war could achieve. Recognizing that Angell made a similar argument before World War I, proponents of MAED have offered two further considerations. Some argue that Angell was right. The costs of war to all parties in World War I did far exceed the benefits the victors reaped. If given the chance to repeat their choices, none would. Since that is now clear, the next time statesmen will be smarter. Others emphasize differences between the earlier case and US-Chinese economic relations today. Levels of trade and investment are similar to those prior to World War I. But supply chains connecting the indispensable producer to the irreplaceable consumer have become so integrated that virtually everything sold in the US, from iPhones to Boeing aircraft, is made with components from China.

Furthermore, the Chinese government has made a "cosmic bet" on an open global marketplace to which it can sell its products and on daily arrivals of tankers delivering oil to power its factories, cars, and planes. All are essential for sustaining the extraordinary rate of economic growth on which the Communist Party's claim to political legitimacy—indeed, its "mandate of heaven"—depends. Both are vulnerable to interruption by the United States. America is not only the major market for Chinese products. Two-thirds of China's oil imports travel across oceans where the US Navy is the guardian and ultimate arbiter—a position it will retain long into the future. War between the US and China, therefore, would certainly mean the end of both economies as we now know them. Even those who find MAED an exaggeration would agree that thickening economic entanglement is creating within both societies influential actors who have big stakes in a productive relationship, which encourages them to become lobbies for peace.

Clue 11: Alliances can be a fatal attraction. From Sparta's reaction to Athens, to Britain's response to Germany, the examples in the Thucydides's Trap Case File show how the dynamic of rise challenging rule can lead parties to seek allies as a counterbalance. Over the past decade, Chinese leaders have been surprised by the virulence of the responses to their surge of assertiveness. Japan, South Korea, Vietnam, and even India have not only become more solicitous of the US, but also more cooperative with each other. Historically, such coalitions have sought to create a balance of power to maintain regional peace and security. But such alliances also create risks —since alliance ties run in both directions. Nowhere is this more vividly displayed than in the decades leading to World War I. As described in chapter 4, in attempting to prevent bloodshed, European statesmen constructed a "doomsday machine" that allowed an otherwise inconsequential assassination to trigger a general war.

The historical record also instructs us that not all treaties are created equal. Defensive alliances are conditional, such as Athens's promise to come to Corcyra's defense if it were the victim of an unprovoked attack, or the US commitment to Taiwan, which is contingent on China being the aggressor. At the other end of the spectrum, the "blank check" the kaiser gave the Austrian emperor emboldened his reckless risk-taking that triggered war in 1914. While the US commitment in Article 5 of the US-Japan mutual defense treaty is not equivalent to the kaiser's guarantee to Austria, one can stump most American diplomats by asking them to explain why not. Given the fact that China's growing power is creating greater demand for US protection in the region, Washington policymakers must carefully review what America's agreements with Asian allies truly entail.

Clue 12. Domestic performance is decisive. What nations do *inside* their borders matters at least as much as what they do abroad. Three factors count most: economic performance creates the substructure of national power; competence in governance allows mobilization of resources for national purposes; and national élan or spirit sustains both. In time, nations with stronger economies, more competent governments, and unified national support have greater impact on the choices and actions of others. In Damon Runyon's cliché: while the race is not always to the swift or the battle to the strong, that is the way to bet.

Britain saw the United States soar from an economy half its size in 1840 to equality in the 1870s, on the way to becoming twice as large by 1914. As noted earlier, this drove realists in the Admiralty to a policy of accommodation. Had the US economy faltered, the nation divided into two, or its government been corrupted or its politics paralyzed over differences like those that led to the Civil War, Britain's role in the Western Hemisphere could have been sustained well into the twentieth century.

Had the Soviet Union been able to sustain economic growth at twice the rate of the US to become the leading economic power in the world, and Communist ideology proved capable of overcoming nationalism in building the "new socialist man," Moscow could have consolidated a position of hegemony not only in Europe but also in Asia. Had its junior partner, Communist China, become the vanguard of Communist expansion through "wars of liberation," as most US policymakers viewed the Vietnam War, a Communist monolith could have overshadowed the US-led "free world." Had the crisis of capitalism that was seen as the principal cause of the Great Depression of the 1930s persisted in the decades after World War II, Western European states could have succumbed to the attraction of socialism's apparently inexorable march, on the one hand, and subversion by the KGB, on the other.

Fortunately, these are just "what ifs." Instead, as Kennan foresaw, free markets and free societies proved more capable of delivering the economic, political, and personal benefits people wanted. Despite several decades of dramatic and frightening ascendency, the Soviet Union failed because its core commitments to command-and-control economics and totalitarian politics could not compete.

Armed with these dozen clues from the past, where do we go from here?

10

WHERE DO WE GO FROM HERE?

In many cases men have been able to see the danger ahead of them. But they have surrendered to an idea that seduced them into an irrevocable disaster . . . by their own folly rather than their misfortune. —Thucydides, Athenians to Melians, 416 BCE

We may have created a Frankenstein. —Richard Nixon

According to the Washington script, this chapter should pivot to propose a new strategy for the United States in its rivalry with China, complete with a to-do list that promises peaceful and prosperous relations with Beijing. But an attempt to shoehorn this challenge into that template would demonstrate only one thing: failure to understand the essence of the dilemma this book has identified.

What America needs most at this moment is not a new "China strategy"—or what passes for strategy in Washington these days—but instead a serious pause for reflection. If the tectonic shift caused by China's rise poses a dilemma of genuinely Thucydidean proportions, then calls for a "more robust" or "muscular" pivot will amount to little more than taking an extra-strength aspirin to treat cancer. If the United States just keeps doing what it has been doing, future historians will compare American "strategy" to illusions that British, German, and Russian leaders held as they sleepwalked into 1914.

There is no "solution" for the dramatic resurgence of a 5,000-year-old civilization with 1.4 billion people. It is a condition, a chronic condition that must be managed over a generation. Constructing a strategy proportionate to this challenge will require a multiyear, multiminded effort. It will be no less ambitious than the four-year debate that ran from Kennan's Long Telegram to Nitze's NSC-68 to shape what ultimately became America's Cold War strategy. It will require insights as penetrating as those from the minds of the "wise men." In short, it will demand something far beyond anything we have seen since the opening to China. This book hopes to provoke a similar debate today. To that end, this chapter offers a set of principles and strategic options for those seeking to escape Thucydides's Trap and avoid World War III.

BEGIN WITH STRUCTURAL REALITIES

Bismarck exaggerated when he described statecraft as essentially listening for the footsteps of God and then grabbing the hem of His garment as He goes by. But statecraft is more a matter of riding waves of history than making them. The clearer leaders are about underlying trend lines, the more successful they can be in shaping the arc of the possible.

In Washington, the first question officials ask about an issue is: What to do? But "don't just stand there, do something" is a political reflex, not a strategic injunction. Strategy insists that diagnosis precedes prescription. You would object if a surgeon prepared to roll you into the operating room right after first discussing your symptoms. Likewise, despite exigencies of recurring crises and political pressure to appear decisive, no president should take seriously the recommendations of policy advisers who have not first demonstrated a deep understanding of the challenge at hand.

When Nixon and Kissinger began exploring an opening to China, no one imagined that in their lifetime it could create an economy as large and powerful as that of the United States. Their focus was America's Soviet adversary, and their purpose, to widen the emerging

Sino-Soviet split in the Communist bloc. And it worked. But as he approached the end of his life and reflected on the course of events, Nixon confided to his friend and former speechwriter William Safire, "We may have created a Frankenstein."[1]

What a monster it may become. In the three and a half decades since Ronald Reagan became president, by the best measurement of economic performance, China has soared from 10 percent the size of the US to 60 percent in 2007, 100 percent in 2014, and 115 percent today. If the current trend continues, China's economy will be a full 50 percent larger than that of the US by 2023. By 2040 it could be nearly three times as large.[2] That would mean a China with triple America's resources to use in influencing outcomes in international relations.

Such gross economic, political, and military advantages would create a globe beyond anything American policymakers can now imagine. American conceptions of international order begin with US military primacy. But why does Washington have the predominant military force in the world today? Because over the past three decades it has invested several times more than all competitors on defense. The 2016 US defense budget exceeds the combined defense budgets of China, Russia, Japan, and Germany. Why has the United States been able to hold the pen in writing the rules of the post–World War II order? While many Americans would like to flatter themselves that it was because of their intelligence, virtue, or charm, the hard fact is that the nation's overwhelming weight has been the decisive factor.

Dramatic shifts in the global economy are making this American-led world order increasingly difficult to maintain. In the years since the financial crisis of 2008 and the global recession, leaders in every nation have insisted that their highest priority was economic growth. Yet the rate of growth has collapsed in major economies the world over. US growth has stagnated, averaging barely 2 percent. The EU economies have fared worse, with total GDP remaining below its pre-recession level until 2016.

Only one major economy has delivered. Though its growth rate has fallen since the 2008 economic crisis, China has continued growing at an average of more than 7 percent annually. As a result, 40 percent of all the growth in the world since 2007 has occurred in just one country. When comparing the power of two competitors, what matters most is not absolute but *relative* growth: how much faster you grow than I do. By this "growth gap," China's performance is even more impressive. Since the financial crisis, this gap between China and the US has actually widened—from an average of 6 percent faster than the US in the decade prior to 2007 to over 7 percent in the years since.

The cardinal challenge in statecraft, it has been said, is to recognize "a change in the international environment so likely to undermine national security that it must be resisted no matter what form the threat takes or how ostensibly legitimate it appears."[3] Is a China bigger and more powerful than the US such a challenge? Is "military primacy" essential for ensuring America's vital national interests? Can the US thrive in a world in which China writes the rules? A world in which China reshapes the international order? As we recognize new structural realities, we must be willing not only to ask but also to answer radical and decidedly uncomfortable questions.

APPLY HISTORY

Applied History is an emerging discipline that attempts to illuminate current predicaments and choices by analyzing historical precedents and analogues. Mainstream historians begin with an event or era and attempt to provide an account of what happened and why. Applied historians begin with a current choice or predicament and analyze the historical record to provide perspective, stimulate imagination, find clues about what is likely to happen, suggest possible interventions, and assess probable consequences. In this sense, Applied History is derivative: dependent on mainstream history in much the same way that engineering depends on physics, or medicine on biochemistry. In our "Applied History Manifesto," my colleague Niall Ferguson and I have proposed that the White House establish a Council of Historical Advisers, analogous to the Council of Economic Advisers.[4] Its first assignment would be to answer three key questions about the rise of China.

The first: What is the US-China competition like? In the capital of the United States of Amnesia, everything is declared to be "unprecedented." But applied historians ask: Have we ever seen anything like this before? If so, what happened in earlier episodes? What insights or clues can we draw from these cases for dealing with the issue at hand? These historians would of course caution busy policymakers against facile analogizing. The temptation to find a fascinating precedent (for example, the rise of Germany), conclude that the rise of China is "just like that," and move directly to apply a prescription is itself a trap. As my late colleague Ernest May never tired of saying, the differences matter at least as much as the similarities.[5]

While the twenty-first century does pose unique problems (and this book argues that the size, speed, and scale of China's rise *is* unprecedented in important respects), all of them have useful analogues — not least the examples in the Thucydides's Trap Case File. As the most influential modern practitioner of Applied History, Henry Kissinger, has cautioned, "History is not, of course, a cookbook offering pretested recipes." It can "illuminate the consequences of actions in comparable situations," but "each generation must discover for itself what situations are in fact comparable."[6]

The second question our White House council should answer is: How did we arrive at what we now call the "China challenge"? What we see today is a snapshot. What about the movie that brought us to this point? Locating the current rivalry in a longer perspective can help uncover the complexity of the issue. It also reminds us that even when the problem has been "solved," underlying issues may remain for years to come. Reviewing the sequence of scenes that brought us to this point will help policymakers resist the American tendency to focus on what they see today, let bygones be bygones, and look solely to the future seeking an immediate answer to the question: What to do?

Third: How do foreign stakeholders perceive the same evolution of events? As the eminent historian Michael Howard has noted, "All we believe about the present depends on what we believe about the past."[7] Not only is it incumbent upon policymakers to understand the relevant history of the issue at hand before acting—they must also try to grasp how their foreign counterparts understand that history.

RECOGNIZE THAT AMERICA'S POST–COLD WAR CHINA STRATEGY IS FUNDAMENTALLY A CONTRADICTION

While the pivot to Asia was one of the Obama administration's most heralded foreign policy initiatives, in reality it was largely a rhetorical repackaging of the strategy that America has followed toward China under both Republicans and Democrats since the end of the Cold War.[8] This strategy is known as "engage but hedge."[9] Its fundamental flaw is that it permits everything and prohibits nothing.

Bureaucratically, this doctrine has allowed each government department to follow its natural inclinations. On the one hand, the Departments of State and Treasury "engage"—eagerly welcoming China as a member of the alphabet soup of international agreements and institutions, from trade, finance, and technology transfer to education and climate. Occasionally, they have called China out for unfair practices. But their overwhelming priority remains building the relationship. So US officials usually overlook persistent Chinese cheating, or accede to Beijing's demands for concessionary terms as a "developing" country. On the other hand, the Department of Defense and intelligence community "hedge." They strive to maintain military superiority, strengthen defense ties to key allies and friends—specifically Japan, South Korea, and India—develop intelligence assets, and plan for conflict with an adversary whose name, like Voldemort's, they are not allowed to speak, but against whom they develop specific weapon systems and operational war plans.

In essence, this strategy envisages a China that follows in the footsteps of Germany and Japan. Like these nations, China is expected to accept its place in the American-led international rule-based order. When pressed to explain their theory, proponents argue that as China becomes wealthier, it will acquire a greater stake in the international system that has allowed it to do so, and thus will in time become a "responsible stakeholder."[10] Furthermore, as China's citizens become wealthier, they will demand greater say in governing themselves, paving the way for democratic reforms of the sort we have seen in Japan, South Korea, and Taiwan.

During the 1970s and 1980s, when the defining challenge for US policymakers was to defeat the Soviet Union, there was a certain logic to strengthening China by supporting its economic growth and even helping build up its military and intelligence capabilities. But when the Cold War ended and the Soviet Union disappeared in 1991, American strategists should have heeded Kissinger's cardinal challenge and asked how fundamental changes in the international environment could undermine vital American interests.[11] Instead, most engaged in a victory lap of triumphalism and forgetfulness. Declarations of a new "unipolar era," and proclamations of the "end of history," in which all nations would embrace the American script and take their places as market-based democracies in the US-designed international order, captured imaginations. On this canvas, Communist China was but an afterthought.

Assessing America's "engage but hedge" strategy, Lee Kuan Yew identified two fatal flaws. First, China is not about to become a democracy. As he put it bluntly, "If it were to do so, it would collapse." Second, comparing China to Germany and Japan misses the fact that the latter two were first defeated in a hot war, occupied by American troops, and governed for a period thereafter by American high commanders who even wrote their constitutions. In contrast, in Lee's words, China will insist on "being accepted as China, *not* as an honorary member of the West."[12]

REVIEW ALL THE STRATEGIC OPTIONS —
EVEN THE UGLY ONES

A "strategy" (in this case, engage but hedge) could only survive over the course of three administrations, Democratic and Republican, if it had roots in both politics and bureaucracy. No one can doubt that engaging China has had huge benefits for American corporations that have employed lower-cost Chinese workers to produce goods, and for American consumers who bought them. Hedging against such a big adversary has allowed the Pentagon to justify a $600 billion annual budget and the major weapon systems to which the military services are wedded.

The question is whether there are significantly different strategic alternatives that might be feasible and preferable to the current one. In the hope of stimulating the imagination of readers, national security officials, and others in the strategic community who bear responsibility for US policy toward China, this chapter concludes with brief sketches of four potential strategic options. These stretch from accommodation (essentially drawing pointers from British policy toward the United States during the twentieth century) to regime change or even splintering of the country (as Britain might have done in dealing with the US had it assisted the Confederacy in the Civil War, and as some believed the US was doing in encouraging Ukraine to move into the embrace of the West). Most of these strategic options may seem impolite or impolitic to consider. Taken together, they suggest a wider range of opportunities for the United States to address an ascendant China.

Accommodate

Accommodation is not a bad word. Opponents seek to conflate it with appeasement. But the two are not synonyms in the realm of strategy. Accommodation is a serious effort to adapt to a new balance of power by adjusting relations with a serious competitor — in effect, making the best of unfavorable trends without resorting to military means. Accommodation comes in two varieties: ad hoc and negotiated.

British policy toward the US in the late nineteenth and early twentieth centuries — after the government concluded that it had to avoid war at virtually any price — provides an example of ad hoc accommodation. It shows how this can be done gracefully, with a clear sense of priorities, and in a way that helps the emerging superpower appreciate overlapping interests. As we saw in chapter 9, Britain's "choice of forbearance" toward the United States was a key factor in avoiding war. Over territorial disputes in Venezuela, for example, Britain ultimately agreed to the US demand that the British accept arbitration under the Monroe Doctrine. Similarly, Britain exempted the United States from the Two-Power Standard, which committed the UK to maintain naval forces equal to those of the next two largest competitors combined.

The Yalta agreement, in which Roosevelt, Churchill, and Stalin drew the borders of postwar Europe, illustrates the possibilities (and pitfalls) of a negotiated accommodation. At the Yalta Conference of 1945, the United States, Britain, and Soviet Union essentially accepted the military facts on the ground. Anticipating public criticism that they had conceded too much to the Soviets, Churchill and Roosevelt persuaded Stalin to accept the Declaration of Liberated Europe — a statement committing the great powers to allow free elections and democratic governance in Eastern European states — in return for acceptance of Russia's 1941 borders and the Moscow-organized Lublin government in Poland.[13] But when a dictator who had never allowed elections in his own country predictably violated that agreement, Roosevelt was accused of betrayal.

If it were exploring accommodation, could the United States agree, for example, to curtail its commitment to Taiwan in exchange for Chinese concessions in the South and East China Seas?[14] Could the US and China come to an understanding over the future of the Korean Peninsula in which the US would withdraw troops from South Korea in exchange for Chinese denuclearization of the North and recognition of a united peninsula under Seoul's authority? Could the US recognize a de facto Chinese sphere of influence around its borders?

Undermine

A strategy to foment regime change within the country, or even divide it against itself, would require leaders in Washington to stretch imaginations further. If the US were to attempt to undermine its rising rival, what means might it employ? Could it openly call into question the legitimacy of the Chinese Communist Party the way Ronald Reagan bluntly called the Soviet Union the Evil Empire in 1983? This might not be as extreme as it sounds. As Kevin Rudd has pointed out, Chinese leaders have long believed Washington will never really accept the legitimacy of the CCP.[15] So why pretend otherwise? And if American leaders go so far as to declare their fundamental opposition to the Chinese government, why not go a step further and attempt to do something about it?

Clearly communism has been exposed as a fraud in every country where it has been tried. Why should a small group that still calls itself Communist rule 1.4 billion fellow citizens? Are Chinese citizens less deserving of the human rights America's Declaration of Independence declares to be the God-given endowment of all people? If democracy is the best form of government for all nations, why not for China? We already know that the Chinese people are adept at democratic governance: 23 million of them have built a successful democracy in Taiwan with a market-based economy that, were it an independent nation, would rank in the top third among UN member states. The United States supported the right of the Scots to hold a free ballot on declaring independence from the United Kingdom, as well as the Kosovars when they separated from Serbia. As a strand in a strategy to divide China and demoralize the regime in Beijing, why not likewise support independence for Tibet and Taiwan? China would undoubtedly react violently to such initiatives. But ruling out this option ignores America's long record of backing independence movements, even over the objections of adversaries—and forfeits leverage.

China now has the world's largest number of Internet users. Smartphones allow Chinese to see (within government limits) the world beyond their borders, as do tourism and the emerging elites' education abroad. When given a choice, Chinese citizens exercise their freedom to go to whichever website they choose, buy what they want, and travel at will. Washington could leverage this nascent preference for political freedom. During the Cold War, the US waged an overt and covert campaign to undermine the legitimacy of the Soviet government and its ideological foundation. Policymakers today could take many pages from that playbook in mounting an effort to bring about regime change in China. For example, the US government could use its cyber-capabilities to steal and then leak through third parties inside China damaging truths about past and present abuses, revealing, for example, how its current leaders became wealthy. The US could cultivate and encourage dissident groups in China, as it did in Soviet-occupied Europe or the Soviet Union itself during the Cold War. Chinese studying in the US are naturally infected with concepts of freedom, human rights, and the rule of law. They could be encouraged to agitate for political change when they returned to China.

In an extreme option, US forces could covertly train and support separatist insurgents. Fissures in the Chinese state already exist. Tibet is essentially occupied territory. Xinjiang, a traditionally Islamic region in western China, already harbors an active Uighur separatist movement responsible for waging a low-level insurgency against Beijing. And Taiwanese who watch Beijing's heavy-handedness in Hong Kong hardly require encouragement to oppose reunification with this increasingly authoritarian government. Could US support for these separatists draw Beijing into conflicts with radical Islamist groups throughout Central Asia and the Middle East? If so, could these become quagmires, mirroring the Soviet intervention in Afghanistan where US-supported mujahideen "freedom fighters" bled the Soviet Union?

A subtle but concentrated effort to accentuate the contradictions at the core of Chinese Communist ideology and the Party's attempt to exert authoritarian control over citizens' increasing demands for freedom could, over time, undermine the regime and encourage independence movements in Taiwan, Xinjiang, Tibet, and Hong Kong. By splintering China at home and keeping Beijing embroiled in maintaining domestic stability, the US could avert, or at least substantially delay, China's challenge to American dominance.

Negotiate a Long Peace

If it were negotiable, the US and China could agree to take a quarter-century hiatus that imposes considerable constraints in some areas of their competition, leaving both parties free to pursue advantage elsewhere. From the Thirty Years' Peace that Pericles signed with the Spartans in 445 BCE to the US-Soviet détente in the 1970s, rivals throughout history have found ways to accept intolerable (but temporally unchangeable) circumstances in order to focus on more urgent priorities, particularly their own domestic affairs.

Nixon and Kissinger's readiness to negotiate an array of agreements that produced what the US and Soviet governments termed "détente" reflected their sense that the US needed breathing space to repair divisions at home driven by the Vietnam War and the civil rights movement. Among these arrangements were SALT (the Strategic Arms Limitations Treaty), which froze the rivals' buildup of the deadliest nuclear-armed missiles; the ABM (Anti-Ballistic Missile) Treaty, which obliged each competitor to forgo defenses against the opponent's missiles and thus acquiesce to a position that left its society vulnerable to destruction by the other; and the Helsinki Accords, which legalized the division of Europe. As Kissinger has explained, a crucial element of détente was linkage: the United States conditioned its concessions on issues of importance to the Soviet Union, such as recognizing East Germany, on Moscow's restraint on issues Washington considered significant—including access to West Berlin and tolerance of American escalation of the bombing campaign in Vietnam.

The political costs of these agreements were substantial. Analysts still remain divided over their merits. Some celebrate them for establishing a new international order in which both Moscow and Washington gave up their ambitions to overthrow each other's regime. Others, however, see the arrangements primarily as having bought time to demonstrate which of the societies and systems of government was superior. Proponents of the latter view who joined the Reagan administration in 1981 saw no contradiction between negotiating further agreements with Soviet leaders while simultaneously seeking to undermine the Evil Empire's regime.[16]

In the current stage of the Chinese-American rivalry, both governments face overwhelming demands at home. Given China's view that progress advances in decades and centuries rather than days and months, it has historically shown a capacity to set problems aside for long periods, as it did in reaching the Shanghai Communiqué in 1972, which effectively set aside the issue of Taiwan, or in 1978 when Deng Xiaoping proposed to Japan that disputes over islands in the East China Sea be shelved for a generation.[17] Americans tend to be less patient. Yet the menu of potential agreements is long and fruitful: a pact to freeze disputes in the South and East China Seas, to affirm freedom of navigation for all ships in all international waters, to limit cyberattacks to agreed domains and exclude others (for instance, critical infrastructure), or to forbid specific forms of interference in each other's domestic politics.

As was the case during Cold War détente, the US and China could link issues to reach agreements that give each more of what it values most. For example, the United States could agree to moderate its criticism of China's human rights violations by ending publication of the State Department's annual human rights report on China and high-level meetings with the Dalai Lama in exchange for constraints on China's practice of espionage for economic gain. If Beijing were prepared to remove antiship and anti-air missiles from its islands in the South China Sea, Washington could limit surveillance operations along China's borders, especially near China's military installations on Hainan Island, as the country's leaders have long demanded. China could agree to end regular patrols near the Senkaku Islands in the East China Sea in return for the US stopping provocative freedom-of-navigation operations in the South China Sea. The US could propose that China freeze island building in the South China Sea, accept limits on the modernization of its submarine fleet and antisatellite weapons, and reduce its amphibious warfare capabilities in exchange for the US slowing or even stopping development of a Conventional Prompt Global Strike capability, delaying deployment or removing advanced missile defense systems in South Korea and Japan, and recognizing Chinese sovereignty over the Paracel Islands. The United States could limit or even end arms sales to Taiwan and withdraw some forces from South Korea if China forces Pyongyang to end further tests of nuclear weapons and long-range missiles.[18]

Redefine the Relationship

In 2012, Xi Jinping proposed to President Obama that they jointly invent a "new form of great power relations," in which the US and China would respect one another's core interests. For Xi, "core interests" meant respecting each other's de facto sphere of influence, which in his view includes not only Taiwan and Tibet, but also China's claims in the South China Sea. Unwilling to accept these terms, the Obama administration rejected this formulation, and President Trump has been equally unsympathetic.[19] However, the US could propose its *own* conception of a new form of great power relations.

In the final years of the Cold War, during a private walk with only Presidents Reagan and Gorbachev and their translators present, Reagan began with a question: If planet Earth were invaded by hostile Martians, how would the Soviet Union and the United States respond?[20] Initially, the Russian interpreter misunderstood Reagan and his translation raised eyebrows: Was Reagan telling Gorbachev that Martians had just invaded Earth? After the confusion was cleared up, Reagan pursued the question. His purpose was to underline the core interests that otherwise deadly adversaries shared.

If we follow Reagan's lead, do the US and China today face threats analogous to an alien invasion—challenges so severe that both sides are compelled to work together? One does not have to stretch too far to answer affirmatively. Four "mega-threats" loom above all: nuclear Armageddon; nuclear anarchy; global terrorism, especially as threatened by Islamic jihadism; and climate change. In confronting each of these, the vital national interests the two powers share are much greater than those that divide them.

Because of the inescapable logic of mutual assured destruction, if the US and China were to stumble into a war in which their full nuclear arsenals were launched, both nations would be erased from the map. Thus their most vital interest is to avoid such a war. Moreover, they must find combinations of compromise and constraint that avoid repeated games of chicken that could inadvertently lead to this dreaded outcome.

Nuclear anarchy poses a distinct mega-threat of its own. A world in which many states have acquired large nuclear arsenals would be a world in which some conflicts go nuclear and some nuclear weapons find their way into terrorist hands. A nuclear war between India and Pakistan could kill hundreds of millions and wreak global environmental havoc. North Korea's sale of a nuclear weapon to the next mutation of al-Qaeda or Xinjiang terrorists, and the explosion of that device in New York City or Beijing, would fundamentally change our world.

President Kennedy identified this threat in 1963, forecasting that by the 1970s there would be twenty-five or thirty nuclear weapon states. Understanding what that would mean for America's survival and well-being, he set in motion a number of initiatives centered around the Non-Proliferation Treaty.[21] Together, these efforts bent this arc of history. Today there are not twenty-five or thirty but just nine nations with nuclear weapons. Thanks to the cooperation of China, as well as Russia, negotiations succeeded in shelving Iran's nuclear aspirations for a decade or more. Nonetheless, the buildup of nuclear weapons and material, particularly in North Korea and Pakistan, is substantially increasing the risk of nuclear terrorism. No states are better positioned to address these challenges than China and the US, especially if they act in concert and can persuade Russia to join them. Resolving proliferation threats by North Korea and Pakistan will diminish the danger of not only nuclear terrorism, but also state-level proliferation in countries like South Korea and Japan. But if they fail to do so, we should expect to see a nuclear bomb explode in a city like Mumbai, Jakarta, Los Angeles, or Shanghai at some point in our lifetimes.[22]

Other types of mega-terrorism pose lesser but still extraordinary threats to the US and China. The driving technological development of the second half of the twentieth century was the integration of engineering and physics that produced everything from the computer chip and the Internet to the nuclear bomb. Its analogue in the twenty-first century is the integration of engineering with genomics and synthetic biology, which has given us not only miracle drugs that target specific cancers, but also biological weapons that could be used by a single rogue scientist to kill hundreds of thousands of people.[23] Nature itself offered a preview of this danger in the SARS epidemic of 2003 and the Ebola plague in Africa in 2014. Now picture a terrorist in a biotech lab creating an antibiotic-resistant smallpox pathogen and releasing it in an airport in Kunming or Chicago. This danger cannot be met by either nation acting alone. Extensive cooperation, through bilateral intelligence sharing, multilateral organizations such as Interpol, and the establishment of global standards will be essential.[24]

The fourth horseman of this prospective apocalypse is the continual emission of greenhouse gases to the point that the global climate becomes incompatible with normal human existence. Scientists have warned that when greenhouse gases reach 450 parts per million, we are likely to see a 3° Fahrenheit increase in global average temperatures, causing catastrophic impacts. Acting alone, there is nothing the US and China can do inside their own borders to meet this slow-motion disaster. Although China and the United States are the two leading carbon emitters, if either were to reduce its carbon emissions to zero while all other nations continued on their present course, the effect on global climate would merely be postponed for several years. Presidents Xi and Obama recognized this fact in forging the US-China agreement that led to the 2016 Paris Agreement, which commits states to cap carbon emissions by 2030 and begin reducing them thereafter. And while the world has celebrated this accord, and rightly so, two harsh realities stand out. First, with current technologies, achieving those targets is impossible. Second, even if all nations fulfill their pledges, global warming will get worse (albeit at a slower rate than if we did nothing).[25] As the two largest economies in the world, the US and China have a special responsibility—and the leverage—to lead the community of nations out of this existential crisis.

These four challenges may seem daunting, perhaps even insurmountable. But fortunately an array of win-win opportunities are available to demonstrate the benefits of cooperation and motivate the US and China to step up to the larger threats. Global trade and investment have unquestionably produced a larger pie with bigger pieces for both nations. How that pie is divided between them, among other countries, and within their own societies is another matter about which debate is intensifying. Support for economic integration is no longer a given, particularly as more and more people believe globalization has left them behind, fueling a surge of populism, nationalism, and xenophobia. Despite their many differences, the US and China have a common interest in managing these rising forces and ensuring that they do not unravel the fabric of the global economy.

More elusive but unquestionably real is an emerging global consciousness among the planet's most active "golden billion" inhabitants. To a degree unseen in history, they have come to share perceptions, norms, and practices. Ubiquitous communication networks have shrunk the globe, allowing elites everywhere to be aware of almost everything, and almost instantly. Smartphones bring images and words from every corner of the earth. Explosions, hurricanes, and discoveries anywhere impact consciousness everywhere. The experience of international travel, not only by the global elite but also by average citizens, is now commonplace. Some 800,000 of China's best and brightest go abroad for their education, 300,000 studying in the US. Pause to think about the fact that the current president of China and his wife sent their only child to college not at Xi's alma matter of Tsinghua University, but rather at Harvard, where she graduated in 2014. How the views of an emerging generation of "internationalists" can be reconciled with the more nationalistic or populist inclinations of their fellow citizens is a puzzle. Finding ways in which the internationalists' understanding of the world can be translated into new forms of cooperation remains among the most intriguing opportunities.[26]

CONCLUSION

—————

If my history be judged useful by those who desire an exact knowledge of the past as an aid to understanding the future—which in the course of human affairs must resemble if it does not reflect it—I shall be content.

—Thucydides, *History of the Peloponnesian War*

Having taught at Harvard for five decades, I have seen thousands of bright students and professors come and go. Hundreds who seemed destined for greatness disappointed, yet hundreds more with fewer advantages soared. First impressions often fail, and trajectories take unanticipated twists and turns.

Henry Kissinger is an apt example. When I began graduate studies at Harvard in 1964, he was my adviser. Kissinger was born to Jewish parents in a small town in Germany, escaped the Nazis by coming to the United States, enlisted in the American army, was enabled by the GI Bill to go to Harvard, and eventually became a professor. Was he destined to one day become America's national security adviser who, with Nixon, engineered the opening to China? Anyone harboring such a thought in 1940 or 1950 would have been out of his mind. So, too, with Bill Gates, who dropped out of Harvard after two years to pursue his passion for computing that became Microsoft. Or Mark Zuckerberg, an indifferent student who spent most of his time creating an online tool for dorm-mates to stay in touch that exploded to become Facebook.

How should we understand these outcomes? The great Greek playwrights like Sophocles, whose tragedies dominated the literary landscape in ancient Greece, thought fate was the answer. In their drama, the gods scripted Oedipus to kill his father and marry his mother. From his assigned role there was no escape. But Thucydides disagreed. He had a distinctly different concept of human affairs. Indeed, he defined a new discipline of history in which men, not gods, were the chief actors. Destiny dealt the hands, but men played the cards.

His history provides a factual record of the choices Pericles and his fellow Athenians made of their own free will. Different choices would have produced different results. Indeed, his purpose in reconstructing the Assembly debate was to teach future statesmen not to accept their fate but to make wiser choices. Athenians did not have to go to war with Sparta in 430 BCE. In fact, almost half the Assembly voted against the alliance that led to war. Could the same Pericles who negotiated the Thirty Years' Peace not have foreseen the conflict between Corinth and Corcyra and taken action to defuse it before it spiraled into war?

In the aftermath of World War I, the kaiser's chancellor Bethmann Hollweg tried to escape responsibility for his actions by claiming that war between Germany and Britain was in the cards. But dealt the same hand, a savvier statesman like Bismarck might have found a way to sustain Germany's secret alliance with Russia, or perhaps even forge an alignment with Britain, to stave off conflict.

In 1936, Hitler violated the Treaty of Versailles and threatened Europe by remilitarizing the Rhineland. Had Britain and France sent a division of troops to enforce the treaty — as Churchill advocated vigorously at the time — German troops would have retreated, the German generals (who had strongly opposed Hitler's reckless move) could have overthrown him, and World War II might never have happened.

The Cuban Missile Crisis presents the starkest counterfactuals of all

—and the lessons most relevant for the current US-China dilemma. From the record of the steps the US and the Soviet Union took, it is not difficult to identify a dozen paths that could have easily ended with nuclear weapons exploding in Washington or Moscow.[1] For example, a Turkish or German NATO pilot in an F-100 fighter bomber loaded with nuclear bombs could have—on his own initiative—by mistake or madness flown to Moscow and dropped his payload. A Soviet submarine with live nuclear warheads in the Caribbean almost mistook US antisubmarine operations as an all-out attack. That commander required no further authorization or code from Moscow to launch his weapons against American cities.

To attempt to manage this inescapable risk of a nuclear confrontation, Kennedy repeatedly overrode the urgings of his advisers, choosing instead to give Khrushchev more time to consider, adapt, and adjust. Thus when an American U-2 spy plane was shot down over Cuba on the final Saturday of the crisis, Kennedy postponed a retaliatory attack in order to attempt a final diplomatic ploy. In doing so, he crafted a unique political cocktail that consisted of a public deal, a private ultimatum, and a secret sweetener—all in defiance of the advice from most members of his National Security Council. If Khrushchev agreed to withdraw the missiles from Cuba (which he had claimed were necessary to defend Cuba from an American invasion), the US would pledge not to invade the island. The private ultimatum gave Khrushchev twenty-four hours to respond, after which the US threatened air strikes to eliminate the missiles. And the secret sweetener insisted that while there could be no quid pro quo, if the Soviets withdrew their missiles from Cuba, the US missiles in Turkey would be gone within six months.

JFK knew that proactive steps to avert such standoffs could come at a high price, including compromising on politically sensitive issues and postponing initiatives that, while not essential, were nonetheless important. But he concluded that the price was worth paying. In his words, the enduring lesson of the Cuban Missile Crisis was: "Above all, while defending our own vital interests, nuclear powers must avert confrontations that force an adversary to choose between a humiliating retreat and nuclear war."[2]

To make similarly wise choices, US leaders will need to muster a combination of hard thinking and harder work. They can begin with four core ideas:

Clarify vital interests. Defending America's vital interests depends first on defining them. To prioritize everything is to prioritize nothing. Yet this is Washington's natural reflex. In a struggle as epic as the one between China and the United States, American leaders must distinguish the vital from the vivid.[3] For example, is maintaining US primacy in the western Pacific truly a vital national interest? Would Americans "bear any burden" to keep China from seizing islands in the South China Sea, or even from reclaiming Taiwan? These are not rhetorical questions. Geopolitical projects — or even responses to crises — decoupled from national priorities are bound to fail.

The German philosopher Nietzsche taught us that "the most common form of human stupidity is forgetting what one is trying to do." In thinking clearly about America's role in the world, we cannot improve on the wise men's Cold War imperative. As noted in chapter 9, that means preserving the US "as a free nation with our fundamental institutions and values intact." That does not require defending every claim made by the Philippines or Vietnam in the South China Sea. It does not even require defending the Philippines. But it does require avoiding nuclear war with China.

Understand what China is trying to do. Applying the logic of Kennedy's counsel, US leaders must also better understand and appreciate China's core interests. In spite of his hard-line rhetoric, when confronted directly, Khrushchev concluded that he could compromise on nuclear arms in Cuba. Likewise, the infamous ideologue Mao proved adept at giving ground when it served China's interests. Xi and Trump both begin with maximalist claims. But both are also dealmakers. The more the US government understands China's aims, the better prepared it will be to resolve differences. The problem remains psychological projection: even seasoned State Department officials too often mistakenly assume China's vital interests mirror America's own. They would be wise to read Sun Tzu: "If you know the enemy and know yourself, you need not fear the result of a hundred battles. If you know yourself but not the enemy, for every victory gained you will also suffer a defeat. If you know neither the enemy nor yourself, you will succumb in every battle."[4]

Cold war has come to be seen as a no-go option in international relations—something to be avoided at virtually any cost. But a quarter century after the dissolution of the Soviet empire (and at a time of renewed angst between Washington and Moscow), it is worth reflecting on the dependable elements of the old US-Soviet relationship. Pretense invites ambiguity; candor breeds clarity. "We will bury you!" and "Evil Empire" left no doubt about where either stood. But such harsh depictions did not freeze meaningful contact, candid conversation, and even constructive compromise. If anything, these claims freed leaders to pursue negotiations from the safety of the moral high ground.

China and the US would be better served not by passive-aggressive "should diplomacy" (calling on the other to exhibit better behavior) or by noble-sounding rhetoric about geopolitical norms, but by unapologetically pursuing their national interests. In high-stakes relationships, predictability and stability—not friendship—matter most. The US should stop playing "let's pretend."

As we saw in chapter 1, many in the United States have been pretending that China's rise is not as spectacular as it really is. They have also been pretending about the raison d'être for China's focus on economic growth. Yes, the Communist Party's survival depends on high rates of growth. But China's emergence as the number-one power in Asia—and its aspiration to be number one in the world—reflects not just the imperative of economic growth but also a supremacist world view bound up in Chinese identity. In his "Letter to My Children," Whittaker Chambers uncovered what he felt was the philosophical driver of revolutionary communism: "It is the great alternative faith of mankind . . . It is the vision of man's mind displacing God as the creative intelligence of the world. It is the vision of man's liberated mind, by the sole force of its rational intelligence, redirecting man's destiny and reorganizing man's life and the world."*[5] While Xi and his Party mandarins no longer preach Marxist-Leninist doctrine, no one should be deluded into thinking that the regime today is a post-ideological movement concerned solely with its own power. Chapter 7 underlined the deeply divergent civilizational values that separate China and the West, an uncomfortable reality that polite diplomacy too often obscures.

Do strategy. In today's Washington, strategic thinking is marginalized or even mocked. President Clinton once mused that in this fast-changing world, foreign policy had become a version of jazz: the art of improvisation. Among the dumbest statements of one of America's smartest presidents—Barack Obama—was his claim that, given the pace of change today, "I don't really even need George Kennan."[6] Though deliberate crafting of strategy does not guarantee success, the absence of a coherent, sustainable strategy is a reliable route to failure.

Policymakers in Washington today often do not even pretend to take strategy seriously. Instead, addressing challenges posed by China, Russia, or Islamic jihadism, they say, "Our lines of effort are . . ." Official national security strategy documents are ignored. Over the past decade, I have yet to meet a senior member of the US national security team who had so much as read the official national security strategies.

Thus, instead of NSC-68, or the Reagan administration's revision, NSDD-75, what guides the Washington agenda on China today are grand, politically appealing aspirations with a list of assorted actions attached. In each case, a serious strategist would judge the stated objective unachievable by any level of undertaking the US can reasonably mount. Current efforts are thus bound to fail.

On China, American policy essentially seeks to cling to the status quo: the Pax Americana established after World War II. Washington

---

* A onetime Soviet spy who defected, Chambers became a fierce anti-Communist, and was awarded the Medal of Freedom by President Ronald Reagan in 1984.

repeatedly, and accurately, reminds the Chinese that this has allowed the longest peace and largest increase in economic well-being Asian nations—and specifically China—have ever seen. But that status quo cannot be sustained when the underlying economic balance of power has tilted so dramatically in China's favor. So America's real strategy, truth be told, is hope.

To conceive and construct a grand strategy proportionate to this challenge will require senior government officials to devote not just their political capital but also their intellectual acumen. Contrary to Obama, US national security strategy *does* need Kennan today—along with modern-day equivalents of Marshall, Acheson, Vandenberg, Nitze, and Truman.

Make domestic challenges central. If Xi and Trump listened to Lee Kuan Yew, they would focus first on what matters most: their domestic problems. What is the single largest challenge to American national security today? What poses the single largest threat to America's standing in the world? The answer to both questions is found in failures of the American political system. Ask the same questions of China and the answers are again the same: failures of governance. Honest observers in both societies are increasingly recognizing that neither "decadent" democracy nor "responsive" authoritarianism is fit for meeting the twenty-first century's severest tests.

I am a congenital optimist about America, but I worry that American democracy is exhibiting fatal symptoms. DC has become an acronym for Dysfunctional Capital: a swamp in which partisanship has grown poisonous, relations between the White House and Congress have paralyzed basic functions like budgets and foreign agreements, and public trust in government has all but disappeared. These symptoms are rooted in the decline of a public ethic, legalized and institutionalized corruption, a poorly educated and attention-deficit-driven electorate, and a "gotcha" press—all exacerbated by digital devices and platforms that reward sensationalism and degrade deliberation. As Abraham Lincoln warned prophetically, a house divided against itself cannot stand. Without stronger and more determined leadership from the president and a recovery of a sense of civic responsibility among the governing class, the United States may follow Europe down the road of decline.

At the same time, I share Lee's devastating critique of China's "operating system." Technology is making its current system of governance obsolete. Young urbanites with smartphones cannot be sustainably governed by Beijing bureaucrats who track every citizen as part of an omnipresent "social credit" system. Lee identified an array of handicaps China will not easily change: the absence of the rule of law; excessive control from the center; cultural habits that limit imagination and creativity; a language "that shapes thinking through epigrams and 4,000 years of texts that suggest everything worth saying has already been said, and said better by earlier writers"; and an inability "to attract and assimilate talent from other societies in the world."[7] His prescription was not American-style democracy (which he thought would lead to China's collapse), but a recovery of traditional mandarin virtues in a government with a strong leader. On that front, Xi's value-centered nationalism may help restore integrity to a Chinese OS that has been hollowed out by rank materialism.

To extend the digital metaphor, both rivals must also reconsider the fitness of their apps for the twenty-first century. In his book *Civilization,* Niall Ferguson identifies six "killer apps"—ideas and institutions that drove the extraordinary divergence in prosperity between the West and the rest of the world after 1500. These are competition, the scientific revolution, property rights, modern medicine, consumer society, and work ethic.[8] While noting China's great reconvergence with the West since 1970, Niall wonders if China can sustain its progress without killer app number three: secure private property rights. I worry that the American work ethic has lapsed into mediocrity, while its consumer society has become decadent.

If the leaders in each society grasped the seriousness of the problems it faced on the home front and gave them the priority they deserved, officials would discover that devising a way to "share the twenty-first century in Asia" was not their most serious challenge.

Will they recognize this reality? Will either or both nations summon the imagination and fortitude to meet their domestic challenges? If they do so, will they be skillful enough to secure their vital interests without stumbling to war? Statesmen seeking to do so will find no better place to start than in rereading Thucydides's *History of the Peloponnesian War*.

Will they succeed? *Ah, if we only knew*. We do know, however, that Shakespeare was right: our destiny lies "not in our stars, but in ourselves."

ACKNOWLEDGMENTS

Recognition of the debts incurred on the intellectual odyssey from which this book emerges would require an essay in itself. From my freshman year at Davidson College when Professor Labban introduced me to Thucydides, to the China Working Group that now meets monthly at Harvard, I have been learning daily in ways that inform this analysis. My senior thesis adviser Crane Brinton (author of *Anatomy of a Revolution*) taught me to recognize patterns in history. Studying analytic philosophy at Oxford, I learned from A. J. Ayer, Isaiah Berlin, Gilbert Ryle, and Peter Strawson the differences between conceptual frameworks and the real world. As a PhD student at Harvard, I had the extraordinary opportunity to be tutored by three legends in applying history to clarify current challenges: Henry Kissinger, Ernest May, and Richard Neustadt. My doctoral thesis examined the Cuban Missile Crisis of 1962 to illuminate the complexities of decision-making in government, as well as the special dangers posed by superpower nuclear arsenals that welded an unbreakable bond between adversaries.

During the Cold War, I had an opportunity to both learn and contribute to understanding this existential threat, and—variously as consultant, adviser, and participant—to develop strategies that ultimately defeated the Evil Empire. I had the privilege of working for President Ronald Reagan and his secretary of defense Caspar Weinberger (for whom I served as special adviser), President Bill Clinton and his secretaries of defense Les Aspen and Bill Perry (for whom I served as assistant secretary of defense), a dozen secretaries of defense from Weinberger to Ash Carter (on whose Defense Policy Board I served), directors of the CIA from Stan Turner (for whom I served as special adviser) to David Petraeus, as well as many more colleagues.

But most of all Harvard, and specifically Harvard's Kennedy School of Government, has nourished and shaped my thinking in general and the ideas in this book in particular. In the late 1970s and 80s, I was honored to serve as the "Founding Dean" of the John F. Kennedy School of Government. Al Carnesale, Joe Nye, and I led the Avoiding Nuclear War Project that enlisted scores of junior faculty and post-docs in an effort to understand how the nuclear competition could be constrained sufficiently to allow deadly adversaries to survive. In the post–Cold War era, I have led Harvard's Belfer Center for Science and International Affairs, where scores of faculty colleagues and fellows have taught me about the most significant challenges in international affairs. Throughout, I have been blessed to be part of what A. N. Whitehead called "the uniting of young and old in the imaginative pursuit of learning."

I continue to benefit from an ongoing tutorial on China from members of the Belfer Center's China Working Group, including Hoss Cartwright, Mark Elliott, Taylor Fravel, Kelly Sims Gallagher, Paul Heer, Alastair Iain Johnston, William Kirby, Roderick MacFarquahar, Meghan O'Sullivan, Dwight Perkins, Stapleton Roy, Kevin Rudd, Anthony Saich, Ezra Vogel, and Odd Arne Westad. For patient help in trying to fathom China's economy, Martin Feldstein has been my lead guide with support from Richard Cooper, Stanley Fisher, Larry Summers, and Robert Zoellick. In the effort to apply history, my co-conspirator in launching Harvard's Applied History Project, Niall Ferguson, has been a most valued colleague, and David Armitage, Drew Faust, Fredrick Logevall, Charles Maier, Steve Miller, Richard Rosecrance, and Stephen Van Evera have offered wise counsel.

As Winston Churchill observed, "Writing a book is an adventure. To begin with it is a toy and an amusement. Then it becomes a mistress, then it becomes a master, then it becomes a tyrant. The last phase is that just as you are about to be reconciled to your servitude, you kill the monster and fling him to the public."

Unlike my earlier books, many people helped me slay this monster. Editor in chief Josh Burek has been a constant source of inspiration, insight, and determination to reach the finish line. His chief lieutenant, Adam Siegel, has demonstrated unflagging good spirit and great skill in managing research assistants and students, including Jieun Baek, Leore Ben-Chorin, Edyt Dickstein, Chris Farley, Paul Fraioli, Eleanor Freund, Eyck Frey-mann, Josh Goldstein, Tess Hellgren, Arjun Kapur, Zachary Keck, Nathan Levine, Wesley Morgan, William Ossoff, Krysianna Papadakis, Sam Rat-ner, Henry Rome, Tim Sandole, and Wright Smith. Special thanks to John Masko, who intrepidly edited the initial draft of the Thucydides's Trap Case File in Appendix 1. Two remarkable emerging scholars made critical contributions: Ben Rhode, who helped me understand the path that led to World War I; and Seth Jaffe, who expertly assessed the original instance of Thucydides's Trap in ancient Greece.

Bob Blackwill, Uri Friedman, Michael Martina, Jim Miller, Joe Nye, Michael Sulmeyer, Mark Toher, Odd Arne Westad, Ali Wyne, and Bob Zoellick reviewed sections of the book and provided valuable comments. The collective feedback of this venerable group resulted in scores of corrections and improvements. The remaining errors are mine alone.

At the Belfer Center, executive directors Gary Samore and Patty Walsh have been superb comrades; they are the major reason the Center did not skip a beat during the drafting of this book. Colleagues Benn Craig, Ari-elle Dworkin, Andrew Facini, Andrea Heller, Henry Kaempf, Simone O'Hanlon, and Sharon Wilke have done yeoman work behind the scenes. Thank you.

Thanks to my agent, Michael Carlisle, who saw the potential of this book early on and never wavered. The Houghton Mifflin Harcourt team deserves extra credit for managing both my manuscript and my mood swings: Larry Cooper, Lori Glazer, Carla Gray, Ben Hyman, Alexander Littlefield, Ayesha Mirza, Bruce Nichols, and Taryn Roeder.

Most of all, I am grateful to my wife Elisabeth who has not only been the love of my life but has become my best friend and most thoughtful reality check in reviewing every chapter.

THUCYDIDES'S TRAP CASE FILE

	Period	Ruling power	Rising power	Domain	Result
1	Late 15th century	Portugal	Spain	Global empire and trade	No war
2	First half of 16th century	France	Hapsburgs	Land power in Western Europe	War
3	16th and 17th centuries	Hapsburgs	Ottoman Empire	Land power in central and Eastern Europe, sea power in the Mediterranean	War
4	First half of 17th century	Hapsburgs	Sweden	Land and sea power in northern Europe	War
5	Mid- to late 17th century	Dutch Republic	England	Global empire, sea power, and trade	War
6	Late 17th to mid-18th centuries	France	Great Britain	Global empire and European land power	War
7	Late 18th and early 19th centuries	United Kingdom	France	Land and sea power in Europe	War
8	Mid-19th century	France and United Kingdom	Russia	Global empire, influence in Central Asia and eastern Mediterranean	War
9	Mid-19th century	France	Germany	Land power in Europe	War
10	Late 19th and early 20th centuries	China and Russia	Japan	Land and sea power in East Asia	War
11	Early 20th century	United Kingdom	United States	Global economic dominance and naval supremacy in the Western Hemisphere	No war
12	Early 20th century	United Kingdom supported by France, Russia	Germany	Land power in Europe and global sea power	War
13	Mid-20th century	Soviet Union, France, and UK	Germany	Land and sea power in Europe	War
14	Mid-20th century	United States	Japan	Sea power and influence in the Asia-Pacific region	War
15	1940s–1980s	United States	Soviet Union	Global power	No war
16	1990s–present	United Kingdom and France	Germany	Political influence in Europe	No war

Sixteen major cases of rise vs. rule. Explore the Harvard Thucydides's Trap Project and access additional materials by visiting http://belfercenter.org/thucydides-trap/.

I. PORTUGAL VS. SPAIN

Period: Late fifteenth century

Ruling power: Portugal

Rising power: Spain

Domain: Global empire and trade

Outcome: No war

> *For most of the fifteenth century, Portugal overshadowed its traditional*
> *rival and neighbor, the Spanish Crown of Castile, by leading the world in*
> *exploration and international trade. By the 1490s, however, a united, re-*
> *juvenated Spain began to challenge Portugal's trade dominance and claim*
> *colonial supremacy in the New World, bringing the two Iberian powers*
> *to the brink of war. An intervention by the pope and the 1494 Treaty of*
> *Tordesillas narrowly staved off a devastating conflict.*

In the mid-fifteenth century, the ambitious prince Henry the Navigator emerged as the chief proponent of Portuguese exploration. He invested in new seafaring technologies and dispatched the Portuguese navy on far-flung expeditions to seek gold, foster new trading partnerships, and spread Christianity. With Portugal's chief rival, Castile, preoccupied with a war over its monarchical succession and its reconquest of the remaining Islamic strongholds on the Iberian Peninsula, Portuguese trading preeminence was secure. Henry therefore had "free hands to undertake a dynamic and coherent policy of expansion"[1] in Madeira, the Azores, and the coastal territories of West Africa. Portuguese mastery of the seas reached its apex in 1488, when the explorer Bartolomeu Dias became the first European to round the Cape of Good Hope, pointing to a future sea route to India and the lucrative East Indies.

But even as Lisbon's empire continued to grow, its Castilian rival was positioning itself to challenge Portuguese supremacy. The dynastic marriage between Catholic monarchs Isabella of Castile and Ferdinand of Aragon in 1469 united those two kingdoms under a single crown and quickly centralized power in the Spanish-speaking world.[2]

In 1492, Ferdinand and Isabella completed their reconquest of the final emirate on the Iberian Peninsula, Granada.

Though Portugal maintained an edge when it came to overseas expansion—Spain's empire extended no farther than the Canary Islands—it did not take long for Spain's rise to worry ruling Portugal. After the 1492 recapture of Granada, Lisbon worried that "the victorious Castilians might now be expected to carry their war into North Africa, posing a threat to Portugal's ambitions in that quarter."[3]

Portugal's concerns grew after Christopher Columbus reached the New World in 1492. Spurned by King John II when he at first appealed to Portugal for support, Columbus turned to Ferdinand and Isabella, who backed him in return for nine-tenths of the revenues from the lands he laid claim to.[4] Columbus's voyages turned Spain into a serious rival for overseas empire.

The balance of power between the two rivals changed almost overnight. According to economic historian Alexander Zukas, "It was clear that conflict would soon arise over the rival claims of Spain and Portugal to lands previously unclaimed by Europeans."[5] Indeed, when rumor arose in Spain that King John, "convinced that the islands which Columbus had discovered belonged to him . . . was already preparing a fleet to take possession of them," war between the two powers seemed likely.[6]

Remembering the bitter lessons of the War of Castilian Succession in the 1470s, in which Castile, Aragon, and Portugal fought for five years to an essential stalemate, Spain turned to the Spanish-descended Pope Alexander VI for arbitration, in whom it found a sympathetic ear. Alexander demarcated a line—about 320 miles west of the Cape Verde Islands—and determined that any new lands discovered east of the line should belong to Portugal, and any west of the line to Spain.[7] The Portuguese, however, were furious with the ruling and refused to abide by it because of its meager share of the New World and the restriction placed on its access to trade routes in India and Africa.[8]

In a last-ditch attempt to avoid war, the two powers agreed to modify the pope's proposal in the 1494 Treaty of Tordesillas. The treaty moved the dividing line westward to the 46th meridian, cutting through modern-day eastern Brazil, and granted Portugal trade access to India and Africa. As historian A. R. Disney has argued, Tordesillas "became a basic charter of empire, defining their respective spheres of 'conquest' and influence well into the eighteenth century."[9] The agreement held despite further exploration of the vast American continent, which revealed that Spain had gotten the far better end of the deal in the Americas.[10]

Why did the two powers not fight, even after Portugal realized that Spain's discoveries would significantly sway the balance of power? One reason was that King John II knew Portugal "could ill-afford another war with Spain,"[11] and Spain too, having just completed its reconquest of Granada, was constrained economically and militarily. The memory of the War of Castilian Succession surely dampened hopes of a decisive victory. But more important, Pope Alexander's bulls carried behind them the threat of papal excommunication, a devastating blow to the prestige of any Catholic monarch. The pope could stave off war because both the Spanish and Portuguese crowns saw their own legitimacy as more important than the balance of power.

The Treaty of Tordesillas survived the test of time.[12] Though Spain and Portugal continued to compete, they recognized a shared interest in excluding other powers from the New World. As Britain, France, and the Netherlands surpassed them in economic and military might, Spain and Portugal increasingly clung to their Vatican-approved positions as guardians of the status quo.[13]

2. FRANCE VS. HAPSBURGS

Period: First half of sixteenth century

Ruling power: France

Rising power: Hapsburgs

Domain: Land power in Western Europe

Outcome: Hapsburg-Valois Wars (1519–59), including Italian War (1521–26)

King Charles of Spain's 1519 election as Holy Roman emperor embold-
ened the rising House of Hapsburg and challenged French preeminence in
Europe. Determined to maintain French influence over Western Europe
and fearful of Hapsburg encirclement, France's King Francis I rallied
his allies to invade Hapsburg-controlled lands, beginning forty years of
intermittent war between the rival land powers that ended with a century
of Hapsburg supremacy.

After dismantling and annexing half of the powerful Duchy of Burgundy in 1477 and the Duchy of Brittany in 1491, France began the
sixteenth century as Western Europe's predominant land power. Its
growing prosperity led Pope Leo X in 1519 to declare that King Francis
I of France "surpassed in wealth and power all other Christian kings."[14]
That year, Francis was a leading contender to succeed Maximilian I as
Holy Roman emperor, but electoral corruption gave the title instead
to the Hapsburg successor, King Charles of Spain. Immediately after
Charles's election — a massive boon for the rising Hapsburgs — Fran-
cis "forecast war — not against the Infidel, but between himself and
Charles."[15]

For Francis, there was much to fear in Charles's appointment. A list
of interrelated feuds between the two rulers — over Navarre (a Hapsburg possession, which Francis claimed), Burgundy (a French possession, which Charles claimed), and control of the Duchy of Milan —
meant that Charles's new advantage posed a serious threat to French
power. It also raised the prospect of encirclement by Hapsburg lands.[16]

The Spanish king's influence — and his neighbors' anxiety — grew
as he consolidated his rule over Hapsburg-controlled parts of the Holy
Roman Empire, the Netherlands, territories in Franche-Comté and
modern-day Italy, and Spain's empire in the New World. "Whether
Charles V aspired to a universal empire or not," historian John Lynch
observes, "the fact remained that even without counting any of the
territories in dispute — Milan and Burgundy — his dominions were already too universal and injured too many interests not to provoke widespread resentment."[17] Francis, according to historian Robert Knecht,

had voiced these concerns prior to Charles's coronation as emperor, and sought the position himself mainly because "if [Charles] were to succeed, seeing the extent of his kingdoms and lordships, this could do me immeasurable harm."[18]

In an effort to reverse Charles's rise, Francis pushed allies to invade Hapsburg-controlled lands in Navarre (part of modern-day northeast Spain and southwest France) and Luxembourg. Charles reacted by enlisting English and papal support against France's aggression, successfully invading French lands in Italy. Francis was captured in the 1525 Battle of Pavia and imprisoned in Madrid. To win release, he had to renounce his claims in Italy, Burgundy, Flanders, and Artois in the Treaty of Madrid of 1526. Charles's growing power and his degrading treatment of the French monarch sent tremors across Europe, making it much easier for Francis to forge a countervailing coalition when he returned to Paris. His alliance included such unlikely partners as the new pope, Clement VII, and Sultan Suleiman of the Ottoman Empire (see case 3). It was insufficient, however, to prevent Charles from invading much of Italy in early 1527, culminating in the shocking sack of Rome and the capture of Pope Clement himself in May.

The struggle between France and the Hapsburgs continued intermittently until the late 1550s, even as the Ottoman Empire rose to threaten Hapsburg power. At that point, having exhausted their finances, both sides agreed to shelve their hostilities. A long peace paved the way for the new Spanish Hapsburg king, Philip II, to enjoy "undisputed supremacy in Christendom,"[19] while France dealt with decades of domestic turmoil in the French Wars of Religion. Conflict resumed during the early 1600s, as King Philip IV of Spain faced a rising France under King Louis XIII. Under his successor, the Sun King, Louis XIV, France became continental Europe's preeminent power once more.

3. HAPSBURGS VS. OTTOMAN EMPIRE
Period: Sixteenth and seventeenth centuries
Ruling power: Hapsburgs

Rising power: Ottoman Empire

Domain: Land power in central and Eastern Europe, sea power in the
    Mediterranean

Outcome: Ottoman-Hapsburg wars, including wars of Suleiman the
    Magnificent (1526–66), Long War (1593–1606), and Great
    Turkish War (1683–99)

> *The rapid expansion of Ottoman territory and resources in the early
> 1500s threatened to upend the status quo of a Hapsburg-dominated
> Europe, particularly as Turkish ambitions to expand into Eastern Europe
> and the Balkans became a reality. This expansion pitted the two powers
> against each other in a series of wars that included the Ottoman seizure
> of much of Eastern Europe and confirmed the empire's rise to continental
> preeminence.*

With the powerful Hapsburg Charles V's election as Holy Roman emperor in 1519, a "universal monarchy, in which the Hapsburgs ruled over a united and once again uniformly Catholic Christendom, seemed a realistic possibility."[20] When Charles defeated France in the Italian War five years later (see case 2), he achieved a dominant position in Europe, controlling Austria, Spain, southern Italy, and the present-day Netherlands. In 1525, in an act of desperation, the vanquished Francis I sought an alliance with the erstwhile enemy of all the European great powers: the Ottoman Empire under Sultan Suleiman the Magnificent. In the words of historian Halil İnalcık, the Ottomans represented to Francis "the only power capable of guaranteeing the existence of the European states against Charles V."[21]

Ottoman ambition was undeniable. Midway through the previous century, Sultan Mehmed the Conqueror had sacked the Byzantine capital of Constantinople, instilling throughout Christian Europe the fear of "an ever more aggressive policy of conquest."[22] At the turn of the sixteenth century, the Second Ottoman-Venetian War transformed the Ottoman Empire into a formidable naval power, with over four hundred ships by 1515 and over one hundred docks on the Black Sea by the early 1520s.[23] Eight years before Francis's plea, the Ottomans completed their conquest of the Mamluk Empire, annexing modern-day Egypt, Syria, and the Arabian Peninsula, and doubling the sultan's territory and tax base. According to Andrew Hess, these conquests "immeasurably strengthened the Ottoman state," providing economic benefits and religious legitimacy in the Islamic world.[24] Using their newfound naval power and wealth, the Ottomans expanded their sphere of influence west into the Mediterranean Sea and northwest toward Vienna.[25] Beyond the walls of Vienna lay Charles's Holy Roman Empire.

In 1526, Suleiman attacked Hungary in the Battle of Mohács, seizing a third of its territory. King Louis II of Hungary died during the retreat. As Suleiman marched on toward the Austrian border, Charles became, as Richard Mackenney puts it, "preoccupied" by the seemingly "invincible and all-conquering" invaders. In 1527, he convoked the Castilian Cortes (Spanish legislature) "to organize the necessary means of defense against the Turks,"[26] whose ultimate goal, Charles knew, was the Holy Roman Empire itself. "It was there that their main enemy, the Hapsburgs, and the German princes who supported them, could be dealt a decisive blow," writes historian Brendan Simms. "Moreover, it was only by occupying Germany that Suleiman could vindicate the Ottoman claim to the legacy of the Roman Empire."[27]

The spark that ignited war between the two powers came quickly. Fearing that the Ottomans would exploit the power vacuum in Hungary following Louis II's death, the Hapsburg archduke of Austria Ferdinand I declared himself king of Hungary and Bohemia. Suleiman responded, with the support of Ferdinand's main rival for the Hungarian succession, John Zápolya of Transylvania, by laying siege to Vienna in 1529.

After twice repelling Ottoman attacks on Vienna but failing to reclaim much territory in Hungary or score any significant naval victories in the Mediterranean, Ferdinand was forced into a humiliating truce at Adrianople in 1547. The terms required him to relinquish most Hapsburg claims to Hungary and pay an exorbitant tribute for those small parts that remained nominally Hapsburg. They also referred to

Charles V not as "Emperor," but only as "King of Spain," allowing Suleiman to proclaim himself the world's true "Caesar."[28]

The Ottoman Empire's victory cemented its position as a principal player in the European political landscape. The empire would continue to test the limits of its expansion in Central Europe and the Mediterranean for the next century and a half, even as it suffered a naval setback in the 1571 Battle of Lepanto. Only at the conclusion of the Great Turkish War in 1699 did the Hapsburg prince Eugene of Savoy manage to gain back most of Hungary and decisively reverse Ottoman expansion in Europe. The Ottomans' protracted decline would last into the twentieth century.

4. HAPSBURGS VS. SWEDEN

Period: First half of seventeenth century
Ruling power: Hapsburgs
Rising power: Sweden
Domain: Land and sea power in northern Europe
Outcome: Part of Thirty Years' War (Swedish involvement, 1630–48)

> *At the time of his election as Holy Roman emperor in 1619, Ferdinand II was the most powerful ruler in Central Europe. His empire, which carried the authority of the papacy, stretched from the Mediterranean to northern Germany. His ascent to power, however, coincided with one of the greatest threats the empire had ever faced: the rise of the Lutheran north. Ferdinand's attempts to quash isolated cases of Lutheran rebellion and reassert Hapsburg rule would eventually grow into the Thirty Years' War. They would also bring him into conflict with the region's fastest-rising power, Sweden.*

During the first half of the seventeenth century, in response to nascent rebellions in the German northern provinces, several Protestant powers outside the Holy Roman Empire—including England and the Dutch Republic—volunteered to finance a militarily powerful Protestant state to confront imperial general Albrecht von Wallenstein in northern Germany. The first king to be given the chance was Christian IV of Denmark. Overmatched, Christian was driven all the way back to the Danish isles, leaving Holy Roman Emperor Ferdinand II even stronger and a ruling force throughout Germany and the rest of northern Europe. Wallenstein's arrival at the shores of the Baltic Sea, along with his plan to assert control in the Baltic by building a Hapsburg northern fleet, seriously alarmed the king of the region's most rapidly rising power, Sweden.

Through wars with Denmark, Russia, and Poland, Swedish king Gustavus Adolphus established himself as one of Europe's most capable commanders. Through a combination of economic growth, military innovation, and territorial expansion, Gustavus transformed Sweden from a poor, backward state into one of Europe's most powerful empires. Between 1590 and 1630, Sweden's small provincial army grew from 15,000 into a force of 45,000.[29] Innovations in the use of artillery and a conscription system (Europe's first) helped to build a well-oiled military machine.[30] His decisive victories over Russia in 1617 and the Polish-Lithuanian Commonwealth in 1625 allowed Sweden to consolidate its control of the Baltics. After capturing a slice of Poland in 1629, Sweden controlled almost "every port of consequence on the southern shore of the Baltic."[31]

The challenge of Sweden's expansionism was not lost on the Hapsburg general. As English historian Samuel Gardiner observes, Wallenstein "had long been alarmed at the danger which threatened him from Sweden . . . for no man could expect that Gustavus would look on quietly, whilst a great military power was forming on the southern coast of the Baltics."[32] According to historian Peter Wilson, Wallenstein "regarded the imperial navy plan as purely defensive," as a means of protecting Hapsburg dominance in northern Europe, for he "genuinely feared Swedish intervention."[33]

What the Hapsburgs considered a defensive measure proved far more provocative than planned. Gustavus lobbied for armed intervention in Germany on the grounds that the Hapsburgs were seeking to contain

Swedish growth and constituted an imminent threat to Swedish security. Gustavus began to see a military standoff as "inevitable."[34] According to Brendan Simms, Gustavus argued before the Swedish Rijkstag that it would be best "to act pre-emptively in order to 'transfer the seat and burdens of war to a place which is subject to the enemy.'"[35] In 1627, he told his nobles: "As one wave follows another, so the popish league comes closer and closer to us. They have violently subjugated a great part of Denmark, whence we must apprehend that they may press on into our borders, if they be not powerfully resisted in good time."[36] As do many rising powers facing containment by an established power, Gustavus accused his enemy of precisely what he was about to do: pursue expansion and make military threats.

Though motivated primarily by security interests, Gustavus solicited financial support by declaring himself the Protestants' champion against the Catholic empire. This approach won him funding from around Europe. Paris, seeking to check Hapsburg power and wishing to maintain influence in a potential postwar order dominated by Sweden, also offered significant support.[37] And so, according to historian Michael Roberts, "the Protestant cause became Sweden's cause too; and the north German coastland became a Swedish interest."[38] Gustavus began his assault at Usedom, near the Polish-German border, in July 1630. The Swedes enjoyed early successes, taking Pomerania and moving inland. Gustavus's ambition grew along with his power: he determined to "emasculate the emperor" and "ensure the emperor was never in a position to pose a danger again."[39]

Although Gustavus himself was killed in action, Sweden won decisive victories, most notably at the Battle of Wittstock in 1636. During the war, Swedish troops occupied half of Germany, and its triumphs were reflected in a favorable settlement at the 1648 Peace of Westphalia. Sweden became the most powerful country in northern Europe and the third-largest country on the Continent (behind Russia and Spain). What historians call Sweden's Age of Greatness lasted into the early eighteenth century.

5. DUTCH REPUBLIC VS. ENGLAND

Period: Mid- to late seventeenth century

Ruling power: Dutch Republic

Rising power: England

Domain: Global empire, sea power, and trade

Outcome: Anglo-Dutch Wars (1652–74)

> *By the time the Dutch Republic was granted full recognition of its independence at the 1648 Peace of Westphalia, it had already emerged as Europe's preeminent trading power. Its dominance of the seas and nascent colonial empire soon brought the republic into conflict with the English, who expanded their holdings in North America and their trading presence in the East Indies. Over several Anglo-Dutch wars at sea, the Dutch Republic's dominance held, continuing until the two countries joined forces in the 1688 Glorious Revolution.*

With trading posts across the Silk Road, South America, West Africa, Japan, and the Pacific islands, as well as colonies in India and what later became New York, the Dutch Republic in the mid-seventeenth century was the world's leader in international commerce. It used this power to construct a "borderless" world order, which enabled the tiny Netherlands to translate high productivity and efficiency into outsized political and economic power. Thus, lucrative trading routes gave the publicly owned Dutch East India Company a leading role in the global spice trade.

Arguably the Continent's most advanced seafaring people, the Dutch built a navy to match their massive overseas trading empire. It would not be long, however, before England, seeking to expand its own share of trade and control of the seas, established rival colonies on the American eastern seaboard. The English also began clawing for access to the spice trade with their own East India Company, while expanding their naval fleet (from 39 major ships in 1649 to 80 by 1651) to protect English shipping. By the 1650s, England's military manpower (which had remained at roughly 20,000 to 30,000 men from 1470 to 1600) had more than doubled, to 70,000, and — in the wake of the English Civil War — became substantially more professional.[40]

England's designs on Dutch economic supremacy were unmistakable. Midway through the coming succession of wars, English general George Monck would say of fighting the Dutch: "What matters this or that reason? What we want is more of the trade the Dutch now have."[41] As historian J. R. Jones explains, "Aggressive foreign and mercantile policies" were also a way in which Charles II's ministers "increased the powers and enhanced the authority of the crown."[42]

Dutch officials were gravely concerned about what they correctly perceived as England's relentless pursuit of both mercantile power and the military means to defend it. As historian Paul Kennedy puts it, Dutch power was "firmly anchored in the world of trade, industry, and finance."[43] Unchecked, England could roll back Dutch control of the seas and threaten the tiny nation's great power status.[44]

Thus an ostensibly economic conflict became a geopolitical one. According to political scientist Jack Levy, this period was characterized by "the transformation of the commercial rivalry into a strategic rivalry that escalated to war . . . Although some interpret the first two Anglo-Dutch naval wars as 'purely commercial,' a purely economical explanation is misleading. The escalatory potential of the economic conflict in fact owed much to the close connection between economic and strategic issues."[45] Historian George Edmundson agrees, writing that each of the two nations was "instinctively conscious that its destiny was upon the water, and that mastery of the seas was a necessity of national existence."[46]

In 1651, the Dutch rejected English attempts at a treaty to unite against the continental Catholic powers, an agreement that may have been intended to gain access to Dutch trade. In response, an increasingly confident English Parliament passed the first Navigation Act, prohibiting any European imports to England carried by third-party ships, and barring foreign ships from carrying imports to England or its colonies from Asia, Africa, or America. The target of this legislation was no secret in either London or The Hague: a large portion of Dutch shipping focused on exactly this sort of activity.

Describing England's actions, sociologist Immanuel Wallerstein explains that "since the Dutch were in fact hegemonic, there were only two possible ways of enhancing English commerce: state assistance to English merchants or state constraint on foreign merchants . . . It is difficult to see how a military test of strength could have been avoided. The provocation to the Dutch was too great, even if the English thought they were being defensive."[47] Tensions boiled over the following year in the North Sea, when a confrontation led England to declare war, beginning the first of three Anglo-Dutch naval wars between 1652 and 1674. Though the conflicts resulted in England's acquisition of New York and the dramatic growth of its navy (adding more than two hundred ships between Charles I's 1649 execution and the Restoration in 1660),[48] the Dutch navy emerged as Europe's mightiest, inflicting a severe defeat on the English with the 1667 Raid on the Medway.

In the end, Dutch sea and trade supremacy held firm, and the Anglo-Dutch rivalry dissolved with the invasion of Britain by Dutch prince William of Orange and the ensuing Glorious Revolution in 1688. The two nations went on to make common cause against William's archenemy, France's Louis XIV.

6. FRANCE VS. GREAT BRITAIN

Period: Late seventeenth to mid-eighteenth centuries

Ruling power: France

Rising power: Great Britain

Domain: Global empire and European land power

Outcome: Nine Years' War (1689–97), War of the Spanish Succession (1701–14), War of the Austrian Succession (1740–48), and Seven Years' War (1756–63)

During the reign of Louis XIV, France became the "preeminent power" in Europe.[49] *Emboldened by its prosperous American colonies and its*

Glorious Revolution, however, Great Britain soon challenged French supremacy in a succession of wars. At first, both Britain's strength and its struggles with France derived mainly from its alliance with the Dutch Republic. But as Britain continued to grow as a trading and naval power that threatened French continental and colonial preeminence, their conflict would stretch across the globe and end in the undisputed imperial hegemony of Great Britain.

Despite Louis XIV's dominant position in Europe by the late seventeenth century, his continual quest for absolute security for France brought him into conflict with a large countervailing coalition of European powers. Although technically at peace with his neighbors, Louis systematically strengthened his position in the 1680s by seizing buffer zones beyond his borders in Strasbourg, Luxembourg, and Casale. These gains were accompanied by a military buildup, indicating an ambition for further conquests. While already possessing Europe's largest army (and by 1689, its largest navy as well), Louis reinforced French fortresses, prepared 36 battalions of infantry for service, and put another 140,000 men on notice.[50]

His ambitions alarmed his neighbors. In 1686, the Dutch prince William of Orange encouraged the Hapsburg Holy Roman emperor Leopold I to form the League of Augsburg, a coalition of powers intended to check further French expansion. In September 1688, the French crossed the Rhine into Phillipsburg. William feared French influence over his father-in-law, the Catholic James II of England, many of whose subjects were disquieted by the prospect of a popish dynasty. He also knew that an England free of James could be a powerful ally in suppressing France's rise. Less than six weeks after Louis crossed the Rhine, William invaded England, with the support of numerous English sympathizers. James fled, and in 1689 the Protestant William became king of England, alongside his wife, Queen Mary.

In early 1689, the League of Augsburg mobilized in response to Louis's crossing of the Rhine the previous autumn. Britain, now united with the Dutch Republic through shared leadership, assumed its place as one of the league's central partners in the Nine Years' War against France (1689–97). In the words of historians Derek McKay and H. M. Scott, William's Glorious Revolution, as it came to be known, brought Britain "decisively on to the continental stage as a military power as well as a diplomatic and naval one."[51]

According to historian Sir George Clark, William and his fellow Augsburg leader, the Holy Roman emperor, "regarded the war as an opportunity to reduce the power of France to a level which could be tolerable to the rest of Europe."[52] Although the war was ultimately successful in blunting Louis's territorial designs, hostilities resumed in 1701 when William and the Hapsburgs rejoined forces in a bid to stop a misguided attempt by Louis to put a fellow Bourbon on the Spanish throne. The alliance was unable to prevent Louis's grandson from assuming the throne, but it succeeded in forcing Louis to cede territory in the New World to Britain in the Treaty of Utrecht.

Partly as a result of its Utrecht acquisitions, Britain reaped substantial economic benefit from its colonies during the 1700s. "Exports to North America rose from a yearly average of £525,000 in the late 1720s to just over £1 million twenty years later," according to historian Lawrence James.[53] The British also benefited from a set of financial reforms based on the Dutch model.[54] Britain's growth had its French competitors greatly concerned. "French officials," as historians Robert and Isabelle Tombs write, "were 'stupefied' and 'obsessed' by British financial power."[55] This economic growth also proved to be a prelude to further military expansion: after the War of the Spanish Succession, the British naval fleet exceeded the strength of the French and Spanish navies combined.[56] Britain's financial power allowed it to raise money quickly in times of conflict. Despite France's formidable land forces, Britain "managed when necessary to outspend France, devoting as much as five times the proportion of its GNP to war as its enemy," as Robert and Isabelle Tombs note.[57]

The rapid growth of Britain's colonial empire in North America led to increasing conflict with the French over rights to trade and territory. Thus the 1740 War of the Austrian Succession (a Central European conflict in which France fought to undermine its longtime enemy the House of Hapsburg, while Britain fought to defend it) spilled over onto the American continent. While the 1748 peace at Aix-la-Chapelle ended that conflict with victory for the Hapsburgs and Britain, it did nothing to abate the French-British rivalry, which, according to the English historian Lawrence James, "persisted and deepened after 1748. The French remained convinced that their antagonist's long-term aim was to stifle their trade and expropriate their colonies."[58] In fulfill-ment of France's fears, Britain underwent a massive military expansion during and after the War of the Austrian Succession, increasing mil-itary spending between 1740 and 1760 by 500 percent, while France managed only a 150 percent increase.[59]

In 1756, the French and British rivalry reignited in the Seven Years' War. Britain's decisive victory over France at the conclusion of that conflict, in 1763, led to a wholesale rearrangement in the balance of power in North America and Europe. Even though it would soon lose much of its American empire—in no small part due to French inter-vention—Britain had overtaken France as Europe's greatest imperial power, a position it would maintain into the Napoleonic era.

7. UNITED KINGDOM VS. FRANCE

Period: Late eighteenth and early nineteenth centuries

Ruling power: Great Britain/United Kingdom

Rising power: France

Domain: Land and sea power in Europe

Outcome: French Revolutionary Wars (1792–1802) and Napoleonic Wars (1803–15)

> *Through ingenuity and control of the seas, Great Britain had, by the end of the eighteenth century, pulled ahead of its rivals to become one of Europe's leading industrialized nations. But beginning with the French Revolution, a reinvigorated French military machine would rise again. Under Napoleon, France would take over much of continental Europe*

and threaten British supremacy, leading Britain and France into violent
confrontation. By funding anti-Napoleonic forces in Europe and fighting
brilliantly at sea, however, Britain managed to avoid invasion and hasten
Napoleon's eventual fall from power.

During the 1780s, Britain's wave of innovation led to domestic industrialization and booming colonial trade, with merchant shipping doubling between 1782 and 1788.[60] By 1793, Britain could rely on 113
ships of the line to protect these trade interests, dwarfing the 76 equivalent ships of Europe's premier mercantile economy, France.[61] It would
not be long, however, before the small island nation faced a fresh challenge from its great rival across the English Channel.

Though the French economy remained backward in the years following the 1789 revolution, its extraordinary political developments
and surging militarism threatened the European status quo.[62] Anxious
over the increasingly radical revolution and the safety of King Louis
XVI and his wife, Marie-Antoinette, Holy Roman Emperor Leopold
II and Prussia's King Frederick William II issued the Declaration of
Pillnitz in 1791, which called on European powers to declare war on
France if the royals were endangered. Intended as a warning, the declaration arguably accelerated conflict, as French radicals, feeling threat-
ened, declared war the following April and successfully invaded the
Austrian Netherlands.

That campaign struck fear across monarchic Europe, especially
because France "proclaimed new war aims calculated to alienate and
alarm not only monarchs, but the entire social hierarchies upon which
their power rested."[63] Corresponding transformations in French military organization, ideology, and aggressiveness confirmed European
anxiety that the country's radicalism would not be contained. France's
shift from aristocratic to popular military leadership opened commis-
sions to new talent and increased enthusiasm for military service; in
1792 alone, the army gained 180,000 new recruits, and a program of
universal conscription the next year swelled the ranks—and revolutionary fervor—further.[64]

This marriage of rising military power and radical politics instilled particular panic in Britain. In a 1793 message to the House of Commons, King George III requested "a further augmentation of his forces by sea and land," as a means of opposing "views of aggrandizement and ambition on the part of France, which would be at all times dangerous to the general interests of Europe, but are peculiarly so, when connected with the propagation of principles which . . . are utterly subversive of the peace and order of all civil society."[65] According to the British historian William Doyle, while the French invasion of the Low Countries had put Britain on notice, the execution of King Louis XVI in January 1793 was the final straw, galvanizing the British to action and prompting Britain to "engineer a grand anti-French coalition."[66] By early 1793, this coalition of European powers was at war, attempting to reverse French territorial gains. These efforts proved unsuccessful: France would augment its territory in the 1790s through annexations in the Netherlands, northern Italy, and through the brief acquisition of America's Louisiana Territory.

British fears of French expansionism rose to the level of existential threat when Napoleon Bonaparte seized power in the 1799 Coup of 18 Brumaire and embarked on a campaign of European domination.[67] Specifically, Napoleon was known to have told the French Directory in 1797 that France "must destroy the English monarchy, or expect itself to be destroyed by [it]," and he pledged to "annihilate England. That done, Europe is at our feet."[68] Britain took these threats seriously. "We are here in daily expectation that Bonaparte will attempt his threatened invasion,"[69] George III confided in 1803. Even when Napoleon failed to invade in the near term, his advances on the Continent reinforced Britain's long-standing conviction that its security required prevention of a hegemonic land power in Europe whose lack of rivals would allow it to divert resources toward a fleet. Prime Minister William Pitt responded with a strategy that, as military historian Michael Leggiere argues, aimed not only "to restore the balance of power in Europe by forcing France to surrender conquests such as the Low Countries," but also to leave Britain as "master of the seas and with a clear monopoly on global trade."[70]

Fortunately for Britain, Napoleon never developed a navy that could supplant British dominance at sea. In 1805, Vice Admiral Horatio Nelson defeated the French fleet at Trafalgar, ending Napoleon's hopes of invading Britain and keeping Britain secure in its role as financial backer of Napoleon's European enemies. Thereafter, as Napoleon continued expanding on the Continent while incurring massive public debt, Britain's economic and diplomatic advantages became increasingly undeniable, and London became the great hope of anti-Napoleonic Europe. As Paul Kennedy explains, "The government in Paris could never be certain that the other continental powers would permanently accept the French imperium so long as Britain — offering subsidies, munitions, and possibly even troops — remained independent."[71] Shaken by his first major land defeat in an ill-advised invasion of Russia in 1812, Napoleon went on to further large-scale defeats and met his final demise at the hands of a British-led coalition at Waterloo in 1815.

8. FRANCE AND UNITED KINGDOM VS. RUSSIA

Period: Mid-nineteenth century
Ruling powers: French Empire (land) / United Kingdom (sea)
Rising power: Russia
Domain: Global empire, influence in Central Asia and eastern
   Mediterranean
Outcome: Crimean War (1853–56)

Throughout the first half of the nineteenth century, Russia instilled fear in Europe as it steadily gained territory and military power. France and the United Kingdom, as established players in global trade with territory and networks in the Middle East and southern Asia, were particularly alarmed by St. Petersburg's recurring efforts to exploit the declining Ottoman Empire. These tensions reached their climax in the Crimean War,

*a conflict that vindicated British and French dominance and revealed the
latent weakness behind Russia's rise.*

Russia achieved highly generous settlements in the aftermath of the
Russo-Turkish wars (1806–12 and 1828–29), adding to its protector-
ates in Eastern Europe and the Caucasus, and expanding its access to
the Black Sea. These wars, along with Russian campaigns in Persia and
Eastern Europe, contributed to a huge expansion of territory: Russia
acquired all or part of modern-day Finland, Poland, Georgia, Azerbai-
jan, and Armenia in the late eighteenth and the first half of the nineteenth centuries alone, coming dangerously close to the centers of European power.[72] As Russian territory grew, so did its military: already
more than twice the size of either France's or Britain's by 1820, Russia's
army grew to be significantly larger than both combined by 1853.[73]

With each advance, fears grew that Russia could threaten the global
balance of power by making Europe's "sick man"—as the tsar called
the Ottoman Empire—a Russian protectorate.[74] The 1829 Treaty of
Adrianople, between St. Petersburg and Constantinople, convinced
Lord Heytesbury, the British ambassador to Russia, that Russia would
soon make the Ottomans as "submissive to the orders of the Tsar as any
of the Princes of India to those of the [British East India] Company."[75]
It was in this spirit that both Britain and France intervened diplomatically on the Ottoman side in the Egyptian-Ottoman War of 1831–33,
fearing that a weakened Ottoman Empire might be vulnerable to Russian pressures.

Russia's repeated attempts to usurp Ottoman power and to assert
influence in Eastern Europe convinced Britain that Russia intended, as
historian Brendan Simms puts it, not only to "partition the Ottoman
Empire, but to dominate Europe as a whole,"[76] and to secure control of
the Dardanelles, which would give its Russian Black Sea fleet a foothold in the Mediterranean. This so-called Eastern Question posed a
strong threat to British naval dominance. Some in Britain even believed
Russia might challenge British colonial power in India.[77]

Henry Kissinger proposes one explanation for British and French anxiety: "Everything about Russia—its absolutism, its size, its globe-spanning ambitions and insecurities—stood as an implicit challenge to the traditional European concept of international order."[78] The anxiety Kissinger identifies was evident even among the general public in France and Britain. In one vivid example, a popular French travel publication at the time described Russia as possessing "inordinate and immense" ambition, with "the design to exercise a tyranny over other nations."[79] Not until it was tested in the crucible of war did either Russia or its competitors recognize that it was a "colossus with feet of clay."[80]

In 1853, Tsar Nicholas I demanded that Sultan Abdulmejid recognize a Russian protectorate over Orthodox subjects in Constantinople and the Holy Land. British diplomats tried to mediate the dispute, but ultimately failed to achieve a settlement agreeable to the Ottoman sultan. When diplomacy failed, the sultan declared war on Russia. The tsar quickly took the offensive, sending troops to occupy the Danube Principalities (modern-day Moldova and Romania) and building up his Black Sea fleet at Sevastopol, the capital of Crimea. After the Russians successfully destroyed an Ottoman fleet at Sinope, Britain and France had seen enough. Despite the tsar's protestations to the contrary, both nations feared the collapse of the Ottoman Empire and the vacuum it would leave for Russian power to fill. For Britain, Russia's capture of Constantinople would pose an intolerable threat to its position in the Mediterranean. Fear of Russian expansion united Britain and France in a joint undertaking that included sending a fleet into the Black Sea and issuing an ultimatum demanding that Russia withdraw from the Principalities. When Russia refused, France and Britain declared war and sent an expeditionary force to Crimea.

Technical and organizational backwardness betrayed Russia in battle. The eventual defeat of Russian forces at Sevastopol shattered the illusion of Russian military superiority, boosted French and British prestige and confidence, and saved the ailing Ottoman Empire for another sixty-five years. As naval historian Adam Lambert concludes, "Britain, France and Russia fought on a global scale for mastery of Europe—a prize that went, temporarily, to the French—and mastery of the world, which the British retained for another two generations."[81]

9. FRANCE VS. GERMANY

Period: Mid-nineteenth century
Ruling power: France
Rising power: Germany
Domain: Land power in Europe
Outcome: Franco-Prussian War (1870–71)

> *Under Napoleon III, France emerged, in historian Paul Kennedy's words, "strong and confident"*[82] *in the second half of the nineteenth century as Western Europe's premier land power. But soon Otto von Bismarck of Prussia, a statesman of rare skill at the helm of a surging economy, pursued ambitions to create a united Germany and usurp France's position. While Bismarck saw war as necessary to unite the German states, France embraced conflict as a means to limit Prussia's prodigious rise. The one-year war vindicated Bismarck's strategic foresight and cemented Germany's status as a great and unified power.*

In 1850, France's colonial empire stretched worldwide, from the Pacific Islands and the Caribbean to West Africa and Southeast Asia. Its domestic manufacturing economy was continental Europe's most productive.[83] Its military expenditures by 1860 exceeded any of its competitors' aside from Russia, and its navy grew so large that, as Paul Kennedy notes, it "at times . . . caused alarm on the other side of the English channel."[84] Also by 1860, France's recent military interventions in Crimea and the Second War of Italian Independence had established Paris as the Continent's major security guarantor. That preeminence, however, would prove short-lived. Ten years later, Napoleon III faced one of the greatest military machines Europe had ever seen: Otto von Bismarck's Prussia.

After defeating Denmark in 1864 and Austria in 1866, Prussia put

France, as historian Michael Howard notes, "in that most dangerous of all moods; that of a great power which sees itself declining to the second rank."[85] While Prussia in 1820 had only one-third the population of France, the annexations of the 1860s saw that proportion balloon to almost four-fifths by 1870. Bismarck also amassed, "thanks to the Prussian use of universal conscription—an army one-third larger than France's."[86] A French historian would later claim that a force resembling the 1.2 million soldiers Bismarck fielded had not been seen "since the legendary armies of Xerxes."[87] Prussia's industrial rise was just as formidable, growing from half of France's iron and steel production in 1860 to overtake it ten years later.[88] Bismarck also developed a rail transportation system to match. According to historian Geoffrey Wawro, these rapid developments "were alarming indicators that threatened a total eclipse of French power."[89] It is therefore no mystery why Prussia "dominated [French] foreign and domestic politics after 1866."[90]

Bismarck's goal was to join his Prussian-dominated North German Confederation with the southern German states of Baden, Württemberg, Bavaria, and Hesse.[91] Ever the master strategist, he concluded that a war against France, which would scare the independent south German states into Prussia's arms, would be a vital step toward German unification. As Bismarck later claimed, "I did not doubt that a Franco-German war must take place before the construction of a United Germany could be realized."[92]

All Prussia had to do was provoke the war. Recognizing Napoleon's alarm at Prussia's rise to his east, Bismarck found an ideal opportunity to stoke French fear even higher by threatening to place a German prince from the House of Hohenzollern on the Spanish throne.[93] France would then face German power on two sides.

The Hohenzollern candidacy and the Ems Telegram (a half-true press dispatch that Bismarck had manipulated to suggest that there had been a confrontation between the Prussian king and the French ambassador) contributed to Napoleon's decision to declare war on Prussia in July 1870. In so doing, France made a strategic error common to ruling powers: taking action it believes will prevent a rising power from surpassing its position but in fact hastening the very reversal of fortune it most fears. France remained confident in 1870 (incorrectly, as it turned out) that it could defeat that Prussian threat, but felt that it needed to fight a preventive war before Prussia rose further.[94] Because the southern German states considered France the aggressor, they joined the North German Confederation, just as Bismarck had anticipated. "There can be no doubt," Michael Howard contends, "that France was the immediate aggressor, and none that the immediate provocation to her aggression was contrived by Bismarck."[95] After a decisive victory, a unified Germany emerged with the strongest army on the Continent. It became, as Brendan Simms writes, "by any standard a colossus."[96] Thus a war that catapulted Bismarck to the ranks of the great statesmen but led to Napoleon's capture and exile initially seemed as good an option for France as it did for Prussia.

10. CHINA AND RUSSIA VS. JAPAN

Period: Late nineteenth and early twentieth centuries

Ruling powers: China and Russia

Rising power: Japan

Domain: Land and sea power in East Asia

Outcome: First Sino-Japanese War (1894–95) and Russo-Japanese
War (1904–5)

Entering the final decade of the nineteenth century, two powers dominated the Asian continent: Qing Dynasty China, for centuries the predominant regional power, and the Russian Empire, a European great power with long-standing ambitions in the Asia-Pacific. But since the Meiji Restoration of 1868, both states had a new threat to fear in the rapidly modernizing island nation of Japan. By 1905, China and Russia had been chastened by two damaging wars against the ambitious Japan, and both had to contend with a new Pacific power whose growth showed no signs of slowing.

Rapid economic growth and military advances facilitated Japan's rise in the late nineteenth century: GNP almost tripled between 1885 and 1899, and military expenditures grew dramatically as Emperor Meiji built a formidable standing army and navy.[97] In 1880, military expenditures accounted for 19 percent of the Japanese budget; by 1886, this figure had risen to 25 percent, and by 1890, 31 percent.[98]

Japan's increasing power heightened its leadership's resentment toward its subordinate position in the region compared to Western powers and China, encouraging a "sense of urgency that they must act more energetically" to extend Japanese influence.[99] Gains in military strength allowed the country's leaders to seriously contemplate territorial expansion in the Pacific islands and on the Asian continent, which would be a direct challenge to Chinese hegemony and Russia's well-known designs on the region. But to project power effectively, the Japanese needed a mainland foothold: the Korean Peninsula.

Beginning in the 1870s, Japan's evolving policies toward Korea served as a barometer of Tokyo's increasing confidence and assertiveness as a rising power. At first, these policies focused primarily on promoting reforms to strengthen the Korean government and its institutions against Chinese intervention, extending Japan's influence while gently drawing Korea away from Beijing. As historian of Japan Peter Duus writes, Korea's strategic significance "was not merely its proximity to Japan but its inability to defend itself against outsiders . . . If Korea remained 'backward' or 'uncivilized,' it would remain weak, and if it remained weak, it would be inviting prey for foreign predators."[100] Yet by the eve of the Sino-Japanese War in 1894, historian Akira Iriye notes, Japan's objective "was no longer the maintenance of a balance between Japan and China, but the ejection of Chinese influence from the peninsula."[101]

Japan's longer-term concerns about Western — and particularly Russian — influence in East Asia corroborated its growing assertiveness. The emperor feared that Russia might respond to Japan's rapid rise by using its new Trans-Siberian Railway (begun in 1891) to intervene in the Korean Peninsula and perhaps even invade Japan.[102] Yamagata Aritomo, a Japanese field marshal and prime minister, put it bluntly in 1893: "Neither China nor Korea is our enemy: it is Britain, France, Russia."[103]

In 1894, a Korean peasant rebellion called the Tonghak Uprising compelled Korea's King Yi Myeong-bok to call upon Chinese troops for help in quelling the violence. Japan—unwilling to see its carefully cultivated influence eroded by Chinese intervention—sent its own troops, bringing them into direct conflict with the Chinese. Japan's military preparedness stunned its opponents, as the emperor's forces quickly expelled the Chinese from Pyongyang, scored an unexpected victory against China's Beiyang naval fleet, and landed in southeast Manchuria, marching northwest into Chinese territory. The Sino-Japanese War concluded one year later in humiliation for Beijing with the Treaty of Shimonoseki, which acknowledged the independence of Korea (a nominal gesture that in reality turned Korea from a Chinese vassal to a Japanese vassal) and ceded Taiwan, the Pescadores Islands, and the Liaodong Peninsula to Japan.

Japanese concerns about Russia's intent to contain their power proved prescient. Unsettled by Japan's smashing victory and the radical terms of the treaty, Russia, France, and Germany staged the Triple Intervention immediately following the settlement. The intervention, to which an embarrassed Japan reluctantly acquiesced, negated the treaty's transfer of southeast Manchuria from China to Japan, keeping the threat of Japanese expansion off Russia's doorstep.

It also, however, hardened Japan's determination to eliminate the Russian threat. "Ever since the humiliation of 1895," writes historian J. N. Westwood, the Japanese government "had been deliberately preparing for an eventual war with Russia."[104] Japan's preparations were dramatic, nearly tripling the emperor's naval personnel in the ten years following the Sino-Japanese War, and increasing his army personnel ninefold.[105] Reacting to Russia's enlistment of French and German support in the Triple Intervention, Japan attempted to head off further European containment by concluding the Anglo-Japanese Alliance with

Britain in 1902. Japan was determined to remove Russia from Manchuria.

Unable to negotiate for the withdrawal of Russian troops, Japan carried out a surprise attack on the Russian fleet at Port Arthur (on the Manchurian coast) in February 1904. The attack ignited the year-and-a-half-long Russo-Japanese War. Once again, Japanese forces won convincingly and achieved their objective of full Russian withdrawal from Manchuria at the resulting Treaty of Portsmouth. With Russia vanquished in Manchuria, Japan cleared away one more obstacle in its route to hegemony in the Pacific.

11. UNITED KINGDOM VS. UNITED STATES

Period: Early twentieth century
Ruling power: United Kingdom
Rising power: United States
Domain: Global economic dominance and naval supremacy in the
          Western Hemisphere
Outcome: No war

> *In the last decades of the nineteenth century, US economic power rose to surpass the world's foremost empire, the United Kingdom, and its growing fleet was a potentially troubling rival to the Royal Navy. As the United States began to assert supremacy in its own hemisphere, Britain, facing the challenges of more proximate threats and maintaining a far-reaching colonial empire, accommodated America's rise. Britain's concessions allowed the US to peacefully achieve dominance in the Western Hemisphere. This great rapprochement laid the groundwork for US-British alliances in two world wars and the enduring "special relationship" both nations now take for granted.*

In the last three decades of the nineteenth century, the United States had risen from the ashes of its civil war to become an economic colossus. American GDP, which exceeded Britain's in the early 1870s, would by 1916 overtake the combined economy of the entire British Empire.[106] Between 1890 and 1914, a rapidly developing United States tripled British levels of energy consumption and iron and steel production, all key measures of industrialization.[107] As prosperity increased US confidence, Washington also became increasingly assertive in the Western Hemisphere, insisting on arbitrating disputes between European and Latin American states. This expanded regional role led to concerns over an impending great power conflict. In late 1895, fear that US involvement in a territorial dispute between Britain and Venezuela would lead to an Anglo-American war caused panic on the New York Stock Exchange.[108] In January 1896, Prime Minister Lord Salisbury advised his finance minister that "a war with America, not this year but in the not distant future—has become something more than a possibility."[109]

The US Navy was still small compared to the Royal Navy, but it was growing (especially after the Spanish-American War and the ascendance of the hawkish Theodore Roosevelt to the presidency). American naval tonnage nearly tripled between 1900 and 1910.[110] The First Lord of the Admiralty acknowledged in 1901 that "if the Americans choose to pay for what they can easily afford, they can gradually build up a navy, fully as large and then larger than ours." With this reality in mind, he argued that "I would never quarrel with the United States if I could possibly avoid it."[111]

To the consternation of the British War Office, the Admiralty quietly exempted the US from the Two-Power Standard that committed the UK to maintaining a number of battleships equal to those of its next two largest competitors combined. The Admiralty was preoccupied with threats closer to home, and did its best to avoid contingency planning for a war with America. In 1904, the First Sea Lord told his civilian superior at the Admiralty that Britain should "use all possible means to avoid such a war," because "under no conceivable circumstances" could it "escape an overwhelming and humiliating defeat by the United States." It was therefore "an utter waste of time to prepare for it."[112]

Salisbury expressed the regret felt by many in Britain for having failed to challenge the American threat earlier: "It is very sad, but I am afraid America is bound to forge ahead and nothing can restore the equality between us. If we had interfered in the Confederate Wars it was then possible for us to reduce the power of the United States to manageable proportions. But *two* such chances are not given to a nation in the course of its career."[113]

Rather than challenge America's rise through war, the UK adapted, managing a "Great Rapprochement." Facing more ominous and proximate threats elsewhere, stretching to defend its imperial possessions, and with no competitors to the US in the Western Hemisphere that it could enlist as allies, Britain had little choice but to accommodate the Americans. It deferred to what many British saw as unreasonable American demands over territorial disputes in Canada and Latin America, lucrative fishing rights, and control of the future Panama Canal. "By the end of 1903," according to historian Anne Orde, "by a series of concessions for which the United States made no return, Britain had acquiesced in American supremacy in the Western hemisphere from Venezuela to Alaska."[114]

Britons would have been justified in resenting the lack of American gratitude for a century of "free security."[115] But London's willingness to compromise helped to heal long-standing hostility between the two nations, enough that when war came in 1914, the US could be an essential source of materiel and finance for Britain. American loans and support during World War I, and Washington's eventual entry into the war as a British ally, proved decisive in defeating Germany.

12. UNITED KINGDOM VS. GERMANY

Period: Early twentieth century
Ruling power: United Kingdom, supported by France and Russia
Rising power: Germany
Domain: Land power in Europe and global sea power
Outcome: World War I (1914–18)

After unification under Bismarck, Germany was the leading military and economic power in continental Europe. It rose further to threaten British industrial and naval supremacy, and to risk unsettling the European balance of power. Though initially intended to earn respect, Germany's surging sea power touched off a fierce naval race with Britain. Anglo-German rivalry, along with a second Thucydides Trap between Germany and a rising Russia to its east, played a vital role in transforming a regional Balkan conflict into World War I.

Between 1860 and 1913, Germany's share of global manufacturing ballooned from 4.8 percent to 14.8 percent, surpassing its chief competitor, the United Kingdom, whose share sank from 19.9 percent to 13.6 percent.[116] Prior to unification in 1870, Germany had produced only half the steel Britain did; by 1914, it produced twice as much as Britain.[117] By the 1880s, Bismarck had obtained colonial possessions in Africa, as well as trading outposts in China, New Guinea, and several islands in the South Pacific. These holdings in no way resembled the scale of the British or French empires, however, and Bismarck was not an enthusiastic imperialist. But the new German emperor, Wilhelm II, who dismissed Bismarck in 1890, was determined that his country become a "World Power"—a status that required a formidable navy.

In the 1890s, German admiral Alfred Tirpitz set a course to rival Europe's premier naval power, Britain. Though intended to secure Britain's respect, Germany's naval buildup frightened British leaders and sparked an intense arms race. The First Lord of the Admiralty, the Earl of Selborne, underlined this concern in 1902: "I am convinced that the great new German navy is being carefully built up from the point of view of war with us . . . [The British ambassador in Germany is convinced that] in deciding on a naval policy we cannot safely ignore the malignant hatred of the German people or the manifest design of the German Navy."[118]

Germany's new fleet affected not only British naval policy but also its whole international outlook. As the historian Margaret MacMillan puts it, "The naval race which Germany intended as a means of forcing

Britain to be friendly instead persuaded the latter not only to outbuild Germany but to abandon its preferred aloofness from Europe and draw closer to France and Russia."[119] Germany's growing power raised the prospect of its being able to eliminate its continental rivals and control the coastline opposite Britain—which, along with any challenge to British naval supremacy, London considered an unacceptable threat.

Berlin confronted a second Thucydidean dynamic in Russia's growing strength. By around 1910, Russia had recovered from its earlier military defeat by Japan and a period of simmering revolutionary unrest, and now seemed to be rising as a revitalized, modern military power right on Germany's borders. In 1913, Russia announced the "grand program" for expanding its army, to be enacted the following year. It was expected that by 1917 the Russian army would outnumber Germany's by three to one. French development of Russia's strategic railways already threatened the entire German war plan. Germany's plan for a two-front war entailed quickly defeating France before turning around to deal with the slow-moving Russian threat. By 1914, heavy French investment had allowed the development of a Russian railway system that would shorten its mobilization period to two weeks, as opposed to the six weeks assumed in the German plan.[120]

Russia's rapid rise, along with a general fatalism about an eventual European war, encouraged an aggressive attitude among Germany's political and military leadership. Many espoused preventive war while there was still a chance to beat Russia, especially since a successful conflict might allow Germany to break out of its "encirclement" by Russia, France, and Britain.[121] Berlin gave its infamous "blank check" to Vienna after the June 1914 assassination of an Austrian archduke in Sarajevo primarily because of the connected fears of its sole ally collapsing if Austria-Hungary did not crush its enemies in the Balkans and the prospect of being helpless in a future conflict against Russia.[122]

Since the outbreak of hostilities, scholars have endlessly debated how to apportion blame for World War I; some even reject the question altogether.[123] Though naming culprits is necessarily simplistic, a pair of Thucydidean rivalries (Germany and Britain, and Germany and

Russia) bears primary responsibility for turning a regional conflict between Austria-Hungary and Serbia into a multiyear continental conflagration.

In 1914, the simultaneous dynamics between London and Berlin, and between Berlin and Moscow, became interlocked. Germany's determination to prop up its ally, forestall the menace of a rising Russia, and thus ensure its own survival led to its declaration of war against the tsar—and his ally, France. In threatening to crush France and overturn the European balance of power, Germany crossed a red line for Britain. In the words of historian Paul Kennedy, "So far as the British and German governments were concerned, the 1914–18 conflict was essentially entered into because the former power wished to preserve the existing *status quo,* whereas the latter, for a mixture of offensive and defensive motives, was taking steps to alter it. In that sense, the wartime struggle between London and Berlin was but a continuation of what had been going on for at least fifteen or twenty years before."[124] Amid a host of other causes for war, none was as destructive as Thucydides's Trap.

13. SOVIET UNION, FRANCE, AND UNITED KINGDOM VS. GERMANY

Period: Mid-twentieth century
Ruling powers: Soviet Union, France, United Kingdom
Rising power: Germany
Domain: Land and sea power in Europe
Outcome: World War II (1939–45)

Adolf Hitler led a simultaneous recovery of Germany's economic power, military strength, and national pride, abrogating the Treaty of Versailles and flouting the postwar order maintained by France and the United Kingdom. Seeking Lebensraum, *or living space, Hitler methodically expanded Nazi dominance over Austria and Czechoslovakia. Recognizing his ambitions too slowly, France and the UK declared war only after*

*Hitler's invasion of Poland, unable to stop German domination of the
Continent until millions of Soviet and American forces turned the tide at
the end of World War II.*

Victorious in World War I, the ruling powers of France and the United
Kingdom spent the 1920s rebuilding their economies and military
strength, while Germany remained subordinate, its power stunted
by the punitive conditions of the Treaty of Versailles. The treaty demanded severe economic reparations and imposed tight constraints
on the German military, prohibiting it from having planes, tanks, and
any more than 100,000 troops. Germany was forced to surrender its
overseas colonies as well as 13 percent of its European territory (and
10 percent of its population), and to submit to Allied occupation of
its industrial core, the Rhineland.[125] Most damaging to German pride
was the "war guilt" clause, which laid blame for the war squarely on
Germany. While "bitterly resented by almost all Germans,"[126] the so-
called "slave treaty"[127] nevertheless "left the Reich geographically and
economically largely intact and preserved her political unity and her
potential strength as a great nation."[128] Only twenty years after the
Great War, Adolf Hitler would use that strength in a second attempt to
overturn the European order.

Hitler "focused relentlessly" on bringing about Germany's rise.[129]
After his National Socialist Party won elections in 1933, Hitler moved
to consolidate his power through extra-democratic means. He justified
himself with a call to marshal "all German national energies" toward
the singular objective of rearmament to secure his vision of *Lebensraum*
for the German people: "He wanted the whole of central Europe and
all of Russia, up to the Volga for German *Lebensraum* to secure Germany's self-sufficiency and status as a great power," as Paul Kennedy
puts it.[130] The military buildup was rapid. When Hitler became chancellor, France and Britain together spent twice as much on defense
as Germany. In 1937, Germany reversed the ratio, spending twice as
much on defense as France and Britain combined.[131] Germany's steep
rearmament was exemplified by its production of military aircraft: in

1933, Germany produced just 368 planes, but by 1938 it had increased production to 5,235, more than the combined output of France and Britain.[132] The German army expanded from 39 divisions in 1936 to 103 divisions in 1939, to a total of 2.76 million men.[133]

Germany's rearmament was first met with a "supine"[134] response from its future adversaries, who showed "little immediate recognition of danger."[135] Despite Winston Churchill's dire and repeated warnings that Germany "fears no one" and was "arming in a manner which has never been seen in German history," Prime Minister Neville Chamberlain saw Hitler as merely trying to right the wrongs of Versailles, and acquiesced to the German annexation of the Sudetenland at Munich in September 1938.[136] Yet Chamberlain's anxiety grew as Hitler's decision to occupy the remainder of Czechoslovakia in March 1939 indicated his broader aims. Chamberlain asked rhetorically: "Is this the end of an old adventure, or is it the beginning of a new? Is this the last attack upon a small State, or is it to be followed by others? Is this, in fact, a step in the direction of an attempt to dominate the world by force?"[137] France, meanwhile, as Henry Kissinger explains, "had become so dispirited that it could not bring itself to act."[138] Stalin decided his interests were best served by a non-aggression pact signed with Germany, which included a secret protocol for the division of Eastern Europe.[139]

One week after agreeing to the pact with Stalin, Hitler invaded Poland, triggering the British and French to declare war on September 3, 1939. The Second World War had begun. Within a year, Hitler occupied France, along with much of Western Europe and Scandinavia. Britain was defeated on the Continent, although it fought off German air assaults. In June 1941, Hitler betrayed Stalin and invaded the Soviet Union. By the time Germany was defeated four years later, much of the European continent had been destroyed, and its eastern half would be under Soviet domination for the next forty years. Western Europe could not have been liberated without the United States, on whose military power it would continue to rely. The war Hitler unleashed was the bloodiest the world had ever seen.

14. UNITED STATES VS. JAPAN

Period: Mid-twentieth century
Ruling power: United States
Rising power: Japan
Domain: Sea power and influence in the Asia-Pacific
Outcome: World War II (1941–45)

> *Imperial Japan, bolstered by decisive victories in the Sino- and Russo-Japanese wars and a growing sphere of influence that included Korea and Taiwan, became aggressively hegemonic in the twentieth century. As Japanese expansion, particularly into China, threatened the American-led "Open Door" order in the Pacific, the United States became increasingly hostile toward Japan in the 1930s. After the US sought to contain Japan by embargoing its raw material imports, Japan attacked Pearl Harbor, drawing the hitherto reluctant Americans into World War II.*

In 1915, Japanese prime minister Okuma Shigenobu used his country's newfound leverage to levy "Twenty-One Demands" against the Republic of China for greater Japanese economic and territorial authority over the Asia-Pacific. These demands posed a deep challenge not only to China but also to the regional order established by America's Open Door policy of 1899. Secretary of State Henry Stimson worried that Japan's claims threatened this order and the American way of life that depended on it.[140]

In pursuit of a "New Order in East Asia," Japan launched an unprovoked campaign to seize Manchuria in 1931. This campaign extended into the heart of China, reaching its ruthless climax in the 1937 Rape of Nanking. Though the US viewed Japan's aggression against an American ally with consternation, President Franklin Roosevelt initially refrained from acting, even as Japan bombed a US ship seeking to rescue Americans near Nanking.

In the next few years, however, the US began to step up aid to China and imposed increasingly severe economic sanctions against

Japan. Since the island nation depended almost totally on imports of critical raw materials such as oil, rubber, and scrap iron, and because it considered territorial expansion vital to the procurement of natural resources and to its future as a great power, Japan's leadership viewed this containment as a mortal threat. As Japanese ambassador Kichisaburō Nomura told Washington on December 2, 1941, "The Japanese people believe . . . that they are being placed under severe pressure by the United States to yield to the American position; and that it is preferable to fight rather than to yield to pressure."[141]

As Japan negotiated with the Axis Powers in Europe, Vichy France, and the Soviet Union for settlements that would allow for easier territorial expansion in Southeast Asia, the US cut off negotiations with Japan. Washington, according to historian Richard Storry, became convinced that Japan was "redrawing the map of Asia so as to exclude the West."[142] As sanctions tightened, American ambassador to Tokyo Joseph Grew insightfully noted in his diary, "The vicious circle of reprisals and counter reprisals is on . . . The obvious conclusion is eventual war."[143]

FDR's August 1941 oil embargo of Japan proved to be the final straw. As former State Department official Charles Maechling explains, "While oil was not the sole cause of the deterioration of relations, once employed as a diplomatic weapon, it made hostilities inevitable. The United States recklessly cut the energy lifeline of a powerful adversary without due regard for the predictably explosive consequences."[144] In desperation, Japanese leaders approved a plan to deliver a preemptive "knockout blow" against the US Pacific Fleet at Pearl Harbor, clearing the way to seize resource-rich territory in Southeast Asia and the Dutch East Indies. As scholar Jack Snyder notes, Japan's strategy reflected its conviction that "if the sun is not ascending, it is descending," and that war with the US was "inevitable" given America's "inherently rapacious nature."[145]

Retrospectively, American statesmen realized the rashness of their oil embargo. As the later secretary of state Dean Acheson put it, America's misreading of Japanese intentions was not of "what the Japanese government proposed to do in Asia, not of the hostility our embargo would excite, but of the incredibly high risks General Tojo would assume to accomplish his ends. No one in Washington realized that he and his regime regarded the conquest of Asia not as the accomplishment of an ambition but as the survival of a regime. It was a life-and-death matter to them."[146] Japan's attack on Pearl Harbor was a partial success in the short term, and Japan went on to enjoy great tactical victories against America and Britain, but the conflict eventually led to its almost total destruction by 1945. Its wars in East Asia cost tens of millions of lives.

15. UNITED STATES VS. SOVIET UNION

Period: 1940s–1980s
Ruling power: United States
Rising power: Soviet Union
Domain: Global power
Outcome: No war

> *In the aftermath of World War II, the United States emerged as the world's undisputed superpower. It controlled half the world's GDP, formidable conventional military forces, and a monopoly on the most destructive instrument of war mankind had ever built: the nuclear bomb. American hegemony, however, was soon challenged by its World War II ally the Soviet Union. Though often tense, the Cold War stands as one of history's greatest successes in escaping Thucydides's Trap. By developing vehicles for competition outside of armed conflict, the two powers peacefully managed the highest-stakes great power competition in history.*

Having liberated the nations of Eastern Europe from Nazi rule at enormous cost, the Soviets felt entitled to carve a sphere of influence out of the ruins of Eastern Europe in the wake of World War II. Deploying Soviet military advisers and intelligence officers to co-opt local politicians, build new Communist Parties, engineer coups, and suppress dissent, the Soviet Union constructed an empire stretching into the middle of Germany and, in Churchill's words, from "Stettin in the Baltic to Trieste in the Adriatic, an iron curtain . . . descended across the Continent."

It soon became apparent to many US policymakers that the Soviet Union, as the historian John Gaddis writes, sought "not to restore a balance of power in Europe, but rather to dominate that continent as thoroughly as Hitler had sought to do."[147] With an overarching position in Europe, Stalin could easily spread his "revolutionary imperial" communism worldwide. Nine months after V-E Day, George Kennan's Long Telegram of February 1946—followed by Winston Churchill's Iron Curtain speech less than two weeks later—identified Soviet communism as an existential threat to the West. Navy Secretary James Forrestal represented the views of many American policymakers when he wrote that Soviet communism "is as incompatible with democracy as was Nazism or Fascism because it rests upon the willingness to apply force to gain the end."[148]

By 1949, the Soviet Union had successfully broken the US nuclear monopoly by testing its own atomic bomb. Eight years later, the USSR launched *Sputnik,* the first artificial satellite sent into space, dealing a blow to America's presumed preeminence in science and technology. The Soviet economy, meanwhile, had begun to surge. Industrial production increased 173 percent over prewar levels by 1950, and annual economic growth (at least as officially reported) averaged 7 percent between 1950 and 1970,[149] prompting fears that the Soviet Union might rival and even surpass the US economically.[150] Paul Samuelson's best-selling 1960s textbook, *Economics: An Introductory Analysis,* projected that Soviet GNP would overtake that of the US by the mid-1980s.[151] Though Samuelson's prediction never came to pass, the USSR did overtake the US in two key areas: military spending and production of iron and steel, both in the early 1970s.[152]

Responding to the challenge, the United States employed all of the traditional instruments of warfare short of bombs and bullets, and many untraditional instruments as well. This confrontation thus came to be known as the Cold War.[153] Despite a number of close calls (for example, the Cuban Missile Crisis) and several proxy wars (in Korea, Vietnam, Afghanistan, and elsewhere), overt conflict between the two militaries was averted.[154] Historians have offered various explanations for why the Cold War never went hot. Most credit the specter of nuclear destruction,[155] while some emphasize the geographic distance between the US and USSR,[156] or the growth of reconnaissance programs that minimized the likelihood of dangerous misunderstandings.[157] Many point to the two countries' mutual recognition of constraints on competition that allowed them to attack each other using all forms of war except direct conflict.[158] Yet another factor that allowed the two powers to escape war was the culture of cooperation that developed around nuclear weapons, beginning with the SALT Treaty in 1972 and culminating with the Reagan-Gorbachev summits of the 1980s. These summits not only reduced the risk of a nuclear accident, but also built a baseline of trust.

In time, the US approach—a strategy of containment sustained over four decades—succeeded. The contrast between the success of free-market democracies and the internal contradictions of command-and-control authoritarianism hollowed out the Soviet regime over several decades. Unable to provide both guns and butter, the Soviet Union collapsed in 1991, and the defining conflict of the late twentieth century ended without bloodshed.

16. UNITED KINGDOM AND FRANCE VS. GERMANY

Period: 1990s–present
Ruling powers: United Kingdom and France
Rising power: Germany
Domain: Political influence in Europe
Outcome: No war

At the conclusion of the Cold War, many expected that a newly reunified Germany would regress to its old hegemonic ambitions. While they were right that Germany was destined for a return to political and economic might in Europe, its rise has remained largely benign. An awareness of how Thucydides's Trap has ensnared their country in the past has led German leaders to find a new way to exert power and influence: by leading an integrated economic order, rather than by military dominance.

When West German chancellor Helmut Kohl broached the question of German reunification at the conclusion of the Cold War, leaders of Europe's status quo powers—the UK and France—balked at the prospect of a newly powerful Germany. For many strategists, the division of Germany at the end of World War II was the enduring solution to the "German problem" that had been at the root of two world wars. NATO's triple mission for Europe, went an oft-repeated quip, was "to keep the Soviets out, the Americans in, and the Germans down."[159]

Britain's and France's anxieties were easy to understand: a reunified Germany would be Western Europe's most populous country and an economic powerhouse. Along these lines, the French ambassador to Germany argued in 1989 that reunification "would give birth to a Europe dominated by Germany, which no one, in the East or West, wants."[160] Prime Minister Margaret Thatcher took these concerns even further, privately telling President George H. W. Bush of her fear that "the Germans will get in peace what Hitler could not get in war."[161] To counter this perceived threat, Thatcher and President François Mitterrand discussed strengthening the alliance between Britain and France. Mitterrand, for example, contemplated "bilateral military and even nuclear cooperation with Britain as a counterbalance."[162] According to former diplomat and scholar Philip Zelikow and former secretary of state Condoleezza Rice, "Europeans, particularly the French, believed that any revival of German power had to go hand in hand with European structures that would keep the German state from endangering France."[163]

As the European leaders foresaw, Germany indeed was able to leverage its economic strength into a position as Europe's strongest political voice, filling the power vacuum left by the collapse of the Soviet Union.

Remarkably, however, this reemergence has so far occurred peacefully. It has also occurred, over time, with British and French support. So how did it happen that, as Henry Kissinger recently observed, "seventy years after having defeated German claims to dominating Europe, the victors are now pleading, largely for economic reasons, with Germany to lead Europe"?[164]

Germany's peaceful rise is mostly due to its broad strategy of assuaging European suspicions through open gestures of good faith and seeking interdependence with its former adversaries. Most importantly, German leaders consciously chose not to redevelop a military presence commensurate with the nation's economic power.

This new path became especially apparent as Germany achieved economic hegemony, becoming a dominant player in Europe's integrated markets and leader of the Frankfurt-based European Central Bank. As former British trade minister Stephen Green notes, Germany channeled its power mainly into influencing Europe's political economy: "In no sense has Germany shown any readiness to play any strategic role in the world of foreign affairs of the kind both the British and the French have taken for granted."[165] A strategy of integration, as international relations scholar Helga Haftendorn describes it, "was to compensate for Germany's gains in power and sovereignty by emphasizing the importance of integrating this potential into a new Europe, creating a 'Europeanized Germany' rather than a 'German Europe.'"[166]

It is important to note, of course, that Germany's pursuit of economic integration began prior to reunification.[167] Furthermore, Germany's decision to forgo a military expansion to match its economic clout was undoubtedly influenced by America's presence as a regional security guarantor and stabilizing force in Europe. Whatever its origins, though, Germany's approach ultimately proved reassuring to its former foes, demonstrating a new ethos characterized by policy analyst Hans Kundnani in *The Paradox of German Power* as "a strange mixture of economic assertiveness and military abstinence . . . In geopolitical terms, Germany is benign."[168]

Recently, instability caused by the fallout from the global financial crisis and an overwhelming surge of immigrants and refugees from Syria and the Middle East have called the existing European system —and German leadership—into question. Regardless of Europe's future, however, or the historically unusual circumstances of America's security presence on the Continent, Germany's approach at the critical moment of power transition provides enduring and important lessons for powers seeking to avoid Thucydides's Trap. Germany has learned that increasing defense spending to match economic development can easily beget conflict, and that continual gestures of goodwill are needed to overcome deep-seated fear between rival nations. Through stability, openness, integration with former adversaries, and a willingness to forgo more traditional shows of power, Germany has managed thus far to escape Thucydides's Trap.

Appendix 2
SEVEN STRAW MEN

In academic debate, scholars frequently prefer to attack straw men rather than contest a stated thesis. The pattern is simple enough: construct a straw man, torch it, and then claim to have refuted the thesis. In response to the September 2015 *Atlantic* essay that previewed this book's argument, critics have repeatedly incinerated the same seven straw men.

1. Inevitability: *Thucydides's Trap claims that war between a rising and a ruling power is inevitable.*

   As stated in the *Atlantic* article and in this book, Thucydides's Trap does *not* claim that war is inevitable. In fact, four of the sixteen cases in the Case File (appendix 1) did not result in war. Moreover, as noted, even in his *History of the Peloponnesian War,* Thucydides's use of the word "inevitable" is clearly meant as hyperbole.

2. Tipping points, tripwires, or turning points: *A specific tipping point during the power transition was passed without war—so Thucydides is wrong.*

   The Thucydides's Trap hypothesis makes no claim about a moment when war will most likely occur. The Thucydidean dynamic is present during the rise, at the point of parity, and after one power has overtaken another.

3. Selection bias: *Thucydides's Trap is guilty of cherry-picking cases to fit its conclusion. It only selected cases that led to war.*

   The Case File includes *all* the instances we have been able to find in the past 500 years in which a major rising power threatened to displace a ruling power. Because this includes the entire universe of the cases (as opposed to a representative sample), the Case File is immune to charges of selection bias. For a detailed discussion of

the Thucydides's Trap methodology, see http://belfercenter.org/
thucydides-trap/thucydides-trap-methodology.

4. Missing cases: *The Thucydides's Trap Case File is incomplete.*

   The Thucydides's Trap Case File is open. Since publishing the
Case File along with the 2015 *Atlantic* article, the website for the
Thucydides's Trap Project has invited readers to suggest additional
cases from other areas of the world, from other, less than major
powers, or from other eras. For the purposes of this inquiry, the
more cases the better, since additional cases can provide additional
insights into the fundamental dynamics of rising vs. ruling powers. To suggest cases, readers can visit http://www.belfercenter.org
/thucydides-trap/case-file.

5. Small data set: *The Thucydides's Trap Case File offers too small a data
   set to support claims about laws or regularities, or for use by social scientists
   seeking to do so.*

   Agreed. The purpose of this inquiry is to explore a phenomenon
—not to propose iron laws or create a data set for statisticians.

6. But what about . . . : *The events and issues in the Case File are "more
   complicated than that."*

   Of course: they always are.

7. Originality: *The concept of Thucydides's Trap is not original.*

   The fact that it is called *Thucydides's* Trap should suggest we
agree. As noted on the website, over the centuries since Thucydides
completed his work other scholars have also contributed to our understanding of hegemonic challenges.

NOTES

1. "The Biggest Player in the History of the World"

1. Henry Kissinger, foreword to *Lee Kuan Yew: The Grand Master's Insights on China, the United States, and the World* (Cambridge, MA: MIT Press, 2013), ix.

2. Lee visited China 33 times from 1976 until his death, while an estimated 22,000 Chinese officials visited Singapore to study its inner workings between 1990 and 2011 alone. See Chris Buckley, "In Lee Kuan Yew, China Saw a Leader to Emulate," *New York Times*, March 23, 2015, http://sinosphere.blogs.nytimes.com/2015/03/23/in-lee-kuan-yew-china-saw-a-leader-to-emulate.

3. Graham Allison, Robert D. Blackwill, and Ali Wyne, *Lee Kuan Yew: The Grand Master's Insights on China, the United States, and the World* (Cambridge, MA: MIT Press, 2013), 42.

4. See World Bank, "Merchandise Imports (Current US$)," http://data.worldbank.org/indicator/TM.VAL.MRCH.CD.WT?locations=CN; World Bank, "Merchandise Exports (Current US$)," http://data.worldbank.org/indicator/TX.VAL.MRCH.CD.WT?locations=CN.

5. China is indeed adding the equivalent of approximately one India to its GDP every two years. For example, China's GDP was $8.6 trillion in 2012 and $10.6 trillion in 2014. In those two years, China added approximately $2 trillion in GDP. Meanwhile, India's GDP was $1.8 trillion in 2012, $1.9 trillion in 2013, and $2 trillion in 2014. GDP data (current prices, US dollars) are from the International Monetary Fund's "World Economic Outlook Database," October 2016, http://www.imf.org/external/pubs/ft/weo/2016/02/weodata/index.aspx.

6. Calculated based on historical GDP growth figures of the Angus Maddison Project. See "GDP Levels in Western Offshoots, 1500–1899," in Angus Maddison, *The World Economy: Historical Statistics* (Paris: OECD Publishing, 2006), 462–63.

7. There are various examples of this productivity gap. The British became sixty-six times more productive in making yarn by using the Hargreaves jenny draw bar, a key innovation of the era that the Chinese failed to adopt. See Joel Mokyr, *The Lever of Riches: Technological Creativity and Economic Progress* (New York: Oxford University Press, 1990), 221. Dutch textile productivity, which was comparable to British productivity during this period, was six times higher than productivity in the most developed region of China, the Yangtze Delta. See Bozhong Li and Jan Luiten van Zanden, "Before the Great Divergence? Comparing the Yangzi Delta and the Netherlands at the Beginning of the Nineteenth Century," *Journal of Economic History* 72, no. 4 (December 2012), 972. Furthermore, warmaking capacity in 1800 was five times higher in Western countries than in Eastern countries, which Ian Morris argues "had a lot to do with why Britain's forces swept China's aside so

easily in the 1840s." See Ian Morris, *Why the West Rules—for Now* (New York: Farrar, Straus and Giroux, 2010), 496, 634–35.

8.   Hillary Clinton, "America's Pacific Century," *Foreign Policy,* October 11, 2011, http://foreignpolicy.com/2011/10/11/americas-pacific-century.

9.   "Remarks by President Obama to the Australian Parliament," November 17, 2011, https://obamawhitehouse.archives.gov/the-press-office/2011/11/17 /remarks-president-obama-australian-parliament.

10. "A Dangerous Modesty," *Economist,* June 6, 2015, http://www.economist .com/news/briefing/21653617-america-has-learnt-hard-way-it-cannot-fix -problems-middle-east-barack.

11. Yi Wen, *The Making of an Economic Superpower: Unlocking China's Secret of Rapid Industrialization* (Hackensack, NJ: World Scientific Publishing, 2016), 2.

12. See "International Car Sales Outlook," in *Improving Consumer Fundamentals Drive Sales Acceleration and Broaden Gains Beyond Autos,* Scotiabank Global Auto Report, September 29, 2016, http://www.gbm.scotiabank.com /English/bns_econ/bns_auto.pdf.

13. See "As China's Smartphone Market Matures, Higher-Priced Handsets Are on the Rise," *Wall Street Journal,* April 29, 2016, http://blogs.wsj .com/chinarealtime/2016/04/29/as-chinas-smartphone-market-matures -higher-priced-handsets-are-on-the-rise/; Serge Hoffmann and Bruno Lannes, "China's E-commerce Prize," Bain & Company, 2013, http:// www.bain.com/Images/BAIN_BRIEF_Chinas_e-commerce_prize.pdf; Euan McKirdy, "China's Online Users More Than Double Entire U.S. Population," CNN, February 4, 2015, http://www.cnn.com/2015/02/03 /world/china-internet-growth-2014/.

14. Candace Dunn, "China Is Now the World's Largest Net Importer of Petroleum and Other Liquid Fuels," US Energy Information Administration, March 24, 2014, http://www.eia.gov/todayinenergy/detail.php?id=15531; Enerdata, "Global Energy Statistical Yearbook 2016," https://yearbook .enerdata.net/; Richard Martin, "China Is on an Epic Solar Power Binge," *MIT Technology Review,* March 22, 2016, https://www.technologyreview .com/s/601093/china-is-on-an-epic-solar-power-binge/.

15. Stephen Roach, "Why China Is Central to Global Growth," World Economic Forum, September 2, 2016, https://www.weforum.org/agenda/2016/09 /why-china-is-central-to-global-growth.

16. Brett Arends, "It's Official: America Is Now No. 2," *MarketWatch,* December 4, 2014, http://www.marketwatch.com/story/its-official-america -is-now-no-2-2014-12-04.

17. Chris Giles, "The New World Economy in Four Charts," *Alphaville Blog, Financial Times,* October 7, 2014, http://ftalphaville.ft.com/2014/10/07 /1998332/moneysupply-the-new-world-economy-in-four-charts/.

18. See PPP description in GDP methodology in "Definitions and Notes," *CIA World Factbook,* https://www.cia.gov/library/publications/the-world -factbook/docs/notesanddefs.html; Tim Callen, "PPP Versus the Market:

Which Weight Matters?" *Finance and Development* 44, no. 1 (March 2007), http://www.imf.org/external/pubs/ft/fandd/2007/03/basics.htm.

19. International Monetary Fund, "World Economic Outlook Database."

20. See, for example, Tim Worstall, "China's Now the World Number One Economy and It Doesn't Matter a Darn," *Forbes,* December 7, 2014, http://www.forbes.com/sites/timworstall/2014/12/07/chinas-now-the-world-number-one-economy-and-it-doesnt-matter-a-darn/; Jeffrey Frankel, "Sorry, but America Is Still No. 1, Even If China Is Bigger," *MarketWatch,* December 5, 2014, http://www.marketwatch.com/story/sorry-but-america-is-still-no-1-2014-12-04.

21. Fischer goes on: "But it is essential to recognize that this is only a first approximation. Particularly for goods that are internationally traded, for example, oil, market exchange rates provide a better yardstick. Moreover, and even more importantly, beyond basic economic capacity many other factors impact a nation's military potential, including its political capacity to tax its citizens and dedicate resources to strengthen its national security posture." This point was underlined by the economist Charles Kindleberger, who wrote: "Whether reparations can be paid or not will depend within fairly large limits of their size, and apart from the application of brute force, on whether the country concerned mounts a cohesive and determined effort to do so. This is not a conclusion that an economist embraces easily." See Charles Kindleberger, *Manias, Panics, and Crashes* (New York: Wiley Investment Classics, 2005), 225–26.

22. International Institute for Strategic Studies, *The Military Balance 2016* (New York: Routledge, 2016), 495.

23. The word "cloud" was generated on the Factiva database, using all headlines from the *New York Times, Wall Street Journal,* and *Financial Times* from October 25, 2013, through October 25, 2016, featuring the words "China" and "growth," or "GDP," or "economy."

24. GDP growth data are from the IMF. The period since the Great Recession is defined as 2010–2016. 2016 figures are IMF estimates from the fund's October 2016 update to the World Economic Database.

25. The percentage of world growth occurring in China is calculated using "GDP, PPP (Constant 2011 International $)," from the World Bank's World Development Indicators. See also David Harrison, "The U.S. May Not Be an Engine of the World Economy for Long," *Wall Street Journal,* March 8, 2016, blogs.wsj.com/economics/2016/03/08/the-u-s-may-be-an-engine-of-the-world-economy-but-perhaps-not-for-long. Harrison highlights that "China singlehandedly accounted for almost a third of the world's growth" in 2013.

26. See World Bank, "Poverty Headcount Ratio at $1.90 a Day (2011 PPP) (% of Population)," accessed November 19, 2016, http://data.worldbank.org/topic/poverty?locations=CN.

27. "Beijing to Cut Number of New Cars," *Xinhua,* October 25, 2016, http://

www.globaltimes.cn/content/1013607.shtml; Hu Shuli, Wang Shuo, and Huang Shan, "Kissinger: China, U.S. Must 'Lead in Cooperation,'" *Caixin,* March 23, 2015, http://english.caixin.com/2015-03-23/100793753.html.

28. Kevin Rudd, "The West Isn't Ready for the Rise of China," *New States-man,* July 16, 2012, http://www.newstatesman.com/politics/international -politics/2012/07/kevin-rudd-west-isnt-ready-rise-china.

29. Evan Osnos, *Age of Ambition: Chasing Fortune, Truth, and Faith in the New China* (New York: Farrar, Straus and Giroux, 2014), 25.

30. From 2011 to 2013, China produced more cement than the US did in the entire twentieth century. See Jamil Anderlini, "Property Sector Slowdown Adds to China Fears," *Financial Times,* May 13, 2014, https://www.ft.com/ content/4f74c94a-da77-11e3-8273-00144feabdc0; See Ana Swanson, "How China Used More Cement in 3 Years than the U.S. Did in the Entire 20th Century," *Wonkblog, Washington Post,* March 24, 2015, https://www.wash ingtonpost.com/news/wonk/wp/2015/03/24/how-china-used-more- cement-in-3-years-than-the-u-s-did-in-the-entire-20th-century/.

31. Eoghan Macguire, "The Chinese Firm That Can Build a Skyscraper in a Matter of Weeks," CNN, June 26, 2015, http://www.cnn.com/2015/06/26 /asia/china-skyscraper-prefabricated.

32. *Economist* Intelligence Unit, "Building Rome in a Day: The Sustainability of China's Housing Boom" (2011), 2, www.eiu.com/Handlers/Whitepaper -Handler.ashx?fi=Building_Rome_in_a_day_WEB_Updated.pdf.

33. Thomas Friedman and Michael Mandelbaum, *That Used to Be Us: How Amer-ica Fell Behind in the World It Invented and How We Can Come Back* (New York: Macmillan, 2012), 3–4.

34. See "China for a Day (but Not for Two)," in Thomas Friedman, *Hot, Flat, and Crowded: Why We Need a Green Revolution — and How It Can Renew Amer-ica* (New York: Picador, 2009), 429–55.

35. Jay Bennett, "Here's an Overpass in Beijing Being Replaced in Under Two Days," *Popular Mechanics,* November 20, 2015, http://www.popular mechanics.com/technology/infrastructure/a18277/beijing-overpass-replaced -in-less-than-two-days/.

36. George Fortier and Yi Wen, "The Visible Hand": The Role of Government in China's Long-Awaited Industrial Revolution," working paper, Federal Reserve Bank of St. Louis, August 2016, 215, https://research.stlouisfed .org/wp/more/2016-016.

37. Ibid.

38. See Virginia Postrel, "California Hits the Brakes on High-Speed Rail Fiasco," *Bloomberg,* June 28, 2016, https://www.bloomberg.com/view /articles/2016-06-28/california-hits-the-brakes-on-high-speed-rail-fiasco; "Taxpayers Could Pay Dearly for California's High-Speed-Train Dreams," *Economist,* March 27, 2016, http://www.economist.com/news/science-and -technology/21695237-taxpayers-could-pay-dearly-californias-high-speed -dreams-biting-bullet.

39. Lu Bingyang and Ma Feng, "China to Build Out 45,000 km High-Speed

Rail Network," *Caixin,* July 21, 2016, http://english.caixin.com/2016-07
-21/100968874.html.

40. See World Bank, "Poverty Headcount Ratio at $1.90 a Day, http://data
.worldbank.org/topic/poverty?locations=CN.

41. According to the most recent IMF estimates from the "World Economic
Outlook Database," Chinese per capita GDP was $8,141 in 2015 and an
estimated $8,261 in 2016.

42. World Bank, "World Bank Group President Says China Offers Lessons in
Helping the World Overcome Poverty," September 15, 2010, http://www
.worldbank.org/en/news/press-release/2010/09/15/world-bank-group
-president-says-china-offers-lessons-helping-world-overcome-poverty.

43. For rise in life expectancy, see Linda Benson, *China Since 1949,* 3rd ed.
(New York: Routledge, 2016), 28; current statistics (1960–2014) in "Life
Expectancy at Birth, Total (Years)," World Bank, http://data.worldbank
.org/indicator/SP.DYN.LE00.IN?locations=CN. For the rise in literacy, see
Ted Plafker, "China's Long — but Uneven — March to Literacy," *Interna-
tional Herald Tribune,* February 12, 2001, http://www.nytimes.com/2001/02
/12/news/chinas-long-but-uneven-march-to-literacy.html; current statis-
tics (1982–2015) in "Adult Literacy Rate, Population 15+ Years, Both Sexes
(%)," World Bank, http://data.worldbank.org/indicator/SE.ADT.LITR
.ZS?locations=CN.

44. The *Economist,* citing research from the Boston Consulting Group, notes
that Asia's wealth is expected to reach $75 trillion by 2020, while North
America's wealth will be $76 trillion. As BCG explains, "The U.S. will re-
main the world's wealthiest country, although North America is expected
to be surpassed by Asia-Pacific (including Japan) soon after 2020." See "The
Wealth of Nations," *Economist,* June 17, 2015, http://www.economist.com
/blogs/freeexchange/2015/06/asia-pacific-wealthier-europe;"Global Wealth
2016: Navigating the New Client Landscape," Boston Consulting Group,
June 2016, https://www.bcgperspectives.com/content/articles/financial
-institutions-consumer-insight-global-wealth-2016/?chapter=2.

45. See Robert Frank, "China Has More Billionaires Than US: Report,"
CNBC, February 24, 2016, http://www.cnbc.com/2016/02/24/china
-has-more-billionaires-than-us-report.html; UBS/PwC, "Billionaires Report, 2016," May 2016, 12, http://uhnw-greatwealth.ubs.com/billionaires
/billionaires-report-2016/. The report finds that China minted 80 billionaires in 2015, which is equal to roughly 1.5 new billionaires per week.

46. Christopher Horton, "When It Comes to Luxury, China Still Leads," *New
York Times,* April 5, 2016, http://www.nytimes.com/2016/04/05/fashion
/china-luxury-goods-retail.html.

47. The 2016 Global Innovation Index, published by Cornell University and
the World Intellectual Property Organization, ranked China's primary and
secondary education system fourth and America's thirty-ninth.

48. Out of the thirty-five OECD countries, the US ranked thirty-first in 2015.
However, it is relevant to note that only four Chinese provinces partici-

pated in the 2015 assessment, while the US score is reflective of nationwide testing. OECD, *PISA 2015 Results,* vol. 1: *Excellence and Equity in Education* (Paris: OECD Publishing, 2016).

49. However, this preliminary study also found that the Chinese lose this critical-thinking advantage throughout college, as American students catch up and the Chinese stay the same. The study was based in part on exams given to 2,700 Chinese students at 11 mainland universities. See Clifton B. Parker, "Incentives Key to China's Effort to Upgrade Higher Education, Stanford Expert Says," *Stanford News,* August 18, 2016, http://news .stanford.edu/2016/08/18/incentives-key-to-chinas-effort-upgrade-higher -education/.

50. "Best Global Universities for Engineering," *U.S. News and World Report,* http://www.usnews.com/education/best-global-universities/engineering ?int=994b08.

51. Te-Ping Chen and Miriam Jordan, "Why So Many Chinese Students Come to the U.S.," *Wall Street Journal,* May 1, 2016, http://www.wsj.com/articles /why-so-many-chinese-students-come-to-the-u-s-1462123552.

52. National Science Board, "Science and Engineering Indicators, 2016" (Arlington, VA: National Science Foundation, 2016), https://www.nsf.gov /statistics/2016/nsb20161/#/report.

53. Richard Waters and Tim Bradshaw, "Rise of the Robots Is Sparking an Investment Boom," *Financial Times,* May 3, 2016, http://www.ft.com /cms/s/2/5a352264-0e26-11e6-ad80-67655613c2d6.html; "World Record: 248,000 Industrial Robots Revolutionizing the World Economy," *International Federation of Robotics,* June 22, 2016, http://www.ifr.org/news /ifr-press-release/world-record-816/.

54. National Science Board, "Science and Engineering Indicators, 2016."

55. China accounted for 38 percent of the global total of patent applications, with as many applications as the next three countries — the US, Japan, and Korea — combined. See "World Intellectual Property Indicators 2016," World Intellectual Property Organization (2016) 7, 21, http://www.wipo .int/edocs/pubdocs/en/wipo_pub_941_2016.pdf.

56. While the US spent $397 billion in 2012 and China spent just $257 billion, Chinese expenditures are projected to skyrocket to $600 billion in 2024, while US spending will remain below $500 billion. See "China Headed to Overtake EU, US in Science & Technology Spending, OECD Says," Organization for Economic Cooperation and Development, November 12, 2014, http://www.oecd.org/newsroom/china-headed-to-overtake-eu-us-in-science-technology-spending.htm.

57. Norman R. Augustine et al., *Restoring the Foundation: The Vital Role of Research in Preserving the American Dream* (Cambridge, MA: American Academy of Arts and Sciences, 2014), 7.

58. See Pierre Thomas, "FBI Director Tells ABC News Whether the US Has the Goods on China," ABC News, May 19, 2014, http://abcnews.go.com

/US/fbi-director-tells-abc-news-us-goods-china/story?id=23787051; "The Great Brain Robbery," *60 Minutes* transcript, CBS News, January 17, 2016, http://www.cbsnews.com/news/60-minutes-great-brain-robbery-china -cyber-espionage/.

59. Thomas Kalil and Jason Miller, "Advancing U.S. Leadership in High-Performance Computing," the White House, July 29, 2015, https:// obamawhitehouse.archives.gov/blog/2015/07/29/advancing-us-leadership -high-performance-computing.

60. "New Chinese Supercomputer Named World's Fastest System on Latest Top500 List," Top500, June 20, 2016, https://www.top500.org/news/new -chinese-supercomputer-named-worlds-fastest-system-on-latest-top500 -list/; James Vincent, "Chinese Supercomputer Is the World's Fastest— and Without Using US Chips," *The Verge,* June 20, 2016, http://www .theverge.com/2016/6/20/11975356/chinese-supercomputer-worlds-fastes -taihulight.

61. See Steven Mufson, "Energy Secretary Is Urged to End U.S. Nuclear Fuel Program at Savannah River," *Washington Post,* September 9, 2015, https:// www.washingtonpost.com/business/economy/energy-secretary-is-urged -to-end-us-nuclear-fuel-program-at-savannah-river/2015/09/09/bc 6103b4-5705-11e5-abe9-27d53f250b11_story.html; Darren Samuelsohn, "Billions Over Budget. Two Years After Deadline. What's Gone Wrong for the 'Clean Coal' Project That's Supposed to Save an Industry?" *Politico,* May 26, 2015, http://www.politico.com/agenda/story/2015/05/billion-dollar -kemper-clean-coal-energy-project-000015.

62. China has also been strengthening its nuclear arsenal. For decades after becoming a nuclear power in 1964, Beijing maintained a small arsenal of silo-based ICBMs, which left it vulnerable to an adversary's first strike. Since the mid-1990s it has been deploying more survivable nuclear forces, most recently road-mobile and submarine-launched ballistic missiles. As a result, the US has been forced to accept a condition of "mutual assured destruction" between China and the United States, similar to the one that existed with the Soviet Union during the Cold War. This was reflected in the 2010 US Nuclear Posture Review's assertion that the US would not take any action that could negatively affect "the stability of our nuclear relationships with Russia or China."

63. Since 1988, China has spent an average of 2.01 percent of GDP on its military, while the US has spent an average of 3.9 percent. See World Bank, "Military Expenditure (% of GDP)," http://data.worldbank.org/indicator /MS.MIL.XPND.GD.ZS.

64. Recall the Rule of 72: divide 72 by the annual growth rate to determine how long it will take to double.

65. International Institute for Strategic Studies, *The Military Balance 2016* (New York: Routledge, 2016), 19.

66. Eric Heginbotham et al., *The U.S.-China Military Scorecard: Forces, Geogra-*

phy, and the Evolving Balance of Power, 1996–2017 (Santa Monica, CA: RAND Corporation, 2015), xxxi, xxix.

67. In remarks to reporters at the May 2012 Strategic and Economic Dialogue in Beijing, Clinton said of the US and China: "We look at the future with great optimism. And we believe that neither of us can afford to keep looking at the world through old lenses, whether it's the legacy of imperialism, the Cold War, or balance-of-power politics. Zero sum thinking will lead to negative sum results. And so instead, what we are trying to do is to build a resilient relationship that allows both of our nations to thrive without unhealthy competition, rivalry, or conflict while meeting our national, regional, and global responsibilities." See "Remarks at the Strategic and Economic Dialogue U.S. Press Conference," US Department of State, May 4, 2012, https://2009-2017.state.gov/secretary/20092013clinton/rm /2012/05/189315.htm.

68. Author's interview with Lee Kuan Yew, December 2, 2011.

69. Robert Blackwill and Jennifer Harris, *War by Other Means: Geoeconomics and Statecraft* (Cambridge, MA: Harvard University Press, 2016), 11.

70. Association of Southeast Asian Nations, "External Trade Statistics," June 10, 2016, http://asean.org/?static_post=external-trade-statistics-3; Shawn Donnan, "China Manoeuvres to Fill US Free-Trade Role," *Financial Times,* November 21, 2016, https://www.ft.com/content/c3840120-aee1-11e6 -a37c-f4a01f1b0fa1.

71. Henry Kissinger, *On China* (New York: Penguin Books, 2012), 28.

72. James Kynge, "China Becomes Global Leader in Development Finance," *Financial Times,* May 17, 2016, https://www.ft.com/content/b995cc7a-1c33 -11e6-a7bc-ee846770ec15.

73. The China Development Bank and the Export-Import Bank of China had outstanding loans of $684 billion internationally by the end of 2014, just below the $700 billion in outstanding loans made in total by the World Bank, the Asian Development Bank, the Inter-American Development Bank, the European Investment Bank, the European Bank for Reconstruction and Development, and the African Development Bank. In addition, China has provided an estimated $116 billion in bilateral and regional development finance, making its total financing of international development significantly greater than the rest of the multilateral banks. See Kevin Gallagher, Rohini Kamal, Yongzhong Wang, and Yanning Chen, "Fueling Growth and Financing Risk: The Benefits and Risks of China's Development Finance in the Global Energy Sector," working paper, Boston University Global Economic Governance Initiative, May 2016, 3–7, http://www.bu.edu /pardeeschool/research/gegi/program-area/china-and-global-development -banking/fueling-growth-and-financing-risk/.

74. See "Our Bulldozers, Our Rules," *Economist,* July 2, 2016, http://www .economist.com/news/china/21701505-chinas-foreign-policy-could -reshape-good-part-world-economy-our-bulldozers-our-rules; Enda Cur-

ran, "China's Marshall Plan," *Bloomberg,* August 7, 2016, www.bloomberg
.com/news/articles/2016-08-07/china-s-marshall-plan.

75. Allison, Blackwill, and Wyne, *Lee Kuan Yew,* 6–7.

2. Athens vs. Sparta

1. Leopold von Ranke's phrase in its original German is *"wie es eigentlich gewe-sen."*

2. Thucydides, *History of the Peloponnesian War,* 1.23.6. Translations of Thu-cydides are from Strassler, who essentially follows Crawley, except where I have adapted them, as here, to more modern English syntax. The three numbers of the citation refer to book, chapter, and line. See Thucydides, *The Peloponnesian War,* ed. Robert B. Strassler, trans. Richard Crawley (New York: Free Press, 1996).

3. Ibid., 1.23.6. For a thoughtful discussion on the Greek word *anankasai* and its meaning in Thucydides's work, see G.E.M. de Ste. Croix, *The Origins of the Peloponnesian War* (London: Gerald Duckworth & Company, 1972), 51–63.

4. Book 1 of *History of the Peloponnesian War* analyzes the path to war. The re-maining seven books chronicle the war itself.

5. Herodotus, *Histories,* 9.10.1.

6. Plutarch, *Moralia,* 241.

7. Thucydides, *History of the Peloponnesian War,* 2.13.6.

8. Ibid., 1.76.2.

9. Ibid., 1.118.2.

10. Ibid., 1.70.2.

11. Ibid., 1.76.2.

12. Paul Rahe, *The Grand Strategy of Classical Sparta: The Persian Challenge* (New Haven, CT: Yale University Press, 2015), 327–36.

13. Thucydides, *History of the Peloponnesian War,* 1.25.4. The original cause of the conflict was wounded pride, Thucydides tells us. The Corinthians felt they had been "treated with contempt" when the Corcyraeans denied them precedence at public sacrifices.

14. Ibid., 1.84.4.

15. Ibid., 1.86.2.

16. Ibid., 1.69.1–4.

17. Ibid., 1.88.1. Adapted from the translation of Rex Warner (1972). Thucyd-ides, *The Peloponnesian War,* ed. M. I. Finley, trans. Rex Warner (New York: Penguin, 1954), 55.

18. Athens even had a formalized system—ostracism—for removing political leaders who had seized too much power.

19. Donald Kagan, *The Peloponnesian War* (New York: Penguin, 2004), 32–34.

20. Thucydides, *History of the Peloponnesian War,* 5.105.2.

21. Among modern scholars, Donald Kagan has provided the most insightful ex-

planation of this point. See Donald Kagan, *On the Origins of War and the Preservation of Peace* (New York: Doubleday, 1995); Donald Kagan, "Our Interests and Our Honor," *Commentary,* April 1997, https://www.commentary magazine.com/articles/our-interests-and-our-honor/.

22. Richard Neustadt, *Presidential Power and the Modern Presidents: The Politics of Leadership from Roosevelt to Reagan* (New York: Free Press, 1990), xix.

3. Five Hundred Years

1. The independent variable in our study is a rapid shift in the balance of power (correlation of forces) between a major ruling power and a rising rival that could displace it. Dominance/primacy/leadership can be in a geographical area (e.g., continental Europe in the sixteenth century for the Hapsburgs) or in a particular domain (e.g., Britain's control of the seas in the nineteenth century). The dependent variable in this inquiry is war, defined according to the standard criteria in the Correlates of War Project as military conflict causing a minimum of one thousand fatalities per year. In identifying and summarizing these cases, we have followed the judgment of leading historical accounts—specifically resisting the temptation to offer original or idiosyncratic interpretations of events. In this project we have attempted to include all instances since the year 1500 in which a major ruling power is challenged by a rising power. In technical terms, we sought not a representative sample but the entire universe of cases. Therefore, as *The Oxford Handbook of Political Methodology* notes: "Insofar as comparative-historical researchers select what can be considered the entire universe of cases, standard issues of selection bias do not arise." A more detailed explanation of the methodology is available at http://belfercenter.org/thucydides-trap /thucydides-trap-methodology.

2. US Department of State, *Papers Relating to the Foreign Relations of the United States and Japan, 1931–1941,* vol. 2 (Washington, DC: US Government Printing Office, 1943), 780.

3. Jack Snyder, *Myths of Empire: Domestic Politics and International Ambition* (Ithaca, NY: Cornell University Press, 1993), 126.

4. Paul Kennedy, *The Rise and Fall of the Great Powers: Economic Change and Military Conflict from 1500 to 2000* (New York: Random House, 1987), 334.

5. Charles Maechling, "Pearl Harbor: The First Energy War," *History Today* 50, no. 12 (December 2000), 47.

6. Bruce Bueno de Mesquita, *The War Trap* (New Haven, CT: Yale University Press, 1987), 85.

7. See Roberta Wohlstetter, *Pearl Harbor: Warning and Decision* (Palo Alto, CA: Stanford University Press, 1962); Gordon W. Prange, *Pearl Harbor: The Verdict of History* (New York: McGraw Hill, 1986).

8. Herbert Feis, *The Road to Pearl Harbor: The Coming of the War Between the United States and Japan* (New York: Atheneum, 1965), 248.

9. B. R. Mitchell, *International Historical Statistics: Africa, Asia and Oceania, 1750–1993* (New York: Macmillan, 2003), 1025.

10. Akira Iriye, "Japan's Drive to Great-Power Status," in *The Cambridge History of Japan,* vol. 5: *The Nineteenth Century,* ed. Marius Jansen (Cambridge: Cambridge University Press, 1989), 760–61.

11. See charts on Japanese military expenditure in J. Charles Schencking, *Making Waves: Politics, Propaganda, and the Emergence of the Imperial Japanese Navy, 1868–1922* (Palo Alto, CA: Stanford University Press, 2005), 47 (1873–1889); 104 (1890–1905).

12. Whereas the Korean king invited the help of the Chinese military, Japan, unwilling to allow China to erode its buildup of regional influence, intervened of its own volition.

13. See Kan Ichi Asakawa, *The Russo-Japanese Conflict: Its Causes and Issues* (Boston: Houghton Mifflin, 1904), 70–82; Peter Duus, *The Abacus and the Sword: The Japanese Penetration of Korea, 1895–1910* (Berkeley: University of California Press, 1995), 96–97.

14. Asakawa, *The Russo-Japanese Conflict,* 52.

15. J. N. Westwood, *Russia Against Japan, 1904–05: A New Look at the Russo-Japanese War* (Albany: State University of New York Press, 1986), 11.

16. Michael Howard, *The Franco-Prussian War* (New York: Methuen, 1961), 40.

17. Geoffrey Wawro, *The Franco-Prussian War: The German Conquest of France in 1870–1871* (New York: Cambridge University Press, 2013), 17.

18. Correlates of War Project, "National Material Capabilities Dataset," version 4, 1816–2007, http://www.correlatesofwar.org/data-sets/national-material-capabilities; J. David Singer, Stuart Bremer, and John Stuckey, "Capability Distribution, Uncertainty, and Major Power War, 1820–1965," in *Peace, War, and Numbers,* ed. Bruce Russett (Beverly Hills, CA: Sage, 1972), 19–48.

19. Wawro, *The Franco-Prussian War,* 17.

20. Ibid, 19.

21. Robert Howard Lord, *The Origins of the War of 1870* (Cambridge, MA: Harvard University Press, 1924), 6.

22. Ibid.

23. Jonathan Steinberg, *Bismarck: A Life* (New York: Oxford University Press, 2011), 284.

24. Henry Kissinger, *Diplomacy* (New York: Simon & Schuster, 1994), 118.

25. Kennedy, *The Rise and Fall of the Great Powers,* 515.

26. George Edmundson, *Anglo-Dutch Rivalry During the First Half of the Seventeenth Century* (Oxford: Clarendon Press, 1911), 5.

27. Ibid.

28. Jack Levy, "The Rise and Decline of the Anglo-Dutch Rivalry, 1609–1689," in *Great Power Rivalries,* ed. William R. Thompson (Columbia: University of South Carolina Press, 1999), 176.

29. Kennedy, *The Rise and Fall of the Great Powers,* 63; ibid., 178.

30. Charles Wilson, *Profit and Power: A Study of England and the Dutch Wars* (London: Longmans, Green, 1957), 23.

31. Ibid., 111.

32. Levy, "The Rise and Decline of the Anglo-Dutch Rivalry," 180.

33. Edmundson, *Anglo-Dutch Rivalry*, 4.

34. María J. Rodríguez-Salgado, "The Hapsburg-Valois Wars," in *The New Cambridge Modern History*, 2nd ed., vol. 2, ed. G. R. Elton (New York: Cambridge University Press, 1990), 380.

35. Ibid., 378. Making war against Muslim "infidels" was a responsibility inherent in the title of Holy Roman Emperor.

36. Ibid., 380.

37. Henry Kamen, *Spain, 1469–1714: A Society of Conflict*, 4th ed. (New York: Routledge, 2014), 64.

38. John Lynch, *Spain Under the Hapsburgs*, vol. 1 (Oxford: Oxford University Press, 1964), 88.

39. Rodríguez-Salgado, "The Hapsburg-Valois Wars," 381.

40. Lynch, *Spain Under the Hapsburgs*, 88.

41. Robert Jervis, "Cooperation Under the Security Dilemma," *World Politics* 2, no. 2 (January 1978), 167–214.

4. Britain vs. Germany

1. Martin Gilbert, *Churchill: A Life* (London: Heinemann, 1991), 239.

2. David Evans and Mark Peattie, *Kaigun: Strategy, Tactics, and Technology in the Imperial Japanese Navy, 1887–1941* (Annapolis, MD: Naval Institute Press, 1997), 147.

3. Within two months of his appointment, Churchill declared that "aviation for war purposes" should become "the most honorable, as it is the most dangerous profession a young Englishman can adopt." Leading by example, he took to flying himself. To secure a reliable source of oil for new warships, Churchill led the government's purchase of a majority stake in the Anglo-Persian Oil Company (later renamed British Petroleum). Gilbert, *Churchill: A Life,* 240–41, 248–49, 251–53, 259–61. Winston S. Churchill, *The World Crisis*, vol. 1 (New York: Scribner, 1923), 125–48.

4. Churchill, *The World Crisis,* 123–24.

5. In seminars at Harvard Kennedy School, I have found that national security professionals and military officers struggle to formulate a feasible plan for Britain to escape this dilemma, even with a century of hindsight.

6. Churchill argued that "viewed in the light of history, these four centuries of consistent purpose amid so many changes of names and facts, of circumstances and conditions, must rank as one of the most remarkable episodes which the records of any race, nation, state, or people can show. Moreover, on all occasions England took the more difficult course. Faced by Philip II of Spain, against Louis XIV under William III and Marlborough, against

Napoleon, against William II of Germany, it would have been easy and must have been very tempting to join with the stronger and share the fruits of his conquest. However, we always took the harder course, joined with the less strong Powers, made a combination among them, and thus defeated and frustrated the Continental military tyrant whoever he was, whatever nation he led. Thus we preserved the liberties of Europe, protected the growth of its vivacious and varied society, and emerged after four terrible struggles with an ever-growing fame and widening Empire, and with the Low Countries safely protected in their independence." Winston S. Churchill, *The Second World War,* vol. 1: *The Gathering Storm* (Boston: Houghton Mifflin, 1948), 207.

7. The factors and events leading to the war are enormously complex and often appear overdetermined. A small sample of the factors that have been indicted as playing a major role include: masculine codes of honor; the elites' fear of domestic chaos that might be solved by a patriotic war; nationalism; Social Darwinistic attitudes and a fatalism, sometimes even an exaltation, of what was portrayed as an inevitable future struggle; a "cult of the offensive"; organizational constraints of military mobilization that promoted diplomatic rigidity; and many others. No single model suffices to explain such a complex event. See Christopher Clark, *The Sleepwalkers: How Europe Went to War in 1914* (London: Allen Lane; New York: Penguin Books, 2012), xxi–xxvii; Margaret MacMillan, *The War That Ended Peace: How Europe Abandoned Peace for the First World War* (London: Profile Books, 2013), xxi–xxii, xxx–xxxi, 605. This chapter's goal is not to adjudicate the claims of competing historical schools or to assign sole responsibility to particular historical actors. Nor is it to "explain" the war in all its complexities. It endeavors, however, to show how Thucydidean stress helped to bring Britain and Germany into a conflict that changed the world forever.

8. Churchill, *The World Crisis,* 17–18.

9. Emphasis added. Gilbert, *Churchill: A Life,* 268. Consider also Christopher Clark's remark on how the "protagonists of 1914 were sleepwalkers, watchful but unseeing, haunted by dreams, yet blind to the reality of the horror they were about to unleash on the world." Clark, *The Sleepwalkers,* 562. For a discussion of how the German military's dreams of war "turned into nightmares, which then happened to become reality," see Stig Förster, "Dreams and Nightmares: German Military Leadership and the Images of Future Warfare, 1871–1914," in *Anticipating Total War: The German and American Experiences, 1871–1914,* ed. Manfred F. Boemeke, Roger Chickering, and Stig Förster (Washington, DC: German Historical Institute; Cambridge and New York: Cambridge University Press, 1999), 376.

10. Gilbert, *Churchill: A Life,* 268.

11. More precisely, as his government later recorded, the king "had repeatedly expressed himself perturbed by what he thought was our persistently unfriendly attitude towards Germany contrasted with our eagerness to run af-

ter France and do anything the French asked." Paul M. Kennedy, *The Rise of the Anglo-German Antagonism, 1860–1914* (London and Boston: Allen & Unwin, 1980), 402–3, 540n73; K. M. Wilson, "Sir Eyre Crowe on the Origin of the Crowe Memorandum of 1 January 1907," *Historical Research* 56, no. 134 (November 1983), 238–41.

12.   MacMillan, *The War That Ended Peace,* 115–16.

13.   The Crowe Memorandum can be found in full as "Memorandum on the Present State of British Relations with France and Germany," January 1, 1907, in *British Documents on the Origins of the War, 1898–1914,* vol. 3: *The Testing of the Entente,* ed. G. P. Gooch and H. Temperley (London: H. M. Stationery Office, 1928), 397–420. Lord Thomas Sanderson, the retired permanent undersecretary at the Foreign Office, contested Crowe's analysis, but was seen to have "taken up the cudgels for Germany," and Crowe's perspective prevailed. See 420–31, and Zara S. Steiner, *Britain and the Origins of the First World War* (New York: St. Martin's Press, 1977), 44–45. For a discussion of the memorandum's significance, see Kissinger, *On China,* 514–22.

14.   Kennedy, *The Rise and Fall of the Great Powers,* 224–26.

15.   London was also the world's financial capital. Ibid., 226, 228.

16.   Niall Ferguson, *Empire: How Britain Made the Modern World* (London: Allen Lane, 2003), 222, 240–44; Kennedy, *The Rise and Fall of the Great Powers,* 226.

17.   MacMillan, *The War That Ended Peace,* 25–28, 37.

18.   In fact, Churchill's first speech had been delivered two years earlier, protesting against attempts by moralizers to conceal various bars in central London. His 1897 speech was, however, what he later called "my (official) maiden effort." Robert Rhodes James, ed., *Winston S. Churchill: His Complete Speeches, 1897–1963,* vol. 1 (New York: Chelsea House Publishers, 1974), 25, 28; Richard Toye, *Churchill's Empire: The World That Made Him and the World He Made* (London: Macmillan, 2010), 4–5; Gilbert, *Churchill: A Life,* 71–72.

19.   Aaron Friedberg, *The Weary Titan: Britain and the Experience of Relative Decline, 1895–1905* (Princeton, NJ: Princeton University Press, 1988); Kennedy, *Anglo-German Antagonism,* 229.

20.   For a recent account of Churchill's adventures in South Africa, see Candice Millard, *Hero of the Empire: The Boer War, a Daring Escape, and the Making of Winston Churchill* (New York: Doubleday, 2016).

21.   Kennedy, *Anglo-German Antagonism,* 265.

22.   Kennedy, *The Rise and Fall of the Great Powers,* 198, 226–28. As Kennedy puts it: "Fin de siècle observers of world affairs agreed that the pace of economic and political change was quickening, and thus likely to make the international order more precarious than before. Alterations had always occurred in the power balances to produce instability and often war. 'What made war inevitable,' Thucydides wrote in *The Peloponnesian War,* 'was the growth of Athenian power and the fear which this caused in Sparta.' But by the final quarter of the nineteenth century, the changes affecting the Great Power

system were more widespread, and usually swifter, than ever before. The global trading and communications network . . . meant that breakthroughs in science and technology, or new advances in manufacturing production, could be transmitted and transferred from one continent to another within a matter of years."

23. Kennedy, *The Rise and Fall of the Great Powers,* 227, 230, 232–33.

24. Hew Strachan, *The First World War,* vol. 1 (Oxford and New York: Oxford University Press, 2001), 13; see also Kennedy, *The Rise and Fall of the Great Powers,* 219–24.

25. Kennedy, *The Rise and Fall of the Great Powers,* 242–44.

26. Ibid., 202.

27. Kenneth Bourne, *Britain and the Balance of Power in North America, 1815–1908* (Berkeley: University of California Press, 1967), 339.

28. Kennedy, *The Rise and Fall of the Great Powers,* 209–15; Kennedy, *Anglo-German Antagonism,* 231.

29. MacMillan, *The War That Ended Peace,* 55, 129–30.

30. George F. Kennan, *The Decline of Bismarck's European Order: Franco-Russian Relations, 1875–1890* (Princeton, NJ: Princeton University Press, 1979), 97–98, 400.

31. Kennedy, *The Rise and Fall of the Great Powers,* 212.

32. Ibid., 199.

33. Germany's GDP was $210 billion in 1910 and Britain's GDP (not including its broader empire) was $207 billion (in 1990 International Geary-Khamis dollars). See "GDP Levels in 12 West European Countries, 1869–1918," in Maddison, *The World Economy,* 426–27.

34. Kennedy, *The Rise and Fall of the Great Powers,* 211.

35. Kennedy, *Anglo-German Antagonism,* 464.

36. Ibid., 293.

37. MacMillan, *The War That Ended Peace,* 101–2. See also Clark, *The Sleepwalkers,* 164–65.

38. Ivan Berend, *An Economic History of Nineteenth-Century Europe: Diversity and Industrialization* (New York: Cambridge University Press, 2012), 225.

39. Clark, *The Sleepwalkers,* 165.

40. Bernard Wasserstein, *Barbarism and Civilization: A History of Europe in Our Time* (Oxford and New York: Oxford University Press, 2007), 13–14.

41. Modris Eksteins, *Rites of Spring: The Great War and the Birth of the Modern Age* (Toronto: Lester & Orpen Dennys, 1994), 70–72. For a discussion of how elite British universities and their alumni were hostile to business and industry, in contrast to higher education in Germany and the US, see Martin J. Wiener, *English Culture and the Decline of the Industrial Spirit, 1850–1980* (Cambridge and New York: Cambridge University Press, 1981), 22–24.

42. For a personal understanding of the scale of German scientific ingenuity, readers should reflect on the fact that half the nitrogen atoms in their body at this moment were originally "fixed" from the atmosphere by the Haber-

Bosch process, which was developed in 1913 and today produces the chemical fertilizer for half of humanity's food supply. Robert L. Zimdahl, *Six Chemicals That Changed Agriculture* (Amsterdam: Elsevier, 2015), 60.

43. Kennedy, *The Rise and Fall of the Great Powers,* 194–96; MacMillan, *The War That Ended Peace,* 54–55.

44. If Germany was late to the table, it was in large part because Bismarck himself was reticent about colonial adventurism, describing Germany as a "saturated" power with other priorities. In the midst of the "scramble for Africa" in the 1880s, he pointed to a map of Europe and told an explorer, "My map of Africa lies here in Europe. Here lies Russia, and here lies France, and we are right in the middle; this is my map of Africa." MacMillan, *The War That Ended Peace,* 80–82; Kennedy, *The Rise and Fall of the Great Powers,* 211–13. For an example of resentment at being denied the global status commensurate with its national power, see General Friedrich von Bernhardi's bestseller *Germany and the Next War* (New York: Longmans, Green, 1912). In the chapter "World Power or Downfall," he explained to his legion of readers that "we have fought in the last great wars for our national union and our position among the Powers of Europe; we now must decide whether we wish to develop into and maintain a World Empire, and procure for German spirit and German ideas that fit recognition which has been hitherto withheld from them."

45. Strachan, *The First World War,* 6.

46. The kaiser dismissed Bismarck for internal reasons, rather than over foreign policy. See Robert K. Massie, *Dreadnought: Britain, Germany, and the Coming of the Great War* (New York: Random House, 1991), 92–99.

47. MacMillan, *The War That Ended Peace,* 74.

48. Kennedy, *Anglo-German Antagonism,* 223–25.

49. Emphasis added. Clark, *The Sleepwalkers,* 151.

50. Nor was *Weltpolitik* itself ever consistently defined. Clark, *The Sleepwalkers,* 151–52; Strachan, *The First World War,* 9–11; MacMillan, *The War That Ended Peace,* 78–81.

51. Clark, *The Sleepwalkers,* 151.

52. Bülow compared naysayers to the proverbial overbearing parent, determined to prevent the next generation from growing up. Kennedy, *Anglo-German Antagonism,* 311.

53. Jonathan Steinberg, "The Copenhagen Complex," *Journal of Contemporary History* 1, no. 3 (July 1966), 27.

54. Emphasis added. MacMillan, *The War That Ended Peace,* 83–84.

55. Michael Howard, *The Continental Commitment* (London and Atlantic Highlands, NJ: Ashfield Press, 1989), 32.

56. Victoria had herself been raised speaking only German until she was three years old. Massie, *Dreadnought,* 3; MacMillan, *The War That Ended Peace,* 58, 84; Joseph Bucklin Bishop, *Theodore Roosevelt and His Time: Shown in His Own Letters* (New York : Scribner, 1920), 253–54. Shortly after their meet-

ing in Berlin, both the kaiser and Roosevelt were reunited in London for the funeral of Edward VII. Edward was succeeded by his son, Wilhelm's cousin, George V.

57. Kiel never quite attained the glamour of Cowes. Queen Victoria's patience had worn thin when she heard of the kaiser's taking umbrage early in his reign at Edward's supposedly insufficient deference toward his imperial nephew. "We have always been very intimate" with Wilhelm, she wrote, but "to pretend that he is to be treated *in private as well* as in public as 'His Imperial Majesty' is *perfect madness!*" MacMillan, *The War That Ended Peace,* 60–65, 84–86; Massie, *Dreadnought,* 152–59.

58. Roosevelt had also noted the kaiser's ambivalence about his uncle, having "a real affection and respect for King Edward and also a very active and jealous dislike for him, first one feeling and then the other coming uppermost in his mind and therefore in his conversation." Bishop, *Theodore Roosevelt and His Time,* 254–55; MacMillan, *The War That Ended Peace,* 86. The kaiser's demand for acceptance was reflected on the national level between the rising and ruling power. As Jonathan Steinberg has argued, "The need of the younger brother or parvenu to be recognized is not a negotiable item, and it is consequently hardly surprising that the British could never quite make out what the Germans wanted, nor arrive at a 'deal' in the ordinary sense of diplomacy. A nation ready to declare war for a few South Pacific islands or a slice of North African territory in which it had minimal interests can simply not be dealt with by the established devices of international accommodation. The Germans wanted what they thought the British had, but they wanted to have it without destroying Britain in the process. Germany could not enjoy [equality] if the British Empire was destroyed to achieve it." See Steinberg, "The Copenhagen Complex," 44–45.

59. See MacMillan, *The War That Ended Peace,* 72, for how another of Wilhelm's nautical metaphors presaged the construction of his own fleet.

60. Mahan's views were shared by Theodore Roosevelt, and his book served as a Bible for those supporting the naval expansion that took place in the US during the subsequent two decades. MacMillan, *The War That Ended Peace,* 87–89.

61. Steinberg, "The Copenhagen Complex," 43.

62. Clark, *The Sleepwalkers,* 149.

63. Kennedy, *Anglo-German Antagonism,* 224.

64. Kennedy, *The Rise and Fall of the Great Powers,* 196, 215.

65. MacMillan, *The War That Ended Peace,* 93.

66. Steinberg, "The Copenhagen Complex," 25.

67. Kennedy, *Anglo-German Antagonism,* 225; Massie, *Dreadnought,* 180.

68. MacMillan, *The War That Ended Peace,* 93; Kennedy, *Anglo-German Antagonism,* 224.

69. Kennedy, *The Rise and Fall of the Great Powers,* 212; Kennedy, *Anglo-German Antagonism,* 422.

70. Kennedy, *Anglo-German Antagonism,* 224.

71. As Margaret MacMillan puts it, "It says something about Tirpitz's narrow focus that he seems to have expected that the British would not notice this very clear hint that they were in Germany's sights." MacMillan, *The War That Ended Peace,* 94; Archibald Hurd and Henry Castle, *German Sea-Power: Its Rise, Progress, and Economic Basis* (London: J. Murray, 1913), 348.

72. In 1897, when the kaiser had asked his government to prepare a secret plan for war against Britain, the proposal called for a surprise attack that seized neutral Belgium and the Netherlands and then used them as a launchpad for invasion of the UK. According to Jonathan Steinberg, although the plan had "strong advocates within the navy," Tirpitz argued that until the German fleet was much stronger, such an invasion would be "insane." Steinberg, "The Copenhagen Complex," 27–28.

73. MacMillan, *The War That Ended Peace,* 94–95.

74. After the war, Tirpitz claimed that "a treaty that was concluded according to the English desire to rule would never have been in accordance with the German necessities. For this, equality would have been the precondition." MacMillan, *The War That Ended Peace,* 78–79, 95–96; Kennedy, *Anglo-German Antagonism,* 226–27.

75. Although the growth of his magnificent fleet would take time, the kaiser looked forward to being able to express himself as he saw fit. As he put it to the French ambassador, when his navy was complete in twenty years, "I shall speak another language." MacMillan, *The War That Ended Peace,* 90, 93, 95–99; Massie, *Dreadnought,* 176–79; Strachan, *The First World War,* 11–12.

76. MacMillan, *The War That Ended Peace,* 89–90; John Van der Kiste, *Kaiser Wilhelm II: Germany's Last Emperor* (Stroud, UK: Sutton, 1999), 121–22; Holger H. Herwig, *"Luxury" Fleet: The Imperial German Navy, 1888–1918* (London and Atlantic Highlands, NJ: Ashfield Press, 1987), 51.

77. Van der Kiste, *Kaiser Wilhelm II,* 122; Herwig, *"Luxury" Fleet,* 51.

78. As Paul Kennedy puts it, "Tirpitz's calculations that Germany could develop a formidable naval force in home waters without the British either noticing it or being able to respond to it was flawed from the start." Kennedy, *Anglo-German Antagonism,* 251–52.

79. Matthew S. Seligmann, Frank Nägler, and Michael Epkenhans, eds., *The Naval Route to the Abyss: The Anglo-German Naval Race, 1895–1914* (Farnham, Surrey, UK: Ashgate Publishing, 2015), 137–38.

80. Britain's increasing alarm about Germany's naval program coincided with a more general souring of London's attitude toward German diplomacy. By 1901, because of Germany's perceived deviousness toward Britain, especially concerning a hoped-for partnership in China, supporters in the cabinet for an Anglo-German alliance had lost much of their earlier appetite. Kennedy, *Anglo-German Antagonism,* 225, 243–46, 252.

81. Ibid., 243–46, 265.

82. MacMillan, *The War That Ended Peace,* 129. The kaiser and Tirpitz claimed that Germany was being singled out, but as the Foreign Office once com-

mented, "If the British press pays more attention to the increase of Germany's naval power than to a similar movement in Brazil—which the Emperor appears to think unfair—this is no doubt due to the proximity of the German coasts and the remoteness of Brazil." Kennedy, *Anglo-German Antagonism,* 421.

83. Friedberg, *The Weary Titan,* 161–80.

84. Kennedy, *Anglo-German Antagonism,* 243–46, 249–50.

85. George W. Monger, *The End of Isolation: British Foreign Policy, 1900–1907* (London and New York: T. Nelson, 1963), 163.

86. Howard, *Continental Commitment,* 33–34.

87. Kennedy, *Anglo-German Antagonism,* 310.

88. Ibid., 424–29.

89. John C. G. Röhl, *Kaiser Wilhelm II: A Concise Life* (Cambridge: Cambridge University Press, 2014), 98.

90. In 1905, Fisher remarked privately that frightening the enemy was the best way to avoid war: "If you rub it in, both at home and abroad, that you are ready for instant war with every unit of your strength in the first line, and intend to be 'first in', and hit your enemy in the belly and kick him when he's down and boil your prisoners in oil (if you take any!) and torture his women and children, then people will keep clear of you. *Si vis pace para bellum,* is what Julius Caesar said, and it's quite true still!" That same year, however, after a minister at the Admiralty announced publicly that "the Royal Navy would get its blow in first before the other side had time even to read in the papers that war had been declared," the kaiser tried to have this politician reprimanded by the British government. Wilhelm's reaction was summed up in remarks to one of his admirals: "Those persons were right who saw in the continued English threats the need to accelerate our naval arms program and those who want to avoid a more rapid course in our fleet development for fear of England are denying any future to the German people." Fisher did not limit his suggestions about preventive attack to the king, telling the head of the Admiralty in 1905 that "if you want to smash up the German Fleet, I am ready to do so now. If you wait five or six years, it will be a much more difficult job." The prime minister said Fisher should be told that "we don't want to smash up the German navy—but to keep it in readiness." Fisher responded: "Very well, remember I have warned you." After the war, Fisher complained that Britain had "possessed neither a Pitt nor a Bismarck to give the order" to "Copenhagen" the German fleet, but there is no evidence that this was ever considered as a real option within the Admiralty. Arthur J. Marder, *From the Dreadnought to Scapa Flow,* vol. 1 (London and New York: Oxford University Press, 1961–70), 111–4; Steinberg, "The Copenhagen Complex," 30–31, 37–39; William Mulligan, "Restraints on Preventative War Before 1914," in *The Outbreak of the First World War: Structure, Politics, and Decision-Making,* ed. Jack S. Levy and John A. Vasquez (Cambridge: Cambridge University Press, 2014), 131–32; MacMillan, *The War That Ended Peace,*

118–19; John Arbuthnot Fisher, *Memories* (London and New York: Hodder and Stoughton, 1919), 4–5.

91. MacMillan, *The War That Ended Peace,* 99.

92. Tirpitz also failed to predict Britain's eventual naval strategy in the war — choosing to blockade Germany rather than seeking decisive battle — and that Germany's submarines, rather than its expensive battleships, would play a much more effective role. MacMillan, *The War That Ended Peace,* 88, 94, 99. Others within Germany were not blind to the flaws in Tirpitz's plan, and, in Paul Kennedy's words, "as the years developed, each of these criticisms was proven correct; yet Tirpitz, with the ear of the Kaiser, refused to acknowledge these arguments. The race would go on regardless." Kennedy, *Anglo-German Antagonism,* 419.

93. Marder, *From the Dreadnought to Scapa Flow,* 74.

94. Strachan, *The First World War,* 17.

95. MacMillan, *The War That Ended Peace,* 86. It was believed that Berlin ascribed any reluctance to match German shipbuilding to "want of national spirit," as Churchill later wrote, "another proof that the virile race should advance to replace the effete over-civilized and pacifist society which was no longer capable of sustaining its great place in the world's affairs." Churchill, *The World Crisis,* 34.

96. Strachan, *The First World War,* 17–18.

97. MacMillan, *The War That Ended Peace,* 116–17.

98. See Marder, *From the Dreadnought to Scapa Flow,* 67.

99. Massie, *Dreadnought,* 407.

100. Ibid., 183.

101. Kennedy, *Anglo-German Antagonism,* 443–44; Steinberg, "The Copenhagen Complex," 40.

102. The Liberal government — which after his defection from the Conservatives included Winston Churchill — faced a widespread lobbying effort to increase naval expenditures. This extended from King Edward, who it was known advocated eight new dreadnoughts, to the popular slogan "We want eight and we won't wait!" In 1909, the government compromised by pledging four dreadnoughts that year, and four the following year if they were deemed necessary. Lloyd George's new taxation prompted political upheaval, but the Liberals eventually triumphed and the expenditure bill passed. MacMillan, *The War That Ended Peace,* 127–29; Strachan, *The First World War,* 26.

103. For a critical discussion of Crowe's perspective, see Clark, *The Sleepwalkers,* 162–64.

104. As Hew Strachan argues, "To use epithets like 'paranoid' and 'fatalistic' of Germany after 1905 . . . does not seem so misplaced." Strachan, *The First World War,* 20.

105. Kennedy, *Anglo-German Antagonism,* 445.

106. Barbara W. Tuchman, *The Guns of August* (New York: Macmillan, 1962), 2.

107. King Edward remarked upon the strangeness of Anglo-German hostility to

Fisher in 1908: "It goes against the grain that we should desert the Saxon for the Celtic Races, who ought to be our natural allies, but I confess that the intense jealousy of one of the former countries and races makes them unfortunately our bitterest enemies." But he hoped that British vigilance would see off any trouble: "I do not despair that if we continue to put our foot down, as we do now, they will accept the inevitable and be friendly with us, but we must never cease keeping our 'weather eye open' across the North Sea!" Arthur J. Marder, *Fear God and Dread Nought: The Correspondence of Admiral of the Fleet Lord Fisher of Kilverstone,* vol. 2 (London: Cape, 1956–59), 170. Wilhelm's full comment to his foreign secretary, on the same day he had received a report from his ambassador in London that Britain would not accept Germany's "crushing" of France and the emergence of a continental hegemon, was that "England will undoubtedly stand behind France and Russia against Germany out of hatred and envy. The imminent struggle for existence which the Germanic peoples of Europe (Austria, Germany) will have to fight out against the Slavs (Russians) and their Latin (Gallic) supporters finds the Anglo-Saxons on the side of the Slavs. Reason: petty envy, fear of our growing big." Fritz Fischer, *Germany's Aims in the First World War* (New York: W. W. Norton, 1967), 32; Holger H. Herwig, "Germany," in *The Origins of World War I,* ed. Richard F. Hamilton and Holger H. Herwig (Cambridge and New York: Cambridge University Press, 2003), 162–63.

108. Churchill, *The World Crisis,* 43–48; Marder, *From the Dreadnought to Scapa Flow,* 239–41; Strachan, *The First World War,* 25–26; Gilbert, *Churchill: A Life,* 233–35; Annika Mombauer, *Helmuth Von Moltke and the Origins of the First World War* (Cambridge and New York: Cambridge University Press, 2001), 126.

109. This was the environment in which Bernhardi produced *Germany and the Next War* (1912), his bellicose bestseller on Germany's frustrated need to be a World Power. As Bernhardi put it: "We not only require for the full material development of our nation, on a scale corresponding to its intellectual importance, an extended political basis, but . . . we are compelled to obtain space for our increasing population and markets for our growing industries. But at every step which we take in this direction England will resolutely oppose us . . . Since the struggle is, as appears on a thorough investigation of the international question, necessary and inevitable, we must fight it out, cost what it may." Any British reader of Bernhardi would find ample cause for concern about Germany's determination to overturn the status quo and the European balance of power — principles Britain was determined to uphold: "There is no standing still in the world's history . . . It is obviously impossible to keep things in the status quo, as diplomacy has so often attempted . . . France must be so completely crushed that she can never again come across our path . . . The principle of the balance of power in Europe, which has, since the Congress of Vienna, led an almost sacrosanct but entirely unjustifiable existence, must be entirely disregarded."

110. The Junkers were the Prussian aristocracy. Before Agadir, Churchill had

been more sanguine about Germany. In 1908, Churchill had shared Lloyd George's caution against increasing naval expenditures. He later wrote that while he and Lloyd George had been correct "in the narrow sense" in their skepticism over projected German naval growth, they were "absolutely wrong in relation to the deep tides of destiny." Gilbert, *Churchill: A Life,* 233–36; Churchill, *The World Crisis,* 33, 43–48; Massie, *Dreadnought,* 819.

111. During the Agadir crisis Britain's leaders had feared a surprise attack by the Germans, but the fleet was apparently scattered and vulnerable. The cabinet realized that the only person who knew the navy's secret war plan was Fisher's successor — and he was on vacation. Churchill found that the Admiralty refused to provide armed protection for the navy's vulnerable munition stores, so on his own initiative he ordered troops to guard them. He authorized the interception of suspect correspondence, and found that "we are the subject of a minute and scientific study by the German military and naval authorities." In August 1911, Churchill sketched out his remarkably prescient thoughts on how a future German attack on France would play out. His timelines were correct almost to the day, and in 1914 one of his colleagues would describe the memorandum as "a triumph of prophecy!" Fisher, although retired, served as the new First Lord's enthusiastic adviser. Gilbert, *Churchill: A Life,* 234–37, 240–42; Marder, *From the Dreadnought to Scapa Flow,* 242–44; Churchill, *The World Crisis,* 44–67.

112. Churchill had added to Cassel that if the Germans were recalcitrant, "I see little in prospect but politeness and preparation." Gilbert, *Churchill: A Life,* 198, 242–45. Demands for British neutrality had been the sticking point in earlier abortive Anglo-German discussions, from 1909 to 1911. The Foreign Office feared that Germany was trying to use naval negotiations as a means of keeping Britain neutral in any future German bid for continental hegemony. The new German chancellor, Theobald von Bethmann Hollweg, also lacked the clout to force Tirpitz to make meaningful cuts to his beloved naval program. See Steiner, *Britain and the Origins of the First World War,* 52–57; MacMillan, *The War That Ended Peace,* 122–24, 507–9; Strachan, *The First World War,* 23; Marder, *From the Dreadnought to Scapa Flow,* 221–33.

113. Tirpitz privately underlined that the ratio did not apply to cruisers. Patrick Kelly, *Tirpitz and the Imperial General Navy* (Bloomington: Indiana University Press, 2011), 326–51, 345; MacMillan, *The War That Ended Peace,* 507–9; Massie, *Dreadnought,* 821–23, 829–31.

114. Kennedy, *The Rise and Fall of the Great Powers,* 203, cited in, and ratios calculated by, Niall Ferguson, *The Pity of War* (New York: Basic Books, 1999), 84.

115. MacMillan, *The War That Ended Peace,* 129.

116. Massie, *Dreadnought,* xxv; MacMillan, *The War That Ended Peace,* 129–30.

117. Michael Howard, *Empires, Nations and Wars* (Stroud, UK: Spellmount, 2007), 5–6.

118. MacMillan, *The War That Ended Peace,* 129–30; Kennedy, *Anglo-German Antagonism,* 231; Steiner, *Britain and the Origins of the First World War,* 57–59.

119. By 1913, the naval race was a manifestation of the fear Britain felt at Germany's rise, not the sole cause of the fear itself. Foreign Secretary Edward Grey recognized that "what Tirpitz said does not amount to much, and the reason for his saying it is not the love of our beautiful eyes, but the extra fifty millions required for increasing the German army." Massie, *Dreadnought,* 829. Some in both countries did feel that relations improved a little from 1912 to 1914, but what has since been labeled an Anglo-German "détente" was illusory. See Kennedy, *Anglo-German Antagonism,* 452.

120. Just as naval budgets reflected German attitudes toward Britain, its army budgets were a telling barometer of Berlin's fears of Moscow. In 1898, German naval expenditures were less than a fifth of the army's budget; by 1911, it had increased to more than half of its size. During the naval race with Britain between 1904 and 1912, the navy's budget had increased by 137 percent, while the army's had risen only by 47 percent. But after this point the pendulum swung back: from 1910 to 1914, the naval budget increased by less than 10 percent, while the army's funding soared by 117 percent. See Herwig, *"Luxury" Fleet,* 75; Quincy Wright, *A Study of War* (Chicago: University of Chicago Press, 1965), 670–71.

121. By 1914 a quarter of all French investment went to a rapidly industrializing Russia. In addition, in 1914 Russian naval expenditures, which had tripled since 1907, overtook those of Germany. Strachan, *The First World War,* 19, 62–63.

122. In December 1912, Helmuth von Moltke, the chief of the German general staff, urged the kaiser to wage war against Russia, "the sooner the better." The German foreign secretary recalled that in the spring of 1914, Moltke told him how "there was no alternative but to fight a preventive war so as to beat the enemy while we could still emerge fairly well from the struggle" —otherwise, he did not know how he would deal with a rearmed Russia. Soon afterward, in May, Moltke told his Austrian counterpart that "to wait any longer means a diminishment of our chances." At the height of the July Crisis, Moltke told the kaiser that they "would never hit it again so well as we do now with France's and Russia's expansion of their armies incomplete." The kaiser himself had wondered a month before Archduke Franz Ferdinand's murder whether it might be advisable to attack the Russians before they could fully rearm. His chancellor Bethmann Hollweg had remarked that Russia "grows and grows and weighs on us like a nightmare," and even advised against planting any trees on his estate, as it would probably soon be in Russian hands. In the summer of 1914, he argued that "were war unavoidable, the present moment would be more advantageous than a later one." Holger H. Herwig, *The First World War: Germany and Austria-Hungary, 1914–1918* (London: Bloomsbury, 2014), 20–24. See also Clark, *The Sleepwalkers,* 326–34.

123. The Austro-Hungarian foreign minister reported to his cabinet that Berlin would support Vienna "even though our operations against Serbia should bring about the great war." Herwig, *The First World War,* 17.

124. The kaiser's decision to support Vienna in early July had also stemmed from his concerns that he had been humiliated in not standing up to his enemies in recent crises. He saw a good opportunity to end Russian influence in the Balkans, even if this led to war with Moscow. When the kaiser read his ambassador's report that Austria planned to attack Serbia in response to the assassination, he annotated it: "Now or never." In late July, as it became clear that Britain would enter the war, Bethmann Hollweg joined the kaiser in trying to limit the extent of Austria-Hungary's intervention in Serbia, suggesting a "halt in Belgrade," but Moltke countermanded his message to Vienna and told the Austrians that both they and Germany should immediately mobilize against Russia. Herwig, *The First World War,* 17–30; MacMillan, *The War That Ended Peace,* 522–33. The extent to which the kaiser had actively sought war with Russia in July 1914 is unclear. It is possible he would have been satisfied merely with Austrian influence triumphing over Russia's in the Balkans. But he had certainly been willing for the dispute to bring about war with St. Petersburg if necessary. See John C. G. Röhl, "Goodbye to All That (Again)? The Fischer Thesis, the New Revisionism and the Meaning of the First World War," *International Affairs* 91, no. 1 (2015), 159.

125. Howard, *Empires, Nations and Wars,* 111; Kennedy, *Anglo-German Antagonism,* 462; Massie, *Dreadnought,* 901–2, 905. In his account of the war, Churchill compared Germany's challenge in 1914 to those of imperial Spain, Louis XIV, and Napoleon, from whose "military domination" Britain had saved Europe. Churchill, *The World Crisis,* 1–2.

126. Kennedy, *Anglo-German Antagonism,* 470.

127. MacMillan, *The War That Ended Peace,* xxiii–xxv, 593.

128. Gilbert, *Churchill: A Life,* 261–64.

129. Churchill had told the cabinet that war was "an appalling calamity for civilized nations to contemplate," but he was still one of the strongest voices for British intervention to defend France. On a personal level, he also relished the excitement of war. Churchill took personal command of military units during the war. In the same letter in which he warned his wife of "catastrophe and collapse," he admitted that "I am interested, geared up and happy." In later comments recorded by one of his intimates, he exclaimed, "My God! This is living History. Everything we are doing and saying is thrilling—it will be read by a thousand generations, think of that! Why I would not be out of this glorious delicious war for anything the world could give me (eyes glowing but with a slight anxiety lest the word 'delicious' jar on me). I say, don't repeat the word 'delicious'—you know what I mean." Gilbert, *Churchill: A Life,* 268–75, 281, 283–86, 294–95, 331–60; Churchill, *The World Crisis,* 245–46.

130. Churchill, *The World Crisis,* vi.

131. Interestingly, Churchill did not believe that an unambiguous advance declaration by Grey that Britain would intervene in the war would have helped to prevent it, as he felt such a declaration would have lacked political support and led to the collapse of the government. He argued that it would have

been impossible to abandon France and Russia, and "in the final crisis the British Foreign Secretary could do nothing but what he did." Churchill, *The World Crisis,* 5–6; Winston S. Churchill, *The World Crisis: The Aftermath* (London: T. Butterworth, 1929), 439–44.

132. Attempting to answer such a question requires counterfactual reasoning. "What ifs" are mind teasers, fascinating to explore — but uncomfortable for many mainstream historians. They are, however, a staple of Applied History. Indeed, as demonstrated (at least to my satisfaction) by the Applied History Project at Harvard, counterfactual reasoning lies at the heart of any historian's assessment of the relative significance of causative factors. The challenge is to be both explicit and rigorous in the process.

133. During the July Crisis Bethmann Hollweg remarked, "A fate beyond human power hangs over Europe and our *Volk.*" In fact, Bethmann Hollweg was well aware of the role he played in starting the war. Less than a year later, he privately confessed to permanent guilt: "The thought never leaves me, I live with *it* constantly." See Herwig, *The First World War,* 23, 30. While Bethmann Hollweg's claim of ignorance was disingenuous and self-serving, it illuminates another paradox: that even when actors are aware of the potentially catastrophic outcome of their conscious decisions, they can feel so compelled by underlying forces that they may later feel they had been powerless.

5. Imagine China Were Just Like Us

1. Edmund Morris, *The Rise of Theodore Roosevelt* (New York: Coward, McCann & Geoghegan, 1979), 21.

2. Memorandum to President William McKinley, April 26, 1897, in *The Selected Letters of Theodore Roosevelt,* ed. H. W. Brands (New York: Cooper Square Press, 2001), 129–30.

3. Morris, *The Rise of Theodore Roosevelt,* 572–73.

4. During TR's presidency, the US intervened three times in Colombia, twice in Honduras and the Dominican Republic, and once each in Cuba and Panama. For summaries of these and other interventions through 1935, see William Appleman Williams, *Empire as a Way of Life* (New York: Oxford University Press, 1980), 102–10, 136–42, 165–67; Barbara Salazar Torreon, "Instances of Use of United States Armed Forces Abroad, 1798–2015," Congressional Research Service, October 15, 2015, https://www.fas.org/sgp/crs/natsec/R42738.pdf.

5. Theodore Roosevelt, "Expansion and Peace," in *The Strenuous Life* (New York: P. F. Collier & Son, 1899), 32.

6. Theodore Roosevelt, "Naval War College Address," Newport, RI, June 2, 1897, http:// www.theodore-roosevelt.com/images/research/speeches/tr1898.pdf.

7. Albert Weinberg, *Manifest Destiny: A Study of Nationalist Expansionism in American History* (Baltimore: Johns Hopkins University Press, 1935), 1–2.

8. Theodore Roosevelt, *The Winning of the West,* vol. 1 (Lincoln: University of Nebraska Press, 1995), 1, 7.

9. Gregg Jones, *Honor in the Dust: Theodore Roosevelt, War in the Philippines, and the Rise and Fall of America's Imperial Dream* (New York: New American Library, 2012), 24. Close to seventy years after Roosevelt's remark, C. Vann Woodward would propose that the "free security" enjoyed by the US— "nature's gift" of the barriers provided by the Pacific, Atlantic, and Arctic Oceans, as well as the protection of the British navy on the Atlantic during the 1880s as American merchant ships plied their goods—had been instrumental to the development of American power and expansionist tendencies. "So long as free land was fertile and arable," Woodward wrote, "and so long as security was not only free but strong and effective, it is no wonder that the world seemed to be America's particular oyster." See C. Vann Woodward, "The Age of Reinterpretation," *American Historical Review* 66, no. 1 (October 1960), 1–19.

10. Theodore Roosevelt, *The Naval War of 1812* (New York: Modern Library, 1999), 151. First published in 1882.

11. Roosevelt, "Naval War College Address."

12. Charles Kupchan, *How Enemies Become Friends: The Sources of Stable Peace* (Princeton, NJ: Princeton University Press, 2010), 74.

13. Edmund Morris, *Theodore Rex* (New York: Random House, 2001), 184.

14. Roosevelt, "Expansion and Peace," 29.

15. Weinberg, *Manifest Destiny,* 429–30.

16. Theodore Roosevelt, "The Expansion of the White Races: Address at the Celebration of the African Diamond Jubilee of the Methodist Episcopal Church," Washington, DC, January 18, 1909, www.theodore-roosevelt.com/images/research/speeches/trwhiteraces.pdf.

17. Theodore Roosevelt, "Fourth Annual Message," December 6, 1904, UCSB American Presidency Project, http://www.presidency.ucsb.edu/ws/?pid=29545; Roosevelt, "The Expansion of the White Races."

18. Theodore Roosevelt, "First Annual Message," December 3, 1901, UCSB American Presidency Project, www.presidency.ucsb.edu/ws/?pid=29542.

19. Joseph Nye, *Presidential Leadership and the Creation of the American Era* (Princeton, NJ: Princeton University Press, 2013), 23.

20. Theodore Roosevelt, "The Strenuous Life," April 10, 1899, http://voicesofdemocracy.umd.edu/roosevelt-strenuous-life-1899-speech-text/.

21. Theodore Roosevelt, "The Monroe Doctrine," *The Bachelor of Arts* 2, no. 4 (March 1896), 443.

22. Louis Pérez Jr., *Cuba in the American Imagination: Metaphor and the Imperial Ethos* (Chapel Hill: University of North Carolina Press, 2008), 30.

23. Beginning in the 1860s, Spain faced a succession of Cuban independence movements: the Ten Years' War (1868–1878), the Small War (1879–1880), and finally the War of Independence (1895–1898), which led to the American intervention.

24. Morris, *The Rise of Theodore Roosevelt,* 513.

25. See William McKinley, "First Inaugural Address," March 4, 1897, Avalon Project, Yale Law School, http://avalon.law.yale.edu/19th_century/mckin1 .asp.

26. Two examples of letters in which Roosevelt expressed a desire to "drive the Spaniards out of Cuba" are found in Morris, *The Rise of Theodore Roosevelt*, 513, 526. For his comments to Mahan, see letter to Alfred Thayer Mahan, May 3, 1897, in Brands, *The Selected Letters of Theodore Roosevelt*, 133. Morris describes McKinley's unease that Roosevelt "would seek to involve the United States in war" on page 560 of *The Rise of Theodore Roosevelt*.

27. Ben Procter, *William Randolph Hearst: The Early Years, 1863–1910* (New York: Oxford University Press, 1998), 103.

28. Morris, *The Rise of Theodore Roosevelt*, 586.

29. See letter to Hermann Speck von Sternberg, January 17, 1898, in Brands, *The Selected Letters of Theodore Roosevelt*, 168.

30. Morris, *The Rise of Theodore Roosevelt*, 607.

31. Jones, *Honor in the Dust*, 10.

32. The inquiry did not specifically accuse Spanish or Cuban actors, but was clear that the explosion was due to external interference from a mine. This has remained a point of controversy ever since; subsequent inquiries have suggested that the explosion was in fact accidental.

33. Mark Lee Gardner, *Rough Riders: Theodore Roosevelt, His Cowboy Regiment, and the Immortal Charge Up San Juan Hill* (New York: HarperCollins, 2016), 175; Morris, *The Rise of Theodore Roosevelt*, 650.

34. In May 1898, American ships had destroyed the Spanish fleet in Manila Bay, achieving an unexpectedly quick victory months before the Cuba matter would be officially settled. When the war ended, the US paid $20 million for the Philippines, then occupied the archipelago, leading to the Philippine-American War, which began in 1899 and lasted until 1902. The newly liberated Cuba, meanwhile, was independent in name only—the country's new constitution granted the US control over Cuba's relations with other countries and guaranteed an American "right to intervene" in the name of maintaining order. The US exercised this right with interventions in 1906–9, 1912, and 1917–22.

35. Daniel Aaron, *Men of Good Hope: A Story of American Progressives* (New York: Oxford University Press, 1951), 268.

36. Describing this period in Roosevelt's presidency, historian Richard Collin writes that "Roosevelt's main task was to convince Europe of America's seriousness." See Richard Collin, *Theodore Roosevelt, Culture Diplomacy, and Expansion: A New View of American Imperialism* (Baton Rouge: Louisiana State University Press, 1985), 101. Elsewhere, Collin has noted Roosevelt's desire to "prevent a strong Germany from replacing a weak Spain in the Caribbean. Roosevelt's big stick . . . was directed at Europe, not Latin America." See Collin's *Theodore Roosevelt's Caribbean: The Panama Canal, the Monroe Doctrine, and the Latin American Context* (Baton Rouge: Louisiana State University Press, 1990), xii. For details of Roosevelt's suspicions about Germa-

ny's designs on Venezuela, see also James R. Holmes, *Theodore Roosevelt and World Order: Police Power in International Relations* (Washington, DC: Potomac Books, 2006), 165–67.

37. Morris, *Theodore Rex,* 186–87.

38. Edmund Morris, "A Few Pregnant Days," *Theodore Roosevelt Association Journal* 15, no. 1 (Winter 1989), 4. The episode is described in detail by Morris in both *Theodore Rex,* 183–91, and "A Few Pregnant Days," 2–13.

39. Morris, "A Few Pregnant Days," 2.

40. The Monroe Doctrine declared that countries in the Western Hemisphere were "not to be considered as subjects for future colonization by any European powers" and warned that the US "could not view any interposition by any European power in any other light than as the manifestation of an unfriendly disposition toward the US." See James Monroe, "Seventh Annual Message," December 2, 1823, UCSB American Presidency Project, http://www.presidency.ucsb.edu/ws/?pid=29465.

41. Stephen Rabe, "Theodore Roosevelt, the Panama Canal, and the Roosevelt Corollary: Sphere of Influence Diplomacy," in *A Companion to Theodore Roosevelt,* ed. Serge Ricard (Malden, MA: Wiley-Blackwell, 2011), 277; Ernest May, *Imperial Democracy: The Emergence of America as a Great Power* (Chicago: Imprint Publications, 1961), 33, 128; Robert Freeman Smith, "Latin America, The United States and the European powers, 1830–1930," in *The Cambridge History of Latin America,* vol. 4: 1870 to 1930, ed. Leslie Bethell (Cambridge: Cambridge University Press, 1986), 98–99.

42. Lars Schoultz, *Beneath the United States: A History of U.S. Policy Toward Latin America* (Cambridge, MA: Harvard University Press, 1998), 112.

43. Letter to Henry Cabot Lodge, December 27, 1895, in Brands, *The Selected Letters of Theodore Roosevelt,* 113. Around the same time, Roosevelt also claimed, "If there is a muss I shall try to have a hand in it myself!" See Brands, *The Selected Letters of Theodore Roosevelt,* 112.

44. The 1895 dispute is described in detail in Schoultz, *Beneath the United States,* 107–24.

45. Roosevelt, "The Monroe Doctrine," 437–39.

46. See Theodore Roosevelt, "Second Annual Message," December 2, 1902, UCSB American Presidency Project, www.presidency.ucsb.edu/ws/?pid=29543.

47. Collin, *Theodore Roosevelt's Caribbean,* 121. The US naval advantage in the Caribbean that December was 53 warships to Germany's 10. See Morris, "A Few Pregnant Days," 7.

48. Rabe, "Theodore Roosevelt, the Panama Canal, and the Roosevelt Corollary," 280; Warren Zimmerman, *First Great Triumph: How Five Americans Made Their Country a World Power* (New York: Farrar, Straus and Giroux, 2002), 426.

49. Theodore Roosevelt, "Charter Day Address," UC Berkeley, March 23, 1911. See *University of California Chronicle,* vol. 13 (Berkeley, CA: The University Press, 1911), 139.

50. Rabe, "Theodore Roosevelt, the Panama Canal, and the Roosevelt Corollary," 274.

51. David McCullough, *The Path Between the Seas: The Creation of the Panama Canal, 1870–1914* (New York: Simon & Schuster, 1977), 250.

52. See Theodore Roosevelt, "Special Message," January 4, 1904, UCSB American Presidency Project, www.presidency.ucsb.edu/ws/?pid=69417.

53. See Schoultz, *Beneath the United States,* 164; Collin, *Theodore Roosevelt's Caribbean,* 239. Although it was the Colombian senate that officially scuttled the plans from moving forward, Roosevelt blamed the country's president, José Marroquín, for not using his influence to push the normally acquiescent senate to approve the treaty.

54. William Roscoe Thayer, *The Life and Letters of John Hay,* vol. 2 (Boston: Houghton Mifflin, 1915), 327–28.

55. Morris, *Theodore Rex,* 273. See Collin's detailed description of the legal memo presented to Roosevelt that advocated this conclusion, in Collin, *Theodore Roosevelt's Caribbean,* 240–43.

56. See Morris, *Theodore Rex,* 275; Rabe, "Theodore Roosevelt, the Panama Canal, and the Roosevelt Corollary," 285.

57. To verify that Bunau-Varilla's revolution could really happen, Roosevelt met at the White House with two army officers he had secretly dispatched earlier in the year to assess the situation in Panama. Posing as tourists, they conducted extensive reconnaissance in the region and reported back that planning for a rebellion was indeed well under way.

58. Morris, *Theodore Rex,* 282–83; McCullough, *The Path Between the Seas,* 378–79.

59. The US maintained its military presence, signaling to the Colombians not to intervene while reminding the Panamanians that their fragile independence relied on continued American support. The exact level of involvement and knowledge of the revolution on the part of Roosevelt is an enduring source of controversy. For detailed accounts, see Morris, *Theodore Rex,* 270–83; Schoultz, *Beneath the United States,* 165–68; Collin, *Theodore Roosevelt's Caribbean,* 254–68; McCullough, *The Path Between the Seas,* 349–86.

60. Schoultz, *Beneath the United States,* 175.

61. Noel Maurer and Carlos Yu, "What T.R. Took: The Economic Impact of the Panama Canal, 1903–1937," *Journal of Economic History* 68, no. 3 (2008), 698–99.

62. Most of this revenue was used to cover the canal's operation and maintenance costs. See McCullough, *The Path Between the Seas,* 612; Eloy Aguilar, "U.S., Panama Mark Handover of Canal," Associated Press, December 14, 1999, http://www.washingtonpost.com/wp-srv/pmextra/dec99/14/panama.htm.

63. Noel Maurer and Carlos Yu, *The Big Ditch: How America Took, Built, Ran, and Ultimately Gave Away the Panama Canal* (Princeton, NJ: Princeton University Press, 2010), 89–92.

64. Roosevelt argued that "the people of Panama had long been discontented

with the Republic of Colombia, and they had been kept quiet only by the prospect of the conclusion of the treaty, which was to them a matter of vital concern. When it became evident that the treaty was hopelessly lost, the people of Panama rose literally as one man" — prompting one senator to retort, "Yes, and the one man was Roosevelt." See McCullough, *The Path Between the Seas,* 382. Later, Roosevelt noted that "some people say that I fomented insurrection in Panama . . . I did not have to foment it; I simply lifted my foot." See Frederick S. Wood, *Roosevelt As We Knew Him* (Philadelphia: J. C. Winston, 1927), 153, quoted in "TR on the Panama Revolution of 1903," *Theodore Roosevelt Association Journal* 15, no. 4 (Fall 1989), 5. As both Morris and Collin point out, Roosevelt frequently reminded his critics that Panama had faced numerous attempted revolutions during the previous decades, and that the Colombian government had often requested US help in maintaining order. Morris, *Theodore Rex,* 273; Collin, *Theodore Roosevelt's Caribbean,* 327. Collin further emphasizes that after 1855, "American naval vessels were always on duty near or at Panama, and at times of insurrection these forces were routinely increased. The American naval presence was not a foreign intrusion but the center of Colombian policy and diplomacy, traditionally serving — at Colombia's behest — as the legal and practical guarantor of Colombia's sovereignty over a consistently ambivalent Panama." See Collin, *Theodore Roosevelt's Caribbean,* 267.

65. Rabe, "Theodore Roosevelt, the Panama Canal, and the Roosevelt Corollary," 287.

66. The correct boundary had long been in question: an 1825 treaty between Russia and Britain established British control over much of the disputed territory, but Russian maps did not reflect the treaty's coordinates. The maps became the de facto guide to the territorial lines, and the British never objected — leaving significant disparities between the "official" and "actual" territorial boundaries.

67. See Tony McCulloch, "Theodore Roosevelt and Canada: Alaska, the 'Big Stick,' and the North Atlantic Triangle, 1901–1909," in *A Companion to Theodore Roosevelt,* ed. Serge Ricard (Malden, MA: Wiley-Blackwell, 2011), 296–300; Christopher Sands, "Canada's Cold Front: Lessons of the Alaska Boundary Dispute for Arctic Boundaries Today," *International Journal* 65 (Winter 2009–10), 210–12.

68. Elting E. Morison, ed., *The Letters of Theodore Roosevelt* (Cambridge, MA: Harvard University Press, 1954), 530. As Senator Henry Cabot Lodge explained: "No nation with an ounce of self-respect" would have willingly ceded what had become valuable territory. "No American president could ever be found," Lodge stated, "who would think for one moment of making such a surrender, and you may rest absolutely assured that it will not be made by Theodore Roosevelt." See John A. Munro, ed., *The Alaska Boundary Dispute* (Toronto: Copp Clark Publishing, 1970), 4.

69. Howard Beale, *Theodore Roosevelt and the Rise of America to World Power* (Baltimore: Johns Hopkins University Press, 1956), 113–14.

70. For a description of the selection of the tribunal's members, see Norman Penlington, *The Alaska Boundary Dispute: A Critical Reappraisal* (Toronto: McGraw-Hill, 1972), 70–81.

71. William Tilchin, *Theodore Roosevelt and the British Empire: A Study in Presidential Statecraft* (London: Macmillan, 1997), 44.

72. Wood, *Roosevelt As We Knew Him,* 115.

73. See "Statement by the Canadian Commissioners" in Munro, *The Alaska Boundary Dispute,* 64; Canadian reactions in Penlington, *The Alaska Boundary Dispute,* 1, 104. The accusation against Alverstone was also leveled by the Canadian members of the tribunal, as Senator Turner recalled: the "debate between Lord Alverstone and his Canadian colleagues at the time was spirited and acrimonious, during which the latter intimated that Lord Alverstone was giving away the Canadian case at the insistence of the English government for diplomatic reasons." See Wood, *Roosevelt As We Knew Him,* 120; Penlington, *The Alaska Boundary Dispute,* 108.

74. Munro, *The Alaska Boundary Dispute,* 86.

75. Frederick Marks III, *Velvet on Iron: The Diplomacy of Theodore Roosevelt* (Lincoln: University of Nebraska Press, 1979), 163n37.

76. Roosevelt, "Fourth Annual Message."

77. Robert Osgood, *Ideals and Self-Interest in America's Foreign Relations* (Chicago: University of Chicago Press, 1953), 144.

78. Negative attitudes and perceptions toward the US are discussed in various sources. Three examples: "By the early 20th century there was already growing concern throughout Latin American societies that the American project contained within it the goal of US domination" (Thomas O'Brien, *Making the Americas: The United States and Latin America from the Age of Revolutions to the Era of Globalization* [Albuquerque: University of New Mexico Press, 2007], 127); by the 1920s, "mistrust and criticism of the behemoth to the north were at an all-time high" (Stuart Brewer, *Borders and Bridges: A History of US-Latin American Relations* [Westport, CT: Praeger Security International, 2006], 99); and 1898–1933 was a time of "virulent hostility" toward the US (Alan McPherson, ed., *Anti-Americanism in Latin America and the Caribbean* [New York: Berghahn Books, 2006], 14).

79. See John Hassett and Braulio Muñoz, eds., *Looking North: Writings from Spanish America on the US, 1800 to the Present* (Tucson: University of Arizona Press, 2012), 46; "Porfirio Díaz," in *The Oxford Dictionary of American Quotations* (New York: Oxford University Press, 2006).

6. What Xi's China Wants

1. Allison, Blackwill, and Wyne, *Lee Kuan Yew,* 2.

2. Ibid., 35.

3. Ibid., 133.

4. Evan Osnos, "Born Red," *New Yorker,* April 6, 2015, http://www.newyorker.com/magazine/2015/04/06/born-red.

5.   Allison, Blackwill, and Wyne, *Lee Kuan Yew,* 17.

6.   Ibid.

7.   Ibid., 2.

8.   Ibid., 3.

9.   Kissinger, *On China,* 2.

10. John K. Fairbank, "China's Foreign Policy in Historical Perspective," *Foreign Affairs* 47, no. 3 (1969); and as summarized in Eric Anderson, *China Restored: The Middle Kingdom Looks to 2020 and Beyond* (Santa Barbara, CA: Praeger, 2010), xiv.

11. John K. Fairbank, "Introduction: Varieties of the Chinese Military Experience," in *Chinese Ways in Warfare,* ed. Frank A. Kiernan Jr. and John K. Fairbank (Cambridge, MA: Harvard University Press, 1974), 6–7; John K. Fairbank, "A Preliminary Framework," in *The Chinese World Order: Traditional China's Foreign Relations,* ed. John K. Fairbank (Cambridge, MA: Harvard University Press, 1968), 2, 4.

12. Kissinger, *On China,* 2–3.

13. Ibid., 9–10, 15. For a student of world order whose doctoral thesis, published as *A World Restored,* analyzed the Congress of Vienna and extolled the virtues of the European concert of power and balance-of-power diplomacy that gave Europe a century of peace, this foreign concept of global order stretched Kissinger's mind. See Henry Kissinger, *World Order* (New York: Penguin Books, 2014).

14. Kissinger, *On China,* 17, 529.

15. The treaty was signed on a gunboat, HMS *Cornwallis,* anchored in the Yangtze River near Nanjing, after the British sailed up the river and seized the Qing government's barges full of tax revenues.

16. China was forced to open ten more ports to foreign trade and cede control of portions of Shanghai and Canton to France and Britain. Jonathan D. Spence, *The Search for Modern China* (New York: W. W. Norton, 1990), 158–62, 179–81; John K. Fairbank, *Trade and Diplomacy on the China Coast: The Opening of Treaty Ports, 1842–1854* (Cambridge, MA: Harvard University Press, 1964), 102–3, 114–33.

17. Kemp Tolley, *Yangtze Patrol: The U.S. Navy in China* (Annapolis, MD: Naval Institute Press, 2013), 30.

18. Stapleton Roy, "The Changing Geopolitics of East Asia," working paper, Paul Tsai China Center, Yale Law School, July 25, 2016, 5, https://www.law.yale.edu/system/files/area/center/china/document/stapletonroy_final.pdf.

19. James L. Hevia, "Looting and Its Discontents: Moral Discourse and the Plunder of Beijing, 1900–1901," in *The Boxers, China, and the World*, ed. Robert Bickers and R. G. Tiedemann (Lanham, MD: Rowman & Littlefield, 2007), 94.

20. Diana Preston, *Besieged in Peking: The Story of the 1900 Boxer Rising* (London: Constable, 1999), 31; "Gift from Peking for the Museum of Art: H. G. Squiers to Present Bronzes and Curios to This City," *New York Times,* Septem-

ber 3, 1901, http://query.nytimes.com/gst/abstract.html/?res=9A07E7DE 153DE433A25750C0A96F9C946097D6CF.

21. Osnos, "Born Red."

22. Ibid.

23. Kerry Brown, *CEO, China: The Rise of Xi Jinping* (London: I. B. Tauris, 2016), 65.

24. Ibid., 72.

25. Ibid., 73–74.

26. Osnos, "Born Red."

27. Chris Buckley, "Xi Jinping Is China's 'Core' Leader: Here's What It Means," *New York Times*, October 30, 2016, http://www.nytimes.com/2016/10/3 1/world/asia/china-xi-jinping-communist-party.html; Jeremy Page and Lingling Wei, "Xi's Power Play Foreshadows Historic Transformation of How China Is Ruled," *Wall Street Journal,* December 26, 2016, http://www .wsj.com/articles/xis-power-play-foreshadows-radical-transformation-of -how-china-is-ruled-1482778917.

28. Allison, Blackwill, and Wyne, *Lee Kuan Yew*, 114.

29. Andrew Nathan, "Who is Xi?" *New York Review of Books,* May 12, 2016, https://www.nybooks.com/articles/2016/05/12/who-is-xi/.

30. Kevin Rudd, "How to Break the 'Mutually Assured Misperception' Between the U.S. and China," *Huffington Post,* April 20, 2015, http://www .huffingtonpost.com/kevin-rudd/us-china-relations-kevin-rudd-report _b_7096784.html.

31. See Liu He's discussion paper from the Belfer Center for Science and International Affairs, "Overcoming the Great Recession: Lessons from China," July 2014, http://belfercenter.org/publication/24397.

32. While India also averaged around 7 percent growth annually since 2008, it was not a "major economy," given that it was not yet one of the world's ten largest economies at the time of the financial crisis.

33. $983 billion was the combined total of economic stimulus and bank bailout funds under Presidents George W. Bush and Barack Obama.

34. International Monetary Fund, "World Economic Outlook Database," October 2016.

35. Robert Lawrence Kuhn, "Xi Jinping's Chinese Dream," *New York Times,* June 4, 2013, http://www.nytimes.com/2013/06/05/opinion/global/xi-jinpings -chinese-dream.html.

36. Osnos, "Born Red."

37. Chun Han Wong, "China's Xi Warns Communist Party Not to Waver on Ideology," *Wall Street Journal,* July 1, 2016, http://www.wsj.com /articles/chinas-xi-exhorts-communist-party-to-hold-fast-to-marxism -1467380336.

38. Allison, Blackwill, and Wyne, *Lee Kuan Yew*, 121.

39. See "Xi: Upcoming CPC Campaign a 'Thorough Cleanup' of Undesirable Practices," *Xinhua*, June 18, 2013, http://news.xinhuanet.com/english /china/2013-06/18/c_132465115.htm; Zhao Yinan, "Xi Repeats Anti-Graft

Message to Top Leaders," *China Daily*, November 20, 2012, http://usa
.chinadaily.com.cn/epaper/2012-11/20/content_15944726.htm; Macabe
Keliher and Hsinchao Wu, "How to Discipline 90 Million People," *Atlantic*,
April 7, 2015, http://www.theatlantic.com/international/archive/2015/04
/xi-jinping-china-corruption-political-culture/389787/.

40. *China Economic Review* online corruption database, http://www.chinaeco
nomicreview.com/cartography/data-transparency-corruption; "Visualizing
China's Anti-Corruption Campaign," ChinaFile.com, January 21, 2016;
"Can Xi Jinping's Anti-Corruption Campaign Succeed?" CSIS China-
Power Project, http://chinapower.csis.org/can-xi-jinpings-anti-corruption
-campaign-succeed/.

41. Josh Chin and Gillian Wong, "China's New Tool for Social Control: A
Credit Rating for Everything," *Wall Street Journal*, November 28, 2016,
http://www.wsj.com/articles/chinas-new-tool-for-social-control-a-credit
-rating-for-everything-1480351590.

42. Joseph Fewsmith, "Xi Jinping's Fast Start," *China Leadership Monitor*,
no. 41, Spring 2013, http://www.hoover.org/sites/default/files/uploads
/documents/CLM41JF.pdf.

43. Xi's China Dream invokes a concept of lost greatness restored that has origins in Chinese literary and intellectual history dating back to at least the
twelfth century. This aspiration toward rejuvenation was the country's driving political currency during the century of humiliation. Qing scholar Feng
Guifen evoked it in 1860 when he asked of Britain and France: "Why are
they so small and yet so strong? Why are we so large and yet so weak? . . .
The intelligence and wisdom of the Chinese are necessarily superior to those
of the various barbarians . . . What we then have to learn from the barbarians
is only one thing, solid ships and effective guns." It was a source of hope,
too, for the "Self-Strengthening Movement," begun the same year, to "revive" China economically and militarily and repel imperial powers. Like a
recurring nightmare, however, the promised dream was crushed before it
could be achieved. See Ryan Mitchell, "Clearing Up Some Misconceptions
About Xi Jinping's 'China Dream,'" *Huffington Post*, August 20, 2015, http://
www.huffingtonpost.com/ryan-mitchell/clearing-up-some-misconce_b
_8012152.html; Jonathan D. Spence, *The Search for Modern China* (New
York: W. W. Norton, 1990), 197.

44. Didi Kristen Tatlow, "Xi Jinping on Exceptionalism with Chinese Characteristics," *New York Times*, October 14, 2014, http://sinosphere.blogs
.nytimes.com/2014/10/14/xi-jinping-on-exceptionalism-with-chinese
-characteristics/.

45. Mark Elliott, "The Historical Vision of the Prosperous Age (*shengshi*)," *China
Heritage Quarterly*, no. 29, March 2012, http://www.chinaheritagequarterly
.org/articles.php?searchterm=029_elliott.inc&issue=029.

46. Jin Kai, "The Chinese Communist Party's Confucian Revival," *Diplomat*, September 30, 2014, http://thediplomat.com/2014/09/the-chinese
-communist-partys-confucian-revival/.

47. Geoff Dyer, *The Contest of the Century* (New York: Vintage Books, 2014), 150–52.

48. Allison, Blackwill, and Wyne, *Lee Kuan Yew*, 14.

49. Dexter Roberts, "China Trumpets Its Service Economy," *Bloomberg Businessweek,* January 28, 2016, http://www.bloomberg.com/news/articles/2016 -01-28/china-trumpets-its-service-economy.

50. Gabriel Wildau, "China: The State-Owned Zombie Economy," *Financial Times*, February 29, 2016, https://www.ft.com/content/253d7eb0-ca6c -11e5-84df-70594b99fc47.

51. Ben Bland, "China's Robot Revolution," *Financial Times*, June 6, 2016, https://www.ft.com/content/1dbd8c60-0cc6-11e6-ad80-67655613c2d6.

52. "Xi Sets Targets for China's Science, Technology Mastery," *Xinhua*, May 30, 2016, http://news.xinhuanet.com/english/2016-05/30/c_135399691 .htm.

53. *Associated Press,* "Air Pollution in China Is Killing 4,000 People Every Day, a New Study Finds," August 13, 2015, https://www.theguardian.com /world/2015/aug/14/air-pollution-in-china-is-killing-4000-people-every -day-a-new-study-finds.

54. World Bank, *Cost of Pollution in China: Economic Estimates of Physical Damages* (Washington, DC: World Bank, 2007), http://documents.worldbank.org /curated/en/782171468027560055/Cost-of-pollution-in-China-economic -estimates-of-physical-damages.

55. John Siciliano, "China Deploys Green 'SWAT Teams' to Meet Climate Goals," *Washington Examiner*, March 19, 2016, http://www.washington examiner.com/china-deploys-green-swat-teams-to-meet-climate-goals /article/2586271.

56. "China Must Quickly Tackle Rising Corporate Debt, Warns IMF Official," *Reuters*, June 10, 2016, http://www.reuters.com/article/us-china-imf-debt -idUSKCN0YX029.

57. Martin Feldstein, "China's Next Agenda," *Project Syndicate*, March 29, 2016, https://www.project-syndicate.org/commentary/china-growth-through -pro-market-reforms-by-martin-feldstein-2016-03.

58. United Nations, Department of Economic and Social Affairs, Population Division, *World Urbanization Prospects: The 2014 Revision, Highlights* (ST /ESA/SER.A/352), https://esa.un.org/unpd/wup/publications/files/wup 2014-highlights.pdf.

59. Martin Feldstein, "China's Latest Five-Year Plan," *Project Syndicate*, November 28, 2015, https://www.project-syndicate.org/commentary/china-new -five-year-plan-by-martin-feldstein-2015-11?barrier=true.

60. Halford Mackinder, *Democratic Ideals and Reality: A Study in the Politics of Reconstruction* (New York: Henry Holt, 1919), 186.

61. Xi Jinping, "New Asian Security Concept for New Progress in Security Cooperation: Remarks at the Fourth Summit of the Conference on Interaction and Confidence Building Measures in Asia," Shanghai, May 21, 2014, http://www.fmprc.gov.cn/mfa_eng/zxxx_662805/t1159951.shtml.

62. Mira Rapp-Hooper, "Before and After: The South China Sea Transformed," Center for Strategic and International Studies, February 18, 2015, https://amti.csis.org/before-and-after-the-south-china-sea-transformed/.

63. Bill Hayton, *The South China Sea* (New Haven, CT: Yale University Press, 2014), 71.

64. Toshi Yoshihara, "The 1974 Paracels Sea Battle: A Campaign Appraisal," *Naval War College Review* 69, no. 2 (Spring 2016), 41.

65. US Department of Defense, "Asia-Pacific Maritime Security Strategy" (August 2015), 16, http://www.defense.gov/Portals/1/Documents/pubs/NDAA%20A-P_Maritime_SecuritY_Strategy-08142015-1300-FINAL FORMAT.PDF.

66. Derek Watkins, "What China Has Been Building in the South China Sea," *New York Times*, February 29, 2016, http://www.nytimes.com/interactive/2015/07/30/world/asia/what-china-has-been-building-in-the-south-china-sea-2016.html.

67. US Department of Defense, "Asia-Pacific Maritime Security Strategy," 17.

68. US trade accounts for $1.2 trillion of the total $5.3 trillion. Bonnie Glaser, "Armed Clash in the South China Sea," Council on Foreign Relations, April 2012, 4, http://www.cfr.org/asia-and-pacific/armed-clash-south-china-sea/p27883.

69. Andrei Kokoshin, "2015 Military Reform in the People's Republic of China: Defense, Foreign and Domestic Policy Issues," Belfer Center for Science and International Affairs, October 2016, vi, http://belfercenter.org/publication/27040.

70. Nomaan Merchant, "Over 1,000 Protest in Front of Chinese Defense Ministry," *Associated Press,* October 11, 2016, http://www.military.com/daily-news/2016/10/11/1-000-protest-front-chinese-defense-ministry.html.

71. Regina Abrami, William Kirby, and F. Warren McFarlan, *Can China Lead?* (Boston: Harvard Business Review Press, 2014), 179.

72. "President Xi Stresses Development of PLA Army," *Xinhua*, July 27, 2016, http://news.xinhuanet.com/english/2016-07/27/c_135544941.htm.

73. Jeremy Page, "For Xi, a 'China Dream' of Military Power," *Wall Street Journal*, March 13, 2013, http://www.wsj.com/articles/SB10001424127887324128504578348774040546346.

74. Iraq's command-and-control systems became so compromised that Saddam Hussein was ultimately forced to use couriers riding motorbikes to deliver his orders to the frontlines. Fred Kaplan, *Dark Territory: The Secret History of Cyber War* (New York: Simon & Schuster, 2016), 22–23.

75. Components of Pillsbury's research for the Defense Department's Office of Net Assessment were published in Michael Pillsbury, *China Debates the Future Security Environment* (Washington, DC: National Defense University Press, 2000). See also *Chinese Views of Future Warfare,* ed. Michael Pillsbury (Washington, DC: National Defense University Press, 1997).

76. As Kokoshin notes: "Commanders and political commissars of the 'major

military regions,' who controlled several provinces at the same time, were an important element safeguarding the central political power of Beijing. These commanders and political commissars were under control of the Main Political Department of the PLA, which reports directly to the Chairman of the Central Military Commission of the PRC. In the event of domestic crisis, commanders and political commissars of the 'major military regions' had a wide variety of opportunities to establish emergency control over the provinces located within these regions . . . One of the core issues faced by the Party and top state officials, when they considered the depth of the military reform . . . was the correlation between the armed forces' capabilities to provide for a more efficient use of military power to pursue foreign policy interests, and the preservation of the role of the PLA in resolving potential internal crises." See Kokoshin, "2015 Military Reform in the People's Republic of China," 22–23, 4.

77. Yang Yong, quoted in Dyer, *The Contest of the Century*, 25.

78. The "Army" in the name People's Liberation Army is a generic term for military forces that include the air force and navy as well as three ground forces (which the US refers to as the "army").

79. M. Taylor Fravel, "China's Changing Approach to Military Strategy: The Science of Military Strategy from 2001 to 2013," in Joe McReynolds, *China's Evolving Military Strategy* (Washington, DC: Jamestown Foundation, 2016), 59–62; Toshi Yoshihara and James Holmes, *Red Star over the Pacific: China's Rise and the Challenge to U.S. Maritime Strategy* (Annapolis, MD: Naval Institute Press, 2010), 60.

80. Holmes and Yoshihara, *Red Star over the Pacific,* 18.

81. In 2015, the Department of Defense renamed Air-Sea Battle the Joint Concept for Access and Maneuver in the Global Commons (JAM-GC), although it is still widely referred to as Air-Sea Battle. Sam Lagrone, "Pentagon Drops Air Sea Battle Name, Concept Lives On," *USNI News*, January 20, 2015, https://news.usni.org/2015/01/20/pentagon-drops-air-sea-battle -name-concept-lives.

82. Eric Heginbotham et al., *The U.S.-China Military Scorecard: Forces, Geography, and the Evolving Balance of Power, 1996–2017* (Santa Monica, CA: RAND Corporation, 2015), xxxi, xxix.

7. Clash of Civilizations

1. Samuel Kim, *China, the United Nations, and World Order* (Princeton, NJ: Princeton University Press, 1979), 38.

2. Helen H. Robbins, *Our First Ambassador to China: The Life and Correspondence of George, Earl of Macartney, and His Experiences in China, as Told by Himself* (New York: E. P. Dutton, 1908), 175.

3. Alain Peyrefitte, *The Immobile Empire,* trans. Jon Rothschild (New York: Knopf, 1992), 10.

4. Kissinger, *On China,* 37.

5. J. R. Cranmer-Byng, ed., *An Embassy to China; being the journal kept by Lord Macartney during his embassy to the Emperor Ch'ien-lung, 1793–1794* (Hamden: Archon Books, 1963), 117.

6. Peyrefitte, *The Immobile Empire,* 170.

7. Ibid., 220.

8. Ibid., 206.

9. Ibid., 227, 306.

10. Qianlong's First Edict to King George III (September 1793), in *The Search for Modern China: A Documentary Collection,* ed. Pei-kai Cheng, Michael Lestz, and Jonathan Spence (New York: Norton, 1999), 104–6.

11. Samuel Huntington, "The Clash of Civilizations?," *Foreign Affairs* 72, no. 3 (Summer 1993), 22.

12. Ibid., 24.

13. Francis Fukuyama, "The End of History?," *The National Interest,* no. 16 (Summer 1989), 3–18.

14. Huntington, "The Clash of Civilizations?," 25.

15. Ibid., 41.

16. Samuel Huntington, *The Clash of Civilizations and the Remaking of World Order* (New York: Simon & Schuster Paperbacks, 2003), 225.

17. Ibid., 169.

18. Ibid., 234.

19. Crane Brinton, *The Anatomy of a Revolution* (New York: Vintage Books, 1952), 271.

20. Huntington, *The Clash of Civilizations,* 223.

21. Ibid., 225.

22. Jeffrey Goldberg, "The Obama Doctrine," *Atlantic,* April 2016, http://www.theatlantic.com/magazine/archive/2016/04/the-obama-doctrine/471525/.

23. Allison, Blackwill, and Wyne, *Lee Kuan Yew,* 42.

24. Harry Gelber, *Nations Out of Empires: European Nationalism and the Transformation of Asia* (New York: Palgrave, 2001), 15.

25. Kevin Rudd, "The Future of U.S.-China Relations Under Xi Jinping: Toward a New Framework of Constructive Realism for a Common Purpose," Belfer Center for Science and International Affairs, April 2015, 12, http://belfercenter.org/files/SummaryReportUSChina21.pdf.

26. William Pitt, Earl of Chatham, Speech in House of Lords, January 20, 1775, http://quod.lib.umich.edu/cgi/t/text/text-idx?c=evans;idno=N11389.0001.001.

27. Richard Hofstadter, *Anti-intellectualism in American Life* (New York: Alfred A. Knopf, 1963), 43.

28. Kissinger, *On China,* 15.

29. Ibid.

30. Thomas Paine, *Common Sense: Addressed to the Inhabitants of America* (Boston: J. P. Mendum, 1856), 19.

31. Neustadt, *Presidential Power and the Modern Presidents,* 29.

32. *Myers v. United States,* 272 US 52 (1926).

33. Lee Kuan Yew, "Speech at the Abraham Lincoln Medal Award Ceremony," Washington, DC, October 18, 2011, https://www.mfa.gov.sg/content/mfa /overseasmission/washington/newsroom/press_statements/2011/201110 /press_201110_01.html.

34. Thomas Jefferson letter to William Hunter, March 11, 1790.

35. Eric X. Li, "A Tale of Two Political Systems," TED Talk, June 2013, https:// www.ted.com/talks/eric_x_li_a_tale_of_two_political_systems/transcript ?language=en.

36. Kissinger, *World Order,* 236.

37. Huntington, *The Clash of Civilizations,* 184.

38. Kissinger, *On China,* 17.

39. Kissinger, *World Order,* 230.

40. George Washington, "Address to the members of the Volunteer Association and other Inhabitants of the Kingdom of Ireland who have lately arrived in the City of New York," December 2, 1783, http://founding.com /founders-library/american-political-figures/george-washington/address -to-the-members-of-the-volunteer-association-and-other-inhabitants/.

41. Yoree Koh, "Study: Immigrants Founded 51% of U.S. Billion-Dollar Startups," *Wall Street Journal,* March 17, 2016, http://blogs.wsj.com/digits/2016 /03/17/study-immigrants-founded-51-of-u-s-billion-dollar-startups/.

42. Allison, Blackwill, and Wyne, *Lee Kuan Yew,* 22–23. Of course, this is not entirely accurate: the American continent may have been undeveloped when Europeans arrived, but it was not "empty."

43. "Notes from the Chairman: A Conversation with Martin Dempsey," *Foreign Affairs,* September/October 2016, https://www.foreignaffairs.com /interviews/2016-08-01/notes-chairman.

44. Kissinger, *On China,* 30.

45. Sun Tzu, *The Art of War,* trans. Samuel B. Griffith (London: Oxford University Press, 1971), 92.

46. François Jullien, *The Propensity of Things: Toward a History of Efficacy in China,* trans. Janet Lloyd (New York: Zone Books, 1999), 26.

47. Sun Tzu, *The Art of War,* 95.

48. Kissinger, *On China,* 23.

49. David Lai, "Learning from the Stones: A *Go* Approach to Mastering China's Strategic, *Shi,"* US Army War College Strategic Studies Institute, May 2004, 5, 28, http://www.strategicstudiesinstitute.army.mil/pubs/display .cfm?pubID=378; Kissinger, *On China,* 23–24.

50. Sun Tzu, *The Art of War,* 14–16.

51. Clinton, "America's Pacific Century."

52. Rudd, "The Future of U.S.-China Relations Under Xi Jinping," 14.

53. M. Taylor Fravel, *Strong Borders, Secure Nation: Conflict and Cooperation in China's Territorial Disputes* (Princeton, NJ: Princeton University Press, 2008).

8. From Here to War

1. To support this claim, some cite Thomas Christensen's *China Challenge*. Christensen effectively explains how changes in global economics and politics are reducing the likelihood of great power war between the United States and China. But Christensen acknowledges that such a conflict is still possible. Moreover, he recognizes that China's increasing military advantages will make successfully managing challenges in the bilateral relationship (like territorial disputes) much more difficult. See Thomas Christensen, *The China Challenge: Shaping the Choices of a Rising Power* (New York: W. W. Norton, 2015), particularly chapters 2 ("This Time Should Be Different: China's Rise in a Globalized World") and 4 ("Why China Still Poses Strategic Challenges") for more extensive discussion of these topics.

2. David Gompert, Astrid Cevallos, and Cristina Garafola, *War with China: Thinking Through the Unthinkable* (Santa Monica, CA: RAND Corporation, 2016), 87, 48–50.

3. Benjamin Valentino, *Final Solutions: Mass Killing and Genocide in the Twentieth Century* (Ithaca, NY: Cornell University Press, 2005), 88.

4. P. K. Rose, "Two Strategic Intelligence Mistakes in Korea, 1950: Perceptions and Reality," *Studies in Intelligence,* Fall–Winter 2001, 57–65.

5. T. R. Fehrenbach, *This Kind of War: A Study in Unpreparedness* (New York: Macmillan, 1963), 184–96.

6. MacArthur's notion, as Fehrenbach describes, was to dispatch naval forces close enough to the Chinese mainland to provoke a violent Chinese response, which could then be used as a pretext for escalation to nuclear weapons.

7. Fehrenbach, *This Kind of War,* 192.

8. Michael Gerson, "The Sino-Soviet Border Conflict: Deterrence, Escalation, and the Threat of Nuclear War in 1969," Center for Naval Analyses, November 2010, 17, https://www.cna.org/CNA_files/PDF/D0022974.A2 .pdf.

9. Ibid., 16–17, 44.

10. Nicholas Khoo, *Collateral Damage: Sino-Soviet Rivalry and the Termination of the Sino-Vietnamese Alliance* (New York: Columbia University Press, 2011), 144.

11. Kissinger, *On China,* 219.

12. Kissinger, *Diplomacy,* 723.

13. Gerson, "The Sino-Soviet Border Conflict," iii.

14. Fravel, *Strong Borders, Secure Nation,* 201.

15. Ibid.

16. Gerson, "The Sino-Soviet Border Conflict," 24.

17. As Chinese scholars correctly point out, Lee's move toward separation also became more accommodating.

18. See Wallace Thies and Patrick Bratton, "When Governments Collide in the Taiwan Strait," *Journal of Strategic Studies* 27, no. 4 (December 2004), 556–

84; Robert Ross, "The 1995–96 Taiwan Strait Confrontation," *International Security* 25, no. 2 (Fall 2000), 87–123.

19. See Jane Perlez, "American and Chinese Navy Ships Nearly Collided in South China Sea," *New York Times,* December 14, 2013, http://www .nytimes.com/2013/12/15/world/asia/chinese-and-american-ships-nearly -collide-in-south-china-sea.html.

20. Henry Kissinger, *A World Restored: Metternich, Castlereagh, and the Problems of Peace, 1812–22* (Boston: Houghton Mifflin, 1957), 331.

21. As Henry Kissinger said in a 2014 interview on PRI's *The World:* "The United States has been engaged in five wars since World War II. In only one of them did it reach its stated objective. In another one, it ended in a stalemate, and from three others, we withdrew unilaterally. I'm talking about the first Iraq War, in which we achieved our objective, the Korean War which ended — that was a kind of a stalemate, and Vietnam, the second Iraq War and Afghanistan — from which we withdrew unilaterally." See "Henry Kissinger Would Not Have Supported the Iraq War If He'd Known What He Knows Now," PRI, September 11, 2014, http://www.pri.org /stories/2014-09-11/henry-kissinger-would-not-have-supported-iraq-war -if-hed-known-what-he-knows-now.

22. "Remarks by Secretary of Defense Robert Gates at the U.S. Military Academy at West Point," February 25, 2011, http://archive.defense.gov /Speeches/Speech.aspx?SpeechID=1539.

23. Carl von Clausewitz, *On War,* ed. Peter Paret, trans. Michael Eliot Howard (Princeton, NJ: Princeton University Press, 1989), 101.

24. Robert McNamara, *In Retrospect: The Tragedy and Lessons of Vietnam*, 2nd ed. (New York: Vintage, 1996), 128–43.

25. See David Sanger, *Confront and Conceal: Obama's Secret Wars and Surprising Use of American Power* (New York: Crown Publishers, 2012).

26. "Kaspersky Lab Discovers Vulnerable Industrial Control Systems Likely Belonging to Large Organizations," Kaspersky Lab, press release, July 11, 2016, http://usa.kaspersky.com/about-us/press-center/press-releases/2016 /Kaspersky-Lab-Discovers-Vulnerable-Industrial-Control-Systems-Likely -Belonging-to-Large-Organizations.

27. Herman Kahn, *On Escalation: Metaphors and Scenarios* (New York: Penguin, 1965), 39.

28. Audrey Wang, "The Road to Food Security," *Taiwan Today,* July 1, 2011, http://taiwantoday.tw/ct.asp?xItem=167684&CtNode=124; "Taiwan Lacks Food Security Strategy," *Taipei Times,* July 26, 2010, http://www.taipeitimes .com/News/editorials/archives/2010/07/26/2003478832.

29. See Ross, "The 1995–96 Taiwan Strait Confrontation," 87–123.

30. This scenario is based on a war game conducted by RAND for *Foreign Policy* magazine. See Dan De Luce and Keith Johnson, "How FP Stumbled Into a War with China — and Lost," *Foreign Policy,* January 15, 2016, http:// foreignpolicy.com/2016/01/15/how-fp-stumbled-into-a-war-with-china -and-lost/.

31. President Obama made this explicit in 2014, stating, "Our treaty commit-
     ment to Japan's security is absolute, and Article 5 covers all territories under
     Japan's administration, including the Senkaku Islands." President Trump re-
     affirmed this commitment shortly after taking office. See "Joint Press Con-
     ference with President Obama and Prime Minister Abe of Japan," April 24,
     2014, https://obamawhitehouse.archives.gov/the-press-office/2014/04/24
     /joint-press-conference-president-obama-and-prime-minister-abe-japan;
     "Joint Statement from President Donald J. Trump and Prime Minister
     Shinzo Abe," February 10, 2017, https://www.whitehouse.gov/the-press
     -office/2017/02/10/joint-statement-president-donald-j-trump-and-prime
     -minister-shinzo-abe.

32. Jeremy Page and Jay Solomon, "China Warns North Korean Nuclear Threat
     Is Rising," *Wall Street Journal,* April 22, 2015, http://www.wsj.com/arti
     cles/china-warns-north-korean-nuclear-threat-is-rising-1429745706; Joel
     Wit and Sun Young Ahn, "North Korea's Nuclear Futures: Technology
     and Strategy," U.S.-Korea Institute at SAIS, 2015, http://38north.org
     /wp-content/uploads/2015/02/NKNF-NK-Nuclear-Futures-Wit-0215
     .pdf.

33. Eli Lake, "Preparing for North Korea's Inevitable Collapse," *Bloomberg,* Sep-
     tember 20, 2016, https://www.bloomberg.com/view/articles/2016-09-20
     /preparing-for-north-korea-s-inevitable-collapse.

34. "Trade in Goods with China," US Census, http://www.census.gov/foreign
     -trade/balance/c5700.html.

35. Michael Lewis, *Flash Boys: A Wall Street Revolt* (New York: W. W. Norton,
     2014), 56–88.

36. Andrew Ross Sorkin, *Too Big to Fail: The Inside Story of How Wall Street and
     Washington Fought to Save the Financial System—and Themselves,* updated ed.
     (New York: Penguin Books, 2011), 59.

37. Andrew Ross Sorkin et al., "As Credit Crisis Spiraled, Alarm Led to Action,"
     New York Times, October 1, 2008, http://www.nytimes.com/2008/10/02
     /business/02crisis.html.

38. David Hambling, "How Active Camouflage Will Make Small Drones In-
     visible," *Popular Mechanics,* November 14, 2015, http://www.popular
     mechanics.com/flight/drones/a18190/active-camouflage-make-small-drones
     -invisible/.

9. Twelve Clues for Peace

1.   "In the fourteenth century, on the eve of the Black Death, the population of
     Portugal probably stood at about 1.5 million, at a reasonable European aver-
     age of some seventeen inhabitants per square kilometer. In 1348, however,
     this figure fell between a third and a half, at which level it was maintained,
     with slight modifications, until about 1460, when a recovery began." See
     Armindo de Sousa, "Portugal," in *The New Cambridge Medieval History,* vol.
     7: *c. 1415–c. 1500,* ed. Christopher Allmand (Cambridge: Cambridge Uni-

versity Press, 1998), 627. Incredibly, an even greater number of Portuguese may have succumbed to the plague: "In Portugal estimates of mortality as high as two-thirds, even nine-tenths, are recorded." See Peter Linehan, "Castile, Navarre and Portugal," in *The New Cambridge Medieval History,* vol. 6: *c. 1300–c. 1415,* ed. Michael Jones (Cambridge: Cambridge University Press, 2000), 637.

2.   A. R. Disney, *A History of Portugal and the Portuguese Empire from Beginnings to 1807,* vol. 2: *The Portuguese Empire* (New York: Cambridge University Press, 2009), 40.

3.   H. V. Livermore, "Portuguese Expansion," in *The New Cambridge Modern History,* 2nd ed., vol. 1: *The Renaissance, 1493–1520,* ed. G. R. Potter (Cambridge: Cambridge University Press, 1957), 420.

4.   Joseph Pérez, "Avance portugués y expansion castellana en torno a 1492," in *Las Relaciones entre Portugal y Castilla en la Época de los Descubrimientos y la Expansión Colonial,* ed. Ana María Carabias Torres (Salamanca, Spain: Ediciones Universidad de Salamanca, 1994), 107.

5.   Alan Smith, *Creating a World Economy: Merchant Capitalism, Colonialism, and World Trade, 1400–1825* (Boulder, CO: Westview Press, 1991), 75.

6.   Christopher Bell, *Portugal and the Quest for the Indies* (London: Constable, 1974), 180.

7.   It is worth noting that Ferdinand and Isabella, on Columbus's first attempt, rejected his request for sponsorship before eventually reconsidering and agreeing to fund his voyage.

8.   Portugal could not risk a recurrence of the costly war it had fought with Castile two decades earlier. The War of Castilian Succession was fought between 1475 and 1479 over the question of whether the Castile-Aragon union would be allowed to stand. If this Castilian civil war reaffirmed Isabella, who was married to Aragonian king Ferdinand, as the next Castilian queen, the union would remain. If supporters of Juana (who was married to Portuguese king Alfonso V) won, Castile would have unified with Portugal instead. Portugal, of course, fought on the side of bringing Juana to the throne rather than Isabella. Therefore, rather than understanding this as a Thucydides's Trap scenario in which fear of rising Castilian power unifying with Aragon prompts Portuguese aggression, we understand this war as a Portuguese attempt to acquire Castile as its own inheritance. For further detail, see note 2 of appendix 1.

9.   Disney, *A History of Portugal and the Portuguese Empire,* 48.

10.   During his two terms, Obama authorized military action in Afghanistan, Iraq, Syria, Libya, Pakistan, Somalia, and Yemen. Meanwhile, US Special Operations forces have provided operational support to hunt down terrorists in at least eight other countries. See Mark Landler, "For Obama, an Unexpected Legacy of Two Full Terms at War," *New York Times,* May 14, 2016, http://www.nytimes.com/2016/05/15/us/politics/obama-as-wartime -president-has-wrestled-with-protecting-nation-and-troops.html.

11.   In the Nicaragua case, when the court found in favor of Nicaragua and or-

dered the United States to pay reparations, the US refused, and vetoed six UN Security Council resolutions ordering it to comply with the court's ruling. US ambassador to the UN Jeane Kirkpatrick aptly summed up Washington's view of the matter when she dismissed the court as a "semi-legal, semi-juridical, semi-political body, which nations sometimes accept and sometimes don't." See Graham Allison, "Of Course China, Like All Great Powers, Will Ignore an International Legal Verdict," *Diplomat,* July 11, 2016, http://thediplomat.com/2016/07/of-course-china-like-all-great-powers-will-ignore-an-international-legal-verdict/.

12. Jacob Heilbrunn, "The Interview: Henry Kissinger," *National Interest,* August 19, 2015, http://nationalinterest.org/feature/the-interview-henry-kissinger-13615.

13. Philip Zelikow and Condoleezza Rice, *Germany Unified and Europe Transformed: A Study in Statecraft* (Cambridge, MA: Harvard University Press, 1995), 207. According to recently declassified Cabinet Office files, Thatcher alarmed the Bush administration by suggesting in 1990 that a British alliance with the USSR might be required as "an essential balance to German power" in Europe. See Henry Mance, "Thatcher Saw Soviets as Allies Against Germany," *Financial Times,* December 29, 2016, https://www.ft.com/content/dd74c884-c6b1-11e6-9043-7e34c07b46ef.

14. Jussi M. Hanhimaki, "Europe's Cold War," in *The Oxford Handbook of Postwar European History,* ed. Dan Stone (Oxford: Oxford University Press, 2012), 297.

15. John Lanchester, "The Failure of the Euro," *New Yorker,* October 24, 2016, www.newyorker.com/magazine/2016/10/24/the-failure-of-the-euro.

16. Andrew Moravcsik, *The Choice for Europe: Social Purpose and State Power from Messina to Maastricht* (Ithaca, NY: Cornell University Press, 1998), 407.

17. In a 1989 speech in Mainz, Germany, Bush proclaimed that "the passion for freedom cannot be denied forever. The world has waited long enough. The time is right. Let Europe be whole and free." See George H. W. Bush, "A Europe Whole and Free," Remarks to the Citizens in Mainz, Germany, May 31, 1989, http://usa.usembassy.de/etexts/ga6-890531.htm.

18. International Monetary Fund, "World Economic Outlook Database."

19. Helga Haftendorn, *Coming of Age: German Foreign Policy Since 1945* (Lanham, MD: Rowman & Littlefield, 2006), 319.

20. Similar questions can be asked about the second great post–World War II anomaly, modern Japan.

21. Bradford Perkins, *The Great Rapprochement: England and the United States, 1895–1914* (New York: Atheneum, 1968), 9.

22. See "GDP Levels in 12 West European Countries, 1869–1918," "GDP Levels in Western Offshoots, 1500–1899," and "GDP Levels in Western Offshoots, 1900–1955," in Maddison, *The World Economy,* 427, 462–63.

23. Kennedy, *The Rise and Fall of the Great Powers,* 200–202, 242–44.

24. The British were dissuaded in part by pro-American public opinion. Ernest

R. May and Zhou Hong, "A Power Transition and Its Effects," in *Power and Restraint: A Shared Vision for the U.S.-China Relationship,* ed. Richard Rosecrance and Gu Guoliang (New York: Public Affairs, 2009), 13.

25. Schoultz, *Beneath the United States,* 115.

26. May and Hong, "A Power Transition and Its Effects," 12.

27. In fact, Britain sought a treaty to arbitrate all future disagreements, which the US administration signed, but the Senate rejected. Perkins, *Great Rapprochement,* 12–19; J.A.S. Grenville, *Lord Salisbury and Foreign Policy: The Close of the Nineteenth Century* (London: Athlone Press, 1964), 54–73; May, *Imperial Democracy,* 52–53, 56–59, 60–65.

28. Bourne, *Britain and the Balance of Power in North America,* 339.

29. Ibid., 351.

30. May and Hong, "A Power Transition and Its Effects," 12–13.

31. Selborne recounted his slight shock at Fisher's vehemence: "'He said . . . he would not spend one man or one pound in the defense of Canada. And he meant it.'" Under Fisher's redistribution of the fleet, the Royal Navy's presence in the Americas was reduced dramatically. Friedberg, *The Weary Titan,* 161–98. Within two years, Canada's land defense had been assigned to the Canadians themselves, and the last British troops withdrawn. Bourne, *Britain and the Balance of Power in North America,* 359–89.

32. Selbourne made this comment in 1901. Bourne, *Britain and the Balance of Power in North America,* 351.

33. Selborne made it clear to his cabinet colleagues that "the standard which I believe now to be the true one is not one which could be publically stated." Friedberg, *The Weary Titan,* 169–80.

34. Ibid., 161–65, 169–74, 184–90.

35. Anne Orde, *The Eclipse of Great Britain: The United States and British Imperial Decline, 1895–1956* (New York: Saint Martin's Press, 1996), 22.

36. May and Hong, "A Power Transition and Its Effects," 13. Some Americans also believed in a natural Anglo-American bond, although they were fewer in number than their British counterparts.

37. MacMillan, *The War That Ended Peace,* 38; May and Hong, "A Power Transition and Its Effects," 13.

38. May and Hong, "A Power Transition and Its Effects," 11–17.

39. Ibid., 14–17.

40. George Will, "America's Lost Ally," *Washington Post,* August 17, 2011, https://www.washingtonpost.com/opinions/americas-lost-ally/2011/08/16/gIQAYxy8LJ_story.html?utm_term=.3188d2889da3.

41. Paul Samuelson, *Economics: An Introductory Analysis,* 6th ed. (New York: McGraw-Hill, 1964), 807.

42. Churchill, *The Second World War,* vol. 3: *The Grand Alliance* (Boston: Houghton Mifflin, 1950), 331.

43. James Forrestal letter to Homer Ferguson, May 14, 1945. See Walter Millis, ed., *The Forrestal Diaries* (New York: Viking Press, 1951), 57.

44. The full text of the Long Telegram is available from the National Security Ar-
     chive at George Washington University, http://nsarchive.gwu.edu/coldwar
     /documents/episode-1/kennan.htm.

45. Bernard Brodie et al., *The Absolute Weapon: Atomic Power and World Order,* ed.
     Bernard Brodie (New York: Harcourt, Brace, 1946).

46. Mark Harrison, "The Soviet Union After 1945: Economic Recovery and
     Political Repression," *Past the Present* 210, suppl. 6 (2011), 103–20.

47. See "GDP Levels in Former Eastern Europe and USSR, 1820–1949" and
     "GDP Levels in Former Eastern Europe and USSR, 1950–2002," in Maddi-
     son, *The World Economy,* 476–77.

48. Robert Gates, *From the Shadows: The Ultimate Insider's Story of Five Presi-
     dents and How They Won the Cold War* (New York: Simon & Schuster, 1996),
     29.

49. High-ranking US officials considered preventive war on at least two occa-
     sions in the first decade of the Cold War. As the argument went, preventive
     war was essential to coerce the Soviets to accept international control of nu-
     clear weapons, and in turn to secure a lasting peace before the Soviets devel-
     oped a robust nuclear capability. In the early months of the Korean War in
     1950, Secretary of the Navy Francis Matthews asserted, "To have peace we
     should be willing, and declare our intention, to pay any price, even the price
     of instituting a war, to compel co-operation for peace." In 1954, shortly af-
     ter stepping down as chairman of the Atomic Energy Commission, Gordon
     Dean wrote, "Can we as a nation and can the now free world permit the So-
     viets to reach this position of power? For reach it she will; and all the fervent
     hopes of free people everywhere will not deny her this terrible capability
     unless those hopes are reduced to action of some sort which forces open the
     Iron Curtain and brings a halt to her enormous weapons program . . . This,
     very bluntly, is the problem of 1953–54." Ultimately, neither Truman nor
     Eisenhower accepted these arguments, with Truman famously quipping,
     "You don't 'prevent' anything by war except peace."

50. As Bernard Brodie wrote, "Thus far the chief purpose of our military estab-
     lishment has been to win wars. From now on its chief purpose must be to
     avert them. It can have almost no other useful purpose." See Brodie et al.,
     The Absolute Weapon, 76.

51. The text of George Marshall's speech at Harvard is available from the OECD,
     http://www.oecd.org/general/themarshallplanspeechatharvarduniversity
     5june1947.htm; the text of NSC-68, "United States Objectives and Pro-
     grams for National Security," is available from the Federation of Ameri-
     can Scientists, http://fas.org/irp/offdocs/nsc-hst/nsc-68.htm. For a more
     detailed overview of US national security strategy and performance in the
     postwar period, see Graham Allison, "National Security Strategy for the
     1990s," in *America's Global Interests: A New Agenda,* ed. Edward Hamilton
     (New York: W. W. Norton, 1989), 199–211.

52. Clausewitz, *On War,* 87.

53. Graham Allison, "Second Look: Lesson of the Cuban Missile Crisis," *Boston Globe,* October 26, 1987, http://belfercenter.org/publication/1334/second _look.html.

54. John Lewis Gaddis, *The Long Peace: Inquiries into the History of the Cold War* (New York: Oxford University Press, 1987), 237–41.

55. For authoritative histories on the shaping of American strategy and interventionism during the Cold War, see John Lewis Gaddis, *Strategies of Containment: A Critical Appraisal of Postwar American National Security Policy* (New York: Oxford University Press, 1982), and Gaddis's *The Cold War: A New History* (New York: Penguin), 2005. For a definitive account of Soviet and American interventions in the Third World during this era, see Odd Arne Westad, *The Global Cold War: Third World Interventions and the Making of Our Times* (Cambridge: Cambridge University Press, 2005). For an illuminating narrative history of American covert operations in the Cold War that were aimed at foreign regime change, see Stephen Kinzer, *Overthrow: America's Century of Regime Change from Hawaii to Iraq* (New York: Times Books, 2006), 111–216.

56. Carmen Reinhart and Kenneth Rogoff, *This Time Is Different: Eight Centuries of Financial Folly* (Princeton, NJ: Princeton University Press, 2009).

57. See Howard Weinroth, "Norman Angell and *The Great Illusion:* An Episode in Pre-1914 Pacifism," *Historical Journal* 17, no. 3 (September 1974), 551–74.

58. Harvard Nuclear Study Group, *Living with Nuclear Weapons* (Cambridge, MA: Harvard University Press, 1983), 43–44.

59. The latter half of the twentieth century saw a succession of cases in which Thucydides would have noted his dynamic at work as states faced an impending change not in the overall balance of power, but in a decisive dimension of military power. In seven cases, when a competitor stood on the threshold of acquiring nuclear weapons, and in time a nuclear arsenal that would pose a genuine existential threat, the nuclear-armed competitor seriously considered preemptive attack. In late 1949, after the Soviet Union tested its first atomic device, the US Air Force chief of staff urged President Truman to authorize a preemptive attack to disarm Moscow. As China approached the nuclear tipping point, the Soviet Union planned to preempt Beijing and even consulted the US about the option. As India, China; as Pakistan, India; as North Korea, the US (with recent secretary of defense Ashton Carter a notable advocate in that case). Only one state executed such plans: Israel. With an "affirmative counter-proliferation policy," it destroyed an Iraqi nuclear reactor in 1981, a Syrian nuclear reactor in 2007, and continues to pose a credible threat to attack Iran's nuclear program today. In this story line, we hear echoes of World War I. Russia's rush to complete major new railroad lines that would allow it to move its huge army rapidly to the German border alarmed the German general staff. When construction was finished, if war occurred, Germany would be forced to fight simultaneously on both its east and west. Today cyber strategists are beginning to imagine

breakthroughs that could, for example, allow one state to shut down the nuclear launch systems of an adversary—creating analogous incentives for preemptive attack.

60. Ronald Reagan, "Statement on the 40th Anniversary of the Bombing of Hiroshima," August 6, 1985, UCSB American Presidency Project, http://www.presidency.ucsb.edu/ws/?pid=3897.

61. "Only Russia and China have the capability to conduct a large-scale ballistic missile attack on the territory of the United States, but this is very unlikely and not the focus of U.S. BMD." See US Department of Defense, "Ballistic Missile Defense Review Report," February 2010, 4, http://www.defense.gov/Portals/1/features/defenseReviews/BMDR/BMDR_as_of_26JAN10_0630_for_web.pdf.

62. Winston Churchill, "Never Despair," House of Commons, March 1, 1955, http://www.winstonchurchill.org/resources/speeches/1946-1963-elder-statesman/never-despair.

63. Philip Taubman, "Gromyko Says Mao Wanted Soviet A-Bomb Used on G.I.'s," *New York Times,* February 22, 1988, http://www.nytimes.com/1988/02/22/world/gromyko-says-mao-wanted-soviet-a-bomb-used-on-gi-s.html?pagewanted=all.

64. Susan Heavey, "Romney: Obama Going in 'Wrong Direction' on China," *Reuters,* February 16, 2012, http://www.reuters.com/article/usa-campaign-china-idUSL2E8DG26A20120216.

65. Michael Warren, "Romney on China's Currency Manipulation," *Weekly Standard,* October 12, 2011, http://www.weeklystandard.com/romney-on-chinas-currency-manipulation/article/595779.

66. Nick Gass, "Trump: 'We Can't Continue to Allow China to Rape Our Country,'" *Politico,* May 2, 2016, http://www.politico.com/blogs/2016-gop-primary-live-updates-and-results/2016/05/trump-china-rape-america-222689.

67. Among those who have used this phrase to characterize US-China relations are Ian Bremmer, "China vs. America: Fight of the Century," *Prospect,* April 2010, http://www.prospectmagazine.co.uk/magazine/china-vs-america-fight-of-the-century; David Rapkin and William Thompson, "Will Economic Interdependence Encourage China's and India's Peaceful Ascent?" in *Strategic Asia 2006–07: Trade, Interdependence, and Security,* ed. Ashley J. Tellis and Michael Wills (Seattle: National Bureau of Asian Research, 2006), 359; and James Dobbins, David C. Gompert, David A. Shlapak, and Andrew Scobell, *Conflict with China: Prospects, Consequences, and Strategies for Deterrence* (Santa Monica, CA: RAND Corporation, 2011), 8–9, http://www.rand.org/pubs/occasional_papers/OP344.html.

10. Where Do We Go from Here?

1. While Nixon used the popular cultural expression, in fact he meant Frankenstein's monster. See William Safire, "The Biggest Vote," *New York Times,*

May 18, 2000, http://www.nytimes.com/2000/05/18/opinion/essay-the
-biggest-vote.html.

2. Belfer Center estimates, based on data (1980–2016) from International
Monetary Fund, "World Economic Outlook Database," October 2016.

3. Kissinger, *Diplomacy,* 812.

4. Graham Allison and Niall Ferguson, "Establish a White House Council
of Historical Advisers Now," Belfer Center for Science and International
Affairs, September 2016, http://belfercenter.org/project/applied-history
-project.

5. To remind us all of the dangers of analogizing, May insisted that when a
precedent or analogue seemed especially compelling, one should pause,
draw a line down the middle of the page, and put "Similar" at the head
of one column and "Different" on the other. If one was unable to identify
three salient points under each, they were to take an aspirin and consult a
professional historian.

6. Henry Kissinger, *White House Years* (New York: Little, Brown, 1979), 54.

7. Allison and Ferguson, "Establish a White House Council."

8. In the mid-1990s, the Pentagon's East Asia–Pacific security strategy, drafted
by Joseph Nye, then the assistant secretary of defense for international security affairs, proposed a version of "engage but hedge" that had a point. On
the one hand, it argued that if the US treated China as an enemy, we would
be assured of having one. So it proposed instead that China be engaged and
integrated into the international system. At the same time, it recognized the
substantial risk that this effort would not succeed. So, on the other hand, the
strategy called for a hedge by strengthening the relationship with Japan and
maintaining "100,000 military personnel . . . to promote our regional strategic interests, and provide evidence of undiminished US commitment and
engagement." See Department of Defense, *The United States Security Strategy
for the East Asia–Pacific Region,* 1998, 59–60.

9. For an overview of its evolution, see Richard Weixing Hu, "Assess-
ing the 'New Model of Major Power Relations' Between China and the
United States," in *Handbook of US-China Relations,* ed. Andrew T. H. Tan
(Northampton, MA: Edward Elgar Publishing, 2016), 222–42.

10. Robert Zoellick, "Whither China: From Membership to Responsibility;
Remarks to the National Committee on U.S.-China Relations," New York
City, September 21, 2005, https://2001-2009.state.gov/s/d/former/zoellick
/rem/53682.htm. While some have misinterpreted Zoellick to say that
China was a responsible stakeholder, he was clear that this was an aspiration,
not an achievement.

11. Kissinger, *Diplomacy,* 812.

12. Allison, Blackwill, and Wyne, *Lee Kuan Yew,* 13, 3.

13. Kissinger, *Diplomacy,* 410–16.

14. Charles Glaser has advocated for such a "grand bargain." See Charles Glaser, "A U.S.-China Grand Bargain?," *International Security* 39, no. 5 (Spring
2015), 49–90.

15. Rudd, *The Future of U.S.-China Relations Under Xi Jinping,* 14. Rudd's analysis of how Chinese leaders view the US is discussed in greater detail in chapter 7.

16. See Gaddis, *Strategies of Containment,* 342–79.

17. In 1978, Deng said of the Senkaku impasse: "It does not matter if this question is shelved for some time, say 10 years. Our generation is not wise enough to find common language on this question. Our next generation will certainly be wiser. They will certainly find a solution acceptable to all." See M. Taylor Fravel, "Explaining Stability in the Senkaku (Diaoyu) Islands Dispute," in *Getting the Triangle Straight: Managing China-Japan-US Relations,* ed. Gerald Curtis, Ryosei Kokubun, and Wang Jisi (Tokyo: Japan Center for International Exchange, 2010), 157.

18. Lyle Goldstein explores these and other ideas in his concept of "cooperation spirals." See Lyle Goldstein, *Meeting China Halfway: How to Defuse the Emerging US-China Rivalry* (Washington, DC: Georgetown University Press, 2015).

19. For an overview of Xi's concept, see Cheng Li and Lucy Xu, "Chinese Enthusiasm and American Cynicism over the 'New Type of Great Power Relations,'" *China-US Focus,* December 4, 2014, http://www.chinausfocus.com /foreign-policy/chinese-enthusiasm-and-american-cynicism-over-the-new -type-of-great-power-relations/. While no Obama administration official formally rejected Xi's proposal, the president and his aides had pointedly stopped using the term by late 2014, after China began constructing islands in the South China Sea. See Jane Perlez, "China's 'New Type' of Ties Fails to Sway Obama," *New York Times,* November 9, 2014, https://www.nytimes.com/2014/11/10 /world/asia/chinas-new-type-of-ties-fails-to-sway-obama.html.

20. Jimmy Orr, "Reagan and Gorbachev Agreed to Fight UFOs," *Christian Science Monitor,* April 24, 2009, http://www.csmonitor.com/USA/Politics /The-Vote/2009/0424/reagan-and-gorbachev-agreed-to-fight-ufos.

21. See Graham Allison, "The Step We Still Haven't Taken to Create a Nuke-Free World," *Atlantic,* March 23, 2014, https://www.theatlantic.com /international/archive/2014/03/the-step-we-still-havent-taken-to-create -a-nuke-free-world/284597/.

22. See Graham Allison, *Nuclear Terrorism: The Ultimate Preventable Catastrophe* (New York: Henry Holt, 2004).

23. Susan Hockfield, "The 21st Century's Technology Story: The Convergence of Biology with Engineering and the Physical Sciences," Edwin L. Godkin Lecture, John F. Kennedy Forum, Harvard Kennedy School of Government, March 12, 2014, iop.harvard.edu/forum/21st-centurys-technology -story-convergence-biology-engineering-and-physical-sciences.

24. See *World at Risk: The Report of the Commission on the Prevention of WMD Proliferation and Terrorism* (New York: Vintage Books, 2008).

25. As a *Nature* analysis of the Paris Agreement and its accompanying individual country pledges (INDCs) pointed out, "The post-2030 challenge to limit warming to below 2 degrees Celsius from current INDC levels is daunting

... Substantial enhancement or over-delivery on current INDCs by additional national, sub-national and non-state actions is required to maintain a reasonable chance of meeting the target of keeping warming well below 2 degrees Celsius." Joeri Rogelj et al., "Paris Agreement Climate Proposals Need a Boost to Keep Warming Well Below 2°C," *Nature* 534, June 2016, 631, 636, http://www.nature.com/nature/journal/v534/n7609/full/nature18307.html.

26.   For an exploration of possibilities in this direction, see Kishore Mahbubani and Lawrence Summers, "The Fusion of Civilizations," *Foreign Affairs*, May/June 2016, https://www.foreignaffairs.com/articles/2016-04-18/fusion-civilizations.

Conclusion

1.   Graham Allison and Philip Zelikow, *Essence of Decision: Explaining the Cuban Missile Crisis*, 2nd ed. (New York: Longman, 1999).

2.   John F. Kennedy, "Commencement Address at American University," June 10, 1963, https://www.jfklibrary.org/Asset-Viewer/BWC7I4C9QUmLG9J6I8oy8w.aspx.

3.   See Robert Ellsworth, Andrew Goodpaster, and Rita Hauser, *America's National Interests: A Report from the Commission on America's National Interests* (Washington, DC: Report for the Commission on America's National Interests, 2000).

4.   Sun Tzu, *The Art of War*, 84.

5.   Whittaker Chambers, "A Witness," in *Conservatism in America Since 1930: A Reader*, ed. Gregory Schneider (New York: New York University Press, 2003), 141.

6.   David Remnick, "Going the Distance: On and Off the Road with Barack Obama," *New Yorker*, January 27, 2014, http://www.newyorker.com/magazine/2014/01/27/going-the-distance-david-remnick.

7.   Allison, Blackwill, and Wyne, *Lee Kuan Yew*, 10.

8.   Niall Ferguson, *Civilization: The West and the Rest* (New York: Penguin, 2011), 12.

Appendix 1: Thucydides's Trap Case File

1.   Pérez, "Avance portugués y expansion castellana en torno a 1492," 107.

2.   In our presentation of this case as a "no war" outcome, it is worth mentioning that the Portuguese did fight in the War of Castilian Succession, a conflict fought between 1475 and 1479 over the question of whether the Castile-Aragon union would be allowed to stand. If this Castilian civil war reaffirmed Isabella, who was married to Aragonian king Ferdinand, as the next Castilian queen, the union would remain. If supporters of Juana (who was married to Portuguese king Alfonso V) won, Castile would have

unified with Portugal instead. Portugal, of course, fought on the side of bringing Juana to the throne rather than Isabella. Therefore, rather than understanding this as a Thucydides's Trap scenario in which fear of rising Castilian power unifying with Aragon prompts Portuguese aggression, we understand this war as a Portuguese attempt to acquire Castile as its own inheritance. Expansion was a greater motivator than fear. There is another issue that separates this war from the Thucydides's Trap case of 1494. In the 1470s, Portugal's overseas empire — and resulting wealth — was increasing at a far higher rate than Castile's. Prior to the war, word of the discovery of gold on Portugal's "Gold Coast" in West Africa had gotten out, and Portugal's lucrative colonial agriculture in the Azores and Cape Verde were well known and growing. A series of papal bulls issued before the war ratified Portuguese control of these lands. After Portugal entered the war, Queen Isabella attacked Portuguese possessions in Africa in an effort to cut Portuguese power down to size. These efforts were ultimately unsuccessful, leaving Portugal a dominant colonial power at the conclusion of the war. This dominance was solidified in the 1479 Treaty of Alcáçovas. Therefore, while the 1492 "no war" scenario we highlight clearly shows the negotiation of an episode in which a rising Spain threatened a ruling Portugal, the colonial battles of the War of Castilian Succession were fought in an era during which both powers were rising: Portugal's colonial rise threatened to shut Spain out of overseas expansion, even as Spain gained territory on the Continent.

3.   Malyn Newitt, *A History of Portuguese Overseas Expansion, 1400–1668* (London: Routledge, 2005), 56.

4.   Christopher Bell, *Portugal and the Quest for the Indies* (London: Constable, 1974), 180.

5.   Alexander Zukas, "The Treaty of Tordesillas," in *Encyclopedia of Western Colonialism Since 1450* (Detroit: Macmillan Reference, 2007), 1088.

6.   Bell, *Portugal and the Quest for the Indies,* 183.

7.   Stephen Bown, *1494: How a Family Feud in Medieval Spain Divided the World in Half* (New York: Thomas Dunne Books, 2012), 146–47.

8.   Considering how little knowledge anyone had of the geography of the Americas at the time, King John's adamant stance against the pope's line of demarcation can be hard to understand. By 1494, neither power knew definitively that the Americas existed at all, let alone that a part of modern-day Brazil lay to the east of the 46th meridian. However, Christopher Bell hypothesizes that Portuguese explorers in the Atlantic prior to 1494 may have actually sighted land when accidentally blown off course on an African voyage, and returned to tell the king about it. Therefore, when King John disputed the 1493 papal bulls, it is possible that "he already knew that there was land across the Atlantic in the southern hemisphere; that, whether it was islands or terra firma, it was suitable for colonization and that it was to be found in the neighbourhood of 36' W." Bell, *Portugal and the Quest for the Indies,* 186.

9.   Disney, *A History of Portugal,* 48.

10. Ferdinand Magellan's 1521 circumnavigation showed that Columbus had not in fact found a westward route to the East Indies, but a new and vast American continent.

11. Bown, *1494,* 155.

12. In fact, it was so effective that it inspired a second, similar treaty. In 1529, Portugal and Spain resolved differences over sovereignty in the Molucca Islands through the Treaty of Zaragoza—a second meridian line dividing Portuguese from Spanish territory, though this time in the Pacific.

13. Jonathan Hart, *Empires and Colonies* (Malden, MA: Polity Press, 2008), 28.

14. Rodríguez-Salgado, "The Hapsburg-Valois Wars," 380.

15. Ibid., 378. Making war against Muslim "infidels" was a responsibility inherent in the title of Holy Roman Emperor. Francis's ability to forecast the coming conflict lends credence to political scientist Dale Copeland's claim that Francis deliberately launched a preventive war against the Hapsburg Empire to prevent it from the rising. See Dale Copeland, *The Origins of Major War* (Ithaca, NY: Cornell University Press, 2000), 215.

16. Henry Kamen, *Spain, 1469–1714* (New York: Routledge, 2014), 65; Copeland, *The Origins of Major War,* 381.

17. John Lynch, *Spain Under the Hapsburgs,* vol. 1 (Oxford: Oxford University Press, 1964), 88.

18. Robert Knecht, *Francis I* (Cambridge: Cambridge University Press, 1982), 72.

19. Rodríguez-Salgado, "The Hapsburg-Valois Wars," 400.

20. Brendan Simms, *Europe: The Struggle for Supremacy* (New York: Basic Books, 2013), 10.

21. Halil İnalcık, *The Ottoman Empire: The Classical Age, 1300–1600* (London: Phoenix Press, 2001), 35.

22. Caroline Finkel, *Osman's Dream: The Story of the Ottoman Empire, 1300–1923* (New York: Basic Books, 2006), 58.

23. Andrew Hess, "The Ottoman Conquest of Egypt (1517) and the Beginning of the Sixteenth-Century World War," *International Journal of Middle East Studies* 4, no. 1, 67; Colin Imber, *The Ottoman Empire, 1300–1650* (New York: Palgrave Macmillan, 2009), 293.

24. Hess, "The Ottoman Conquest of Egypt," 70.

25. Ibid., 55.

26. Richard Mackenney, *Sixteenth-Century Europe: Expansion and Conflict* (New York: Palgrave Macmillan, 1993), 243.

27. Simms, *Europe,* 11.

28. Imber, *The Ottoman Empire,* 54.

29. Geoffrey Parker, *Europe in Crisis, 1598–1648* (Ithaca, NY: Cornell University Press, 1979), 70.

30. Ibid., 210–11.

31. Michael Roberts, "Sweden and the Baltic, 1611–54," in *The New Cambridge Modern History,* 2nd ed., vol. 4, ed. J. P. Cooper (New York: Cambridge University Press, 1970), 392–93.

32. Samuel Rawson Gardiner, *The Thirty Years' War, 1618–1648* (London: Longmans, Green, 1912), 105.

33. Peter Wilson, *The Thirty Years War: Europe's Tragedy* (Cambridge, MA: Harvard University Press, 2009), 431.

34. Erik Ringmar, "Words That Govern Men: A Cultural Explanation of the Swedish Intervention into the Thirty Years War" (PhD diss., Yale University, 1993), 157.

35. Simms, *Europe,* 15.

36. Michael Roberts, *Gustavus Adolphus* (London: Longman, 1992), 59–60.

37. Geoffrey Parker argues that Gustavus managed essentially to extort massive financial support from France out of fear that Swedish success might block France out of the postwar settlement: "France could not take the risk that Gustavus might achieve, without her help, a position of dominance from which the map of Germany might be redrawn . . . French envoys . . . promised Sweden 1 million livres annually for five years, to finance a war for 'the safe-guarding of the Baltic and Oceanic Seas, the liberty of commerce, and the relief of the oppressed states of the Holy Roman Empire.' The treaty, which was published immediately, together with a note that France had paid 300,000 livres on the spot, created a sensation . . . It was widely acclaimed as a masterstroke of Swedish diplomacy." See Parker, *Europe in Crisis,* 219.

38. Roberts, "Sweden and the Baltic, 1611–54," 392.

39. Wilson, *The Thirty Years War,* 462.

40. Kennedy, *The Rise and Fall of the Great Powers,* 63, 56.

41. Wilson, *Profit and Power,* 107.

42. J. R. Jones, *The Anglo-Dutch Wars of the Seventeenth Century* (New York: Routledge, 1996), 8.

43. Kennedy, *The Rise and Fall of the Great Powers,* 67.

44. It is important to remember that both powers' pre-Smithian understanding of mercantilist economics did not yet admit to the possibility of free trade leading to mutual benefit. F. L. Carsten explains that the Dutch were reacting to "the idea of the domination of the British seas against the system, or the lack of the system, which the Dutch called the principle of free seas and which they upheld wherever their commercial power was or could be expected to be supreme. Only after many years and after the opening of new possibilities did it begin to be realized that world commerce itself could be expanded and that two capitalist and competing states could thrive without destroying each other." See E. H. Kossmann, "The Dutch Republic," in *The New Cambridge Modern History,* 2nd ed., vol. 5: *The Ascendancy of France, 1648–88,* ed. F. L. Carsten (Cambridge: Cambridge University Press, 1961), 283.

45. Levy, "The Rise and Decline of the Anglo-Dutch Rivalry," 176, 189.

46. Edmundson, *Anglo-Dutch Rivalry During the First Half of the Seventeenth Century,* 5.

47. Immanuel Wallerstein, *The Modern World-System II: Mercantilism and the Consolidation of the European World-Economy, 1600–1750* (Berkeley: University of California Press, 2011), 77–78.

48. Wilson, *Profit and Power,* 78.

49. John A. Lynn, *The Wars of Louis XIV, 1667–1714* (Harlow, UK: Longman, 1999), 17.

50. Kennedy, *The Rise and Fall of the Great Powers,* 99; Sir George Clark, "The Nine Years War, 1688–1697," in *The New Cambridge Modern History,* 2nd ed., vol. 6: *The Rise of Great Britain and Russia, 1688–1715,* ed. J. S. Bromley, (New York: Cambridge University Press, 1970), 223.

51. Derek McKay and H. M. Scott, *The Rise of the Great Powers, 1648–1815* (London: Longman, 1983), 46. The Glorious Revolution tends to refer not only to William's deposal of James, but also to a range of constitutional reforms granting more power to Parliament. William was generally content to approve these, as his priority was to harness English resources for the war with France.

52. Clark, "The Nine Years War," 230.

53. Lawrence James, *The Rise and Fall of the British Empire* (New York: St. Martin's Press, 1996), 66.

54. John Brewer, *The Sinews of Power: War, Money and the English State, 1688–1783* (London: Unwin Hyman, 1989), xvii.

55. Robert Tombs and Isabelle Tombs, *That Sweet Enemy: The French and the British from the Sun King to the Present* (London: William Heinemann, 2006), 51.

56. James, *The Rise and Fall of the British Empire,* 58.

57. Tombs and Tombs, *That Sweet Enemy,* 45.

58. James, *The Rise and Fall of the British Empire,* 66.

59. Tombs and Tombs, *That Sweet Enemy,* 46.

60. Kennedy, *The Rise and Fall of the Great Powers,* 120.

61. David Chandler, *The Campaigns of Napoleon* (New York: Macmillan, 1966), 208.

62. In late-eighteenth-century France, economic progress to rival Britain's, according to historian François Crouzet, "was almost completely lacking. This decisive British superiority in ingenuity and willingness to innovate is the basic fact which accentuated the structural discrepancy between the two economies during the second part of the eighteenth century." See François Crouzet, *Britain Ascendant: Comparative Issues in Franco-British Economic History* (Cambridge: Cambridge University Press, 1990), 12.

63. William Doyle, *The Oxford History of the French Revolution* (Oxford: Oxford University Press, 2002), 197.

64. Ibid., 198, 204–5.

65. William Cobbet, ed., *Cobbett's Parliamentary History of England: From the Norman Conquest, in 1066, to the Year 1803,* vol. 30 (London: T. C. Hansard, 1806), 239.

66. Doyle, *The Oxford History of the French Revolution,* 200–202.

67. Napoleon enlarged the French army to more than triple its 1789 levels by 1815. See Kennedy, *The Rise and Fall of the Great Powers,* 99.

68. Charles Downer Hazen, *The French Revolution and Napoleon* (New York: Henry Holt, 1917), 251–52.

69. Norman Longmate, *Island Fortress: The Defense of Great Britain, 1603–1945* (London: Hutchinson, 1991), 291.

70. Michael Leggiere, *The Fall of Napoleon* (Cambridge: Cambridge University Press, 2007), 2.

71. Kennedy, *The Rise and Fall of the Great Powers,* 124.

72. Such a rate of expansion is hardly unprecedented in Russian history: Russia "expanded each year by an amount larger than the entire territory of many European states (on average, 100,000 square kilometers annually) from 1552 to 1917." See Kissinger, *World Order,* 53.

73. Correlates of War Project, "National Material Capabilities Dataset." See Singer, Bremer, and Stuckey, "Capability Distribution, Uncertainty, and Major Power War," 19–48.

74. Orlando Figes, *The Crimean War: A History* (New York: Metropolitan Books, 2010), 40.

75. Ibid.

76. Simms, *Europe,* 221.

77. Figes, *The Crimean War,* 48.

78. Kissinger, *World Order,* 50.

79. Astolphe de Custine, *Letters from Russia,* ed. Anka Muhlstein (New York: New York Review of Books, 2002), 647.

80. Alexander Polunov, Thomas Owen, and Larissa Zakharova, eds., *Russia in the Nineteenth Century: Autocracy, Reform, and Social Change, 1814–1914,* trans. Marshall Shatz (New York: M. E. Sharpe, 2005), 69.

81. Adam Lambert, *The Crimean War: British Grand Strategy Against Russia, 1853–56* (Manchester, UK: Manchester University Press, 1990), 27.

82. Kennedy, *The Rise and Fall of the Great Powers,* 120.

83. Ibid., 149.

84. Ibid., 183.

85. Howard, *The Franco-Prussian War,* 40.

86. Wawro, *The Franco-Prussian War,* 19.

87. Howard, *The Franco-Prussian War,* 22.

88. Correlates of War Project, "National Material Capabilities Dataset." See Singer, Bremer, and Stuckey, "Capability Distribution, Uncertainty, and Major Power War," 19–48.

89. Wawro, *The Franco-Prussian War,* 19.

90. Simms, *Europe,* 241.

91. Steinberg, *Bismarck,* 281–82.

92. Otto von Bismarck, *Bismarck, the Man and the Statesman, Being the Reflections and Reminiscences of Otto, Prince von Bismarck, Written and Dictated by Himself After His Retirement from Office,* trans. A. J. Butler (New York: Harper & Brothers, 1898), 57.

93. There is scholarly debate over the extent to which Bismarck intended the Hohenzollern candidacy to lead to war against France. It is fairly widely agreed, however, that Bismarck did desire war and that the candidacy, whether through coincidence or master plan, formed "the centerpiece of this quest for a confrontation." See S. William Halperin, "The Origins of the Franco-Prussian War," *Journal of Modern History* 45, no. 1 (March 1973), 91.

94. Jasper Ridley, *Napoleon III and Eugenie* (New York: Viking, 1980), 561.

95. Howard, *The Franco-Prussian War,* 40.

96. Simms, *Europe,* 243.

97. Mitchell, *International Historical Statistics,* 1025.

98. See charts on Japanese military expenditure in Schencking, *Making Waves,* 47 (1873–1889), 104 (1890–1905).

99. Iriye, "Japan's Drive to Great-Power Status," in *The Cambridge History of Japan,* vol. 5: *The Nineteenth Century,* ed. Marius Jansen (Cambridge: Cambridge University Press, 1989), 760–61.

100. Duus, *The Abacus and the Sword,* 49.

101. Iriye, "Japan's Drive to Great-Power Status," 764.

102. S.C.M. Paine, *The Sino-Japanese War of 1894–1895: Perceptions, Power, and Primacy* (Cambridge: Cambridge University Press, 2003), 77.

103. Stewart Lone, *Japan's First Modern War: Army and Society in the Conflict with China, 1894–95* (London: St. Martin's Press, 1994), 25.

104. Westwood, *Russia Against Japan,* 11.

105. Schencking, *Making Waves,* 104.

106. Adam Tooze, *The Deluge: The Great War, America, and the Remaking of the Global Order, 1916–1931* (New York: Viking, 2014), 13.

107. Kennedy, *The Rise and Fall of the Great Powers,* 200–201.

108. May, *Imperial Democracy,* 57–59.

109. Bourne, *Britain and the Balance of Power in North America,* 339.

110. Kennedy, *The Rise and Fall of the Great Powers,* 203.

111. Bourne, *Britain and the Balance of Power in North America,* 351.

112. Friedberg, *The Weary Titan,* 197.

113. MacMillan, *The War That Ended Peace,* 38.

114. Orde, *The Eclipse of Great Britain,* 22. See also May and Hong, "A Power Transition and Its Effects," 12–13.

115. In his description of "free security," C. Vann Woodward notes that the "costly navy that policed and defended the Atlantic was manned and paid for by British subjects for more than a century, while Americans enjoyed the added security afforded without added costs to themselves." Woodward, "The Age of Reinterpretation," 2.

116. Kennedy, *The Rise and Fall of the Great Powers,* 202.

117. Kennedy, *Anglo-German Antagonism,* 464.

118. Seligmann, Nägler, and Epkenhans, eds., *The Naval Route to the Abyss,* 137–38.

119. MacMillan, *The War That Ended Peace,* xxvi.

120. By 1914, a quarter of all French investment went to a rapidly industrializing Russia. Strachan, *The First World War,* 19, 62–63.

121. Herwig, *The First World War,* 20–24.

122. The German emperor worried that he had been humiliated in not standing up to his enemies in recent crises and saw a good opportunity to end Russian influence in the Balkans, even if this led to war with Moscow. Herwig, *The First World War,* 21–24; MacMillan, *The War That Ended Peace,* 523.

123. For example, Clark, *The Sleepwalkers,* xxi–xxvii, 561.

124. Kennedy, *Anglo-German Antagonism,* 470.

125. Margaret MacMillan, *Paris 1919: Six Months That Changed the World* (New York: Random House, 2003), 465.

126. Richard J. Evans, *The Third Reich in Power, 1933–1939* (New York: Penguin, 2005), 4.

127. Kennedy, *The Rise and Fall of the Great Powers,* 288.

128. William Shirer, *The Rise and Fall of the Third Reich: A History of Nazi Germany* (New York: Simon & Schuster, 2011), 58.

129. Evans, *The Third Reich in Power,* 705.

130. Kennedy, *The Rise and Fall of the Great Powers,* 305; Antony Beevor, *The Second World War* (London: Weidenfeld & Nicolson, 2012), 5.

131. Stephen Van Evera, *Causes of War: Power and the Roots of Conflict* (Ithaca, NY: Cornell University Press, 1999), 95–96.

132. Kennedy, *The Rise and Fall of the Great Powers,* 324.

133. Zara Steiner, *The Triumph of the Dark: European International History, 1933–1939* (New York: Oxford University Press, 2011), 835.

134. Beevor, *The Second World War,* 4.

135. Gerhard Weinberg, *A World at Arms: A Global History of World War II* (New York: Cambridge University Press, 2005), 22.

136. Winston Churchill, *Never Give In!: Winston Churchill's Speeches,* ed. Winston S. Churchill (New York: Bloomsbury, 2013), 102–3.

137. "Speech by the Prime Minister at Birmingham on March 17, 1939," Yale Law School Avalon Project, http://avalon.law.yale.edu/wwii/blbk09.asp.

138. Kissinger, *Diplomacy,* 294.

139. See Beevor, *The Second World War,* 17–21.

140. Kennedy, *The Rise and Fall of the Great Powers,* 334.

141. US Department of State, *Foreign Relations of the United States and Japan,* 780.

142. Richard Storry, *Japan and the Decline of the West in Asia, 1894–1943* (London: Macmillan, 1979), 159.

143. Feis, *The Road to Pearl Harbor,* 248.

144. Maechling, "Pearl Harbor," 47.

145. Snyder, *Myths of Empire,* 126, 5.

146. Dean Acheson, *Present at the Creation: My Years in the State Department* (New York: Norton, 1969), 36.

147. Gaddis, *The Cold War,* 15.

148. Forrestal letter to Homer Ferguson, see Millis, ed., *The Forrestal Diaries,* 57.

149. Wilfried Loth, "The Cold War and the Social and Economic History of the Twentieth Century," in *The Cambridge History of the Cold War,* vol. 2, ed. Melvyn Leffler and Odd Arne Westad (New York: Cambridge University Press, 2010), 514.

150. Secretary of State John Foster Dulles began to worry that it would be "very difficult to stop Communism in much of the world if we cannot in some way duplicate the intensive Communist effort to raise productivity standards." See H. W. Brands, *The Devil We Knew: Americans and the Cold War* (New York: Oxford University Press, 1993), 70.

151. Samuelson, *Economics,* 807.

152. Correlates of War Project, "National Material Capabilities Dataset"; Singer, Bremer, and Stuckey, "Capability Distribution, Uncertainty, and Major Power War," 19–48.

153. Many scholars—from those in the "revisionist" school to respected cold warriors like George Kennan—have argued that the United States overreacted to the Soviet threat. Plenty of historical evidence supports this view. The Thucydides's Trap, however, does not require that the ruling power's perception of the rising power's rise be rational or proportionate to the threat. It simply requires that the rising power be at least *somewhat* rising, and that its rise is sufficient to inspire fear in the ruling power. Both conditions are, in this case, well satisfied.

154. During the rare cases in which the two powers fought covertly, as when Soviet pilots flew bombing sorties over South Korea during the Korean War, they were loath to admit it for fear of the potentially devastating consequences of nuclear escalation.

155. See Campbell Craig and Fredrik Logevall, *America's Cold War* (Cambridge, MA: Harvard Belknap, 2009), 357; Melvyn Leffler, *For the Soul of Mankind* (New York: Hill and Wang, 2007), 465; Gaddis, *The Cold War,* 261.

156. See Gaddis, *The Long Peace,* 225.

157. Ibid., 232.

158. See Graham Allison, "Primitive Rules of Prudence: Foundations of Peaceful Competition," in *Windows of Opportunity: From Cold War to Peaceful Competition in US-Soviet Relations,* ed. Graham Allison, William Ury, and Bruce Allyn (Cambridge, MA: Ballinger, 1989).

159. Jussi M. Hanhimaki, "Europe's Cold War," in *The Oxford Handbook of Postwar European History,* ed. Dan Stone (Oxford: Oxford University Press, 2012), 297.

160. Moravcsik, *The Choice for Europe,* 407.

161. Zelikow and Rice, *Germany Unified and Europe Transformed,* 207.

162. Moravcsik, *The Choice for Europe,* 408.

163. Zelikow and Rice, *Germany Unified and Europe Transformed,* 47.

164. Heilbrunn, "The Interview: Henry Kissinger."

165. Stephen Green, *Reluctant Meister* (London: Haus Publishing, 2014), 299.

166. Haftendorn, *Coming of Age,* 319.

167. As Martin Dedman notes, "The objective of safely incorporating a revived

German economy into Western Europe, in the absence of any formal peace settlement with the defeated, belligerent former Germany, was solved through economic integration: the creation of common markets originally in coal and steel in 1951 and in industrial goods in 1957. This meant that the recovery of German economic power did not pose a political or military threat to Europe in the 45 years following World War II (whereas Japan's rise to economic superpower status has alarmed its Asian neighbours)." See Martin Dedman, *The Origins and Development of the European Union, 1945–2008* (New York: Routledge, 2009), 2.

168. Hans Kundnani, *The Paradox of German Power* (London: C. Hurst, 2014), 102–3, 107.

INDEX

Page numbers in italics refer to figures.